INTERNATIO

Featuring over 20 new entries, *International Relations: The Key Concepts*, now in its second edition, is the essential guide for anyone interested in international affairs. Comprehensive and up to date, it introduces the most important themes in international relations in the post-9/11 era. Key areas cover international criminal law, human rights, the developing world (the Arab League, African Union), globalization and strategic studies. New entries include:

- English School
- Digital Divide
- War on Terror
- Bush Doctrine
- International Criminal Court
- Legitimacy
- Global Warming
- Unilateralism

Featuring suggestions for further reading as well as a unique guide to web sites on international relations, this accessible guide is an invaluable aid to an understanding of this expanding field; ideal for the student and non-specialist alike.

**Martin Griffiths** is Associate Professor at the Department of International Business and Asian Studies at Griffith University, Australia. He is the author of *Fifty Key Thinkers in International Relations*, also available from Routledge.

**Terry O'Callaghan** is Senior Lecturer in the School of International Studies at the University of South Australia.

**Steven C. Roach** is Assistant Professor of International Affairs in the Department of Government and International Affairs at the University of South Florida. He is the author of *Politicizing the International Criminal Court: The Convergence of Politics, Ethics, and Law* (2006), *Cultural Autonomy, Minority Rights, and Globalization* (2005), and editor of *Critical Theory and International Relations: A Reader* (2007).

# ALSO AVAILABLE FROM ROUTLEDGE

# INTERNATIONAL RELATIONS

## The Key Concepts
### Second Edition

*Martin Griffiths,*
*Terry O'Callaghan*
*and*
*Steven C. Roach*

Routledge
Taylor & Francis Group

LONDON AND NEW YORK

First published 2002
by Routledge
Second edition published 2008
by Routledge
2 Park Square, Milton Park, Abingdon, Oxon OX14 4RN

Simultaneously published in the USA and Canada
by Routledge
270 Madison Ave, New York, NY 10016

*Routledge is an imprint of the Taylor & Francis Group, an informa business*

© 2002, 2008 Martin Griffiths, Terry O'Callaghan and Steven C. Roach

Typeset in Bembo by
HWA Text and Data Management, Tunbridge Wells
Printed and bound in Great Britain by
TJ International Ltd, Padstow, Cornwall

*British Library Cataloguing in Publication Data*
A catalogue record for this book is available from the British Library

*Library of Congress Cataloging-in-Publication Data*
A catalog record for this book has been requested

ISBN10: 0–415–77436–5 (hbk)
ISBN10: 0–415–77437–3 (pbk)
ISBN10: 0–203–93408–3 (ebk)

ISBN13: 978–0–415–77436–9 (hbk)
ISBN13: 978–0–415–77437–6 (pbk)
ISBN13: 978–0–203–93408–1 (ebk)

# CONTENTS

# PREFACE TO SECOND EDITION

This second edition of *International Relations: The Key Concepts* provides students of international relations with short introductory essays to the concepts and issues that are most likely to be encountered in the study of international relations. It builds on the central aim of the first edition, by updating many of the essays of the key concepts and adding several concepts associated with important new debates in international relations. In doing so, it addresses many of the new concepts associated with the post-9/11 era, including the Bush Doctrine, Enemy Combatants, Pre-emption, War on Terror, Axis of Evil, Jihad, etc. Such an era has also provided a novel context for studying the importance of existing concepts that were not stressed in the first edition (i.e. unilateralism and torture), yet have come to shape and define US foreign policy during the post-9/11 era.

The revised version also includes additional concepts and institutions associated with four areas of international relations: (1) the developing world (Mercosur, African Union, Arab League), (2) international criminal law (International Criminal Court (ICC) and International Criminal Tribunals), (3) Human Rights (Human Security), and (4) strategic studies (Coercion). Accordingly, the second edition seeks to be more inclusive without being comprehensive, more relevant than simply being up to date. In all, there are 21 concepts that have been added to this new edition (10 that have been dropped from the first edition). Together, they reflect a wider array of relevant and previously under-emphasised introductory essays and an expanded range of important new debates in international relations.

Given the expanded scope of this edition and the historical importance of the post-9/11 era, I have included a brief introduction that discusses several emergent challenges and the central debates in the field of international relations. In addition, I have updated and expanded the list of web sites to reflect the rapidly growing number of non-governmental organisations, research institutes, and academic journals in international relations.

Steven C. Roach
University of South Florida
March 2007

# INTRODUCTION
## International relations: conceptual issues and challenges

International relations (IR) is the study of the political and social interaction of state, non-state actors, and individuals. In recent years, the increasing interaction among these actors, coupled with advances in informational technology and the spread of **human rights**, have raised many new questions for IR scholars, practitioners, and students. For instance, why do states now elect to delegate more of their authority to the international level? How does this process explain the capacity of international institutions, notably the **United Nations** (UN), **World Trade Organisation** (WTO), and the **International Criminal Court** (ICC), to address the social, economic, legal, and humanitarian problems that cut across nation-state boundaries? Moreover, which theories in IR allow us to best explain the changing dynamics of international issues such as environmental pollution, humanitarian emergencies, global terrorism, the AIDS/HIV pandemic, the proliferation of nuclear weapons and trade disputes? And how should we apply IR theory to devise effective policies that can resolve the serious effects of these global problems?

To address these questions, we need to first appreciate the importance of international relations theory. Theory, in this sense, offers the conceptual tools to accomplish three basic tasks: to analyse the impact of rules and decisions on state behaviour; to understand the changing dimensions and limits of power structures, institutions and order, including the role of greater transparency (access to information) and accountability; and to promote the ideals of justice, greater social inclusion, and equality. In short, theory is about describing reality and generating the historical and practical knowledge needed to resolve problems and promote the above ideals. Whether this means applying a rigorous, scientific assessment of the effects of low educational standards on civil wars in Africa during the 1990s, or understanding the oppression of women in Taliban-controlled Afghanistan (1996–2001), it is essential that theory be employed to understand the increasingly complex policy and ethical challenges facing state and international political leaders.

Today, policymakers confront the ongoing challenge of building consensus around complex issues related to maintaining and promoting international peace and security. In light of the 9/11 attacks on the World Trade Center and Pentagon, US foreign policy now, more than ever, requires new strategic priorities and thinking to address global problems. And while there is no easy solution or fix per se, we also need to be wary of the limits and political fallout of relying too heavily on military solutions to resolve our problems. Nowhere is this perhaps more evident than with the unprecedented formulation of enemy combatants, which has allowed the United States government to engage in reported acts of torture that violate the Geneva Conventions and other well established international legal mechanisms.

Thus, of the many challenges facing international policymakers and political leaders, the **global war** on terrorism is arguably the most pressing (though global warming may also be considered equally important). Here, we must continue to strike some credible balance between international and domestic security concerns and the need for justice, ethics, civil rights, and freedom. How students and scholars effectively engage this task will of course depend on how they appreciate the historical and theoretical meaning of concepts and issues. Or, alternatively, how they are able to link the issues and concepts with the relevant policy and theoretical debates that inform and shape their meaning and significance in international relations. Below are three of the principal theoretical debates in IR with which all IR students need to be acquainted. Together, they show how IR scholars and practitioners frame the basic questions and issues of their research and policy analysis regarding power politics, interests, identities, values, and new norms and practices (i.e. **sovereignty**, **human rights**, and environmental protection) in international relations.

## FRAMING THE ISSUES: THEORETICAL DEBATES

The origins of the first debate can be traced back to the early studies of international politics in the United Kingdom and United States during the 1930s and 1940s. At this time, E. H. Carr's *The Twenty Years Crisis* emerged as one of the most important texts of International Relations (Carr, 1946). Carr, for instance, argued that the failure of the **League of Nations** to contain aggression symptomised the tension between the League's adherence to the ideals of peace and democratic order and the political realities of national aggression. By neglecting the latter, the League failed to take stock of the political and social realities that conflicted with and often undermined the enactment of these principles. Realists, therefore, believed that political interests needed to be defined in terms of power objectives;

whilst idealists insisted on the need to formulate and implement international principles of peace and tolerance.

Naturally, the devastating effects of the Second World War had convinced many that violence and war could not be ignored. In fact, they argued, it was precisely the abiding adherence to moral principles that for some had become the very source of national aggression and conflict. Hitler, for instance, invoked the League Covenant's encoded democratic principle of the right to self-determination to justify the conquest of the Sudetenland (to uphold the right to self-determination of German nationals living in this area). In the United States and United Kingdom, therefore, political realism became the established conceptual framework for studying international order and relations among states. It was based on two tenets: 1) that states defined their political interests in terms of power; ✓ and 2) that order reflected a delicate yet diplomatically engaged effort to work with, and harness the normative and structural constraints of the balance of power (in the international realm) to prudent foreign policy making. As one of the first texts to offer a systematic study of the power relations among states, Hans Morgenthau's *Politics Among Nations* focused on the relationship between political power interests and the laws and mechanics of the balance of power (Morgenthau, 1948). Other prominent diplomats, most notably George Kennan and John Herz would go on to formulate the policy of containment (of Soviet influence) and the security dilemma (in which one state's attempts to make itself more secure only leads to greater insecurity), respectively.

By the 1950s and 1960s, however, a second great debate would arise, which pitted historians and behavioural (positivist) social scientists. The latter, in this case, stressed the use of statistical analyses and hypothesis testing to test and measure the impact of rules and events on state behaviour. In taking issue with this scientific priority, historians argued that the international system was an evolving process, requiring a historically based analysis of the changing laws and rules of the inter-state system. Despite this general disagreement, however, realism remained the dominant paradigm in international relations theory.

The term 'paradigm' came to prominence in the philosophy of science in the 1960s, primarily through the work of Thomas Kuhn (1970). Briefly, he argued that a paradigm consists of a set of fundamental assumptions about the subject-matter of science. A paradigm is both enabling and constraining. On the one hand, it helps to define what is important to study and so a paradigm is indispensable in simplifying reality by isolating certain factors and forces from a multitude of innumerable possibilities. On the other hand, a paradigm is constraining since it limits our perceptual field (what we 'see' as the most important actors and relationships in a particular field of study). In examining the history of science, Kuhn argued that what he called *normal* science proceeded on the basis of particular paradigms, the truth of whose assumptions were taken for granted. A paradigm is therefore a mode of thinking within a field of inquiry that regulates scientific activity, sets the standards for research, and generates consensus, coherence, and unity among scholars. For Kuhn, periods of normal science are punctuated by periods of *revolutionary* science as scientists confront problems (or *anomalies*) that cannot be solved within the terms of the dominant paradigm. A new period of normal science can only resume on the basis of a 'paradigm-shift': the establishment of a new set of assumptions to account for anomalies that could not be accommodated within the assumptions of the old paradigm.

Although Kuhn had little to say about the social sciences, many scholars in the latter domain quickly seized upon his arguments in order to strengthen and clarify the historical, organisational, and sociological foundations of their own disciplines. Students of international relations were no different in this regard. Arend Lijphart was among the first to import the Kuhnian notion of a paradigm into international relations. Writing in the early 1970s, he argued that the general pattern of development in international relations **theory** paralleled Kuhn's version of theoretical progress in the natural sciences. He described the traditional paradigm in terms of state **sovereignty** and international **anarchy**. For Lijphart, **realism** had such a ubiquitous presence in the field that it qualified as a paradigm. Not only did it set out the key questions, determined the core concepts, methods and issues, it also shaped the direction of research.

Still, by the 1970s, realism came under sustained attack from both liberals and radicals or structuralists. The result was a broad disagreement among three competing views, or *inter-paradigm debate*, concerning the adequacy of the dominant realist paradigm. Writers use different terms to refer to the various 'paradigms' within the debate. The following table helps to clarify the terms used.

| Realism | Liberalism | Marxism |
|---|---|---|
| Power politics | Interdependence | Structuralism |
| *Realpolitik* | Pluralism | Dependency |
| | | Radicalism |

Again, for *realists*, relations among states take place in the absence of a world government. The international system is anarchical, and international relations are best understood by focusing on the distribution of **power** among states. Despite their formal legal equality, the uneven distribution of power means that the arena of international relations is a form of 'power politics'. Power is hard to measure; its distribution among states changes over time and there is no consensus among states about how it should be distributed. Nonetheless, international relations is a realm of necessity (states must seek power to survive in a competitive environment) and continuity over time. It should be noted here that with Kenneth Waltz's *Theory of International Politics* (1979), realism stresses the structural properties of anarchy such as competition among units and distribution of capabilities across states. Structural realism, in this sense, employed these structural properties or variables to derive causal patterns in state behaviour and long-term stability of the international system.

In contrast to realists, then, *liberals* see international relations as a potential realm of progress and purposive change (Keohane *et al.*, 1984). They value individual freedom above all else, and believe that the state ought to be constrained from acting in ways that undermine that freedom. For them, states learn to cooperate under anarchical conditions by bargaining with other states and, in the process, calculate the short-term costs of cooperating against the long-term benefits of cooperating on issues ranging from trade (GATT and now the WTO) to the environment. Domestically, the power of the liberal constitutional state is limited by its democratic accountability to its citizens, the need to respect the demands of the economic marketplace, and the rule of law. Liberals believe that despite the difficulties of replicating these constraints at the international level, they must be established to promote stability among, as well as within, sovereign states.

Finally, *radicals* or structuralists are primarily concerned with the sources of structural inequality allegedly inherent in the international system, as well as the ways in which it might be overcome. Often inspired by, but not limited to, the Marxist tradition of thought, they examine how international relations among states make possible (and tend to conceal) the inequities of a global capitalist system (Cox, 1981; Wallerstein, 1974–89). In contrast to liberals, radicals are not content with international reforms that are limited to regulating relations among states, particularly if they rely on the capacity and the will of the great powers. Radicals believe that both realism and liberalism serve to maintain the basic distribution of power and wealth. They think that students need to reflect far more critically on the historical conditions underlying inequality between global *classes*, the material and ideological forces that sustain it, and the potential for revolutionary change towards a just world order.

Nonetheless, the growing complexity of world politics, especially in the aftermath of the fall of the Soviet Union in 1991, the rise of informational technology, and the spread of democracy fuelled a growing trend toward pluralism in the field of IR. Pluralism, in this sense, stressed the importance and meaning of identity, politics, and the social interaction of states and other important international players (**NGO**s, social movements, and grassroots organisations). As such, the shift from positive and scientific methods to one stressing interpretation and knowledge marked a (third) debate between post-positivist/epistemological approaches (Lapid, 1989).

Post-positivism, in this sense, refers to a broad term that encompasses a diverse range of theoretical perspectives that have proliferated in the field since the late 1970s, including **critical theory**, **constructivism**, **feminism**, and **postmodernism** as well as the debate in normative international relations theory between cosmopolitanism and communitarianism (Wendt, 1999; Walker, 1993; Linklater, 1998; Sylvester, 1994). Despite their differences, all these 'isms' can be seen as part of a post-positivist era in the study of international relations. All this means is that positivism is no longer dominant in shaping the nature and limits of contemporary international relations theory, although the debate between supporters and opponents of positivism remains a controversial issue. Rather than explore all the manifestations of post-positivism, students should be clear what positivism is (or was!) in the field. Here it is important to distinguish between epistemology and methodology. The term epistemology comes from the Greek word *epistēmē*, meaning knowledge. In simple terms, epistemology is the philosophy of knowledge or of how we come to know. Methodology is also concerned with how we come to know, but is much more practical in nature. Methodology is focused on the specific ways that we can use to try to understand our world. Epistemology and methodology are intimately related: the former involves the philosophy of how we come to know the world and the latter involves the practice.

Positivism can also be characterised as a philosophical movement emphasising three factors: science and scientific method as the only sources of knowledge, a sharp distinction between the realms of fact and value, and a strong hostility towards religion and traditional philosophy. Positivists, for instance, believe that there are only two sources of knowledge (as opposed to opinion): logical reasoning and empirical experience. A statement is meaningful if and only if it can be proved true or false, at least in principle, by means of the experience. This assertion is called the verifiability principle. The meaning of a statement is its method of verification; we know the meaning of a statement if we know the conditions under which the statement is true or false. In a positivist view of the world, science is seen as the way to get at truth, to understand the world well enough so that we might predict and control it. The world and the universe are deterministic. They operate by laws of cause and effect, which we can discern if we apply the unique approach of the scientific method. Science is largely a mechanistic or mechanical affair. We use deductive reasoning to postulate theories that we can test. Based on the results of our studies, we may learn that our theory.

The only shared characteristic among those who call themselves 'post-positivists' in the study of international relations is a rejection of one or more aspects of positivism. Beyond that, post-positivism defies easy summary. It is perhaps best seen as a multidimensional attempt to broaden the epistemological and methodological horizons of the field. Although this attempt has led to claims by some scholars that the study of international relations has fallen into disarray, most scholars have welcomed the move towards post-positivism, even if they remain suspicious of some of its manifestations in international relations theory. In short, then, post-positivists seek to interrogate the discursive practices of **hegemonic** and exclusionary practices of international politics and to question the conceptual boundaries of **sovereignty**, **anarchy**, and **legitimacy**.

In recent years, some IR scholars have begun to debate whether **critical theory** and other non-paradigmatic approaches are in fact policy relevant, that is, if the ideas of some critical theorists such as Jürgen Habermas can be made more policy relevant (Waever, 1996; Diez and Steans, 2005). For some, this trend constitutes a new emerging debate in IR, a fourth debate that seeks to bridge science and critical reasoning and to provide a new reflexive policymaking framework for promoting social justice. Whether or not this new debate will provide the basis for a new critical scientific paradigm is not entirely clear. However, it does reflect the ongoing challenge of bridging the gap between much of IR theory and policymaking, which has made IR an intriguing, evolving field of study.

# LIST OF KEY CONCEPTS

African Union
alliance
anarchy
appeasement
Arab League
arms control
arms trade
axis of evil
balance of power
beggar-thy-neighbour policies
Bretton Woods
Bush doctrine
capital controls
capitalism
citizenship
clash of civilisations
CNN factor
coercion
cold war
collective security
communism
communitarianism
concert of powers
constructivism
containment
cosmopolitanism
crisis
critical theory
debt trap
decolonisation
democratic peace
democratisation

dependency
deterrence
development
diaspora
digital divide
diplomacy
disarmament
distributive justice
embedded liberalism
end of history
enemy combatant
English School
ethnic cleansing
ethnicity
euro
European Union (EU)
exploitation
extraterritoriality
failed state
feminism
foreign aid
foreign direct investment (FDI)
free trade
functionalism
genocide
geopolitics
global civil society
global governance
global warming
globalisation
great powers
Group of Eight (G8)

hegemonic stability theory
hegemony
historical sociology
human rights
human security
humanitarian intervention
idealism
imagined community
imperialism
integration
interdependence
International Criminal Court (ICC)
international criminal tribunals
international law
International Monetary Fund (IMF)
international political economy
international society
irredentism
isolationism
jihad
just war
League of Nations
legitimacy
levels of analysis
liberal internationalism
loose nukes
managed trade
Marxism
mercantilism
mercenary
Mercosur
misperception
modernisation theory
multilateralism
multinational corporation (MNC)
mutually assured destruction
    (MAD)
nation–state
national interest
nationalism
newly industrialising countries
    (NICs)

non–governmental organisation
    (NGO)
non–tariff barrier (NTB)
North Atlantic Treaty
    Organisation (NATO)
nuclear proliferation
order
Organisation for Economic
    Cooperation and Development
    (OECD)
Organisation for Security and
    Cooperation in Europe (OSCE)
Organisation of Petroleum
    Exporting Countries (OPEC)
peace-building
peacekeeping
Peace of Westphalia
peace studies
perpetual peace
political risk
population growth
postmodernism
power
pre-emption
preventive diplomacy
prisoners' dilemma
public goods
realism
reciprocity
recognition
refugees
regime
regional trade blocs
regionalism
relative gains/absolute gains
rogue state
safe haven
sanctions
secession
security
security dilemma
self-determination

sovereignty
structural adjustment programme
   (SAP)
structural violence
superpower
sustainable development
terrorism
theory
Third World
torture
tragedy of the commons

unilateralism
United Nations (UN)
war
war crime
war on terror
wars of the third kind
weapons of mass destruction
women in development (WID)
World Bank
world-system theory
World Trade Organisation (WTO)

# INTERNATIONAL RELATIONS

## AFRICAN UNION

Many of the least-developing countries of the world are located in Africa. Over the years, Africa has experienced increasing civil conflict, mass starvation, refugee crises, corruption, drought, and the effects of HIV/AIDS. This has made the task of promoting and maintaining peace and security on the continent all the more complex and even dire. As the principal regional organisation charged with this task, the African Union (AU) has struggled to contain and manage the effects of these crises, albeit with little apparent success.

The blueprint for the AU was the Organisation for African Unity (OAU), which was established in 1963. Its central aim was to unify the newly independent African states around a common set of goals, notably the pooling of resources for the purposes of fostering rapid social and economic development. Legally, the OAU incorporated many of the legal principles of the **UN** Charter into its own charter, including the territorial integrity of states, the duty of non-intervention, and the sovereign equality of states. By the late 1960s, however, the OAU would be tested on many political fronts. Perhaps most important was the Biafran secessionist movement in Nigeria in 1967, which forced the OAU leaders to intervene on behalf of the Nigerian government. Additionally, there was the divisive issue of apartheid and residual colonial states. Here, though, the OAU would work with the UN to condemn and overturn apartheid and to pressure the colonial regime of Rhodesia.

During the 1980s, rising interest rates on foreign loans would impose a severe economic burden on many postcolonial African states, many of which would be forced to pay an amount on the interest that equalled nearly 25 per cent of their overall GDP. Not surprisingly, this had the effect of undermining the social and economic development of many African states, thereby complicating the OAU's mission and engendering what many now refer to as *neocolonialism*.

Nonetheless, on 9 September 1999, OAU authorities responded to the worsening conditions by calling on its members to establish the African Union (AU). The hope was that a reconstituted or updated OAU could effectively address the emerging challenges of the post-Cold War era, including the resurgence of civil war and the HIV/AIDS pandemic. As such, when the AU was formally established in 2002, it was based on three initiatives: the Sirte Extraordinary Session, which established the African Union; the Lomé Summit, or the Constitutive Act of the Union; and the Lusaka Summit that designed the blueprint for implementing the Union. Many of the objectives set forth in the Constitutive Act reaffirmed the

AU's determination to promote the UN Charter principles. Among the main objectives of the African Union are:

- to defend the sovereignty, territorial integrity, and independence of its Member States;
- to accelerate the political and socio-economic integration of the continent;
- to promote peace, security, and stability on the continent;
- to promote democratic principles and institutions, popular participation, and democratic governance;
- to promote and protect human and peoples' rights in accordance with the African Charter on Human and Peoples' Rights;
- to establish the necessary conditions for enabling the continent to play its proper role in the global economic and international negotiations.

The AU, therefore, was the culmination of efforts by the OAU to address the changing global conditions, including the spread of democracy, human rights, and globalisation. In 1980, for instance, the OAU adopted the Lagos Plan, which implemented programmes and strategies for self-reliance and development. This was soon followed by the adoption in 1981 of the African Charter on Human and Peoples' Rights, which recognised a communal or peoples' right to development. Of particular note here is the fact that the recognition of a peoples' right to development comprised one of the central themes of the third generation of **human rights**: namely, the debate between collective and individual rights.

However, by the 1990s, African leaders faced a range of serious and grave crises, ranging from environmental degradation to the HIV/AIDS crisis. The HIV/AIDS pandemic, for instance, has already killed an estimated 40 million people, many of whom were women and children. This health issue has only served to compound Africa's problems by increasing its dependency on outside donor countries of the North for cheap and affordable anti-retroviral drugs. Moreover, examples of political crises/divisions within African nations, in particular South African President Mbeki's controversial position on the false link between HIV and AIDS, and the Rwandan **genocide** which occurred in the spring of 1994 killing nearly 800,000 Tutsis and moderate Hutus, have highlighted the problem of political will and consensus formation.

Given these rising threats, it is not difficult to see why the leaders of the OAU felt compelled to establish the AU to address these crises. Yet, the issues facing the African Union remain daunting. For instance, the AU has shown little ability to contain the genocide in the Darfur region, where it has deployed a small peacekeeping force to monitor and stop genocide. Its failure to stop the violence ultimately prompted the UN Security Council to adopt a resolution mandating the implementation of peacekeeping operations in the region.

It also remains unclear if the African Union can become a high-profile global player. With rampant state corruption in many countries and the abusive practices of transnational corporations, there are few signs that the African Union can achieve the initial goals set forth by the OAU. One still encounters, for instance, the effects of the free market ideology of the **World Bank** and **IMF**, in particular the **structural adjustment programmes** (SAP) of the 1980s and 1990s, which were intended to privatise state economies, but only ended up diverting funds away from the social sector. What is more, much of Africa continues to remain at an economic disadvantage in trade matters, in part because of many African states' failure to diversify their economies, and also because of the **WTO**'s inability to resolve the issue of subsidies that have long favoured the workers of developed countries at the expense of those in developing countries.

*See also:* **dependency; development; genocide; globalisation; human rights; international law; sovereignty; United Nations**

*Further reading:* Mathews, 2001; Parker and Rukare, 2002; Tieku, 2004

## ALLIANCE

An agreement between two or more states to work together on mutual security issues. States enter into such cooperative security arrangements in order to protect themselves against a common (or perceived) threat. By pooling their resources and acting in concert, the alliance partners believe that they can improve their overall power position within the international system and their security relative to states outside the alliance.

Alliances can be either formal or informal arrangements. A formal alliance is publicly recognised through the signing of a treaty in which the signatories promise to consider an attack on any one of them as equivalent to an attack on all of them. The **North Atlantic Treaty Organisation (NATO)** is a good example of a formal security alliance. Informal alliances are much looser and less stable and rely, to a large extent, on the word of the parties involved and ongoing cooperation between them. The latter may entail, among other things, joint military exercises, the sharing of strategic information, or promises of assistance during a military crisis. Informal alliances can also take the form of secret agreements between leaders.

There are a number of benefits in forming alliances. First, they can offset the cost of defence. It is much cheaper for a state to ally itself with a stronger state that possesses a nuclear capability than it is for that state to build and maintain its own infrastructure, technological expertise, and weapons delivery systems. This makes alliances especially attractive to small, vulnerable states. Second, alliances can provide increased economic benefits through increased trade, aid, and loans between alliance partners. The deployment of foreign military personnel can also be beneficial to a local economy.

From the point of view of the **great powers**, alliances can provide them with a strategic advantage with respect to their actual or potential enemies. The United States, for example, entered into a number of bilateral alliances after 1945 in order to gain landing rights, access to ports, and the use of military facilities in strategically important locations around the periphery of the former Soviet Union. Alliances can thereby help to **contain** an enemy and control a region of strategic interest. In addition, alliances can be useful in maintaining **hegemonic** control over one's allies, encouraging them to 'bandwagon' with the great power as opposed to 'balancing' against it!

The lifespan of alliances varies. Some last for many years. This may have to do with a long-lasting perception of threat, similarity of political systems between member states, or the existence of a powerful **hegemon**. Other alliances decay fairly quickly. The so-called 'Grand Alliance' between Britain, the former Soviet Union, and the United States during the Second World War is a good example. It lasted only as long as Hitler remained a threat to world peace. As soon as Germany was defeated in 1945, the alliance broke down. Also, a state may bow out of an alliance if it no longer feels that its partners can fulfil the terms of the alliance. Finally, leadership and ideological changes among member states may undermine an alliance.

**Liberal internationalists** from Immanuel Kant onwards have argued that alliances are a source of conflict between states. After the end of the First World War, US President Woodrow Wilson suggested that alliances drew states into webs of intrigue and rivalry. On the other hand, realists tend to argue that states form alliances based on their **national interests**. A change in the national interest can and should prompt states to rethink the terms of their alliance membership. Alliances should be regarded as highly flexible arrangements that can play an important role in maintaining the **balance of power**.

It is important to note that alliances are not simply beneficial security arrangements for 'peace-loving' states. They can be used to promote aggression as well. The alliance between Germany, Italy, and Japan during the Second World War is a good example. Moreover, alliances may themselves be provocative instruments of foreign policy. It may well be the case, for example, that an alliance between two states is regarded as a hostile act by a third state. Under these circumstances, an alliance may lead to an arms race. It is for this reason that some states (such as Sweden and Switzerland) have traditionally pursued a policy of neutrality and non-alignment in Europe.

*See also:* **balance of power; cold war; collective security; concert of powers; national interest; North Atlantic Treaty Organisation; realism; security dilemma**

*Further reading:* Reiter, 1996; Snyder, 1997; Walt, 1997

## ANARCHY

In everyday usage, this term evokes images of chaos, violence, and lawlessness. Derived from the Greek word *anarkhos*, meaning 'without a ruler', a state of anarchy can be said to prevail when there is no government to keep the peace. Anarchy is often associated with periods of revolutionary upheaval and extreme social and political turbulence. Some science fiction writers and film-makers are fond of employing the idea to depict the future of the human race. In this sense, anarchy is the complete opposite of civilised conduct and expresses an extremely pessimistic view of human potential.

Students of international politics use the term in a more specific way. International politics is said to be anarchical because no single state or coalition of states has absolute control over the entire system. There is no central government, and the peculiar character of the units operating within the international system is that they are **sovereign** and autonomous states, responsible for their own fate even though they may not control it. They exercise legitimate control and authority over their own territory and answer to no higher **power**. They determine when it is appropriate to fight, when to make peace, and when to act in concert with others.

Thomas Hobbes was the first modern political philosopher to describe international relations as anarchical. While it is true that his political philosophy is primarily concerned with the problem of **order** within the state, his description of the international 'state of nature' has had a major influence on the development of international relations **theory**.

Hobbes uses the idea (sometimes called the 'domestic analogy') of a state of nature to show why rational individuals would and should prefer to live under an absolute and supreme power than live in a world without order. According to him, the state of nature is one of misery and hardship in which individuals continually struggle for survival. No matter how strong and powerful they may be, they are incapable of completely securing themselves against attack. Under these conditions, there is no time for leisure, social communion, or civilised behaviour. Life (which he famously described as 'nasty, brutish and short') is spent perpetually trying to outwit competitors in order simply to stay alive. This state of affairs is so oppressive that it is in the interest of rational individuals to give up their natural freedom and rights in return for protection and **security** against others granted by an all-powerful ruler or *Leviathan*.

It is easy to see how this pre-social condition is often said to be applicable to international relations, particularly among **realists** in the field. They argue that the absence of a supreme power capable of enforcing order across the entire system means that individual states are in a permanent state of insecurity and must be prepared to do whatever they can to survive in this hostile self-help environment. The relationship between anarchy and war, then, is extremely close.

Today, the realist interpretation of the consequences of anarchy for international relations is much debated in international relations theory. Some **liberal internationalists**, for example, agree that anarchy is important, but argue that realists tend to exaggerate its effects on state behaviour. Similarly, **constructivists** accept that anarchy is the characteristic condition of the international system, but argue that, by itself, it means nothing. For example, an anarchy of friends is quite different from an anarchy of enemies, but both are possible. In short, the nature and effects of anarchy among states depend a great deal on the particular **level of analysis** that different theories focus on, and how they justify the character and relationship between different levels.

*See also:* **constructivism; international society; levels of analysis; liberal internationalism; prisoners' dilemma; realism; relative gains/absolute gains; war**

*Further reading:* Bull, 1995; Hobbes, 1988; Milner, 1991; Powell, 1994; Waltz, 1979; Wendt, 1992

## APPEASEMENT  ✓

Appeasement is an extremely problematic foreign policy goal. It is based on the assumption that acceding to the demands of aggressive states will prevent **war** from breaking out. The folly of this approach lies in the fact that aggressive states are rarely satisfied in this way. Capitulating to their demands simply feeds their thirst for **power**, making them stronger. In the long run, such a policy is likely to increase the risk of war rather than reduce it.

Britain and France pursued a policy of appeasement with Adolf Hitler throughout most of the 1930s. Hitler had never made a secret of his expansionist (and racist) aims in Europe. They are clearly spelt out in his book *Mein Kampf* (My Struggle). In the late 1930s he orchestrated a propaganda campaign against the Czechoslovak government, claiming that it was persecuting the Sudeten Germans. There was a grain of truth in this claim. The Sudeten Germans were excluded from government positions for linguistic reasons and many Sudeten Germans were unhappy about this discrimination. Hitler took advantage of the situation to promote further unrest among the Sudeten Germans. Consequently, he demanded that Sudetenland be turned over to German control. Of course, this was totally unacceptable to the Czechs. But Hitler continued to press his claims against Czechoslovakia. The Western states, eager to avoid another European war, insisted on an international conference to settle the matter. On 30 September 1938 the Munich Agreement was signed and control of the Sudetenland passed to Germany, with France and Britain guaranteeing the newly drawn borders of Czechoslovakia. Hitler also pledged not to go to war with Britain. Within six months, Hitler had invaded Czechoslovakia and controlled the whole country.

As a consequence of the Munich Agreement, Hitler consolidated his grip on Eastern Europe and invaded Poland the following year. Clearly, the policy of appeasing Hitler had failed dismally. Rather than forestalling war in Europe, the Munich Agreement actually made war possible by tipping the **balance of power** in Germany's favour. Had the West been prepared to go to war to protect Czechoslovakia against Germany, a full-scale world war might have been averted. This is, of course, conjecture. But there is no doubt that the annexation of the Sudetenland made Hitler a more formidable enemy than he otherwise might have been.

The moral which policymakers and scholars have drawn from this unsavoury affair is that the international community must not accommodate aggressive and unreasonable states. To do so is to court disaster. But while this holds true in the case of Nazi Germany, it is important not to rule out conciliation altogether. There may well be occasions when appeasement is an appropriate policy option. It is conceivable that a state may have legitimate grievances which should be heard and accommodated. One of the dangers with ruling out accommodation and conciliation is that it may actually increase the possibility of **misperception** and leave a state with no other option but to go to war. Moreover, there is now a tendency for government elites to use the example of Munich to defend their own aggressive foreign policies. It is no accident that US policymakers revisited the Munich case as a way of justifying their involvement in Iraq and in the former Yugoslavia during the 1990s. But it is as important not to be swayed by such rhetoric as it is to recognise that a policy of appeasement can have dangerous outcomes.

Whether a policy can be condemned as a form of appeasement is ultimately context-dependent. Each case needs to be evaluated on its merits.

*See also:* **balance of power; misperception; prisoners' dilemma**

*Further reading:* Carr, 1946; McDonough, 1998; Robbins, 1997

## ARAB LEAGUE

The Arab League was established in 1945 to promote the common interests of Arab states. As a voluntary association of member states, it is designed to implement social, cultural, and political programmes and to maintain the collective unity of those states with majority Arab populations. As such, the Arab League represents the governing body of the Arab nation, which stretches from the Middle East to North Africa down to the Southeastern African equatorial region. Currently, the League consists of the following 22 members: Egypt, Iraq, Lebanon, Saudi Arabia, Syria, Jordan, Yemen, Algeria, Bahrain, Comoros, Djibouti, Kuwait, Libya, Mauritania, Morocco, Oman, Qatar, Somalia, Sudan, Tunisia, and the United Arab Emirates. Although not a state, the Palestinian Liberation Organisation (PLO) has long remained a member of the League. Perhaps more importantly, the struggle for Palestinian statehood continues to draw broad and unflagging support among the current member states of the League. Indeed, many Arab leaders have publicly declared that peace in the Middle East will ultimately depend on the resolution of the Israeli–Palestinian conflict. Still, it remains unclear if all Arab authorities will elect to recognise the **legitimacy** and **sovereignty** of the Israeli state. For instance, Hamas, the majority political party in the Palestinian Authority, refuses to recognise Israel's right to exist, which has prompted the EU to impose trade sanctions on the Palestinian Authority.

Structurally, the Arab League consists of a Council, which deliberates and votes on resolutions, and Economic Cooperation bodies. Whilst its day to day operations are run by the Secretary General, each member state recognises the special parameters of Arab state sovereignty. In this case, virtually all the constitutions of Arab states refer to the state as independent and sovereign, whilst recognising Islam as the state religion, and proclaiming Arabic as the official language. As such there is no Arab nation-state *per se*: only one Arab nation to which all Arab states and people belong.

This theme of Arab nationhood has long provided an important source of Pan Arabism. During the 1950s and 1960s, Abu Nasser, the leader of Egypt, used his leadership skills and charisma to promote a powerful brand of Arab socialism. Nasser, for instance, saw Arab socialism, or the struggle to promote social equality within and among Arab states, as providing an essential counterweight to US imperialism in the region. Although many Arab states remain largely committed to promoting these values, oil revenues from **OPEC** have brought closer economic ties among the corporate elites and Arab state leaders. Moreover, it could be argued that such favourable economic developments have allowed Arab states to tolerate the strong US military presence in the region. Whether or not oil revenues are the key source of this presence is an issue that cannot be entirely ignored.

What is more, internal political stability in the Middle East region continues to be threatened in a number of ways, including the threat of global **jihad** posed by Al Qaeda and the external pressures for political (democratic) reform. The Iraq War (2003–) has also exposed the often volatile effects of imposing democracy on Arab states, suggesting that overcoming authoritarianism in this region will require time and patience. And while there are signs of democratic political change, including Saudi Arabia's decision to hold municipal elections in the summer of 2004, the Arab League continues to hold a rather fragile consensus on the need for democratic change.

In addition to the problem of internal political change, the issue of **sovereignty** continues to strain relations among state members. The League's decision in 1990 to issue a resolution in support of the US-led multilateral intervention of Kuwait led to sharp divisions within the League. While many members saw Saddam's actions as violating Arab state sovereignty, others saw the intervention as an extension of US imperialism in the region. More recently, the Arab League has shown an increasing willingness to critique US policies in the region, including its handling of the Iraq War, and has remained united in its stiff opposition to the Israeli state's occupation of the West Bank. In the case of the latter, however, it has shown little, if any effective resolve, short of issuing declarations that support the UN Security Council's resolution of condemning Israel's occupation of the West Bank. Still, the League continues to exercise an important influence on the region. On a local level, for instance, it has helped shape school curricula and create a regional telecommunications union that has brought many social and economic benefits to various regions.

*See also:* **collective security; jihad; Organisation of Petroleum Exporting Countries (OPEC); sovereignty; war on terror**

*Further reading:* Barnett, 1998; Hourani, 1991

## ARMS CONTROL

One way of dealing with the proliferation of weapons is through negotiated arms control agreements, which have a long history in international relations. The Athenians, for example, entered into a range of arms control measures with the Spartans almost 2,500 years ago. In the early nineteenth century, the Rush–Bagot Treaty (1817) demilitarised the border between the United States and Canada. The number of arms control agreements increased markedly in the twentieth century, however. This is partly due to the advent of nuclear weapons and the danger of a nuclear **war** between the **superpowers**. But the problem of the horizontal spread of weapons among states – both conventional and nuclear – has also been an important stimulus to arms control.

Arms control is different from **disarmament**. Advocates of the latter argue that the only way to ensure peaceful international relations is to eliminate weapons from the calculations of states. In contrast, the purpose of arms control is purely regulatory. Its goal is not to construct a new world **order**, but to manage the existing one. Indeed, arms control may go hand in hand with an increase in the numbers and types of weapons among states.

Controlling the proliferation of weapons can be accomplished in a number of ways, and different treaties embody different strategies. These include:

1  limiting the number and kinds of weapons that can legally be used in war;
2  limiting the potential for destruction after war has broken out by reducing the size of arsenals;
3  reducing the overall number of weapons;
4  banning technologies which may have a destabilising effect on the **balance of power**;
5  developing confidence-building measures.

Typically, arms control agreements ban certain classes of weapons and weapons systems, place upper limits on the number of weapons that states may possess, limit the size and destructive power of weapons, ban the production of weapons that will increase the likelihood of war, and stop or at least slow the development of new technologies. They also include new methods of communication, verification, and compliance. Since 1945, many arms control agreements have focused on the proliferation of nuclear, chemical, and biological weapons, the problems associated with anti-ballistic missile systems, and on reducing the frequency of nuclear tests around the world. Some of the most famous agreements include:

- the 1925 *Geneva Protocol* banning the use of gas and bacteriological weapons;
- the 1959 *Antarctic Treaty* preventing states from using Antarctica for military purposes;
- the 1968 *Nuclear Non-Proliferation Treaty* (NPT) limiting the transfer of nuclear weapons and allied technologies to non-nuclear states;
- the 1972 *Biological Weapons Convention* banning the manufacture and possession of biological weapons;
- the 1972 *Strategic Arms Limitation Talks* (SALT 1) controlling the development and use of anti-ballistic missile systems;
- the 1989 *Conventional Forces in Europe* (CFE) *Treaty* limiting the number of conventional arms that could be deployed in Europe;
- the 1991–2 *Strategic Arms Reduction Talks* (START 1) reducing the size of the superpowers' nuclear arsenals;
- the 1993 *Chemical Weapons Convention* (CWC) requiring that signatories destroy their chemical weapons stocks within a decade;
- the 1998 *Anti-Personnel Landmines Treaty* (APLT).

But while there is little doubt that arms control played an important role in reducing tensions between the superpowers during the cold war, the history of that period reveals a number of problems with arms control agreements. Most importantly, accurate verification is difficult. Put bluntly, states often cheat. They sometimes fail to disclose the full extent of their weapons stocks, build secret installations, and move their weapons around. They can also be uncooperative and evasive with on-site inspectors. Even with technical advances such as satellite surveillance, it is impossible to be certain that states will abide by the terms of their agreements. The spectre of mistrust haunts all arms control agreements.

Closely allied to this problem is the propensity of states to disregard arms control agreements after they have signed them. Although the United States has signed the 1993 Chemical Weapons Convention, for example, it has developed substantial quantities of chemical weapons since then. This raises the issue of the enforceability of arms control agreements. How does the international community enforce arms control agreements in a world of **sovereign** states? Short of armed intervention, there are few credible options available. **Sanctions**, economic inducements, and diplomatic persuasion have all been tried, but their overall success is difficult to gauge. At any rate, even if these sorts of **coercive** measures work against small, economically weak states, it is difficult to see how the international community could enforce such agreements against the United States, China, or Russia.

These problems highlight the extremely fragile nature of arms control agreements. It is for this reason that a number of scholars have expressed scepticism about their contribution to international stability. Perhaps the biggest problem is the unequal distribution of power in the international system. A number of countries in the **Third World** have argued that arms control agreements, like the 1968 Non-Proliferation Treaty (NPT), are a way for the First World to maintain its stranglehold over the international system. Rather than leading to a reduction in the incidence of war and to a lessening of international tension, arms control ensures the continued subservience of many of the world's less powerful states. Whether one agrees with this view or not, it is certainly a powerful criticism and one not likely to change in the near future.

*See also:* **arms trade; cold war; deterrence; disarmament; mutually assured destruction; nuclear proliferation; security dilemma; weapons of mass destruction**

*Further reading:* Adler, 1992; Freedman, 1981; Gallagher, 1998; Pierre, 1997

## ARMS TRADE

It is somewhat ironic that the five permanent members of the **United Nations**' Security Council (i.e. those nominally responsible for maintaining international peace and security) are also among the biggest suppliers of conventional weapons to other states in the international system. Although many observers talked about a peace dividend after the **cold war**, and hopes were raised that arms industries could be converted from the production of deadly weapons to more peaceful uses, the arms trade persists as a vibrant industry in the twenty-first century. The United States remains the biggest arms supplier in the world. It has consistently controlled more than half the arms trade market over the past decade, and its sales of weapons are worth approximately US$20 billion per year. For all the concern raised over Russian arms exports, they comprise less than one-tenth of the world trade in arms. Aside from the United States, Britain and France are major players in the industry, and China's exports in arms have been increasing steadily over the past few years.

The arms trade refers to the transfer, from one country to another, of arms, ammunition, and combat support equipment. Such transfers are usually conducted on a commercial basis or on the basis of military assistance programmes. The recipients are normally governments, although a large network of black-market channels has arisen to supply insurgents, separatist groups, and other paramilitary organisations. Whilst **Third World** countries account for two-thirds of all arms imports, the main recipients of the arms trade are located in the Middle East. Today, Israel, Saudi Arabia, and Kuwait are the main importers of weapons from the West.

The end of the cold war was a major blow for the arms trade industry, which has shrunk to about half of its value in the 1980s. As a consequence many defence industries face a distinctly uncertain future. With the contraction of military forces among **NATO** member states (including the United States and Great Britain), arms exports have become more essential to the industry while at the same time generating political controversy and public debate.

In large part the controversy reflects the attempt by the industry to achieve an 'ethical' approach to arms sales. Critics claim that arms sales assist repressive states in perpetrating **human rights** abuses, that they cause wars, that they result in increased war casualties, and that they impede economic development. They point to the increase in small arms sales, which have killed an estimated 500,000 people worldwide. In 2003, for instance, the United States and **European Union** were the biggest exporters of small arms. Representatives of the arms trade industry take a different position. They argue that to withdraw unilaterally from the arms trade has the potential to inhibit the development of exporting states' technological base, and thus undermine defence and foreign policy objectives. They also point out that repressive states do not need expensive, high-tech modern weaponry to abuse their citizens or to engage in genocide; such weaponry is unsuitable for that purpose. After all, up to 800,000 people were slaughtered in Rwanda in 1994, most of whom were killed with primitive machetes. Arms sales can be destabilising but they can also be stabilising; the ultimate underlying causes of instability are always political. Moreover, they claim that there is no evidence of a correlation between the levels of arms exports and the numbers of casualties in wars. Supporters also argue that while weapons purchases may direct some resources away from civilian use in the Third World, they have not prevented economic development. Finally, they suggest that whilst the export of arms can be used for the purposes of repression, those weapons can also be used to deter aggression and to maintain regional **balances of power**. Of course, such arguments are entirely self-serving, but they are worth bearing in mind if only because the burden of proof lies with those who support the arms trade rather than its opponents.

There have been some important developments in recent years to regulate the arms trade. These include efforts to control the export of long-range ballistic missiles and land mines, and the promotion of greater transparency in the reporting of arms transfers. In 1991 the **United Nations** General Assembly voted to establish an annual register of imports and exports of major weapons systems, although the register remains a voluntary instrument. Little work has been done, however, to regulate the growing black market in arms transfers.

*See also:* **arms control; cold war; disarmament; foreign aid; war; wars of the third kind**

*Further reading:* Craft, 1999; Kaldor, 1999; Klare and Lumpe, 1998; Krause, 1992; Laurance, 1992

## AXIS OF EVIL

President George W. Bush introduced this term in his 2002 State of the Union Address to refer to Iraq's, Iran's, and North Korea's intent to attack the United States with weapons of mass destruction. Examples of other political axes include most notably the axis powers of the Second World War. Here though, the term 'axis' reflected the coordination of common strategies and policies; whilst in the case of the axis of evil, one encounters little if any policy coordination among the rogue states. As such, the Axis of Evil provides a strategic measure for linking 'evil' with the intent of state leaders to use weapons of mass destruction against other states. Metaphorically, then, it represents a common axle of evil intent around which the threat of the rogue states turns. Such an axle, it could be said, divides civilised and uncivilised states in a manner analogous to the **clash of civilisations**, and is intended to demonstrate which particular states constitute the gravest potential threat to the values of the civilised world.

Not long after President Bush's State of the Union Address, attempts were made to expand the list of states belonging to the axis of evil. In his speech delivered on 6 May, the then Undersecretary of State, John K. Bolton, announced that Libya, Syria, and Cuba all showed signs of sponsoring terrorism or a willingness to pursue weapons of mass destruction with the intent of threatening the United States. Whilst Cuba strongly denied manufacturing any such weapons, Libya promptly announced its plans to dismantle its programme of weapons of mass destruction.

Accordingly, the axis of evil might be best characterised as the use of a metaphorical symbol to demonise the enemy. Here one encounters the stark and perilous dichotomy creating an us versus them distinction: where deep-seated fear fuels the perception of another state's intention to use their weapons of mass destruction. It is this dichotomy, however, that exposes the apparent rift between the Bush administration's neo-conservative doctrine and that of political **realism**. The primary difference in this respect is the pronounced exigency of removing the constraints associated with self-preservation and the balance of power; and the corresponding failure to structure prudent foreign policy in accordance with these constraints.

Carl Schmitt (1880–1972), a prominent German political scientist, argued that outside threats of conquest posed a constant challenge to the political survival of the state. He theorised that the concept of the political was based on the friend/enemy relationship, a term that presupposed the possibilities of war and the attendant need to preserve the political sovereignty of the state from a foreign invasion. Whilst Schmitt largely reserved this distinction for deterring threats, as opposed to launching an aggressive war, the axis of evil can be seen as an extended metaphor for reserving the absolute right to preserve the political values of freedom and democracy.

Some might argue that the axis of evil is largely a self-fulfilling prophecy; that it represents how the Bush administration's own lack of forgiveness or sensitivity provides the very source of the rogue state's evil intentions. Moreover, in a world of imperfect information, evidence of a country's intent to use weapons of mass destruction can have dire consequences, as the Iraq War has shown. More importantly, we need to distinguish between the evil state and the people or innocent civilians of that state. Given the present course of the Iraq War and recent warnings of another potential attack against Iran, there remains much concern that the axis of evil label will continue to threaten friendly relations, good will, and diplomacy between and among states.

*See also:* **Bush doctrine; clash of civilisations; pre-emption; unilateralism; war; war on terror; weapons of mass destruction**

*Further reading:* Casebeer, 2004; Cummings, 2004; Difilippo, 2004; Hayden and Lansford, 2003

## BALANCE OF POWER ✓

No concept in the study of international relations has been discussed more often than this one. It has been defined in so many ways, however, that it has become an ambiguous idea. Used objectively or descriptively, the term indicates the relative distribution of power among states into equal or unequal shares. Traditionally, it refers to a state of affairs in which no one state predominates over others. Prescriptively, it refers to a policy of promoting a power equilibrium on the assumption that unbalanced power is dangerous. Prudent states that are at a disadvantage in the balance of power will (or at least should) form an **alliance** against a potentially **hegemonic** state or take other measures to enhance their ability to restrain a possible aggressor. Also, one state may opt for a self-conscious balancing role, changing sides as necessary to preserve the equilibrium. A balance of power policy requires that a state moderate its independent quest for power, since too much power for one state may bring about self-defeating reactions of fear and hostility from other states.

All balance of power systems have certain conditions in common:

1    a multiplicity of sovereign states unconstrained by any legitimate central authority;
2    continuous but controlled competition over scarce resources or conflicting values;
3    an unequal distribution of status, wealth, and power potential among the political actors that make up the system.

Inequality and the ever-present threat of violence combine to give the dominant and the subordinate states a shared but unequal interest in preserving the **order** of the system, whose equilibrium protects their **sovereignty**. The balance of power is a kind of compromise among states that find its order preferable to absolute chaos, even though it is a system that favours the stronger and more prosperous states at the expense of sovereign equality for all of them.

**Great powers** play the leading roles in balance of power systems because of their preponderant military force and their control of key technologies. A dominant or hegemonic state will often try to justify its position either by providing certain **public goods** for other states (such as a beneficial economic order or international **security**), or because it embraces values that are common to a set of states. Great powers reap a disproportionate share of the benefits of the system, but they also bear a greater responsibility as its regulators.

It is common to make some key distinctions about the balance of power. First is the distinction between unipolarity, bipolarity, and multipolarity.

- *Unipolarity* is a situation in which one state or **superpower** dominates the international system. Many would argue that the United States is in this position today.
- *Bipolarity* exists when two states or blocs of states are roughly equal in power. The term is often applied to the period of the cold war between the United States and the Soviet Union, although it is misleading. Simply because the two superpowers were both more powerful than all other states, they were not equally as powerful as each other. The Soviet

pole was far weaker than its rival in economic terms, although its ability to engage in a sustained nuclear arms race with its rival and project its conventional military power abroad concealed its underlying weakness.

- *Multipolarity* refers to a situation in which there are at least three great powers. The classic example is nineteenth-century Europe. In this case, one state's greater military and economic strength does not necessarily give it preponderance because weaker states can combine against it.

A second important distinction is between regional or local balances and the balance of power in the international system as a whole. Although historians have often spoken of the European balance of power in the eighteenth and nineteenth centuries as if it were the whole of international relations, this was effectively true only for the brief period when European states dominated the rest of the world. Today, we have a number of *regional* balances overlaid by a *unipolar* pattern.

A third distinction is between a *subjective* and an *objective* balance of power. One of the great difficulties of evaluating the balance of power in the twenty-first century is that power resources are unevenly distributed among the great powers and there is no simple correspondence between possession of a resource and the ability to control outcomes as a consequence. For example, whilst the United States is overwhelmingly dominant in terms of military power, economic power is much more evenly distributed between the United States, Western Europe, and Japan.

One of the most contested issues in the study of international relations is the relationship between the balance of power and the stability of the international system. One should note that the term 'stability' is itself contested! For example, it can mean peace but it can also refer to the endurance of a particular distribution of power regardless of how peaceful it is. Some scholars argue that multipolarity is less stable than unipolarity or bipolarity. Under multipolarity, threats are allegedly more difficult to evaluate, and there is a tendency for states to 'pass the buck' and rely on others to balance against an emerging state. On the other hand, when power is concentrated among one or two superpowers that compete at a global level, they are likely to export their rivalry abroad. For example, although the United States and the former Soviet Union never fought a war directly with each other, over 20 million people died in the **Third World** as the superpowers intervened in a series of so-called 'proxy wars' in the second half of the twentieth century.

The debate between supporters and opponents of particular balance of power systems is inconclusive for two main reasons. First, the distribution of power among states is a variable located at a structural **level of analysis**. Its relationship to outcomes at the level of relations among states has to be determined in light of the character of the great powers and their particular relationships. Second, since the origins of the modern state system in the seventeenth century, there are too few cases of different systems across which one can make meaningful comparisons. The balance of power is a dynamic concept which, in practice, has to be understood in context. For example, it is difficult to draw conclusions about the allegedly bipolar balance of the cold war when so much of the competition between the United States and the former Soviet Union revolved around the novel challenges of the nuclear era

*See also:* **alliance; anarchy; clash of civilisations; cold war; concert of powers; geopolitics; great powers; levels of analysis; mutually assured destruction; power; realism; superpower**

*Further reading:* Haas, 1953; Kegley and Raymond, 1992; Layne, 1993; Mearsheimer, 1990; Wagner, 1993; Waltz, 1979; Wilkinson, 1999

# BEGGAR-THY-NEIGHBOUR POLICIES

Governments sometimes pursue policies at the expense of other states that they believe will be in their own country's short-term **national interest**. However, if other countries follow their example, such beggar-thy-neighbour policies can be self-defeating. A good analogy is crowd behaviour in sports. If your view of the action is blocked by the person sitting in front of you, it is in your interest to stand up and get a better view, even if by so doing you prevent those behind you from seeing what is going on. However, if everyone stands up then the situation is no better than it would have been if they had remained seated, only now it is more uncomfortable. The term is applicable to many situations in international relations, although it is generally used to illustrate some of the dynamics that contributed to the Great Depression in the 1930s, and as a warning to governments that may be tempted to pursue similar policies in the future.

In the face of dramatic economic problems, and in particular the combination of stagnant or declining production and rising unemployment, the major advanced **capitalist** states pursued three beggar-thy-neighbour policies in the late 1920s and 1930s. Each country took steps to maximise its exports while at the same time minimising its imports.

First, in the 1920s the preferred method of rationing imports was fiscal deflation, as governments raised taxes and reduced spending. Fiscal deflation works by acting to reduce domestic expenditure. The idea is that if a state cuts its spending by, say, 10 per cent, then it will cut its import bill by 10 per cent. The argument was that fiscal deflation would lead to a low-wage, low-tax environment that would enhance the competitiveness of a country's export sector. The problem is that, when every country was doing the same thing, no country could gain a competitive advantage but all countries would move into a deflationary spiral because spending was falling everywhere. Exports decreased. Poverty also increased, especially amongst primary producers.

Second, governments unilaterally devalued their currency, thereby hoping that their exports would be cheaper for overseas consumers, and domestic consumers would reduce expenditure on expensive imports. Devaluation became more popular than fiscal deflation as the Depression progressed. This became possible as countries left the fixed exchange rate system known as the gold standard. Those countries that devalued earlier (e.g. Britain) recovered from the Depression much more quickly than the late devaluers did. Competitive devaluations have been cited by some writers as a key cause of the Depression. Certainly the devaluation of Britain in 1931 had an adverse impact on the United States in 1932. But the world's states could not devalue all at once, so devaluations cannot do the kind of damage that fiscal deflation can do.

Third, governments raised tariffs on imports, thereby encouraging domestic consumption of domestic production and hopefully reducing unemployment. Sometimes this was done on an empire-wide basis, such as Britain's imperial preference system. Throughout the 1920s, tariff protection did exist, but at the same levels as in the pre-First World War economy. Thus, the 1920s were not a decade of protectionism. It was the countries that resisted devaluation that turned first to tariff protection (e.g. the United States, which devalued in 1933) or exchange controls (e.g. Germany). Protection is the most direct way to ration imports, and there was a wave of protectionism in the 1930s. Some commentators have argued that tariff protection ultimately paved the way for the recovery of the international economy. Protectionism was a result of the Depression, not a cause. Even J. M. Keynes, the most famous economist of the era, favoured national self-sufficiency in 1933. He saw that each country had to find its own solution, but that no country could risk a reflation unless it could ensure that the extra spending would lead to domestic employment growth.

Keynes understood that the international economy could not recover until each national economy was restored to full health. The immediate problem was to reverse the disastrous effects of the beggar-thy-neighbour fiscal deflations that had caused the declines in world commodity prices, world trade volumes, and the values of financial assets. His blueprint for the recovery of the international economy was presented to the international conference at **Bretton Woods**, New Hampshire, in 1944.

This problem was a major concern for the architects of the Bretton Woods system, and that concern increased after the collapse of the system in the early 1970s. However, it receded when inflation became a major challenge. Because of the implications for price stability, countries were unwilling to use their exchange rates to export unemployment since this would simply contribute to domestic inflation.

At the beginning of the twenty-first century, the threat of competitive devaluations is much more serious than at any time since the 1970s, because the danger now (as in the 1930s) is deflation, not inflation. There were some signs of deflation during the currency crisis in Europe in the early 1990s when some countries pulled out of the European Monetary System (EMS) and devalued their currencies. This is why it is important to have expansionary policies in the countries with external surpluses. This was a crucial factor after the Asian economic collapse in 1997. Fortunately, two factors have inhibited the resort to beggar-thy-neighbour policies in this crisis. First, China did not devalue its currency to make its exports more competitive relative to other Asian countries. Second, the United States was still enjoying rapid economic growth and was therefore able to absorb exports from Asian countries despite the ongoing recession in Japan. Nonetheless, it is still too soon to write off the experience of beggar-thy-neighbour policies as a footnote to the history of the Great Depression.

*See also:* **Bretton Woods; embedded liberalism; hegemonic stability theory; multilateralism; regional trade blocs**

*Further reading:* Hall and Ferguson, 1998; Keylor, 1992; Kindleberger, 1973

## BRETTON WOODS

Even before the declaration of war on the axis powers (Germany, Italy, and Japan) in 1942, officials in Washington were pondering the shape and character of the post–1945 international economic system. Policymakers came to believe that the Great Depression and the rise of fascism were in part a consequence of countries pursuing discriminatory trade policies during the interwar years. By 1941, an open trading regime had become a major foreign policy goal of the Roosevelt administration. This was clearly spelt out in the text of the Atlantic Charter. Article IV states that all countries should have 'access, on equal terms, to the trade and to the raw materials of the world which are needed for their economic prosperity'.

This approach also underpinned the 1942 Lend–Lease agreement with Britain. The Lend–Lease Act allowed the President to transfer munitions and other war-fighting material to those countries fighting the axis powers. In the case of Britain, however, this was conditional on its acceptance of a new postwar international economic order.

The most significant step in putting this foreign policy goal into practice came just before the end of the Second World War. In August 1944 the United States, Britain, and 42 other countries met at Bretton Woods, a small resort town in New Hampshire, to sketch out the rules and formal institutions that would govern their trade and monetary relations. The main architects of the conference were Harry White of the US Treasury and John Maynard Keynes, Britain's leading economist.

Formally known as the International Monetary and Financial Conference of the United and Associated Nations, Bretton Woods made decisions that were instrumental, not only in bringing about the economic recovery of Europe, but in establishing a framework for commercial and financial conduct which continues to be influential today. Delegates from the former Soviet Union attended, but had little effective say in the discussions. Given their longstanding antipathy to **capitalism**, it was not surprising that the Soviets would not accept the institutional arrangements agreed to by the other participants. It is also important to bear in mind that the US had become the predominant military and economic power. Since the late 1930s its industrial output had doubled, it had achieved full employment, and it was well on the way to winning the war in Europe and the Pacific. It also had the largest standing army among the Western states and possessed the only functioning economy of any global significance. Thus, while Bretton Woods was meant to be a victors' conference, the United States set the agenda and dominated the proceedings. The US, for example, rejected Keynes's idea of creating a central world currency reserve which would redistribute trade surpluses to those countries in financial deficit. Instead, the Americans pushed for a liberal system based on capital mobility and **free trade**.

The meetings at Bretton Woods resulted in a range of measures to stabilise the international financial system and facilitate the expansion of trade. More specifically, the Bretton Woods system included the creation of three formal institutions: the International Bank for Reconstruction and Development (IBRD), commonly known as the **World Bank**; the **International Monetary Fund** (IMF); and the General Agreement of Tariffs and Trade (GATT). The World Bank was initially designed to offer assistance in the form of loans to those countries devastated by the Second World War. The IMF was set up to oversee the management of fixed exchange rates between member states. GATT was set up to break down discriminatory trade practices. The distinctive feature of the Bretton Woods system, however, was the fixing of exchange rates. All the world's currencies were valued (by the IMF) in terms of US dollars, and gold was used to set the value of the dollar. In 1945, the US held around 75 per cent of the world's reserve gold stocks (approximately US$25 billion). Under the agreement, the US promised to convert dollars into gold on demand.

Although Bretton Woods was remarkably successful in reviving an international economy destroyed by war, it was seriously flawed as a long-term economic strategy. The convertibility of dollars into gold was initially meant to give stability to the financial system. As US dollars were shipped abroad in the form of aid and to pay for goods for US consumers, foreign reserve banks would convert them into gold. By 1970, US gold stocks dropped to US$10 billion. Essentially, Bretton Woods failed to provide enough new gold to compensate for the growth in world trade. The Bretton Woods system formally came to an end in 1971 when Richard Nixon announced that the US would no longer exchange dollars for gold. From that point on, currencies began to float freely against each other.

Despite its formal demise, much of the framework of the Bretton Woods system remains. The World Bank, the IMF, and the **World Trade Organisation** (GATT's successor) continue to play a central role in setting the norms and rules of international monetary and trade relations. But rising rates of unemployment, worries about growth sustainability, and increasing levels of poverty in Africa, Asia, and Latin America are leading to calls for a new Bretton Woods conference. Whether this happens is still an open question. The ideology of globalisation would seem to run counter to such a proposal. There is no doubt, however, that the conference held in New Hampshire in 1944 has been a major influence on the economic character of the world since 1945.

*See also:* **beggar–thy–neighbour policies; capital controls; capitalism; embedded liberalism; International Monetary Fund; multilateralism; regional trade blocs; World Bank; World Trade Organisation**

*Further reading:* Hawes, 1990; Helleiner, 1996; Schild, 1995

# BUSH DOCTRINE ✓

The Bush doctrine represents a sweeping overhaul of US foreign policy and a highly aggressive plan to reshape world **order** in the wake of the 9/11 attacks on the World Trade Center and Pentagon. Unlike other US governmental doctrines, such as the Truman doctrine, which advocated containment in the form of military and economic assistance to any country threatened by Soviet aggression, the Bush doctrine moves beyond containment and defence to one of offence or aggressive action aimed at eliminating the enemy or terrorism. In many ways, the doctrine redefines traditional *Realpolitik* to the extent that it applies US military **power** to restructure international **security** in terms of US **national interests**. Unsurprisingly, then, it has stirred controversy overseas. Many, for instance, argue that the doctrine reflects a new age of **imperialism** or Empire; and that the doctrine has resulted in the over-extension of US power overseas, or what Paul Kennedy has referred to as 'imperial over-stretch'.

There are four identifiable pillars of the doctrine.

- The spread of democracy;
- Threat and preventive **war**;
- **Unilateralism**;
- American **hegemony**.

The first pillar represents the forcible spread of democracy to other states. In the context of the invasions of Afghanistan and Iraq, the Bush administration has sought to implement new democratic **regimes**, albeit with mixed results. In these cases, democratic stability and institution-building have been hampered by the resurgence of the Taliban and Al Qaeda. As this result suggests, democracy remains a delicate political process, and, when imposed by an outside power, often fuels resentment and distrust of that foreign occupying power.

The second pillar refers to the strategic nature of preventative war. Here the aim is twofold: to launch an attack or war that will disable the target's ability to attack in the future; and to deter other states that might wish to strike the hegemon with weapons of mass destruction. The Bush administration has insisted that the only way to prevent **terrorism** is to eliminate the threat before it materialises. Whilst it is unclear if the use of military **coercion** has provided an effective deterrent, military **pre-emption** has managed to instil fear and anxiety in many foreign countries concerning US intentions.

The third pillar, by comparison, represents the United States's capacity to act unilaterally to promote its national interests. Unilateralism characterises one country's willingness and capacity to act alone to achieve its military, political, and/or economic goals. The idea here is that unilateralism constitutes a more efficient and streamlined framework for conducting war against another state(s). Sometimes, however, the hegemonic power's unilateralist agenda can result in the erosion of this power. This may, for instance, take the form of opposition by other major power players, or give rise to an insurgency, or resistance movement by allowing that group to focus its hatred on one power. Nonetheless, unilateralism typically requires an assertive hegemon: a particular willingness to deploy military, economic, and political resources.

Finally, the fourth pillar refers to US hegemony. By hegemony, we are referring to the concentration of power in one state and the capacity of the state to use that power to project and sustain its power. Hegemony does not simply refer to excessive concentration of military power, but also to the capacity of actors to use their economic and cultural advantages to exact consent from less powerful states. When the Soviet Union collapsed in 1991, for example, the US became the world hegemon, whilst its cultural and economic influence rapidly increased overseas. Under the Bush doctrine, US hegemony has come to represent the US' determination to use its military superiority to actively enforce world order and to punish any **rogue state** that fails to comply with US demands.

Thus, one broad criticism of American hegemony, as exercised under the Bush doctrine, has been its failure to accommodate the needs or wishes of other states. A hegemon, for instance, must attach priority to securing the willingness of other states to abide by its moral and strategic goals and rules, lest it risk losing the support of these other states. Accordingly, the lack of political accommodation in this respect can make an important difference in whether a hegemon maintains its power and influence overseas. The greatest challenge facing the Bush doctrine, then, is not the elimination of terrorism, but the need to balance its aggressive objectives against the need to accommodate other states' foreign policy interests.

*See also:* **anarchy; axis of evil; clash of civilisations; containment; global governance; hegemony; imperialism; national interest; pre-emption; security; unilateralism; war on terror**

*Further reading:* Dombrowski and Payne, 2003; Ikenberry, 2002; Jervis, 2003; Kennedy, 1987; Monten, 2005

## CAPITAL CONTROLS

A broad range of measures that governments undertake to restrict the movement of capital and money across their national borders. In an era of allegedly accelerating globalisation, and in light of the Asian financial collapse of the late 1990s, international political economists are debating the pros and cons of capital controls. Such controls are not new, although their use has been on the decline since the late 1960s. The debate was sparked by the decision of the Malaysian government to impose capital controls in 1998 to prevent volatile capital flows in and out of its economy, particularly speculative capital. Controls on capital flows are usually imposed for two reasons: first, as part of macroeconomic management to reinforce or substitute for other monetary and fiscal measures, and second, to attain long-term national development goals, such as ensuring that residents' savings are locally invested or to reserve certain types of investment activity for residents.

Capital controls may be imposed on capital leaving a country or entering it. The former include controls over outward transactions for direct and equity investments by residents and/or foreigners. For example, restrictions on the repatriation of capital by foreigners can include specifying a period before such repatriation is allowed, and regulations that phase the repatriation according to the availability of foreign exchange. Residents may be restricted as to their holdings of foreign stocks, either directly or through limits on the permissible portfolios of the country's investment funds. Law can also restrict bank deposits abroad by residents. Alternatively, bank accounts and transactions denominated in foreign currencies can be made available to residents, and non-interest-bearing capital reserve requirements can be imposed on deposits in foreign currencies, thus reducing or eliminating the interest paid on them and therefore diminishing their attractiveness. The main purpose of controls over capital outflows is to thwart attempts to shift between currencies during financial crises, which can exacerbate currency depreciation.

Controls on capital flowing into a country have been imposed by both rich and poor states, although for different reasons. When freer capital movements were allowed from the 1960s onwards, large capital inflows posed problems for rich states such as West Germany, the Netherlands, and Switzerland, boosting the demand for their currency and hence making their exports more expensive for overseas consumers. Consequently, they imposed controls such as limits on bank deposits for non-residents.

More recently, some developing countries facing problems due to large speculative capital inflows have also resorted to controls. In 1992 Chile subjected foreign loans entering the country to a reserve requirement of 20 per cent (later raised to 30 per cent). In other words, a certain proportion of each loan had to be deposited in the central bank for a year without earning any interest. In 1994 Brazil imposed a tax on foreign investment in the stock market, and increased the tax on foreign purchases of domestic fixed-interest investments. Similarly, in the same year the Czech Republic taxed banks' foreign exchange transactions, and also imposed limits on short-term borrowing abroad by its banks and other firms. Malaysia imposed capital controls over inflows in 1994 and again in 1998, despite widespread concern in the international finance community.

The debate over the wisdom of imposing capital controls is conducted between those who believe that the state should not interfere with the market, and others who argue that capital controls remain one of the few remaining tools with which governments can attempt to regulate international capital movements that have increased dramatically in recent years. Among economists, the tendency is to argue against them, for five main reasons.

First, they demonstrate an obvious disregard of investors' rights to decide where and how to invest. Second, they drastically reduce the incentive of foreigners and residents to invest when they cannot be sure when they will be able to get their earnings or investments out of a country with capital controls in place. Third, capital controls remove the discipline of the market, which allegedly constantly evaluates and rewards countries that pursue sound, pro-growth policies and penalises those that do not. Fourth, capital controls tend to grow, because when governments ration foreign exchange they limit not only capital inflows but also consumers' ability to purchase imports. Finally, controls allegedly isolate emerging economies and, if allowed to linger, cut off the country imposing them from worldwide economic growth.

One of the most notable features of the world economy is that labour is plentiful and capital is in short supply. Opponents of capital controls argue that achieving greater capital mobility and moving towards full financial market **integration** are central steps to world economic development. This provides the best prospects for transforming the small pool of world savings into the required stock of investment capital.

On the other hand, supporters of capital controls believe that the costs have to be weighed against the benefits of reducing extreme volatility in the movement of speculative capital. Remedies for debtor states whose currency is subject to speculative attack all involve pain to the debtor country, and the costs of capital controls may be lower in some circumstances than the standard prescriptions of the **International Monetary Fund**, which usually involve higher domestic interest rates. Emergency restrictions on capital flows might be the best policy if international investors can be assured that they are not imposed as long-term solutions to a country's economic problems.

Ultimately, the debate over capital controls is unlikely to be resolved definitely in favour of one side or the other. The increasing integration of global capital markets makes it difficult to sustain fixed or managed exchange rates by individual states. Thus for most countries the move towards more free-floating rates is valuable. But since there are also costs from too free a flow of short-term capital, there is a need for capital controls as one tool of macroeconomic policy.

*See also:* **Bretton Woods; capitalism; development; foreign direct investment; globalisation; International Monetary Fund**

*Further reading:* Edwards, 1997; Kahler, 1998; Ries and Sweeney, 1997; Schulze, 2000

# CAPITALISM ✓

Every society has some method of organising its material life. It must produce the goods and services that are deemed useful and/or desirable by the society and then must distribute them for consumption. Societies have accomplished the management of material life in vastly different ways, which are sometimes referred to as *social formations*. The feudalism of Western Europe in the middle ages, the centralisation of production and distribution decisions in the Soviet Union, and the capitalism of modern Japan, Western Europe, and the United States are all examples of different social formations. One of the ways in which social formations such as feudalism, capitalism, or Soviet-style socialism differ is in the control and use of the social surplus. There is a social surplus whenever a society is able to produce more than is needed to sustain material life at the established standard of living. The pyramids of ancient Egypt, the public buildings and vast armies and navies of the Roman Empire, and the ornate cathedrals of medieval Europe are all evidence of a social surplus.

When we examine different social formations and look for the method that each has used to orchestrate its material life, a pattern emerges. There are three basic methods of organisation: *tradition, command,* and the *market.* In the modern world, every actual social formation is to some degree a mixture of all three organisational principles. Modern capitalism is a market-based social formation because the market is the primary organising principle, yet we can find plenty of examples of command and some examples of tradition even here. For example, you may select an occupation based on family traditions. Most farmers also have farmers for parents. And there are certainly elements of command in modern capitalism. Government commandeers, through taxation, the resources to provide for defence, a system of courts, education, and much of our infrastructure (such as roads and harbours). In extreme cases, such as major **wars**, government may commandeer labour directly through the military draft.

Like feudalism, or the slavery-based systems of the ancient world, or socialism, capitalism is a set of social relationships that organise the material life of a society. It is a particular social formation. We can define a social formation in two ways: historically, and by identifying the major features that distinguish it from other social formations. Historically, capitalism is the social formation that began to replace feudalism in parts of Western Europe between 1400 and 1800. With the Industrial Revolution, which started in Britain in the mid-1700s, capitalism became the dominant social formation in the world – in part through conquest and colonisation and in part due to the drive of national leaders to increase their country's power through industrialisation (Japan, for example). The term 'capitalism' only came to be widely used in the later nineteenth century.

We can also identify three major features of capitalism that set it apart from other social formations. First and foremost is capital itself and the drive of capitalists to amass more capital. Capital differs greatly from forms of wealth that were common before capitalism. A feudal baron's castle was certainly a form of wealth, but it was not capital. It did not produce anything – in fact its construction and maintenance absorbed workers who could have been producing more agricultural goods instead. A microchip fabrication plant is different. It is both wealth and capital. It will produce goods that will more than recompense its owners for the costs of building and operating it (or so they hope and expect). This extra compensation, called profit, will enable the owners to build more chip factories.

Second, markets provide information, predictability, and order. If prices and profits fall in one sector of the economy, production will fall in that sector. If prices and profits increase in a sector of the economy, then (other things being equal) production will increase in that sector. If one type of skilled labour is scarce, increasing wages will induce more workers to acquire that skill at the same time that they will induce capitalists to look for new ways to replace this type of labour with machinery or computer programs.

Third, capitalism has two forms of **power**: market and state. As noted above, there is a command element in modern capitalism. But what separates capitalism from other social formations is the way in which the market element and the command element have been separated. We even have different social sciences for each of the sources of **power**: economists study the power that emanates from the market while political scientists study the power that emanates from the state. Note that this would not be true of feudalism or of Soviet-style socialism.

While any social formation must develop a certain degree of stability, social formations have also changed. Feudalism waned and was replaced with capitalism. The Soviet Union disintegrated and its former components are now in a transition phase. Capitalism is a particular type of market system, so we must examine the nature of markets and market systems before we can understand capitalism.

Human societies have always produced goods and services, but they have not always produced commodities. This is an important distinction. A commodity is a good or service that is produced in order to sell it. If you paint your own house, you have produced a service. But if you paint someone else's house for a fee, the house-painting service has become a commodity. The market can only orchestrate the production and distribution of commodities – so the market can only become a major orchestration force when most goods and services have become commodities. So we must not confuse the existence of markets with market systems. For most of history, markets have existed on the fringes of society while command and tradition supplied most of the orchestration of material life. While markets have been around a long time, market systems have not. For most of their history, markets have been on the periphery of material life, not at its centre. The centre of material life was dominated by work on the land. Only since the beginning of the Industrial Revolution has it been possible for societies to feed themselves with anything less than about 80 per cent of their populations working the land.

There are three steps on the road to capitalism. First, the market must penetrate material life, turning the pig as the peasant's bacon into the pig as the peasant's income. Second, labour and land (otherwise known as the factors of production) must themselves become subject to the market process. Only then can the third step proceed: the capitalist can hire labour and rent land in order to reduce costs by operating on a larger scale than the peasant family.

Capitalism is the dominant social formation in the world today, but its future remains uncertain. In particular, it is unclear how the relationship between states and markets will evolve. We live in an era when the state appears to be subordinate to the global market, but capitalism is not a self-sustaining economic order, and its ability to generate wealth depends on the capacity and willingness of states to manage the instability and inequality that capitalism generates at a global level.

*See also:* **Bretton Woods; communism; dependency; development; distributive justice; embedded liberalism; end of history; globalisation; Marxism; world-system theory**

*Further reading:* Gilpin, 1987; Greider, 1998; Heilbroner, 1994; Landes, 1999

## CITIZENSHIP

A citizen enjoys the full privileges and rights accorded by the state constitution or under public law. Such privileges typically refer to the right to vote, hold high office, the receipt of a passport, the right to leave and enter a country freely, equal protection under the law, etc. Whilst many people become a citizen at birth, others are granted citizenship after emigrating to the host country. Citizenship laws require, in most cases, the individual to speak the language proficiently, to have resided in the state for a period of time, and to know the law(s) of the country or the principles and rights encoded in the constitution. Constitutions and/or public law, therefore, provide the particular legal basis of citizenship. Under Germany's Basic Law (German Constitution), for instance, immigrants must be of German descent if they are to become a German citizen.

But while citizens are granted public protection, not all citizens are treated equally, at least not in practice (*de facto*). It is true that most, if not all state constitutions offer clauses of 'equal representation' or 'equal treatment under the law' to their citizens. However, there is no absolute guarantee that citizens will be afforded the same treatment under the law. In some cases, constitutions permit discrimination of ethnic, racial, and national groups, as in the case of Turkey's constitution with respect to Kurdish rights. In others, such as the United States constitution, the limits of the colour blind principle may require the use of racial classification to affirm the rights of individuals belonging to disadvantaged groups. Regardless of the difference, however, there remains the thorny issue of whether a constitution can protect, and in some cases, actively promote the rights of individual members of minority groups.

In *Multicultural Citizenship*, for instance, Will Kymlicka addresses this issue by proposing to level the playing field for ethnic groups and (indigenous) national minority groups. He argues that (shared) cultural values and beliefs are intrinsic to how we define our political loyalties and attachments to the **nation–state**. This explains why many individuals, who have suffered a long history of discrimination and abuse, have not elected to assimilate into the dominant national culture, and why many express their loyalties to the immigrant communities or ethnic groups, as opposed to the state or higher international political authority. To redress these built-in disadvantages, then, Kymlicka proposes a group-differentiated system of rights consisting of: (1) national autonomy; (2) polyethnic rights; and (3) special representation. Together, such rights form the basis of a multicultural society in which oppressed national minorities are entitled to provincial autonomy, and immigrant groups to polyethnic rights and special representation (affirmative action).

Transnationally, citizenship has become a topic of much discussion. For example, the European Union now offers a general set of parameters of citizenship, including an EU passport and a single economic currency, the **euro**. Its evolving framework also features many new institutional forums that allow nationals of member states to participate in higher office. The EU parliament, for instance, comprises parties with no national origin or cause. In addition, the EU also consists of a Court of Justice (European Court of Justice) and has recently adopted (although not ratified) an EU constitution. Although the Netherlands and France voted against ratification of the constitution, the future process of ratification reflects the emergent shift in loyalties from the nation-state to the transnational level. Thus, the issue that arises is whether national identity, or one's allegiance to the nation-state, can be transformed into a transnational one. Jürgen Habermas, for instance, argues that the solidification of an EU identity will depend on a number of important prerequisites, including the entry into force of an EU constitution, greater communicative networks (media), the adoption of an official single language, and a strong sense of solidarity and sympathy among the citizens of the **EU**.

Similarly, international relations theorists, or **cosmopolitans,** have grappled with the transformation of political communities and the possibilities of world citizenship. Andrew Linklater, for instance, argues that national loyalties and attachments continue to be transformed into the individual's loyalties to global society (universal moral principles). Facilitating this transformation has been the rise of the internet and other forms of informational technology that have enabled the individual to communicate across state boundaries. Yet, whilst such technologies have helped to transform political communities, there remains the difficult question of how world citizenship can be fully realised in the absence of strong state cooperation and consensus-building.

*See also:* **communitarianism; distributive justice; euro; European Union; global civil society; global governance; globalisation**

*Further reading:* Baubock, 1996; Beder, 1995; Habermas, 1999; Kymlicka, 1995; Linklater, 1998

# CLASH OF CIVILISATIONS ✓

Samuel Huntington's article 'The clash of civilizations?' was published in the journal *Foreign Affairs* in 1993 and resulted in a heated academic and public debate. Three years later the book with the same title, now without the question mark, appeared. The appeal of Huntington's **theory** is his attempt to develop an all-encompassing construct that explains not only the conflicts of the present and future, but also the key features of the international political system. Since it also touches upon intrastate conflicts, its implications reach beyond international relations.

There have been a number of 'world images' of international politics predicted for the twenty-first century. On the one hand, some of the more optimistic students of **globalisation** and the alleged spread of democracy see the world's peoples coming closer together in economic, political, and cultural terms. On the other hand, more pessimistic analyses have focused on the gap between 'zones of peace and **war**' and clashes between emerging **great powers** in a multipolar era.

Huntington's diagnosis belongs in the pessimistic camp, although it is distinctive in its focus on civilisations as the main unit of analysis. Huntington argues that the world is divided into a number of such civilisations. They are Western, Latin American, African, Islamic, Sinic, Hindu, Christian Orthodox, Buddhist, and Japanese. Within some of these civilisations, there is a core state, often possessing nuclear weapons. Sinic civilisation has China as its core; Japan has its own civilisation. Western civilisation has linked cores in the United States, France, Germany, and the United Kingdom. Russia is the core state of Orthodox Christianity. In contrast, Islam lacks a core state, as does Latin America and Africa. In the future, we can expect conflicts to emerge along the major fault-lines between civilisations: Orthodox versus Western Christianity and Islam; Muslim versus Hindu; Sinic versus Hindu. Africa and Latin America will remain on the sidelines.

Huntington defines a civilisation as the broadest grouping of people beyond the level distinguishing humans from other species. A civilisation is defined by common objective elements – language, history, religion, customs, and institutions – as well as by people's self-identification.

Huntington is particularly concerned about the challenge that Islam poses to the West, both because its birthrate is higher than that of other civilisations and because of the resurgence of its popularity in the wake of the 9/11 attacks. Moreover, its rejection of Western values and American influence means that these two civilisations are bound to clash at some point. If China allies with Islamic states against the United States, the danger of war will be very high.

Huntington offers some guidelines or rules of conduct to avoid such a fate. The core states should abstain from intervening in the internal affairs of other civilisations; they must mediate disputes that could turn into wars on fault-lines between civilisations; and all civilisations should work to identify shared values. As for the West, Huntington urges the United States to strengthen its alliances with others in the Western bloc, and avoid weakening its distinctive cultural values. Huntington is no supporter of multiculturalism and the politics of respect among different minorities.

As one might expect, the argument has been criticised on a number of grounds. First, it has been pointed out that to reduce the number of civilisations to eight or nine does not seem serious. The mention of a possible African civilisation is dubious. Africa is a rich mosaic of cultures; so is Europe. And Europe is not the same as North America. What Huntington lumps together as Western civilisation has considerable internal fractures. Civilisations are not monolithic blocs. Some, for example Islam, are defined primarily by their religious inspiration; in others, such as the Confucian civilisation, the relationship between the religion inspiring them and the political force they exert is less clear. In Western civilisation, Catholic or Protestant versions of Christianity form part of the cultural landscape, although citizens of Western states are deeply divided with regard to religious beliefs. In each of Huntington's civilisations there are trends of thought that follow confessional lines, and others that follow secular lines – a subject of lively debate today in countries such as Turkey and Italy.

Besides religion, cultural splits make it difficult to look at civilisations as politically compact blocs. Huntington talks of Latin American culture but ignores, for example, the division between the Spanish and native cultures. There are also considerable splits between social groups that benefit from the international economic system and those it discriminates against. On the African continent, oligarchies share Western values and cultural preferences while other groups make do with socially devalued lifestyles far removed from modernity. Who represents African civilisation, the English- or French-speaking communities, or the masses that speak only local languages and lack access to Western technologies?

The second major criticism levelled at Huntington's argument is that the relationship between states and civilisations remains unclear. If civilisation is the true independent variable, why did it give way to **power** relationships between states during the **cold war**? Furthermore, Huntington's own analysis of alignments between, say, China and Islam explicitly crosses civilisational boundaries and reflects the interests of powerful states. One might then argue that military power and the balance of power among states could overwhelm the influence of culture and religion.

Finally, critics have argued that Huntington underestimates the enduring strength of Western civilisation, global **capitalism**, and **interdependence**. Whilst his vision does alert us to the ways in which cultural values can exacerbate particular conflicts (e.g. between the former Soviet Union and Afghanistan, and during the wars in the Gulf in 1991 and in Yugoslavia over the past decade), it remains flawed in some important respects.

*See also:* **balance of power; cold war; democratic peace; end of history; geopolitics; global civil society; globalisation; hegemony; jihad**

*Further reading:* Herzog, 1999; Huntington, 1993, 1996; Rashid, 1998; Walt, 1997

## CNN FACTOR

Ted Turner dedicated the Cable News Network (CNN) on 1 June 1980, calling the round-the-clock news operation 'America's news channel'. Using satellites to deliver CNN to cable operators around the country meant that Turner could reach American consumers without having to build a conventional network of local broadcast affiliates to rebroadcast his programmes over the airwaves. Unfortunately for Turner, only about 20 per cent of US television households could receive cable television, and his new 24-hour news channel reached only 1.7 million of those households – far fewer than were needed to make a profit.

The pace at which Ted Turner lost money only accelerated 18 months after CNN's launch, when the company created Headline News, a second 24-hour news network. Predictions of a failure were common among media analysts, who wondered if Turner had sufficiently deep pockets to allow him to lose money for years to come. By the mid-1980s Turner had spent more than US$70 million keeping CNN and Headline News afloat. Yet by 1985, Turner's original news channel was reaching more than 33 million households – four out of five US cable homes – and nearly 40 per cent of all US TV homes. Headline News had 18 million subscribers. These numbers were vital to CNN's economic success because larger audiences mean greater advertising revenues. By the mid-1980s, CNN and Headline News were fast becoming important parts of a growing family of networks making up the Turner Broadcasting System. Shortly after Turner's failed bid that same year to buy CBS, which would have vastly increased the audience for CNN programming, Turner returned to the strategy of expanding audiences through the creation of still more cable-based news and entertainment networks. For Turner, it was a relatively simple matter to combine the CNN and Headline News domestic signals and put them on an international satellite in 1985, thus creating CNN International. Today, CNN has an annual budget of US$400 million, 2,500 employees, and 150 correspondents based in 29 bureaux around the world, all of whom can report via satellite to 145 countries.

When Ted Turner ordered that the flag of the United Nations should fly at CNN's 1980 dedication ceremony (along with the flags of the United States and the state of Georgia), he gave a hint of his ambition to create an international news service. The significance of CNN's global expansion became most evident during the Gulf War in 1991, when its wall-to-wall coverage not only produced the company's highest ratings, but led to much talk of a CNN factor, whereby the network was thought to be inadvertently shaping news events by virtue of its aggressive live television coverage. CNN built much of its reputation as a credible source for international news on the basis of its on-the-spot reporting from such locales as Tiananmen Square in Beijing in May 1989, Baghdad under siege in January 1991, and the Parliament Building in Moscow in August 1991. These and numerous instances to follow also led to CNN's reputation as a news company whose very presence can shape the outcome of the events it covers.

There are two issues around which the alleged CNN factor is debated. The first concerns its impact on international relations. Some observers argue that it was pivotal in explaining the manner and speed with which the **cold war** ended. In the late 1980s, visions of **capitalist** prosperity invaded Eastern Europe by way of TV, underscoring the economic decay in **communist** states. In 1989, the Berlin Wall was demolished, an event unimaginable just a few years earlier. Thanks to satellites and instant global communications, images of the celebration circulated around the world. In the wake of the Soviet breakup, popular revolts brought down one communist government after another in Eastern Europe; news pictures of one uprising inspiring the next. Similarly, when pro-democracy demonstrations broke out in Tiananmen Square in 1989, CNN satellites beamed the dramatic footage around the world live. The United States quickly condemned the massacre that followed and briefly imposed trade sanctions. By contrast, a previous violent crackdown on Chinese dissenters in 1986 drew no response from Western leaders, largely because there were few cameras there.

However, it is easy to exaggerate television's impact on foreign policy. Stark television reports of human suffering can occasionally prompt a decision to send humanitarian aid. But television pictures rarely convince governments to take decisive military action to end the conflicts that give rise to the suffering, such as the war in Bosnia (1992–5), no matter how heart-rending the images.

The second issue of debate is whether the CNN factor, to the extent that it exists, is positive or negative. While Western leaders celebrate the CNN factor in the former Soviet Union, many bemoan its influence on their own governments. Television can educate the public and focus attention on trouble spots that may otherwise be ignored. But television also encourages policymakers to react quickly, perhaps too quickly, to a **crisis**. Whether this is the case partly depends on the degree to which governments have a clear set of policies in place. When they do, they can use the CNN factor to their own advantage.

During the 1991 Gulf War, for example, the Pentagon realised that television news images, selectively controlled and released, could be used to promote the military's agenda instead of working against it. By restricting access to the front lines (which it did not do during the Vietnam War) and by providing its own video news releases, the military featured the precision of high-tech weapons and downplayed the human consequences of war. After the war, it came to light that only 7 per cent of the bombs dropped on Iraq were so-called 'smart bombs'. The remainder were conventional bombs that often produce widespread civilian destruction. It has also been suggested that images of Patriot missiles knocking Iraqi Scuds out of the night-time sky over Tel Aviv created a public perception of the wonders of American military technology and persuaded the Israelis to refrain from attacking Iraq, which would have shattered the allied coalition. Nonetheless, the CNN factor has undoubtedly convinced military planners in the United States that they must fight short and relatively bloodless wars, at least in terms of American casualties if not of their opponents'.

*See also:* **cosmopolitanism; diplomacy; wars of the third kind**

*Further reading:* Badsey, 2000; Giboa, 2005; Moeller, 1999; Robinson, 2002; Strobel, 1996, 1997

# COERCION

Coercion involves the study of threats and demands that encourage the adversary to either reverse its action or stop what it has been doing. Unlike **deterrence**, which stresses the prevention of an attack or the use of threats by state A to dissuade its enemy, state B, from attacking, coercion consists of the use of threats by state A, or the coercer (e.g. state **hegemon**, **NATO, UN**), to reverse an act of aggression by state B. To coerce a state, then, means to employ a range of diplomatic and military options. These may include economic/trade sanctions, blockades, embargoes, and precision air-strikes. The threat of exercising these options serves as either an inducement to the transgressor state to stop what it is doing, or as punishment for not taking the steps to comply with the coercer's demands. Such options, therefore, reflect the costs and benefits of calculated threats, and are often referred to as *ex ante* demands. The *ex ante* mix of punishment and inducements, in this case, can either take the form of a carrot/stick or tit for tat approach. Yet, depending on the seriousness of the violation, the coercer will typically issue an ultimatum in order to place greater pressure on the coerced to comply with its demands.

At stake, then, is the credibility of the coercer. For should the coercer fail to act or enforce its demands, then it necessarily risks losing its political and military credibility, and allowing, in the process, the coerced state to call the bluff of the coercer. According to Lawrence Freedman, credibility involves an important strategic choice between the costs of compliance and non-compliance, or rather the deliberate and purposive use of overt threats to influence the strategic choice of another. According to Freedman, strategic coercion is based on two main objectives: (1) to study the forms of punishment needed to reverse or stop the action of the adversary; and (2) to assess the responsiveness of the coerced to the coercer's threat, or the different ways in which the target constructs its views of reality. Both objectives, in his view, require a deeper understanding and appreciation of the strategic dynamics of coercion.

Rivalling this conception of coercion is Alexander George's theory of coercive diplomacy, which stresses the need for inducements and punishments to convince the enemy that the costs of non-compliance will outweigh the costs of compliance. An essential task of coercive diplomacy is to dissuade the enemy to continue to do what it is doing. Compared to George's theory, Freedman's concept of strategic coercion stresses the range of options available to the target. In this case, the target's responsiveness, in Freedman's view, depends on the balance of control and consent. More often than not, the target will resist the coercer by choosing to counter-coerce the coercer's tactics. This can dramatically raise the costs of punishment or enforcement and require various military and non-military options aimed at convincing the coerced that counter-coercion may be too costly and ineffective.

Coercive diplomacy is derived from Thomas Schelling's concept of 'compellance'. Compellance, as understood here, involves the use of military capabilities or punishment to force the enemy to comply with the coercer's demands. By favouring the benefits that come with the actual display of force, compellance is intended to deny the coerced state either the available opportunities or time to counter the tactics of the coercer. In short, compellance is about foregoing the costs of inducements associated with coercive diplomacy. Robert Pape, for instance, argues that denial (i.e. threat to launch a massive ground force invasion) creates in the enemy the rapid loss of will or morale to resist the coercer. Similarly, a 'shock and awe' option, as illustrated during the early stages of the Iraq War when the US-led alliance of the willing bombed the headquarters of the Iraqi government in Baghdad, represents a form of brute, overwhelming force. Like denial, it relies on the use of brute military force to win an early surrender. The danger, as one might expect with such strategies, is that brute force is never failsafe. The coercer, for instance, may underestimate the extent and degree of the enemy's resistance, thereby exposing the excessively high costs of using brute force. Indeed, as some have argued, the main problem with compellance is that it accepts the risk of severe consequences, should the target choose to resist the coercer's offensive threats.

Coercion, therefore, is a situation that involves crisis escalation and de-escalation. The most prominent cases in this regard are the Cuban Missile Crisis, the Vietnam War, the Gulf War, the Kosovo and Iraq War. Whilst it is often difficult to assess the degree of success in these cases, in part because of the high human and economic costs associated with military coercion, it is widely agreed that the Kosovo War was a successful case of coercive diplomacy. Likewise, the Cuban Missile Crisis in October 1962 illustrates how US President John F. Kennedy forced Vladimir Kruschev, the Soviet leader, to reverse his decision to install missile launchers and warheads in Cuba. Only later would it be revealed that Kennedy had withdrawn American long-range warheads and launchers from Turkey, as a carrot, or inducement to Kruschev to reverse his action.

In recent years, military coercion has involved a complex mix of military and humanitarian objectives, or what some have referred to as 'humanitarian coercion'. The most well-known case of this type of coercion is the Kosovo War. Whilst many lauded the use of military coercion and/or coercive diplomacy to stop Milosevic's ethnic cleansing of the ethnic Albanians, the war highlighted the conflict between military objectives and the political aims of the war (to stop humanitarian suffering). Moreover, it is widely agreed that President Clinton's initial decision to remove the option of ground troops encouraged Milosevic to withstand NATO air strikes, or to *counter-coerce* NATO's coercive tactics by using refugees as human shields. Still, there is little denying that human rights will continue to complicate the objectives of military coercion. But it is also true that in order to stop humanitarian emergencies some form of military coercion will be required.

*See also:* **crisis; deterrence; humanitarian intervention; pre-emption; preventive diplomacy; realism; sanctions; security; sovereignty**

*Further reading:* Byman and Waxman, 2002; Freedman, 1998; George and Simons, 1994; Pape, 1996; Roach, 2005b

# COLD WAR

A period in international history (beginning soon after the end of the Second World War and ending in the early 1990s), as well as a description of the overall relationship between the United States and the Soviet Union during that period. Although the cold war is fast fading into history, divergent interpretations of its character continue to shape expectations about some central features of contemporary international relations. For example, those who expect a world without extreme ideological conflict to be essentially harmonious tend to see the period of the cold war as inherently antagonistic.

There are three main views about the cold war. Each of them generates a set of discrete claims about the causes of the cold war, the nature of the cold war, the end of the cold war, and its legacy in contemporary international relations.

Perhaps the most popular view is that the cold war was an intense struggle for **power** between the superpowers. The word '**war**' implies tension, armed conflict, and a zero–sum relationship between the **superpowers**. The word 'cold' refers to the presence of factors that allegedly restrained the confrontation and prevented a 'hot' war. Conventional historiography is based on a definition of the cold war that assumes a high level of East–West tension with the threat of escalation to nuclear conflict. Of course, there is a great deal of debate among those who share this overall view about who was to blame for the cold war. A common distinction is between *orthodox* and *revisionist* historians.

According to the orthodox argument, the cold war was a struggle between conflicting universal values. In the West, the concepts of a market economy and a multi-party democracy were cherished. In the East, single party statism and a command administrative economy were highly valued. The obvious conflict of ideas and obstinate nature of those who defended them were the driving forces behind the conflict. Within this broad school of thought, the behaviour of the Soviet Union during and after the Second World War was a crucial impetus to the cold war. The policies of **containment** followed by the United States were defensive reactions to an inherently aggressive and expansionist enemy. In the absence of nuclear weapons and the condition of **mutually assured destruction** (MAD), the cold war might well have turned 'hot' on a number of occasions. Fortunately, the Soviet Union was unable to sustain its competition with the United States, and this inability was the main reason for the collapse of the cold war system. Nonetheless, the timing of that collapse was due in no small measure to the preparedness of the United States and its allies to match or exceed Soviet escalations of the arms race. Now that the cold war is over, the United States dominates the international system. In light of the benign nature of American **hegemony**, such dominance is not a matter of great concern.

Revisionists agree with orthodox scholars about the nature of the cold war, but reverse the focus of blame. Revisionism became popular in the 1960s during the Vietnam War, but it remains a marginal school of thought within the United States. Revisionists emphasise the power of the United

States during and after 1945. For example, although the United States lost 400,000 lives during the Second World War, the USSR lost 27 million lives. The American economy benefited from the war whilst the Soviet economy was almost destroyed. According to some revisionists, Soviet behaviour was merely a defensive attempt to build a legitimate **security** zone in Eastern Europe, whilst the United States was trying to reconstruct the international economic system for its own **national interests**. In short, the cold war was a period of American dominance whose legitimacy was based on a mythical Soviet 'threat'. True, the Soviet Union's inherent economic weaknesses were crucial in explaining its collapse in 1991, but the end of the cold war could have occurred much earlier and without the horrendous expense of the arms race. The post-cold war era is a very dangerous time, since the United States now has no challenge to its military might, nor any political challenge to its own views about the most desirable international **order**.

In contrast to the view that the cold war was inherently antagonistic, regardless of who was the main instigator, an opposing school of thought suggests that the cold war was (in retrospect) very useful to both sides. For the United States, it solved the problem of what to do about Germany and Japan, both of whom were key states in bringing about the Second World War. For the Soviet Union and the United States, the cold war permitted a de facto solution of the German problem by freezing the social/political contours of Europe, both East and West. The perpetuation of the cold war was also useful for maintaining a strict nuclear hierarchy between the superpowers and their allies, as well as between nuclear states and non-nuclear states. The theoretical possibility of nuclear conflict subordinated actual conflicts within the respective blocs to the interests of 'global stability' ensured by the superpowers. Finally, powerful domestic interests on each side sustained the cold war. For example, within the United States, the arms race strengthened sectors of the military–industrial complex, justified intervention abroad, facilitated the establishment of the national security state, and elevated the Presidency over other institutions of the US federal government. On the other side of the Iron Curtain, the cold war justified domestic repression, subordinated the civilian to the military sectors of society, and maintained an authoritarian system of government predicated on the demands of **geopolitical** 'catch-up'.

Although there is some truth in the main claims of all these schools of thought, they share a tendency to exaggerate the degree of coherence and foresight in the planning and implementation of foreign policy. The cold war was a period of genuine conflict *and* cooperation between the superpowers. It arose out of a long period of geopolitical turmoil in Europe, whose internal conflicts eventually subordinated that continent to two extra-European superpowers with very different social systems and little diplomatic familiarity with each other. Some conflict between them was inevitable, and was exacerbated by the tendency of each to suspect the worst of the other.

Also, it should be remembered that as a period of history, the cold war coincided with the onset of the nuclear era as well as **decolonisation**, both of which raised the stakes in the competition. Nonetheless, despite all the factors that kept the superpowers apart, they did share some important common interests that moderated their competition, particularly after the Cuban missile crisis in 1962, when many feared that a nuclear war would break out. The division of Europe, **arms control**, the shared interests in ensuring that real wars in the **Third World** would not lead to direct conflict between them, all these factors ensured a degree of moderation in the cold war. However, as was demonstrated during the era of *détente* (relaxation of tensions) in the late 1960s, it was very difficult for the superpowers explicitly to acknowledge their shared interests in such a way as to end the confrontation once and for all. In so far as the cold war was a war, clearly the former Soviet Union as well as communism were the losers. On the other hand, in an era when the problems of world order are greater than the capacity of any state to respond to them effectively, and in light of the evidence suggesting that the cold war relationship could best be described as an adversarial partnership, it is important not to exaggerate the fruits of victory for the United States and its allies.

*See also:* **alliance; appeasement; arms control; balance of power; communism; containment; decolonisation; deterrence; embedded liberalism; end of history; great powers; misperception; North Atlantic Treaty Organisation; peace studies; superpower; Third World**

*Further reading:* Booth, 1998; Crockatt, 1995; Gaddis, 1997; Isaacs and Downing, 1998; Lundestad, 1997; Walker, 1993; Westad, 2000

## COLLECTIVE SECURITY

The basic principle behind this concept can be summed up in the phrase 'one for all and all for one'. As a means of maintaining peace between states, the legal and diplomatic organisation of collective security can be located midway between the two extremes of an unregulated **balance of power** and a world government. Although the idea of a single world government is sometimes entertained as a solution to the problem of **war**, it is extremely unlikely to be brought about by conscious design. The idea of collective security is attractive because it seeks to bring about some of the alleged benefits of a world government without altering the essential features of an **anarchical** states system.

In formal terms, collective security refers to a set of legally established mechanisms designed to prevent or suppress aggression by any state against any other state. This is achieved by presenting to potential/actual aggressors the credible threat, and to potential/actual victims the reliable promise, of effective collective measures to maintain and if necessary enforce the peace. Such measures can range from diplomatic boycotts to the imposition of **sanctions** and even military action. The essence of the idea is the collective punishment of aggressors through the use of overwhelming **power**. States belonging to such a system renounce the use of force to settle disputes among themselves but at the same time promise to use collective force against any aggressor. In all other respects states remain **sovereign** entities.

The purpose of a collective security system is to maintain peace among the members of the system, not between the system and outsiders. For example, **NATO** is not a collective security system. It is an **alliance**, or perhaps it could be called a collective defence system. Ideally, in a global collective security system alliances are unnecessary. Collective security allows states to renounce the unilateral use of force because they are assured of assistance if a state illegally uses force against them. Simultaneously, it requires that all states participate in enforcing sanctions against an aggressor.

There are three reasons why many commentators (and sometimes states) have found the idea of collective security attractive. First, it promises security to all states, not just some of the most powerful. Ideally, all states have an incentive to join such a system, since they are all subject to the threat of war. Second, in principle collective security provides much greater certainty in international relations, at least in promoting a concerted response to war. Third, collective security is focused on an apparently clear problem, that of aggression, which is typically defined as the military violation of the territorial integrity and political independence of member states.

The first major attempt to implement a system of collective security took place at the end of the First World War, with the signing of the **League of Nations** Covenant. With Article 10 of the Covenant, peace was guaranteed and together with Article 16, which provided the threat of counteraction, they formed the core of collective security. Every member state was asked in Article 10 to guarantee the territorial and political integrity of all other member states. To secure this promise, each member state was (according to Article 16) automatically at war with an aggressor. The sorry history of the League of Nations in failing to maintain international peace and security (its successor, the **United Nations**, does not even mention the term 'collective security' in its Charter) reflects some fundamental problems with this concept as a means to maintain peace.

First, unless collective security really is universal, and in particular includes the most powerful states in the system, it is unlikely to be effective. If the latter are outside the system, then other states cannot rely on collective security to protect themselves from the **great powers**. This was particularly the case in the interwar period. The United States never joined the system, and other great powers (including the Soviet Union, China, Germany, and Japan) were never permanent members of the system.

Second, the effectiveness of collective security depends on states sharing the view that peace is 'indivisible'. Aggression against any state is meant to trigger the same behaviour amongst members, regardless of where it takes place or the identity of aggressor and victim. This view was shared by many states at the end of the First World War in light of the manner in which that war had spread so rapidly and the degree of destruction it had caused. Nonetheless, it remains somewhat idealistic to believe that collective security can totally replace the balance of power and the calculations of national interest. For example, the refusal of some states to impose sanctions against Italy after its invasion of Abyssinia (Ethiopia) in December 1934 was due to their belief that Italy could still be a useful ally against Germany.

Third, despite its apparent simplicity, the term 'aggression' is notoriously difficult to define in practice. For example, Japanese treaties with China allowed Japan to keep troops stationed on Japanese railways in Manchuria and those troops had the right of self-defence. When a bomb exploded on a railway near the city of Mukden in September 1931, the Japanese took over the city and soon had control over the whole province of Manchuria. China claimed that Japan had committed aggression. Japan claimed that it was acting in self-defence. It took the League a whole year to determine who was right, by which time the Japanese had succeeded in setting up their own puppet state in the area.

Finally, the concept of collective security is deeply conservative. It is dedicated to the maintenance of the territorial status quo, identifying 'aggression' as the worst crime in international relations, and it assumes that peaceful mechanisms of territorial change exist which make war unnecessary. In the twenty-first century, when war within states rather than between them is likely to be the norm, collective security is unlikely to provide a solution even if the great powers share its basic assumptions.

*See also:* **alliance; anarchy; concert of powers; idealism; just war; League of Nations; sanctions; sovereignty; United Nations**

*Further reading:* Butfoy, 1993; Buzan, 1991; Claude, 1967; Lepgold and Weiss, 1998; Mearsheimer, 1994/5; Saroosh, 1999; Sloan, 1998

## COMMUNISM

This concept has been interpreted in a variety of ways – as a political philosophy, a utopia, an existing system of political and economic rule, a philosophy of history, and as a revolutionary ideology of change diametrically opposed to **capitalism** and liberal democracy. Students of international relations have tended to think of it as the official ideology of the former Soviet Union (1917–91) and China (1949–).

The term derives from the Latin word *communis* which means 'belonging to everyone'. In theory, a communist society is organised in such a way that individuals share in the fruits of their labours equally and hold property in common. Individuals contribute what they can and consume only what they need. They treat each other equally and fairly, regardless of gender, age, or nationality. There is no need for the coercive **power** of the state to keep individuals under control, and the acquisitive behaviour that is characteristic of liberal capitalist societies becomes unthinkable. Needless to say, this vision has never been fully realised in practice. There have, however, been a number of relatively successful, small-scale rural *communes*, suggesting (at least to communists!) that human beings have the capacity to join together in one harmonious political union.

Contrary to popular belief, Karl Marx wrote very little on the precise characteristics of a developed communist society since he was more concerned with understanding the nature of capitalism and the historical forces that would eventually lead to the abolition of private property. But he did claim that in a communist society it would be possible to hunt in the morning, fish in the afternoon, rear cattle in the evening, and debate after dinner.

As an organised modern political force, communism began in the nineteenth century and became a global ideology during the early part of the twentieth century. Much of its success was due to the efforts of Lenin. His major contribution to communist theory and practice was in elaborating the crucial role of the 'vanguard party'. This highly skilled and dedicated group of revolutionaries would carry the revolution forward. As a temporary dictatorship of the proletariat, the vanguard party would represent the true interests of all workers. Its function was to teach the workers, organise them, and eventually lead them out of their alienated and debased existence under capitalism.

Lenin had an opportunity to put his ideas into practice in Russia after the success of the Bolshevik Revolution in October 1917. When in power, however, the vanguard party became a dictatorship, and a particularly brutal one at that. In addition, the rhetoric of world revolution promoted by the Soviet Union antagonised and worried many leaders of capitalist states. Indeed, so concerned were the Americans, French, and the British that they joined the so-called 'White Russians' in a war of intervention against the Bolsheviks in 1918–19. Much of the **cold war** antagonism between the Soviet Union and the United States can be traced back to this episode in the history of American and European foreign policy.

The Soviet leadership not only proclaimed the need to spread communism around the world, it also actively supported communist parties and trade union movements in Europe, funded revolutionary activities in Asia, Africa, and Latin America, and ultimately engaged in a massive arms race with the West. On other occasions during the cold war, Soviet leaders were more measured in their rhetoric, speaking about the possibility of peaceful co-existence between communism and capitalism. Nevertheless, from the perspective of the West, both the Soviet Union and China represented a fundamental threat to Western values. Today, after the collapse of communism as a global ideology, the prospect of realising Marx's utopian vision remains as distant as it was in the late nineteenth century.

*See also:* **capitalism; cold war; distributive justice; end of history; Marxism**

*Further Reading:* Berki, 1983; Blackburn, 1991; Marx and Engels, 1999; Ulam, 1992

## COMMUNITARIANISM

Over the last couple of decades, communitarian thought has emerged as an important and diverse set of arguments in political **theory** directed largely against certain versions of modern liberal political theory. This critique, however, is part of a broader project aimed at showing the state of malaise that afflicts contemporary moral discourse.

The communitarian critique of liberalism has at least four facets. First, communitarians argue that the liberal priority given to procedural rights over substantive ideas of justice is flawed, for it fails to understand the way that human beings are constituted by the ends they choose, the values they hold, and the communities in which they live. Second, liberalism represents a form of asocial individualism that fails to understand the extent to which a person's identity only makes sense as part of a community and which also underestimates the significance which communal goods have for individuals. Third, communitarians question the universalism of liberalism. They argue that no theory of justice can apply universally and cross-culturally. Fourth, communitarians are suspicious about the moral priority that some liberals give to individual choice. If individual choice is simply a question of subjective preference, then there is no rational justification for determining whether one way of life is better or worse than any other.

The centrepiece of the communitarian argument is the proposition that human beings only develop their characteristically human capacities within 'society'. The individual does not exist prior to society. Society is what shapes us, gives our lives meaning, and makes us fully human. It is a necessary condition for individuals becoming moral agents and fully responsible, autonomous beings. For communitarians, failure to understand this leads to a loss of community spirit and political agency. The communitarians are picking up on an ancient idea that human beings are by nature political animals. To conceive of individuals as asocial and to deny that their choices are a result of their social embeddedness is to end up with a very truncated notion of what it means to be fully human.

In recent years, communitarian thought has attracted the attention of students of international relations. Its significance lies in the fact that it can form the basis of a moral defence of the sovereign **nation–state**. If human beings are socially embedded, and individuals cannot be fully human outside a shared community, then the form of social organisation which most clearly expresses the shared values of the community (assuming that the nation–state does so!) must have some moral worth. Contrary to a **cosmopolitan** view, then, the nation–state cannot be regarded as morally irrelevant. The difference between the two positions turns, to a large extent, on where one locates the ultimate source of moral value. For cosmopolitans, it is the individual human being who is the site of moral value, not particular political communities.

One of the most interesting aspects of communitarian arguments in the study of international relations is their compatibility with certain interpretations of political **realism**. What is interesting and controversial about such interpretations is that they omit from consideration so much of what most scholars (particularly in the United States) would deem to be central to this school of thought. Realism cast in terms of communitarianism focuses primarily on the concept of a person, the moral standing of states, and the appropriate site of principles of justice (universalism versus particularism). Recently, Amitai Etzioni, one of the most prominent theorists and practitioners of communitarianism in the United States, has sought to extend communitarianism to the global level. He argues that a new global architecture, consisting of the **UN, ICC, EU,** and Kyoto Protocols, represents the normative synthesis between Eastern values (social order and equality) and Western values (liberal autonomy and individual rights). In his view, such an architecture seeks to resolve problems that states cannot resolve alone, emphasises the need for foreign policy rooted in self-constraint, and calls for greater respect and understanding of the values and rights of individuals and peoples of different cultures.

*See also:* **cosmopolitanism; distributive justice; nation–state; nationalism; realism; theory**

*Further reading:* Brown, 1992a; Cochran, 1995a; Etzioni, 2004; Mulhall and Swift, 1992; Thompson, 1992

## CONCERT OF POWERS ✓

In the early 1990s the idea of a concert of powers became popular as a recipe for managing relations between the **great powers** and for providing a semblance of **global governance** in a world without a formal government. The best-known example of such a concert was established in the early nineteenth century, and those who argued that a similar concert could be established after the **cold war** have used this as a basis for their claims.

In 1815 the Concert of Europe was created as a mechanism to enforce the decisions of the Congress of Vienna. It was composed of the Quadruple Alliance that had defeated Napoleon and ended his **imperial** adventures in Europe. The **alliance** consisted of four main great powers – Russia, Prussia, Austria, and Britain. In 1818 France was formally admitted to the club, but it had already played an important role in the settlements of 1815. The main priorities for the great powers of the era were to establish a stable **balance of power** in Europe to preserve the territorial status quo, and to sustain 'legitimate' conservative governments in the heart of the European continent.

Over the next 30 to 40 years the members of the Concert met regularly to consult and negotiate solutions to their disputes and to deal with broader threats to the Concert as a whole.

As an exercise in sustained great power cooperation, the Concert was remarkably successful in its aims, at least until the middle of the nineteenth century. It managed to suppress revolutionary uprisings in Spain and Italy in 1820 and 1822, and to contain France from achieving supremacy in Europe. Ultimately, differences between the great powers of the era, and their joint failure to suppress forces of revolutionary change within their own borders, brought the Concert to an end. There are differences of opinion over when precisely the Concert ceased to function. Some scholars argue that the outbreak of the Crimean War in 1853 signified its downfall. This was the first major armed conflict in Europe after the settlement at Vienna. Moreover, it represented an expansionist move against the weak Ottoman Empire by Russia that was contrary to the very purpose of the Concert. Others argue that despite periodic crises, the Concert managed to persist in a variety of forms until the outbreak of the First World War in 1914, and after the members of the Concert had become rivals in two competing alliances.

After the end of the cold war, and particularly in the years immediately following the end of the Gulf War in 1991, a number of observers raised the possibility that a new concert could be established among the great powers of the present era – the United States, Russia, China, Japan, and the leading states of the **European Union**. The ability of these states to cooperate in forcing Iraq to reverse its annexation of Kuwait raised hopes that they could continue to collaborate to sustain international **order**. There are, however, a number of differences between the great powers of the early nineteenth century and those of today.

First, the Concert of Europe was composed of five roughly equal great powers. Today, it is much harder to evaluate the distribution of power in international relations. No longer is there such a close link between military power and political influence, so it is difficult to determine the appropriate criteria for membership of a contemporary concert.

Second, the Concert of Europe was established in part to deal with a military and political threat in the heart of Europe. After the collapse of the Soviet Union, it is difficult to identify any state sufficiently threatening to the great powers to generate an incentive for any of them to form a new concert of powers.

Third, all the members of the Concert of Europe shared certain conservative values. Despite their differences, which increased as the years went by, they accepted the system of the balance of power as the common framework of their endeavours. Today, the balance of power is global rather than merely regional, and it is not difficult to identify important differences between the states often identified as potential members of a contemporary concert. Whilst they all share some common interests, it remains unclear whether any normative consensus about a legitimate international order exists among them. In light of the overwhelming superiority of the United States today, it is unlikely that other great powers (particularly China) would want to join a concert that is bound to be dominated by one state.

This is not to suggest that something approximating a concert of powers does not exist or could not be developed further in the years to come. The great powers of the twenty-first century do share some common interests such as an aversion to nuclear war, global terrorism, the use of military force to change territorial boundaries, and the threat of a global economic collapse. The question is whether those interests are sufficient to generate the cooperation necessary to address these issues.

*See also:* **alliance; balance of power; collective security; diplomacy; great powers; order**

*Further reading:* Craig and George, 1990; Holsti, 1992; Rosecrance, 1992

## CONSTRUCTIVISM ✓

Constructivism is a distinctive approach to international relations that emphasises the social, or intersubjective, dimension of world politics. Constructivists insist that international relations cannot be reduced to rational action and interaction within material constraints (as some **realist**s claim) or within institutional constraints at the international and national levels (as argued by some **liberal internationalists**). For constructivists, state interaction is not among fixed **national interests**, but must be understood as a pattern of action that shapes and is shaped by identities over time. In contrast to other **theoretical** approaches, social constructivism presents a model of international interaction that explores the normative influence of fundamental institutional structures and the connection between normative changes and state identity and interests. At the same time, however, institutions themselves are constantly reproduced and, potentially, changed by the activities of states and other actors. Institutions and actors are mutually conditioning entities.

According to constructivists, international institutions have both regulative and constitutive functions. Regulative norms set basic rules for standards of conduct by prescribing or proscribing certain behaviours. Constitutive norms define a behaviour and assign meanings to that behaviour. Without constitutive norms, actions would be unintelligible. The familiar analogy that constructivists use to explain constitutive norms is that of the rules of a game, such as chess. Constitutive norms enable the actors to play the game and provide the actors with the knowledge necessary to respond to each other's moves in a meaningful way.

States have a corporate identity that generates basic state goals, such as physical **security**, stability, **recognition** by others, and economic **development**. However, how states fulfil their goals depends upon their social identities, i.e. how states see themselves in relation to other states in **international society**. On the basis of these identities, states construct their national interests. Constructivists accept that **anarchy** is the characteristic condition of the international system, but argue that, by itself, it means nothing. For example, an anarchy of friends is quite different from an anarchy of enemies, but both are possible. What matters is the variety of social structures that is possible under anarchy. It is important to understand that states may have many different social identities, that these can be cooperative or conflictual, and that state interests vary accordingly. States define their interests in the process of interpreting the social situations in which they are participants. Thus, one might argue that the **cold war** relationship between the United States and the Soviet Union was a social structure wherein the two principals identified each other as enemies and defined their national interests regarding each other in antagonistic terms. When they no longer defined each other in these terms, the cold war ended.

Constructivism emphasises that the international system consists of social relationships as well as material capabilities. Indeed, social relationships give meaning to material capabilities. Intersubjective systemic structures consist of the shared understandings, expectations, and social knowledge embedded in international institutions. It should be understood that by 'institutions', constructivists mean much more than actual organisations. Instead, they regard an 'institution' as a stable set or 'structure' of identities and interests. Institutions are fundamentally cognitive entities that do not exist apart from actors' ideas about how the world works. Institutions and states are therefore mutually constituting entities.

Institutions embody the constitutive and regulative norms and rules of international interaction; as such, they shape, constrain, and give meaning to state action and in part define what it is to be a state. At the same time, institutions continue to exist because states produce and reproduce them through practice. States usually assign meanings to social situations on the basis of institutionally defined roles. Constructivism suggests that state identities and interests – and how states relate to one another – can be altered at the systemic level through institutionally mediated interactions.

Constructivists focus most of their attention on institutions that exist at a fundamental level of international society, such as **international law**, **diplomacy**, and **sovereignty**. However, **regimes** are also important. Constructivists argue that these regimes also reproduce constitutive as well as regulative norms. They help to create a common social world for interpreting the meaning of behaviour. A regime's proper functioning, however, also presupposes that the more fundamental institutions are already in place, making its activities possible. These regimes, therefore, do not create cooperation; they benefit from the cooperative effects of much deeper structures.

As a theoretical approach, constructivism is difficult to employ. Constructivism, for example, does not predict any particular social structure to govern the behaviour of states. Rather, it requires that a given social relationship be examined, articulated and, ultimately, understood. When this is done, then it may be possible to predict state behaviour within that particular structure. However, if these predictions prove false, it could be that the governing social structures were not properly understood or have simply changed. Thus, realist descriptions of the implications of anarchy proceed from an interpretation of international society as a Hobbesian 'state of nature'. This is a description of a set of social relationships that give meaning to the material capabilities of states.

If constructivism's utility as an explanatory **theory** remains unclear, it is still productive as a theoretical framework. How and why particular social structures and relationships develop among different states is a matter for historical research and analysis. Past interactions between states set the context for the present, and may produce fairly rigid identities and interests, but such an outcome is not inherent to the logic of the international political structure. The relationship between agents and structures is at the heart of the 'agent–structure debate' between constructivism and other schools of thought in the study of international relations.

*See also:* **anarchy; levels of analysis; national interest; realism; theory**

*Further reading:* Adler, 1997; Biersteker and Weber, 1996; Carlsnaes, 1992; Hopf, 1998; Katzenstein, 1996a; Koslowski and Kratochwil, 1994; Lapid and Kratochwil, 1996; Wendt, 1992, 1999

# CONTAINMENT ✓

The fundamental goal of US national security policy *vis-à-vis* the former Soviet Union during the cold war. One of the chief architects of this goal, who later became a stern critic of the means employed to achieve it, was George Kennan. At the end of the Second World War Kennan was employed as a staff officer in the American embassy in Moscow. In February 1946 he sent a secret cable to Washington. After analysing the history and nature of the Soviet regime, he concluded that unless prevented, it would probably expand into the **power** vacuum in central and western Europe. He reminded the US government that America had fought two wars in the twentieth century to prevent all of Europe coming under the control of a single militaristic regime. He suggested that this danger could arise again, and he recommended that Soviet expansionism be contained by American policies while there was yet time to do so without having to fight again.

Kennan's analysis and his recommendation of the containment concept were not immediately accepted in Washington. It was still US policy to work with the Soviets and to try to make the **United Nations** (UN) succeed. But his articulate and obviously thoughtful essay was circulated first around the State Department, then more widely through the government. Kennan himself was recalled to Washington to explain his ideas further. As the months passed and Soviet actions in Europe disappointed and frustrated American hopes more and more, Kennan's view gained ground. His analysis provided a way of understanding what was occurring and why the ideal of organising world politics in the framework of the UN system was failing. As the course that the United States was trying to take in the world proved more and more impossible, Kennan's approach gained favour as an alternative. By the winter of 1947 it was largely accepted by policymakers and incorporated into a formal document establishing it as a fundamental goal of the United States. As the cold war escalated thereafter, containment of the Soviet Union became the very bedrock of US foreign policy. So that the American public could better understand the premises of US policy, Kennan published an edited version of his long cable, with secret information about the USSR removed. Entitled 'The Sources of Soviet Conduct', it appeared in the July 1947 issue of *Foreign Affairs*, at the time the only important American journal devoted to international relations and foreign policy. The article's author was named as 'Mr X', but it soon became widely known that the article presented what was now the American government's view. As the main justification for containment to appear in public, the 'Mr X' article is probably the most famous essay on US foreign relations in the twentieth century.

In retrospect it is easier than it was at the time to see exactly what containment was and was not. Kennan argued the need to imprison Soviet influence within approximately its existing boundaries, and he justified this with a careful analysis of Soviet practice, **communist** doctrine, and the threat that an expansion of Soviet power in Europe could pose. But containment was offered as a policy only in a loose sense of the term. It was really a concept and a policy goal. Which among many possible foreign policies and/or military policies would accomplish the goal of containment was not disclosed either in the cable or the 'Mr X' article.

In later years, George Kennan dissociated himself from many of the specific policies of the United States that were often justified in the name of containment. He argued that containment could and should be pursued by the firm defence of military–industrial 'strong points' in Western Europe and Japan, rather than the 'perimeter' of Europe and Asia. He also emphasised the need to rely on economic rather than military tools to achieve containment. Uppermost in Kennan's mind was his concern that the US contain itself from becoming a heavily militarised state. For him, there was a crucial difference between the Soviet threat and that of communism in general, particularly when the latter was used as an ideology of liberation by many states in the **Third World**. In Europe the Soviet threat was less one of military invasion than the appeal of its political system to ordinary citizens struggling with the devastation and economic poverty caused by the Second World War. Thus while he supported the provision of economic aid to Western Europe in the late 1940s, Kennan opposed the escalation of the arms race in the early 1950s and became a trenchant critic of US national **security** policy in the 1970s and 1980s.

Containment of the Soviet superpower was the watchword of Western policies during the cold war. During that era, regional conflicts were generated as proxy conflicts which performed the essential service of preventing a direct confrontation between the superpowers. That bipolar superpower world is now gone, and regional wars are no longer seen as proxy conflicts. If there are new containment policies, they are now directed towards regional conflicts – less because there is greater moral concern to prevent loss of life than out of the perceived need to prevent regional conflicts from spreading, from involving weapons of mass destruction, and from drawing in external combatants.

*See also:* **appeasement; cold war; communism; isolationism; rogue state**

*Further reading:* Gaddis, 1982; Litwak, 2000; Smith, 2000

# COSMOPOLITANISM

Cosmopolitanism has ancient roots in Western civilisation. The idea of a 'cosmopolis', or universal city, played a central role in Stoic philosophy as well as in Christianity. A number of social and political theorists have recently resurrected the concept, most of whom present it as part of a new politics of the left, and as an alternative to ethnocentric **nationalism**. A call for some kind of cosmopolitanism in international relations has also re-emerged due to an increasing awareness of transnational realities on various levels. For instance, at a broad global level, many political agendas (including human rights, crime, and the environment) are beyond the capacity of any one country to deal with effectively. On an immediate personal level, many individuals are now more prone to articulate complex affiliations and allegiances to issues, people, places, and traditions that lie beyond the boundaries of their resident state. For all these reasons a renewed interest in cosmopolitanism is understandable.

For some **theorists**, cosmopolitanism refers to possibilities surrounding global democracy and world **citizenship** or new frameworks for cooperation among transnational social movements. Others invoke cosmopolitanism to advocate a non-**communitarian** politics of overlapping interests, challenging conventional notions of belonging, identity and citizenship. The rapidly expanding number of publications regarding cosmopolitanism reveals three main ways in which the concept is elaborated.

First, cosmopolitanism refers to a sociocultural condition, as in references to a 'cosmopolitan world'. More people travel further than ever before, and they are increasingly exposed to new customs, cuisines, and fashions. In this sense, however, cosmopolitanism is a condition that applies to only a fraction of humanity who can afford it. A common stereotype of cosmopolitans depicts privileged, politically uncommitted elites – made up of wealthy corporate managers and (a few!) academics and intellectuals – who maintain their condition on the basis of independent wealth and a globetrotting lifestyle. In this characterisation, cosmopolitanism is a matter of consumption, an acquired taste for music, food, fashion, art, and literature from all parts of the world.

Second, cosmopolitanism refers to an ideology or philosophy. Contemporary political philosophers tend to divide themselves into communitarians, who believe that moral principles and obligations are or should be grounded in specific groups and contexts, and cosmopolitans. The latter urge us to see ourselves as 'citizens of the world', creating a worldwide moral community of humanity committed to universal ideals of human rights. A variant of this wide-ranging argument is whether cosmopolitanism can be reconciled with nationalism and patriotism. Is it possible to combine them via some form of cosmopolitan patriotism, which celebrates different ways of being while sharing a commitment to the political culture of a single state? Or are they doomed to clash, forcing individuals to make a choice between them?

Third, the concept is used to refer to a political project, a new order of transnational political structures exercising what is sometimes described as 'cosmopolitan democracy'. The concept implies a layer of **global governance** which limits the **sovereignty** of states and yet is not itself a world state. Cosmopolitan institutions would co-exist with states and would override their authority in particular spheres of activity. The institutions most studied for their potential to assist in the realisation of such a cosmopolitan project are the **United Nations** and the **European Union**. Most of the work on this topic remains somewhat abstract. An interesting exception is the work of Martha Nussbaum, who has elaborated a detailed vision of cosmopolitan education. In the study of international relations, David Held is the leading scholar and proponent of cosmopolitan democracy. Held, for instance, distinguishes among three types of cosmopolitanism: political, legal, and liberal. His aim here is to elaborate on the duties, institutional prerogatives, moral rights, and ethico-political factors that have contributed to a new constitutional world **order**.

*See also:* **CNN factor; communitarianism; critical theory; European Union; functionalism; global governance; liberal internationalism; nationalism; perpetual peace; United Nations**

*Further reading:* Archibugi *et al.*, 1998; Brown, 1992a; Caney, 2001; Heater, 1996; Held, 2002; Hutchings and Dannreuther, 1999; Jones, 1999; Nussbaum, 1997; Toulmin, 1990

# CRISIS

The term 'crisis' is often used to draw attention either to a particular problem – such as the 'environmental crisis' – or to a dispute or set of disputes between states, such as 'the East–West crisis' or even 'the 20 year crisis' of the 1920s and 1930s. When used in these ways for dramatic effect, the notion of crisis may be overused, generalised, and thereby trivialised. It shares this problem with other words such as 'disaster' or 'tragedy'. In the study of international relations, however, the concept has taken on a very specific meaning, and has been the subject of a large body of **theory**.

Crisis implies a moment of crucial decision in the context of immense danger. Historically, the word is usually associated with grave illness. It refers to the moment or turning point from which a patient must either begin to recover or descend towards death. In other words, it is an episode in an illness with a close relationship to death, but death is not inevitable. In international relations, a crisis is a brief period of time when one or more parties to a conflict perceive an imminent threat to vital interests and a very short time to react to the threat. Crises between states are periods during which there is a sharply increased likelihood of **war**. Crises are quite sudden transformations of 'normal' relations between states. They may escalate and result in war or may be dealt with in such a manner that war is averted and the status quo ante restored. A crisis is therefore a necessary phase between peace and war, but one from which war does not necessarily result.

The academic literature on international crises grew rapidly following the Cuban missile crisis in October 1962, a period of the **cold war** when the **superpowers** came very close to a hot war over Soviet attempts to deploy nuclear missiles in Cuba. Much of the theoretical work on crises was inspired both by the need to learn important lessons from the episode and by the recognition that similar crises might occur, given the ongoing hostility between the United States and the Soviet Union. This is also a grave limitation on our understanding of crises, since the characteristics of the cold war and its two chief protagonists are now a thing of the past.

Most of the literature on international crises focuses on processes of decision-making, although it also includes a variety of attempts to model crises as a bargaining game between states. Whilst the latter tends to treat the state as a unified rational actor during a crisis, the former isolates decision-makers and closely examines how they make and implement decisions under the psychological and organisational stresses typical of a crisis. In general, analysis is inspired by a prescriptive interest in identifying effective strategies of crisis management. Whilst much of the theory on crisis management is developed at a high level of abstraction, four aspects of crisis decision-making are particularly pertinent.

First, much has been learnt about the psychological effects of crises on decision-making. Psychological experiments indicate that increasing stress produces an inverted U-curve of decision-making efficiency. Some stress can improve an individual's performance. Too much stress can inhibit it, leading to sloppy consideration of information and policy alternatives.

Second, there are some common tendencies that affect decision-makers during a crisis. They often fit their interpretation of the crisis to match their pre-established fears and hopes. They see and hear what they want to see and hear. Perceptions are ordered through pre-set belief systems that are both valuable and potentially dangerous. They can lead to wishful thinking and faulty analysis.

Third, there are some patterns of behaviour that can arise through the dynamics of small policy-making groups. The concept of 'groupthink' refers to the psychological internalisation of group norms exacerbated by the group's hierarchical, cohesive, and insulated structure. Symptoms include an illusion of invulnerability; rationalisation of contradictory information; self-righteousness; stereotyping of outsiders; self-censorship; and a tendency towards unanimity.

Finally, much has been learnt about the difficulty of controlling crises. Foreign policy is often the result of predetermined 'standard operating procedures' that are implemented through complex bureaucratic and administrative procedures. Individual decision-makers must operate in a complex web of relationships, and crises may develop in ways that are not within the control of those formally responsible for foreign policy.

Despite the voluminous literature on crisis decision-making, progress in understanding has been hampered by a number of problems. Whilst it is relatively simple to define a crisis in the abstract, in practice the distinction between normality and crisis is difficult to draw. Moreover, since the common definition of a crisis refers to what often does not take place (i.e. crisis escalation towards war), the identification of crises is a complex matter. In the absence of a scholarly consensus over how to measure the occurrence of crises, it is difficult to generate reliable explanations or predictions about how they either escalate or are coped with. Finally, it is worth noting that the focus on decision-making tends to obscure important political factors that often contribute to both the onset and fate of crises among states. These include the **balance of power**, the extent to which the political systems of states resemble one another, their historical relationship, and overall familiarity with what is at stake for the other party.

*See also:* **cold war; diplomacy; misperception; preventive diplomacy**

*Further reading:* Allison and Zelikow, 1999; Janis, 1972; Lebow, 1990; Robinson, 1996; Welch, 1989

## CRITICAL THEORY

Critical theory refers to a set of Marxist-based critical analyses of international theory and practice. The term, which was officially coined in 1937, refers first and foremost to the works of the Frankfurt Institute of Social Research or the 'Frankfurt School'. Established in Frankfurt, Germany in 1923 the school critically analysed the relationship between fascism and the authoritarian personality, and the impact of science and technology on critical reason. The most important early thinkers of the school included Max Horkheimer, Theodor Adorno, and Herbert Marcuse. In time, they would embrace a pessimistic view of the prospects of democracy and revolution. However, it was precisely this view that would inspire Jürgen Habermas, a second generation theorist of the school, to recover the progressive elements of reason by theorizing about the intersubjective relationship between rationality and democracy and the role of communication in building rational consensus amongst citizens.

In his effort to create an alternative foundation to positivism, Habermas distinguishes three 'knowledge-constitutive interests' which he derives from various aspects of social existence. The first are *technical* cognitive interests. These are motivated by our material needs for existence which lead to an interest in prediction and control of the environment. This interest constitutes the empirical, analytical sciences. Second, Habermas identifies *practical* cognitive interests, which are generated by the desire for increasing mutual, intersubjective understanding. This interest led to the development of fields of study that are concerned with the meaning of language, symbols, norms, and actions. The third category consists of *emancipatory* cognitive interests, derived from the human ability to engage in reflective reasoning. Through the process of self-reflection, we can perceive society as a site of **power** struggles which constrain the realisation of human potential. Thus, we have an interest in liberation. Emancipatory cognitive interests constitute critical theory. Habermas's emphasis on emancipatory interests does not mean that any theory that promotes emancipation is 'true'. Because he does not accept that 'anything goes', some independent criterion of validity – a theory of truth – is needed. Habermas's concept of truth is established by rational consensus. What is true is what is agreed to be true, but this consensus must have specific rational features, otherwise truth loses all meaning.

Among others, Robert Cox has drawn on critical theory in the study of international relations. Cox affirms the connection between knowledge and interests. Furthermore, he stresses the need for reflexivity. Theory must be able to scrutinise itself. Cox distinguishes two perspectives on theory depending on its purpose. The first is *problem-solving theory*, in which theory serves as a guide to find solutions to problems from the point of view of, and within, its own framework. The second is *critical theory*, in which the presumptions of the theory itself and the process of theorising are reflected upon. To do so means to open up the possibility of choice. It is then possible to choose a different perspective which involves different presumptions and seeks to realise different values from problem-solving theory. Cox is a central figure in elaborating the goals of critical theory in international relations. Critical theory questions the dominant world **order** by taking a reflective stance on the framework of this order. By doing so it also questions the origins and **legitimacy** of political and social institutions and the way they change over time. History is perceived as a continuous process of change. Critical theory seeks to determine which elements are universal to world order and which are historically contingent.

For Andrew Linklater, another leading critical theorist in the field, questions of inclusion and exclusion are central to international relations. He is not in favour of the system of **sovereign** states, because of their exclusionary character. Instead, Linklater advocates a community of humankind. Therefore, he wants to construct new forms of international political relations that are able to include all people on equal grounds. For him, the normative purpose of critical theory is to facilitate the extension of moral and political community in international affairs. Critical theory – with its emphasis on rational communication – provides a way of supporting a tolerant universalism, which is inclusive without denying or extinguishing cultural diversity and difference.

The implicit, normative goal of the realisation of human potential gives direction to critical theory. Habermas assumes not only that there exists such a thing as human potential that can be realised, but also that society can move progressively towards this realisation, which he self-evidently claims to be a universal desirable goal. Habermas believes in social evolution and ethical progress through learning how to use universal moral principles to resolve conflicting claims about the organisation of social and political life.

Finally, it is important to distinguish between critical theory and **postmodernism**. To many postmodernists, notions of ethical progress and moral universality are wholly arbitrary. They feel that the perceived self-evidence of moral and ethical progress and universality have led to the structural exclusion of groups and ideas, and to totalitarian truth claims. Habermas (and those scholars in international relations who have been inspired by him) aims for progression towards the realisation of human potential by trying to find a way to overcome differences through rational consensus based on rational argument.

*See also:* **cosmopolitanism; postmodernism; theory**

*Further reading:* Brown, 1994; Devetak, 1995; Haacke, 1996; Hoffman, 1987; Jahn, 1998; Linklater, 1992; Neufeld, 1993; Roach, 2007; Wyn Jones, 2001

# DEBT TRAP

A situation in which a state has to spend much of its earnings from trade on servicing its external debts rather than on economic and social **development**. This is one of the most crippling problems for **Third World** countries (or more accurately, the vast majority of their citizens). The origins of the debt trap for poor states lie in the formation of the **Organisation of Petroleum Exporting Countries (OPEC)** in 1973 and the dramatic rise in oil prices that year. The OPEC states deposited their new oil wealth in Western banks. Since idle money loses against inflation (which was rising rapidly at the time), the banks needed to find countries to take loans. Many states in Eastern Europe and the Third World borrowed huge sums of money in the expectation that interest rates would remain stable.

The expectation was shattered by two trends in the global economy over the next 20 years. First, the fixed exchange rate system that had been established after the Second World War collapsed, and states began to use interest rates to stabilise their exchange rates. Second, interest rates rose in the 1980s in response to trade and budget deficits in the United States. This triggered a recession in many industrialised states, thereby reducing export markets for poor states. As their export earnings fell, debt repayment obligations rose, leaving much of Africa and Latin America in a state of financial bankruptcy. In the recession the price of raw materials, on which many poorer states depend for earning foreign exchange, collapsed. Debts incurred were so large that they needed new loans to finance them.

Between 1982 and 1990 US$927 billion were advanced to poor states but US$1,345 billion were remitted in debt service alone. The debtor states began the 1990s 60 per cent more in debt than they were in 1982. Sub-Saharan Africa's debt more than doubled in this period. When the issue of debt remission or debt forgiveness is raised, Western banks have argued that it would create what economists call 'moral hazard' – failing to honour debts would simply encourage poor states to continue borrowing in the expectation that they would never have to repay their debts. On the other hand, some commentators argue that moral hazard should cut both ways. Overborrowing is overlending, and creditors should pay their share of the costs of mistakes made in the 1970s.

By 1997 Third World debt totalled over US$2.2 trillion. The same year US$250 billion was repaid in interest and loan principal. The debt trap represents a continuing humanitarian disaster for some 700 million of the world's poorest people. During the last decade the world's most heavily indebted continent, Africa, has experienced falling life expectancies, falling incomes, falling investment levels, and rising infant and maternal mortality rates.

In October 1996 the first real attempt was made to deal with the problem when the **World Bank** and the **International Monetary Fund (IMF)** won agreement from their Boards of Governors for the establishment of the Highly Indebted Poor Country (HIPC) Initiative. At its launch, the policy offered the promise of poor countries achieving a 'robust exit' from the burden of unsustainable debts. Campaigning groups and **non-governmental organisations (NGOs)** welcomed this policy as the first comprehensive approach to debt write-offs with an enormous potential for poverty reduction. The Initiative is open to the poorest countries, namely those that:

1   are eligible only for highly concessional assistance such as from the World Bank's International Development Association (IDA) and the

IMF's Poverty Reduction and Growth Facility (formerly called Enhanced Structural Adjustment Facility);

2 face an unsustainable debt situation even after the full application of traditional debt relief mechanisms;

3 have a proven track record in implementing strategies focused on reducing poverty and building the foundation for sustainable economic growth.

The HIPC debt initiative is the first debt reduction mechanism that promises to deal with the ongoing debt trap in a comprehensive and concerted way. It is designed to tackle not only commercial debt and debt owed by HIPCs to bilateral creditors, but also – and this is new – debt owed to **multilateral** creditors: the World Bank, the IMF, and the regional development banks. The central aim of the HIPC initiative is to enable highly indebted poor countries, whose debt burdens are too high to be dealt with by traditional debt reduction mechanisms, to achieve a sustainable debt level within a period of six years. During this six-year period, a country must implement a World Bank/IMF-supported **structural adjustment programme**. At the 'decision point', which marks the end of the first three years, creditors reexamine the country's debt problem and determine whether it can exit the HIPC scheme or, if it cannot, how much debt relief it will need to reach a sustainable level of debt at its 'completion point', three years down the line.

What is a sustainable level of debt? This has been defined by the World Bank/IMF as a level at which a country is able to meet its current and future debt repayment obligations in full without compromising economic growth and without resorting to rescheduling or building up arrears in the future. In the HIPC scheme, a country undergoes a Debt Sustainability Analysis (DSA), on the basis of which it is decided exactly how much debt relief is needed for the country to fulfil the sustainability targets of the initiative: a debt burden within the range of 200–250 per cent of the country's annual exports and a debt service of 20–25 per cent of annual exports.

The cost (and therefore debt relief provided) under the scheme is approximately US$30 billion, to be divided in half between bilateral and multilateral creditors. With regard to its implications for overall debt reduction, a rough estimate suggests that after HIPC and traditional debt relief, the value of public debt in the 33 countries likely to qualify – presently estimated at about US$90 billion – would be reduced by about half.

*See also:* **dependency; development; distributive justice; failed state; foreign aid; International Monetary Fund; structural adjustment programme; World Bank**

*Further reading:* Dent and Peters, 1999; George, 1988, 1991; Payer, 1991

## DECOLONISATION

The process whereby a colonial society achieves constitutional independence from imperial rule. It is the reverse of colonisation – a process whereby one state occupies the territory of another state and directly rules over its population. Although it has a very long history (the Greeks, for example, set up colonies around the Mediterranean several hundred years before Christ), it is the period of European expansion into Africa, Asia, the Americas, and the Pacific between the fifteenth and the early twentieth century that is generally associated with colonialism as a system of rule.

There are a number of reasons why European states pursued such a policy. They were driven by the desire for raw materials and natural resources, new markets and investment opportunities, and concern over the imperial ambitions of their rivals in Europe. **Balance of power** considerations often helped to fuel European colonialism.

As a system of rule, colonialism was often violent and repressive. It tended to undermine indigenous cultural and religious beliefs, led to the emergence of new class structures, and weakened traditional social bonds. People in the colonies were sometimes forced to speak languages other than their own, to conform to legal and political norms foreign to them, and were often regarded as racially inferior by their colonial overlords. However, some would argue that colonialism has not been a wholly negative occurrence. In some cases it brought economic **development** and **modernisation**, advancements in medicine and agriculture, and political liberalism and democracy to the less-developed world. Whether these 'positives' outweigh the long-term suffering of the colonised societies is a debatable point.

Decolonisation amounts to the granting or return of **sovereignty** to the colony. In contemporary terms, decolonisation is most often associated with the achievement of political independence of Africa and much of Asia from the European states after 1945. It began in earnest in the early 1950s and continues up to the present day. Between 1980 and 1989, for example, Britain granted independence to Zimbabwe, Belize, Antigua, and Brunei. East Timor has only just become independent after 25 years of colonial occupation by Indonesia. One might also regard the end of Soviet rule over Eastern Europe as part of a process of decolonisation.

There are a number of reasons why decolonisation occurred during this period. First, the European states were financially and militarily exhausted after the Second World War and could no longer endure the costs of maintaining colonial empires in faraway corners of the globe. France and Belgium are exceptions here. They hung on to their colonies with much more determination than the British. Second, the United States pressured the European states into divesting themselves of their colonies. Third, **self-determination** was an important political ideal in international relations throughout the twentieth century and it took root in the colonies and fed resistance movements. The British in India (1940–7), the French in Indo-China (1946–54) and Algeria (1954–62), the Dutch in Indonesia (1945–9), and the Belgians in the Congo (1959–60) are just some of the many examples where the colonial states became involved in difficult and protracted struggles against local insurgents. Fourth, public opinion within Europe began to turn against colonial domination. Finally, the **United Nations** began to support the process with its 1960 Declaration on Decolonisation.

Five aspects of decolonisation are worth highlighting. The first is the role played by **nationalism** in arousing and maintaining popular support against colonial rule. Second, the speed at which colonies achieved independence after 1945 varied greatly. In some cases, it was achieved relatively quickly. In others the transition to self-rule was a gradual process. Third, it is quite difficult to determine when decolonisation begins and ends. Does it begin with revolutionary opposition in the colony and end the moment the colonising power departs? Or does it also include the long period of adjustment after the imperial power returns control to the colony? Fourth, different colonies have had to employ different strategies to achieve independence. The Palestinian Liberation Organisation (PLO) has used international **terrorism**, Mahatma Gandhi preached non-violent resistance to British rule in India, and Ho Chi Minh had to fight a long guerrilla war, first against the French and then the United States. Fifth, decolonisation has not always been accomplished easily or been successful. Exiting colonial states often left the former colonies ill-equipped for self-rule, power vacuums have been created leading to vicious and intractable civil wars, and local economies and markets have withered.

It is perhaps worth making one final point. Achieving independence has not necessarily meant the end of foreign intervention. Economic ties have continued through trading relations, and European **multinational corporations** (MNCs) have continued to flourish in former colonies. Indeed, some scholars argue that the formal end of colonialism was followed by subtle forms of *neo-colonialism*.

*See also:* **cold war; dependency; development; failed state; imperialism; self-determination; United Nations; wars of the third kind**

*Further reading:* Ashcroft *et al.*, 1998; Betts, 1998b; Lundestad, 1997; Roach 2005a; Waites, 2000

## DEMOCRATIC PEACE ✓

Democracies do not (or virtually never) go to **war** with one another. In the 1990s the idea of a democratic peace was the subject of much debate, tending to focus on three issues:

1   Is there a direct causal relationship between democracy and peace?
2   If there is, what best explains the relationship?
3   What are the implications of the relationship for world **order**?

In the twentieth century, democracy refers to a system of government characterised by:

*   regular elections for the most powerful government positions;
*   competitive political parties;
*   near-universal franchise;
*   secret balloting;
*   respect for civil liberties and political rights (or basic **human rights**).

Prior to the twentieth century, scholars have relaxed this definition in light of the marked absence of secret balloting, competitive political parties, and the limited nature of the franchise. If a democracy refers merely to a state with periodic, competitive elections which also acknowledges a body of citizens with equal rights, it is clear that democracies rarely, if at all, go to **war** with one another. If one defines an international war as a military engagement in which 1,000 people or more are killed, then 353 pairs of states engaged in such wars between 1816–1991. None was between two democracies: 155 pairs involved a democracy and a non-democratic country, and 198 involved two non-democratic states fighting each other.

The significance of these empirical facts is unclear. Do they expose a deep and persistent feature of democracy or are they a mere statistical curiosity, like the fact that no two countries with McDonald's franchises went to war prior to 1999? This precarious relationship between McDonald's franchises and peace collapsed when **NATO** attacked Yugoslavia in March 1999. Unlike this relationship, however, the lack of war between democracies has been tested in different ways for other periods, other definitions of democracy, and other ways of defining war. In each case it has been significant.

It remains unclear, however, whether democratic states do not fight one another *because* they are democratic. Some scholars argue that the relative peace between democracies can be explained on the basis of other factors. For example, it could be argued that the lack of war between democracies during the **cold war** was really due to the overwhelming threat from the Soviet Union. On the other hand, even if this alleged threat accounted for the particular lack of war between democracies since 1945, what about other periods?

If one accepts that there is a causal link between democracy and peace, a variety of factors have been suggested to explain it. First, it could be argued that democratic leaders are restrained by the resistance of their people to bearing the costs and deaths of war. However, if this were true, democracies would be peaceful with all kinds of states, since wars against non-democracies are just as unpleasant as wars against democracies. But democratic states fight as often as other states do; their peaceful tendencies are only alleged to extend to one another. The putative law that democracies do not fight one another stands out because the evidence is conclusive that democratic states have been involved, proportionately, in as many wars as non-democratic states.

Second, the diversity of institutions and relations within and between democracies creates checks and balances and cross-pressures inhibiting belligerence among them. Whilst this may well be a contributing factor to the democratic peace, it also has a dark side. Democracies are not monolithic; they are divided into many agencies, some of which operate in secrecy and are really authoritarian subsystems connected only at the top to democratic processes. Examples are the military, especially in wartime, and secret services such as the Central Intelligence Agency (CIA).

The most plausible explanation is cultural. The presence of a democratic culture of negotiation and conciliation means that in their interaction with other democracies, democratic leaders are basically dovish. They share the same values, and thus are more willing to negotiate than fight. Disagreements among the citizens of a democracy are resolved through compromise and negotiation rather than conflict and coercion. When confronted with international disputes, democracies seek to resolve them in the same ways. Democracies **reciprocate** attempts at compromise and enjoy peaceful relations with one another. Because undemocratic states do not follow norms of compromise, however, democracies distrust them and treat them with hostility.

The final issue in the debate revolves around the implications of the relationship for world **order**. Optimists believe that democracy will spread around the world, which in turn will therefore become more peaceful. Pessimists note that democratic states are generally hostile towards non-democratic states. Unless today's democracies actively encourage the process of **democratisation**, there will not be a peaceful world order; at best, democracies will enjoy peace among themselves but the rest of the world will remain plagued by war. Even more revealing is the fact that democratic peace scholars have focused almost exclusively on the relationship between violent conflict and different types of political systems. Some scholars argue that democratic peace theorists have little if anything to say concerning the prerequisites for building liberal, democratic institutions.

It will take a large investment of resources by democracies to help other states democratise. Such aid will be more forthcoming only if there is a wider understanding among the democracies that by providing it, they are not only promoting the freedom and prosperity of other countries but also peace and non-violence.

*See also:* **clash of civilisations; cold war; democratisation; end of history; levels of analysis; liberal internationalism; order; perpetual peace; realism; war**

*Further reading:* Brown *et al.*, 199; Doyle 19836; Gowa, 1995; Paris, 2006; Ray, 1995; Russett, 1993; Weart, 1998

## DEMOCRATISATION

The processes associated with the spread of democracy around the world from its core in Western Europe and North America. With the end of the **cold war** came a period of optimism concerning the prospects for democracy in the **Third World**. At the beginning of the twenty-first century much of that optimism has disappeared. Although many Third World countries have experienced the opening stages of a transition process to democracy, a large number of them remain stuck in the initial phases of the process. Although no comprehensive setback for democracy has taken place, there are no prospects for any substantial democratic progress either.

It is important to distinguish between *electoral* democracy and *liberal* democracy. Liberal democracy is a system of government that meets the following conditions:

- meaningful and extensive competition among individuals and organised groups (especially political parties) for all effective positions of government **power**, at regular intervals and excluding the use of force;
- a highly inclusive level of political participation in the selection of leaders and policies, at least through regular and fair elections, such that no major (adult) social group is excluded;

- a level of civil and political liberties – freedom of expression, freedom of the press, freedom to form and join organisations – sufficient to ensure the integrity of political competition and participation.

Over the past 30 years there has been some democratic progress. Democratic transitions began in Southern Europe in the 1970s; they came to include Latin America in the early 1980s and then Eastern Europe, Africa, as well as parts of Asia in the late 1980s and early 1990s. There are more countries today than ever before with some measure of democracy and the ideological popularity of democracy has never been greater. Very few authoritarian rulers would actively defend traditional, authoritarian modes of rule (North Korea and Iraq are possible exceptions). In the large majority of cases, authoritarianism is justified with reference to its supposedly positive sides of creating e.g. order, stability, growth, and welfare.

Yet it is also clear that much of the democratic progress is shallow: it is a thin veil over political and social structures and institutions that have changed little since the days of authoritarianism. Electoral democracies may hold periodic elections and thus demonstrate some measure of political competition and popular participation, but large parts of the population are often kept out of the political process. Moreover, the military and other important parts of the state are frequently isolated from democratic control, the media may be censored, and the courts may be corrupt and ineffective. In short, elections take place but democracy has not developed in most other respects. Examples of electoral democracies are Brazil, Burkina Faso, Congo, El Salvador, Indonesia, Kenya, Malaysia, Russia, Tanzania, Turkey, Ukraine, and Zambia.

While the number of electoral democracies has increased steadily, the number of liberal democracies has remained almost unchanged. There were 76 liberal democracies in 1991 and 79 in 1996. In other words, elections are held in many countries, but the process of liberal democratisation is not moving forward. At the same time, the quality of democracy has deteriorated in a number of countries with a long-term democratic experience: Venezuela, Colombia, India, and Sri Lanka. On the other hand, there are some positive trends in parts of Eastern Europe. Economic and political relations with Western Europe are developing rapidly. The attraction of closer cooperation with the European Union will help prevent any widespread deterioration of democratic conditions. In that sense, Eastern Europe's external environment is conducive to democracy. That is not the situation in South and East Asia. In China, economic growth rates remain high, but corruption among political and economic elites is an increasingly severe problem. Political repression of any dissident voice is swift and severe, including numerous executions. Corruption is a major problem in many other countries in the region as well, including Thailand, the Philippines, and Indonesia.

The most spectacular setbacks for early and frail democratic openings have been in Sub-Saharan Africa, where **ethnic** violence in some cases has led to the breakdown not merely of democracy, but also of state authority altogether, as in Rwanda and Somalia. In several cases, the fragile democratic opening has itself fuelled violent conflict. In many African countries, new, weak parliaments tend to become merely another player in the old, authoritarian system of personal rule.

There are two main constraints on democratisation. First, it is extremely difficult if not impossible to graft democracy on to countries lacking a stable political community. For instance – if an election is legitimate, then the state must clearly be seen as legitimate, and that is rarely the case in Africa. Second, liberal democracy emerged in Western Europe in tandem with the expansion of **capitalism** and the rise of a middle-class constituency. It developed in opposition to medieval, hierarchical institutions – the despotic monarchies whose claim to all-powerful rule rested on the assertion that they enjoyed divine support. Liberal democrats attacked the old system on two fronts. First, they fought for state power and the creation of a sphere of civil society where social relations including private business and personal life could evolve without state interference. An important element in this respect was the support of a market economy based on respect for private property. The second element was the claim that state power was based not on natural or supernatural rights but on the will of the **sovereign** people. Ultimately, this claim would lead to demands for democracy – that is, for the creation of mechanisms of representation that assured that those who held state power enjoyed popular support. The tradition that became liberal democracy was liberal first (aimed at restricting state power over civil society) and democratic later (aimed at creating structures that would secure a popular mandate for holders of state power). Even when the focus was on democracy, liberals had various reservations. They feared that democracy would impede the establishment of a liberal society. Today, in many countries there is a real tension between attempts to promote democracy, and the increasingly global rather than local dynamics of capitalism. In many states, powerful middle classes have yet to develop, and it is unclear whether the European and North American experience can be duplicated on a global level.

*See also:* **democratic peace; end of history; globalisation; liberal internationalism**

*Further reading:* Cox *et al.*, 2000; Dahl, 1989; Diamond, 1996; Holsti, 1996; Nadia, 1996; Pinkney, 1993

## DEPENDENCY ✓

Explaining low levels of **development** in Latin America, Asia, and Africa has been an enduring concern for scholars and policymakers. In very broad terms, two types of explanation have been put forward. The first type – encapsulated in **modernisation theory** – focuses on factors internal to countries in the **Third World**. According to modernisation theorists, they lack certain qualities that are necessary for development, which itself should be measured as economic growth. Such qualities include access to capital, high rates of saving, an industrial infrastructure, and technical expertise. The second type of explanation – which includes dependency **theory** – not only rejects the orthodox focus on development as economic growth in favour of a much greater emphasis on equality and the fulfilment of basic needs, but also focuses on **power** asymmetries between the First World and the Third World. In other words, underdevelopment is a consequence of factors external to Third World countries.

The concept of dependency was developed in the 1960s and 1970s to account for these structural inequalities in global wealth and power. Dependency theory draws on the work of the structural school of international political economy developed in the 1930s by the Latin American economist Raul Prebisch. The foremost exponent of dependency theory in North America is Andre Gunder Frank, although others such as Fernando Cardozo and Theotonio Dos Santos were important in Latin America.

The dependency theorists not only rejected modernisation theory but also radically undermined Karl Marx's view that **capitalism** is able to promote development everywhere. Dependency refers to exogenously imposed conditions whereby the exposure of Third World states to **foreign direct investment** (FDI), unequal trade agreements, interest payments on debt, and the exchange of raw materials for higher-priced manufactured goods creates structurally unequal relations between the core and the periphery. Gunder Frank argued that FDI creates a 'sucking out' effect, whereby wealth is systematically transferred from the periphery to the core. The result is chronic underdevelopment. Capitalism is a **world-system** within which the metropolitan core manages to expropriate the meagre economic surpluses from 'satellite' countries, thereby producing simultaneously the development of the former and the underdevelopment of the latter. Third World countries are underdeveloped because they are structurally dependent within the world capitalist system.

Underdevelopment, in turn, manifests itself in two ways. The first is in uneven development. Certain sectors of Third World countries receive the lion's share of FDI, leaving other sectors weak. The second is the introduction of a Western class system into the Third World. Foreign capital creates a 'comprador bourgeoisie', a technocratic class of individuals who do the bidding of foreign capital at the expense of the local economy.

Since the 1970s, dependency theory has been heavily criticised. Marxists attacked it for confusing a mode of production (capitalism) with a mode of exchange (the market). More importantly, dependency theory assumed that development was impossible under conditions of underdevelopment, but the rise of the **newly industrialising countries** (NICs) largely discredited this argument. In addition, some scholars claimed that dependency theory confused dependency with underdevelopment, whereas it can be shown that some countries such as Canada are both dependent and developed.

Although dependency theory is no longer as influential as it was 30 years ago, the language of core and periphery still infuses left-wing critiques of **globalisation**. Despite the criticisms, the concept itself remains important. However, dependency must not be used as a blanket concept to explain all the evils of underdevelopment everywhere. The extent of dependency varies between different countries, requiring careful study of concrete situations instead of trying to expose a single universal mechanism of exploitation applicable to all peripheral countries.

*See also:* **debt trap; decolonisation; development; exploitation; foreign aid; imperialism; modernisation theory; Third World; women in development; world-system theory**

*Further reading:* Blomstrom and Hettne, 1984; Leys, 1996; Smith, 1979; Tornquist, 1998

## DETERRENCE

In its simplest form, deterrence consists of the following threat, intended to dissuade a state from aggression: 'Do not attack me because if you do, something unacceptably horrible will happen to you.' In other words, deterrence is a form of persuasion in military strategy. To convey such a threat, the deterrer must decide what constitutes an attack, and must then decide what level of response would be adequate to deter it. This in turn depends on the deterrer's estimation of the adversary's intentions and the values it places on them. For deterrence to succeed, the threat must also be credible. Not only must the potential aggressor believe that the costs of an attack would be higher than its benefits, but also that there is a significant likelihood that such costs would indeed be incurred.

As a strategy, deterrence is often contrasted with defence. The latter focuses on military capabilities rather than intentions. While deterrence works by the threat of punishment, defence works by denying the enemy's ability to achieve its objectives once an attack has begun. It was only with the advent of nuclear weapons that such a distinction could be made in peacetime. Before the arrival of **mutually assured destruction** (MAD), the terms 'deterrence' and 'defence' simply referred to different time periods. Prior to an attack, military forces are supposed to deter an enemy. After the attack, when deterrence has failed, they are used to actively resist the attack.

In light of the unacceptable costs of nuclear **war**, military strategists and planners have devoted a great deal of attention to the requirements of deterrence in the nuclear age. Strange as it may seem, the main problem with the concept of nuclear deterrence is that (fortunately) no two nuclear-armed states have gone to war with each other using their nuclear weapons. The result is that none of the alleged requirements of nuclear deterrence is derived from a tested empirical **theory**. What theory has been developed is therefore deductive rather than inductive. No one knows for sure what kind of attacks, or what kind of behaviour in general, the possession of nuclear weapons deters. Nor is there any reliable answer to the question 'How many nuclear weapons are enough?'. This is because the credibility of a deterrent threat depends on the perceptions of the adversary rather than the deterrer. Nevertheless, there are three issues that, although debated at some length in the context of the **cold war**, remain central to debates about nuclear deterrence in the post-cold war era.

First, there is much debate over the scope of nuclear deterrence, and the dilemmas associated with attempting to deter threats not only to one's own state, but also to one's allies. During the cold war, for example, the United States engaged in a strategy of *extended* deterrence. Not only were its nuclear forces intended to deter a direct nuclear attack (or first strike) on its territory, but it was also believed that they could deter the Soviet Union from non-nuclear aggression against US allies in Western Europe, as well as a range of 'provocative' behaviour by the Soviet Union and China. This is sometimes referred to as *general* deterrence as opposed to *immediate* deterrence directed against an imminent threat.

Second, there is no consensus in the literature on how best to make nuclear deterrence credible in the eyes of an adversary. There is a complex trade-off between credibility and effectiveness in thinking about *nuclear* deterrence. An available response to attack, which is very low in credibility, might be sufficient to deter if it poses a very severe **sanction** (e.g. massive retaliation) or if the aggressor's prospective gain carries very little value for it. On the other hand, a threatened response that carries a rather high credibility but poses only moderate costs for the aggressor may not deter if the aggressor places a high value on its objective and anticipates a good chance of attaining it. During the cold war, advocates of 'minimal deterrence' debated with those who suggested that the United States should be prepared to fight a nuclear war with the Soviet Union in order to deter it. Nuclear deterrence strategy has long been plagued by the paradox that if deterrence should fail and war should begin, then it would not be rational actually to carry out a threat of nuclear retaliation upon which deterrence is based. Once attacked, a rationally calculating player has nothing to gain by massive retaliation.

Third, there has always been a heated debate over the levels and types of nuclear weapons necessary to achieve nuclear deterrence. On the one hand, many commentators believe that nuclear war is so unthinkable that nuclear-armed states co-exist in a situation of existential deterrence. As long as political leaders acknowledge the irrationality of nuclear weapons as instruments of war, and as long as it is impossible to defend oneself against a nuclear attack or to launch a nuclear attack in the realistic expectation of preventing any nuclear retaliation (otherwise known as second strike invulnerability), nuclear deterrence is not difficult to achieve. Other commentators argue the opposite case, claiming that the paradox of deterrence provides scope for an enemy to strike first. The choice between suicide or surrender should be avoided by blurring the so-called 'firebreak' between nuclear and conventional weapons, and having available a variety of options to deter a variety of attacks.

During the cold war these three issues were debated at some length, and there is a voluminous literature on the subject. Thankfully, the cold war ended without a nuclear war. Nonetheless, as long as nuclear weapons exist, the same issues will remain pertinent in the future. If we have learnt anything from the experience of nuclear deterrence over the last 50 years, it is that deterrence is not merely a stockpile of weapons. A nuclear strategy allegedly based on this concept neither ensures the continuation of peace nor allows political leaders to ignore the international context that makes deterrence necessary. Even so, where nuclear deterrence offerred a fairly simple, productive model of deterrence, deterrence in general, especially during the post-cold war period, has become increasingly complex. No longer is it possible to dissuade would-be **terrorists**, much less national elites who may wish to commit **ethnic cleansing**. This of course makes the monitoring of existing nuclear stockpiles all the more crucial.

*See also:* **arms control; coercion; cold war; collective security; disarmament; International Criminal Court; misperception; mutually assured destruction; nuclear proliferation; security dilemma**

*Further reading:* Freedman, 1981; Lebow and Stein, 1998; Morgan, 2003

## DEVELOPMENT

The word 'development' is open to a great deal of controversy. To many, it can appear patronising, especially when distinguishing between countries that are developed and those that are described as 'developing' or 'undeveloped'.

One way that development is often measured is in terms of changes in gross national product (GNP) per capita and comparative GNPs between countries. A country is said to be developing if its GNP is increasing. If the gap between its GNP and those of the so-called 'developed' countries is decreasing, the country is said to be moving from being a less developed country to being a highly developed country. On these terms, the **newly industrialising countries** (NICs) such as Singapore, South Korea, Taiwan, and Hong Kong are sometimes said to be rapidly reaching, and in some cases surpassing, Western standards of development.

However, there are many problems with measuring development purely in terms of GNP per capita. Is the country as a whole really developing if the wealth disparity in the country is increasing, despite increases in aggregate GNP per capita? While the richest in the society may be getting substantially richer, the majority of the population may see no change in their living standards. Similarly, can a country be said to be developing if economic growth is achieved at a cost to future generations in terms of the using up of unrenewable resources and the pollution of the air, land, and water? For example, the economic growth of many countries in the former Eastern bloc in the post-1945 period was achieved to a large extent with little care about the environment.

Another problem with the economic growth concept of development is that it ignores political liberties and the type of government that is presiding over the development. Many of the newly industrialising countries have had authoritarian governments during their period of growth. Can a country be said to be developing if its citizens are politically oppressed and have basic **human rights** denied, such as freedom of speech? The growth seen in the Chinese rush for industrialisation in the 1950s and 1960s was at the expense of the welfare of the population who suffered widespread famine and terrible living conditions.

Thus simply looking at GNP per capita is not an adequate way of measuring development. Economic growth may be one factor that constitutes development, but development does not simply involve economic growth and not all economic growth can be classed as development. Politically, the term 'development' has often been used to imply a move towards Western systems of economy and government or towards a Western style of living. But some observers claim that it can be very patronising to assume that Westernisation is the only path to development.

Perhaps a better way to measure development is in terms of the satisfying of basic needs of all members of the society. That is, the provision of shelter, food, clean water, health and medicine, access to education, and other important elements that go to make up an acceptable standard of living. If a country moves to being able to provide these things, then it can be said to have developed. On this basis, many of the African countries can be seen as underdeveloped in not being able to provide these essentials.

One way of measuring development as the provision of basic needs is by looking at the number of people living at or below the poverty line. This is useful in looking at changes within a country over time, as it is an indication of the distribution of wealth in a particular country. However, as a country becomes richer, the standard by which poverty is measured will increase. What constitutes poverty in Germany is very different to what constitutes poverty in the Sudan.

In conclusion, development does not simply involve economic growth. One needs to examine the cost of such growth, the distribution of any increase in wealth, and the provision of essentials to achieve a decent standard of life for all.

Human development is a process of enlarging people's choices. The most critical of these wide-ranging choices are to live a long and healthy life, to be educated, and to have access to resources needed for a decent standard of living. Development enables people to have these choices. The process of development should at least create a conducive environment for people, individually and collectively, to develop their full potential and to have a reasonable chance of leading productive and creative lives in accord with their needs and interests.

Underdevelopment is obviously extensive. Depending on where we draw the line between developed and underdeveloped, the underdeveloped world makes up about three-quarters of the world's population. We should also take note of the persistence of underdevelopment. The membership of the exclusive club of rich countries has not changed much between 1900 and the present.

Why should we in the advanced industrialised states be concerned about the prospects for the development of the rest of the world? First are the obvious humanitarian reasons – can we really enjoy our wealth when poverty is the normal condition of most of the world? Second, our economic self-interest calls for rapid development of the rest of the world: our export markets will thereby grow and there will no longer be the lure of low wages to siphon away our jobs. Last, a more developed world is likely to be a more peaceful world.

*See also:* **debt trap; democratisation; dependency; failed state; foreign aid; modernisation theory; newly industrialising countries; population growth; sustainable development; Third World; World Bank; world-system theory**

*Further reading:* Handelman, 1999; Little, 2001; Mehmet, 1999; Sen, 1999

## DIASPORA

The study of global diasporas is a growing academic field that is not confined to any one academic discipline in the social sciences. Once considered the preserve of Jewish studies and the US immigrant story, the study of the physical movements of groups around the world now includes Chinese, Korean, Latino, Indian, and countless cultural groups residing outside their original homelands. A hallmark of diaspora studies is the examination of cultural continuities and adaptations characteristic of such movements. Scholars are primarily concerned with how well diasporic groups retain their home cultures and how much is lost in the process of absorption into another culture. In an era of **nationalism**, **globalisation**, and increased flows of immigrants and **refugees**, one can expect diasporas to attract greater scholarly attention in the study of international relations than has been the case thus far.

The term 'diaspora' was originally coined to describe the circumstance of Jews who lived outside Palestine after the Babylonian exile. Since then, its scope has been enlarged to include any group that has been scattered far from its original homeland, with most attention paid to the descendants of Africans who were forcibly removed from Africa and brought to the New World as slaves in the seventeenth century. Today, diasporas also refer to an 'exile community', with a rank and file membership.

In light of the diversity of the diasporic experience, however, it would be futile to insist on an exclusive definition of what is and what is not a diaspora. Instead, it is more useful to note that there are different types of diaspora, and it is important to distinguish between them. There are three main types. First, one can identify *victim* diasporas, such as Jews, Armenians, and Africans. These are groups whose history is one of systematic oppression in which they have either fled or been forcibly removed from their homeland. Second, there are *labour and imperial* diasporas, such as the Indians and British, respectively. Many groups have moved from their place of origin and established communities overseas as a consequence of the history of **imperialism**. In the case of the British diaspora, these are often descendants of British colonial administrators who have remained in former colonies rather than returning home. Finally, there are *trade* diasporas such as the overseas Chinese or Lebanese, groups whose entrepreneurial skills have enabled them to flourish outside their country of origin.

Given this diversity of experience, is it possible to make any useful generalisations about diasporas? Not really. What can be said is that diasporas share a common problem of cultural identity to which they respond in vastly different ways. Diasporic identity points in two directions – the place of origin and the location of domicile. Members of diasporas have often never been to their homeland, whilst the experience of assimilation in their new home can exacerbate rather than alleviate the sense of marginality for which it was supposed to be the cure. The condition of the diaspora is thus an interesting state of suspension. Their nationality is rarely fixed or definitive. Instead, they represent forms of sociocultural organisation that transcend and even pre-date the state, itself a relatively new form of political organisation born about 400 years ago. Still, diasporas often serve a political function when it comes to the spread of democracy or political modernisation of the home country. Indeed, exile communities have proved particularly adept in getting their host government to apply pressure on their home countries. In successful cases, the leaders of the group may become the new leaders of the new regime (of the home country).

*See also:* **ethnicity; globalisation; nation-state; nationalism; refugees**

*Further reading:* Cohen, R., 1995, 1997; Okpewho *et al.*, 1999

# DIGITAL DIVIDE

One crucial result of the unequal distribution of wealth between the countries in the Northern and Southern hemispheres (North and South) has been the disproportionate concentration of informational technology services in the developed countries. The technological disparity between the North and South is what characterises the digital divide. Currently, UNESCO reports that roughly 80 per cent of developing countries lack the availability of the internet or other basic technological devices, including telephones and faxes. This has led to significant concern that the technological gap between the North and South will continue to increase, thereby worsening the disparity in wealth and knowledge. As such, higher incomes, increased access to information (via the internet), and education will continue to favour the countries of the North; whilst the South will continue to lag behind the North, burdened by the cost and time associated with technological underdevelopment.

Accordingly, the digital divide reflects a recent and often complex trend in international relations. For Pippa Norris, it is a 'multidimensional phenomenon' consisting of three broad aspects:

- a global divide, or the divergence of internet access in the developing and developed countries;
- a social divide that involves the gap between rich and poor;
- a democratic divide, or the lack of internet access restricting the people's capacity to mobilise and participate in the political affairs of its government.

Given these features, the digital divide represents an increasingly daunting challenge. The questions that arise are as follows: will the technological gap direct much needed resources away from the South? And can the divide be narrowed through greater technological diffusion or the channelling of resources to the countries in the South? Underlying these questions is the disagreement regarding the extent of the (negative) impact of the digital divide. While many believe that the divide will only worsen existing economic and social relations between the North and South, others remain far more optimistic, believing that the internet will have a transformative impact on the economies of the South. As this claim suggests, the internet represents a novel but crucial means of mobilising citizens in the developed countries. For it allows people to access information and knowledge and to connect with one another at a far lower cost than traditional forms of media. And while some may dispute the positive aspects of the internet, there is little denying the fact that the internet has played a key role in mobilising citizen groups, particularly in developed countries. News blogs, for instance, allow more citizens to communicate with one another, and have arguably influenced policymaking and public opinion. However, critics of news blogs insist that it allows inadequately researched news information to dictate discussion, diverting attention away from traditional sources of news media such as newspapers and radio.

Nonetheless, it is important to stress the internet's transformative political economic role. As the democratic divide shows, the internet will impact policymaking in three principal ways: (1) to bring together individuals and supporters of a cause in a more cohesive fashion; (2) to provide public information; and (3) to place direct pressure on politicians and policymakers. As such, many see the internet as playing a powerful role in calling attention to the social plight of oppressed ethnic and religious groups in developing countries. In the mid-1990s, for instance, the internet provided a key communicative link between the Zapatistas of the Chiapas rebellion in January 1994 (Mexico) and the rest of the world. Others such as the spiritual religious group Falun Gong in China have used the internet to call attention to their oppression by the Chinese government.

It is of course true that the lack of access to the internet remains an important source of underdevelopment. However, this should not divert attention away from the task of developing innovative, long-term solutions to bridging the divide. In recent years, for instance, companies have established local internet kiosks in villages; and it is hoped that micro-credit finance or low interest loans to local entrepreneurs in the developing world will expand the range of digital opportunities in education.

*See also:* **African Union; debt trap; development; foreign aid; globalisation; International Monetary Fund; Marxism; modernisation theory; newly industrialising countries; Third World; United Nation**s

*Further reading*: Norris, 2001; Servon, 2002; Warschauer, 2004

# DIPLOMACY

In a broad sense, diplomacy is the entire process through which states conduct their foreign relations. It is the means for allies to cooperate and for adversaries to resolve conflicts without force. States communicate, bargain, influence one another, and adjust their differences through diplomacy. It is interesting to note that serious confrontations between the **great powers** since 1815 have ended in force only about 10 per cent of the time. The routine business of international affairs is conducted through the peaceful instrument of diplomacy.

In a more narrow sense, diplomacy is the implementation of foreign policy, as distinct from the process of policy formation. Diplomats may influence policy, but their main task is to negotiate with the representatives of other countries. Ambassadors, ministers, and envoys are official spokespersons for their country abroad and the instruments through which states maintain regular direct contact. Although messages are rapidly transmitted from one state to another today, personal, face-to-face encounters can put a stamp of privacy and authenticity on diplomatic exchanges. Formal diplomacy is a regularised system of official communication between states: the exchange of ambassadors, the maintenance of embassies in foreign capitals, the dispatch of messages through officially accredited emissaries, participation in conferences and other direct negotiations.

The importance of diplomacy arises from the fact that most foreign policies are stated very generally, without spelling out measures for implementation. A good diplomat must adapt such policy mandates to the circumstances of the moment. Moreover, there are numerous occasions when the demands of a particular situation might justify an exception to policy, and for this a state often relies on the wisdom of its diplomatic officers in the field. Few governments pursue a perfectly consistent policy that is articulated with a single voice. It falls to the diplomats to reconcile the competing voices and to give coherence, emphasis, and interpretation to their state's foreign policy.

Diplomacy has two faces. It is the vehicle through which a state asserts itself and represents its concerns to the world; it is also one of the principal means for conciliating competing **national interests**. In other words, diplomacy aims to further a state's particular goals whilst preserving international **order**. It is the tool that states use to get their way without arousing the animosity of other states. Diplomats must constantly balance the needs to protect their state's interests and to avoid conflict with other states.

There are three main functions of diplomacy – intelligence gathering, image management, and policy implementation. An embassy gathers information on the thinking of the local political leadership, the state of the local economy, the nature of the political opposition – all of it critical for predicting internal problems and anticipating changes in foreign policy. Diplomatic representatives are the 'eyes and ears' of their government; their cables and reports form part of the raw material from which foreign policy is developed. Diplomacy also aims at creating a favourable image of the state. Modern communication makes it possible to shape perceptions and attitudes around the globe. States today have vast public relations apparatuses whose purpose is to place their actions and policies in a favourable light. Foreign embassies supply local news media with official interpretations and try to avoid negative publicity or explain it away. Finally, diplomats administer the overseas programmes of the state. They negotiate military basing rights, facilitate foreign investment and trade, supervise the distribution of economic aid, and provide information and technical assistance.

Some scholars argue that over time, there has been a marked decline in the importance of formal ambassadors. In the days when travel and communications were primitive, ambassadors had a great deal of authority and discretion in the implementation of foreign policy. They might be stationed abroad for many years without receiving new instructions or returning home. Today overseas envoys receive large numbers of cables and instructions on a daily basis. Heads of state communicate directly with one another by telephone. Top policymakers often negotiate directly with each other (*summit* diplomacy) or they send special envoys (*shuttle* diplomacy). Henry Kissinger, Secretary of State under Presidents Nixon and Ford, raised shuttle diplomacy to a high art in the 1970s. As a result, the ambassador has become less important in the realm of 'high politics' – particularly in areas of military **security** – than in the past.

On the other hand, the growth of **interdependence** among states, and the expansion of the old Eurocentric state system into a global **international society**, has brought in its wake the emergence of an increasingly **multilateral** style of diplomacy. Multilateral management is essential for many issues that involve cooperative arrangements among governments. This is the case in such areas as **nuclear proliferation**, **arms control**, trade regulation, and the suppression of **terrorism**. The **United Nations** and other intergovernmental organisations convene periodic conferences to deal with problems of food, **population growth**, the environment, and other issues of global concern. Since most of the less developed countries make the greater part of their diplomatic contacts at the United Nations, many issues of modern diplomacy are addressed in this multilateral forum.

*See also:* **CNN factor; concert of powers; crisis; globalisation; international law; international society; misperception; multilateralism; reciprocity; recognition**

*Further reading:* Barston, 1996; Craig and George, 1990; Eban, 1998; Eldon, 1994; Kissinger, 1994; Sharp, 1999

## DISARMAMENT

The attempt to eliminate or radically reduce armaments. It can be distinguished from the concept of **arms control**, which entails restraint but not necessarily reduction in the number and kinds of weapons available to states. Most disarmament proposals are based on the assumption that weapons are an important source of conflict in themselves. Historically, disarmament has taken place in two contrasting ways.

First, after a **war**, disarmament has often been *imposed* on the defeated state by the victor. For example, in 1919 the Treaty of Versailles limited the German army to 100,000 troops, thereby effectively eliminating an army that could be capable of offensive activity. A similar restriction was placed on Germany and Japan after the Second World War. Historically, the victors have been unable to remain united and unwilling to act together to enforce these prohibitions. Nazi Germany established training areas and munitions factories in the Soviet Union after the First World War without suffering any penalties, and as the cold war intensified after 1945, a primary concern of US foreign policy became rebuilding the military might of Japan and West Germany.

The other type of disarmament is *voluntary* disarmament, in which states seek to negotiate a mutually acceptable framework within which all parties will reduce the size of their military establishments. While the ultimate logic of disarmament points to the total elimination of all weapons, three main types of disarmament plans can be identified. The first is typified by attempts to reduce the size of the German armed forces to the bare minimum. A second type of disarmament is General and Complete Disarmament (GCD), which seeks the total elimination of all weapons. If this ever happened, the fundamental nature of international relations would be radically transformed. Unfortunately, GCD is usually associated with extreme **idealism**, although there are historical examples of such proposals. During the Reykjavik Summit in 1986, General Secretary of the former Soviet Union Mikhail Gorbachev proposed – and President Reagan of the United States accepted – a plan for the elimination of all nuclear-armed ballistic missiles by 1996. Although the plan was never implemented, it did increase public support for Gorbachev at a time when many people feared that the nuclear arms race was reaching dangerous levels of intensity.

A third form of disarmament is *regional* disarmament. It seeks to reduce or to eliminate weapons from a particular geographic area. Over the last five decades regional disarmament plans have frequently taken the form of proposals for nuclear-free zones. A major barrier to the successful negotiation of such agreements is that, once a state in a region has acquired nuclear weapons, it is difficult to prevent others from doing likewise. This was the main problem that ultimately prevented the implementation of the often proposed South Asian Nuclear-Free Zone. Today, both India and Pakistan possess nuclear weapons, and the proposal looks very unlikely to be implemented in the foreseeable future. However, the history of regional disarmament is not all hopeless. Four main regional agreements remain in effect. In 1967 the Treaty for the Prohibition of Nuclear Weapons in Latin America, also known as the Treaty of Tlatelolco, was signed. This treaty prohibits the testing, possession, and deployment of nuclear weapons in the region. Similarly, the 1959 Antarctic Treaty bans the use of Antarctica for military purposes, including nuclear testing. In 1971 a treaty was signed banning states from placing nuclear weapons on the seabed, and in 1967 a similar treaty prohibited states from placing nuclear weapons in earth orbit or stationing them in outer space.

While the existence of such treaties may provide supporters of disarmament with some hope that they can be extended, it should be pointed out that treaties such as those just mentioned are not strictly about disarmament. Rather, they represent agreements by states not to develop weapons that they were not planning to build in the first place, and not to deploy weapons in areas that are of peripheral strategic value. Were these conditions ever to change, it is unlikely that the mere existence of such treaties would deter states from breaking them.

There are two main problems with the concept of disarmament. First, it is not clear that the underlying assumption that arms cause war is correct. In the 1980s, many supporters of the Campaign for Nuclear Disarmament (CND) and European Nuclear Disarmament (END) claimed that the nuclear arms race was out of the control of politicians. They advocated unilateral nuclear disarmament in order to break the cycle of the arms race. However, the end of the cold war has been followed by radical arms reductions by the great powers, suggesting that arms races are caused by underlying political conflicts. Disarmament proposals that treat only the symptoms of a problem rather than its causes are unlikely to work. A second problem with the concept is the difficulty of verifying disarmament agreements. In the absence of reliable verification, disarmament can make the world a more dangerous place. Having said that, disarmament is most likely to proceed when there is a consensus among states that the possession of particular weapons can no longer be justified and when there exist reliable systems of verifying agreements. Arguably, the most likely weapons that states will agree to disarm in the near future are anti-personnel landmines, although much work remains to be done to achieve this limited goal.

*See also:* **arms control; collective security; deterrence; idealism; security dilemma**

*Further reading:* Arnett, 1994; Berdal, 1996; Karp, 1992; Wittner, 1995

# DISTRIBUTIVE JUSTICE

Normative principles designed to allocate goods in limited supply relative to demand. The principles vary in numerous dimensions. They vary *vis-à-vis*: which goods are subject to distribution (income, wealth, opportunities, etc.); the nature of the subjects of the distribution (individuals, states, etc.); and the basis on which the goods should be distributed (equality, according to individual characteristics, according to free market transactions, etc.). The following five principles have been at the core of recent debates in normative international relations theory: strict egalitarianism; the Difference Principle; welfare-based principles; deserts-based principles; libertarian principles.

### Strict egalitarianism

One of the simplest principles of distributive justice is that of strict or radical equality. The principle says that every person should have the same level of material goods and services. The principle is most commonly justified on the grounds that people are owed equal respect, and that equality in material goods and services is the best way to give effect to this ideal of equal respect.

The problem with strict egalitarianism is that there will be many other allocations of material goods and services which will make some people better off without making anybody else worse off. For instance, a person preferring apples to oranges will be better off if she swaps some of the oranges from her bundle for some of the apples belonging to a person preferring oranges to apples. Indeed, it is likely that everybody will have something they would wish to trade in order to make themselves better off. As a consequence, requiring identical bundles will make virtually everybody materially worse off than they would be under an alternative allocation. There are a number of other criticisms made of strict equality principles: that they unduly restrict freedom; that they do not give best effect to equal respect for persons; that they conflict with what people deserve; and that everyone can be materially better off if incomes are not strictly equal. It is this fact which partly inspired the Difference Principle.

### The Difference Principle

The most widely discussed theory of distributive justice in the past three decades has been that proposed by John Rawls in his seminal work, *A Theory of Justice* (1971). Rawls proposed the following two principles of justice:

1 Each person is to have an equal right to the most extensive total system of equal basic liberties compatible with a similar system of liberty for all.

2 Social and economic inequalities are to be arranged so that they are both:

   (a) to the greatest benefit of the least advantaged, and

(b)  attached to offices and positions open to all under conditions
of fair equality of opportunity.

(Rawls 1971: 60)

The main motivation for the Difference Principle is similar to that for
strict equality: equal respect for persons. Opinion divides on the size of the
permissible inequalities which should be allowed by the Difference
Principle, and on how much better off the least advantaged would be under
the Difference Principle than under a strict equality principle. Rawls is not
opposed to the principle of strict equality *per se*; his concern is about the
absolute position of the least advantaged group rather than their relative
position. If a system of strict equality maximises the absolute position of the
least advantaged in society, then the Difference Principle advocates strict
equality. If it is possible to raise the position of the least advantaged further
by inequality of income and wealth, then the Difference Principle
prescribes inequality up to that point where the absolute position of the
least advantaged can no longer be raised.

The importance of Rawls in the history of political theory is now
widely acknowledged. Charles Beitz (1979) argues that the Difference
Principle is equally pertinent to the international arena, despite the fact that
Rawls does not extend it beyond particular liberal societies that can be
described as particular communities in which individuals cooperate for
their mutual advantage. For Beitz and other cosmopolitan thinkers,
distributive justice should apply at a global level among all individuals and
not be limited to what states can agree to distribute on a just basis.

### Welfare-based principles

Welfare-based principles are motivated by the intuition that what is of
primary moral importance is the level of welfare of people. Advocates of
welfare-based principles view the concerns of other theories – equality, the
least advantaged, resources, desert-claims, or liberty – as secondary
concerns. They are only valuable in so far as they increase welfare, so that all
distributive questions should be settled according to which distribution
maximises welfare. However, 'maximises welfare' is imprecise, so welfare
theorists propose particular welfare functions to maximise. Although there
are a number of advocates of alternative welfare functions, most
philosophical activity has concentrated on a variant known as
utilitarianism. This **theory** can be used to illustrate most of the main
characteristics of welfare-based principles.

Historically, utilitarians have used the term 'utility' rather than 'welfare'
and utility has been defined variously as pleasure, happiness, or
preference-satisfaction. So, for instance, the principle for distributing
economic benefits for preference utilitarians is to distribute them so as to

maximise preference-satisfaction. The welfare function for such a principle has a very simple theoretical form: it involves choosing that distribution maximising the arithmetic sum of all satisfied preferences, weighted for the intensity of those preferences.

The basic theory of utilitarianism is one of the simplest to state and understand. Much of the work on the theory therefore has been directed towards defending it against moral criticisms, of which two are particularly important.

The first is that utilitarianism fails to take the distinctiveness of persons seriously. Maximisation of preference-satisfaction is often taken as prudent in the case of individuals – people may take on greater burdens, suffering, or sacrifice at certain periods of their lives so that their lives may be better overall. The complaint against utilitarianism is that it takes this principle, commonly described as prudent for individuals, and uses it on an entity, namely society, which is unlike individuals in important ways. While it may be acceptable for a person to choose to suffer at some period in her life (be it a day, or a number of years) so that her overall life is better, it is often argued against utilitarianism that it is immoral to make some people suffer so that there is a net gain for other people. In the individual case, there is a single entity experiencing both the sacrifice and the gain. Also, the individuals who suffer or make the sacrifices choose to do so in order to gain some benefit. In the case of society as a whole, there is no single experiential entity – some people suffer or are sacrificed so that others may gain.

A related criticism of utilitarianism involves the way it treats individual preferences or interests referring to the holdings of others. For instance, some people may have a preference that some minority racial group should have fewer material benefits. Under utilitarian theories, in their classical form, this preference or interest counts like any other in determining the best distribution. Hence, if racial preferences are widespread and are not outweighed by the minorities' contrary preferences, utilitarianism will recommend an inegalitarian distribution based on race.

## Deserts-based principles

The different deserts-based principles of distribution differ primarily according to what they identify as the basis for deserving. Most contemporary proposals fit into one of three broad categories:

1 *Contribution*: People should be rewarded for their work activity according to the value of their contribution to the social product.
2 *Effort*: People should be rewarded according to the effort they expend in their work activity.

3   *Compensation*: People should be rewarded according to the costs they incur in their work activity.

The specification and implementation problems for deserts-based distribution principles revolve mainly around the deserts bases: it is difficult to identify what is to count as a contribution, an effort, or a cost, and it is even more difficult to measure these in a complex global economy.

The main moral objection to deserts-based principles is that they make economic benefits depend on factors over which people have little control. The problem is most pronounced in the case of productivity-based principles – a person's productivity seems clearly to be influenced by many factors over which the person has little or no control.

### Libertarian principles

Most contemporary versions of the principles discussed so far allow some role for the market as a means of achieving the desired distributive pattern – the Difference Principle uses it as a means of helping the least advantaged; utilitarian principles commonly use it as a means of achieving the distributive pattern maximising utility; deserts-based principles rely on it to distribute goods according to deserts, etc. In contrast, advocates of libertarian distributive principles rarely see the market as a means to some desired pattern, since the principle(s) they advocate do not propose a 'pattern' at all, but instead describe the sorts of acquisitions or exchanges that are themselves just. The market will be just, not as a means to some pattern, but in so far as the exchanges permitted in the market satisfy the conditions of just exchange described by the principles. For libertarians, just outcomes are those arrived at by the separate just actions of individuals; a particular distributive pattern is required for justice at no stage, neither as a starting point nor as an outcome.

The obvious objection to libertarianism is that it is not clear why the first people to acquire some part of the material world should be able to exclude others from it (and, for instance, be landowners while others become the wage labourers).

Whatever principle of distributive justice one prefers, it must be noted that the allocation of goods within a single society or state is more easily accomplished than across the international state system. The hierarchical nature of domestic society means that authorities can (in theory) adjust the distribution of goods. This is not the case in international relations. There is no overarching authority to allocate goods according to principles of justice. Yet it is here that the greatest inequalities exist. The diminishing share of global income going to the world's poorest people is a cause of great concern and has given rise to demands for a significant redistribution of goods and services from the rich countries to the poorest ones. As one might expect, the strengths and weaknesses of competing principles of distributive justice, and their applicability to international relations, are central issues in the contemporary study of international relations.

*See also:* **communitarianism; exploitation; human rights; theory**

*Further reading:* Beitz, 1979; Kymlicka, 1990; Rawls, 1971, 1999

## EMBEDDED LIBERALISM ✓

For the purpose of understanding this concept, the terms 'embedded' and 'liberalism' have specific meanings. Liberalism refers to a consensus among advanced industrial states about the desirability of maintaining open trade and therefore the need to minimise protectionism and other beggar-thy-neighbour policies. At the same time, the word 'embedded' refers to a parallel consensus about the purpose of open or free trade. In so far as the latter promotes greater efficiency and higher levels of economic growth, these values should not be pursued in ways that hinder governments from fulfilling their role of providing social and economic welfare to their citizens. In other words, the economy should be regulated so that states can continue to pursue macroeconomic policies that minimise unemployment and redistribute income on behalf of the least well-off members of their societies. Thus the word 'embedded' modifies the extent to which liberalism is often associated with policies and arguments designed to minimise the role of the state *vis-à-vis* the market. The concept of embedded liberalism is consistent with what is sometimes known as *social liberalism*, according to which the cardinal value of individual freedom from coercion by the state has to be balanced against the positive freedom that the state can promote by intervening in society to ensure some measure of equality among its citizens.

In the twentieth century, two political economists, Karl Polanyi and John Ruggie, have examined this concept in some depth. In his famous text published just before the end of the Second World War, Karl Polanyi explored what he called a 'double movement'. The first movement was the creation of a new type of **capitalist** society following the industrial revolution of the eighteenth century. Successive governments took concrete steps to create *laissez-faire* capitalism. The commodification of land, the creation of a competitive labour market, and the gradual removal of administrative restrictions on the market all hastened the onset of a market society. The second movement took place after the First World War when, in response to the challenge of Marxism and the inequities of a market society, governments began to acknowledge their responsibilities for providing some measure of social and economic welfare. Polanyi was particularly concerned to show that this double movement by the state was not from a stance of non-intervention to one of intervention. The division between the state and the market was not a natural one: it had to be created, sustained, and justified by successive governments.

Polanyi's arguments were taken up in the study of the international political economy by John Ruggie, whose name is most closely associated with the concept of embedded liberalism in the study of international relations since the Second World War. Writing in the 1980s, he argued that the agreements signed at **Bretton Woods** represented a form of embedded liberalism at the international level. The international economic **order** among advanced industrialised states reflected not just the overwhelming **power** of the United States, but also a common purpose not to repeat the economic collapse of the 1930s. The **multilateral** agreements underlying trade liberalisation were supposed to be consistent with a high degree of domestic intervention in the economy. Governments did promote a division of labour to achieve comparative advantages and gains from trade, but since they were also committed to counter socially disruptive domestic adjustments, they encouraged trade mainly within continents and within particular economic sectors. They deliberately traded off gains from free trade for the purpose of domestic stabilisation. Similarly, states agreed to control flows of speculative capital across their borders on the shared assumption that finance should be the servant rather than the master of economic production.

Today, most scholars argue that the postwar era of embedded liberalism is over. We are now in the midst of a period reminiscent of the late nineteenth century. Once again, governments are pursuing policies across North America and Western Europe to disembed the market from state control. Freedom of global capital movements, the deregulation of markets for goods and labour, and other policies consistent with 'neo-liberalism' are becoming the norm. In turn, capital mobility makes it increasingly difficult for governments to pursue the kind of policies that were typical of the 1950s and 1960s. Whatever their ideological values may be on the spectrum from Left to Right, Western governments are following similar policies to ensure the approval of the global finance markets.

It remains to be seen whether the current movement away from the embedded liberalism of the postwar era can be sustained. As long as the most important economies of the world – particularly the United States – continue to grow, we are unlikely to see a sharp reversal of current trends. On the other hand, if the global economy encounters severe problems in the future, it may be that governments will have to construct a new Bretton Woods for the twenty-first century.

*See also:* **Bretton Woods; cold war; free trade; globalisation; International Monetary Fund; managed trade; multilateralism; regionalism**

*Further reading:* Gill, 1995; Polanyi, 1944; Ruggie, 1982, 1997, 1998

## END OF HISTORY

This concept is closely associated with Francis Fukuyama, who was largely unknown to most scholars in the field until he published *The End of History and the Last Man* (1992). The book itself was a response to the attention paid to an article the author had published three years earlier. Almost overnight, the phrase 'end of History' was used as a synonym for the 'post-**cold war** era' and Fukuyama became an instant intellectual celebrity. In a sense this was unfortunate, as the subtleties of his argument were often lost in the ensuing debate. Fukuyama did *not say* that 'History' had come to an end in the sense that politics, **war**, and conflict would no longer take place. Nor did he argue that the collapse of **communism** would guarantee that all states would become liberal democracies. The subtleties of his argument – an ingenious blend of political philosophy, historical analysis, and tentative futurology – can only be gleaned from a careful reading of the text, something that too many commentators have neglected to do. Once one grasps the underlying pessimism of Fukuyama's argument, it is not helpful to celebrate or condemn him on the erroneous assumption that his book is merely an exercise in triumphalism at the end of the cold war.

By the phrase 'end of History', Fukuyama is referring to the history of systematic thought about legitimate first principles governing political and social organisation. His argument is primarily a normative one. At the end of the twentieth century, the combination of liberal democracy and **capitalism** has proved superior – in fact and morally – to any alternative political/economic system, and the reason lies in its ability to satisfy the basic drives of human nature.

According to Fukuyama, human nature is composed of two fundamental desires. One is the desire for material goods and wealth. The other, more fundamental desire is for recognition of our worth as human beings by those around us. Capitalism is the best economic system for maximising the production of goods and services and for exploiting scientific technology to create more wealth. Economic growth, however, is only part of the story. Fukuyama appeals to the German philosopher G. W. F. Hegel's concept of *recognition* and his theory of teleological history to account for the superiority of liberal democracy over its rivals in the political arena. Whilst economic growth can be promoted under a variety of political regimes, including fascist and communist ones, only liberal democracies can meet the fundamental human need for recognition, political freedom, and equality. It was Hegel who contended that the 'end of History' would arrive when humans had achieved the kind of civilisation that satisfied their fundamental longings. For Hegel, that end-point was the constitutional state. In his version, Hegel appointed Napoleon as his harbinger of the 'end of History' at the beginning of the nineteenth century. Fukuyama argues that we need to recover the philosophical **idealism** of Hegel and abandon the philosophical materialism of Marx and his followers, who believed that socialism was necessary to overcome the economic inequality of capitalist societies. Fukuyama also finds in Hegel a more profound understanding of human nature than can be gleaned from the ideas of such philosophers as Thomas Hobbes and John Locke, who privileged self-preservation above recognition.

In addition to Hegel, Fukuyama invokes Plato and Alexandre Kojève, Hegel's most famous interpreter in the twentieth century. From Plato, Fukuyama borrows the notion of *thymos*, variously translated as 'spiritedness', 'courage', or 'desire'. *Megalothymia* is the *thymos* of great men, the movers of history such as Caesar and Stalin. In contrast, *isothymia* is the humble demand for recognition in the form of equality rather than superiority. History is a struggle between these thymotic passions. The genius of liberal democracy is that it represents the end-point of the struggle. The master–slave dialectic is a primary motor of history, which can never be stable as long as human beings are divided between masters and slaves. The latter will never accept their subordinate status and the genius of capitalist liberal democracy is its ability to reconcile the thymotic passions. Instead of superiority and dominance, society provides for political equality. Those who still strive for dominance have the capitalist pursuit of wealth as their outlet.

Fukuyama also relies on the interpretation of Hegel by Alexandre Kojève, the Russian exile and political philosopher. Writing in the 1940s, Kojève argued that the welfare state had solved the problems of capitalism identified by Marx. Capitalism has managed to suppress its internal contradictions. Furthermore, it not only provides material prosperity, but also homogenises ideas and values, thus undermining the clash of ideology among states, in turn reducing the threat of war. Hegel himself did not believe that the end of war within states could be replicated at the international level. Kojève and Fukuyama argue that whilst wars will not disappear, the homogenisation of values among the **great powers** will promote peace among the most powerful states, and these are the only ones that matter from a long-term perspective.

Fukuyama's philosophical views are elaborated in conjunction with a detailed examination of the allegedly inexorable trend towards liberal democratic forms of government in the twentieth century. He argues that in Southern Europe, Latin America, parts of Asia, and Eastern Europe, free-market economics and parliamentary democracy are, with some important exceptions, becoming the norm. He claims that there were only 13 liberal democracies in 1940, 37 in 1960, and 62 in 1990. He also traces the decline of war among democratic states over time, arguing that peace between states correlates closely with their convergence towards liberal democratic norms.

But the 'end of History', according to Fukuyama, is not necessarily welcome news. Despite the victory of liberal democracy as a normative model over its rivals, Fukuyama is concerned that the subordination of *megalothymia* to *isothymia* may be also the pursuit of equality at the expense of the pursuit of excellence. If there is too much equality, and no great issues to struggle for, people may revolt at the very system that has brought them peace and security. We cannot subsist merely on equal rights and material comfort alone, else we become what Fukuyama (echoing Nietzsche) calls 'last men'. At the end of the book Fukuyama sounds a note of warning. Unless there are ways to express *megalothymia* in those societies lucky enough to have reached the 'end of History' (and according to his own statistics, less than one-third of all states have arrived thus far), liberal democracy may atrophy and die.

*See also:* **capitalism; clash of civilisations; cold war; communism; democratic peace; democratisation; globalisation; liberal internationalism; perpetual peace**

*Further reading:* Anderson, 1992; Brown, 1999; Drury, 1992/3; Fukuyama, 1992; Halliday, 1992; Williams *et al.*, 1997

# ENEMY COMBATANT

Also referred to as an unlawful combatant, an enemy combatant is a fighter whose hostile activities fall outside the scope of the laws of war. The definition appears in an unprecedented Bush administration executive order issued just after the 9/11 attacks on the World Trade Center and Pentagon, and applies principally to those fighters taken from the field of battle in Afghanistan, Iraq, and surrounding areas. Many of these fighters have been designated as either Al Qaeda operatives or people suspected of abetting the terrorists; hence active and hostile enemies to the US.

It is vital to stress, then, that enemy combatants are not afforded the same treatment as prisoners of war under the Geneva Conventions of 1949.

Geneva Convention III, Relative to the Treatment of Prisoners, and IV, Relative to the Protection of Civilian Persons in Time of War, both provide various protections for prisoners of war, including the right to legal counsel, adequate food and water, and freedom from harsh interrogation tactics. Such rules of war ( *jus in bello*) also serve to reinforce the **reciprocity** between and among states and to protect civilians from the effects of war.

We therefore need to see an enemy combatant as not simply a legal term, but also, and perhaps most importantly, as a political, strategic tool of the current Bush administration. The strategic rationale in this case is that the **war on terror** needs to be waged in the most efficient manner, especially if this means preventing leaks of classified information that might jeopardise the government's war strategies. Yet, the human costs involved are as follows: the deprivation of suspected combatants or terrorists of civil rights, such as *habeas corpus*, the foregone right to legal counsel (due process), and the use of harsh interrogation tactics to extract information from prisoners being held at Guantanamo Bay and other CIA facilities. By labelling these suspected terrorists as enemy combatants, it could be argued that the Bush administration has sought to devise its own rules of war in response to the threats posed by global terrorism.

But the new rules raise three important political questions. First, does the US President possess the authority to detain a person indefinitely without legal counsel or *habeas corpus*? Second, does an enemy combatant status justify harsh interrogation tactics? Or alternatively, do such tactics unduly challenge the reciprocity principle by encouraging states to ignore the legal obligation of protective treatment of prisoners of war? Third, should a US *citizen*, who is taken from the field of battle, be treated as an enemy combatant? The issue here is whether the US President reserves the right to suspend the constitutional rights of his own citizens, and if his decision violates the checks and balances and bill of rights of the constitution.

In 2004, the US Supreme Court heard two cases involving the legality of the status of enemy combatants: *Hamdi vs. Rumsfeld*, and *Rasul vs. Bush*. The attorneys for the defendant in the first case argued that the detention of Yaser Esam Hamdi, a US citizen, who was seized in Afghanistan during the hostilities between the Taliban and US, violated due process agreements; and that pursuant to the Geneva Convention III, Hamdi was entitled to be treated as a prisoner of war. The second case called attention to the *habeas corpus* right of non-citizens, particularly those from friendly countries or countries not engaged in hostilities with the US. The US Supreme Court concluded in the latter case that the Bush administration could not detain the prisoner without some degree of due process. It made this recommendation by calling on the Bush administration to implement military tribunals to hear the cases of the accused. However, in the autumn of 2006, the Republican-controlled US Senate passed the Military Commission Act, which barred all aliens from accessing US federal courts.

It is important to note that the US Supreme Court typically (albeit not always) defers to the Executive Branch's constitutional authority to devise and conduct foreign policy. Complete deference in this case characterises some of the Supreme Court justices' defence of the Bush administration's executive order concerning enemy combatants. Still, the legal status of enemy combatants remains a highly controversial and unprecedented legal term. Not only does it conflict with many provisions of international law; it also appears to violate the Bill of Rights of the US constitution.

*See also:* **Bush doctrine; international law; just war; pre-emption; sovereignty; unilateralism; war on terror**

*Further reading:* Lelyveld, 2007; Martinez, 2004; Mofidi and Eckert, 2003; Sloss, 2004

## ENGLISH SCHOOL

The origins of the English School can be traced back to the late 1930s. Unlike theories rooted in the behaviouralist tradition or positivist theory, the English School represents a synthesis of moralist and rationalist approaches. It is, in other words, a school of thought that focuses on the moral, political, and social properties and rules of the international system, and that shows how these properties and rules both constitute and constrain state interest and action. Although the name of the school was not officially coined until the early 1980s, the school continued to evolve in the 1960s and 1970s, with the writings of Hedley Bull, John Vincent, and Martin Wight. In perhaps his most well-known work, *The Anarchical Society*, Bull sought to demonstrate the nature of the moral and normative rules with which states learn to cooperate, and to shed light on the normative constraints of international order and decisionmaking.

Generally speaking, the school comprises three traditions of political theory: Grotianism, Kantianism, and Hobbesianism. Grotianism, which is based on the writings of Hugo Grotius, a Dutch lawyer and statesmen of the early seventeenth century, represents the rationalist strand of thinking in the school. By contrast, Kantianism and Hobbesianism signify the universalist and **realist** strands of thought in the school, respectively. Each of these traditions refers to a different set of structural principles that comprise an explanatory framework for understanding international politics. Whilst Grotianism refers to the rational constraints of domestic law on the state and international society (rationalism), Hobbesianism represents the anarchical character of the international system: more particularly, the warlike conception of the interstate society rooted in the distrust and heated competition between and among states. Kantianism, in contrast, represents the moralistic and universal strand of English School thinking, in which international solidarity is characterised by the duty to act in accordance with international principles of accountability and equal respect.

It is important to stress the differing strands of thought in the English School. Here one encounters two fundamental strands in English school thinking: solidarism and particularism. Whereas the solidarists prioritise **collective security** and **cosmopolitan** right in their analysis, particularists emphasise the normative value of state **sovereignty**, or rather, the incentives that arise from asserting and preserving state sovereignty through cooperation.

By the 1980s and 1990s, the solidarist strand assumed an arguably more prominent role in English School thinking; especially in the context of the debate concerning the objectives and duties associated with **humanitarian intervention**. Solidarists, such as Tim Dunne and Nick Wheeler, challenged the particularist version of humanitarianism advocated by Vincent, by stressing the collective responsibility to protect the rights of severely abused peoples. This debate would generate increasing discussion of the issue of whether the transition from an international to world society required broader sociological and institutional analyses of the **global civil society**.

Barry Buzan, for instance, argues that the focus on **human rights**, while generating many important insights, is only one essential area of study. Equally important are the economic sources of international and world society, which address the role of **NGOs**, and other non-state actors, such as **terrorist** groups. Whether one agrees with Buzan's efforts to design a systematic English School theory, his argument does call attention to certain limits in English School theory. Perhaps more important, his critique underscores the resurgent interest in English School theory during the post-**cold war** era, and the prospects of expanding English School theory, particularly in terms of explaining and understanding the evolving role of ethics, social values, global **power**, and universalist notions of solidarity and peace.

*See also:* **international society; legitimacy; liberalism; rationalism; realism; sovereignty; theory; United Nations**

*Further reading:* Bull, 1995; Buzan, 2004; Dunne, 1998; Little, 2000; Ralph, 2005; Wheeler, 2000; Wight, 1991

## ETHNIC CLEANSING

When ethnic populations are minorities in territories controlled by rival ethnic groups, they may be driven from the land or (in rare cases) systematically exterminated. By driving out the minority ethnic group, a majority group can assemble a more unified, more contiguous, and larger territory for its **nation-state**. This is what many ethnic Serbs did through the policy of ethnic cleansing after the break-up of Yugoslavia. Indeed, the very term 'ethnic cleansing' was coined in the context of the dissolution of Yugoslavia. It is a literal translation of the expression *etnicko ciscenje* in Serbo-Croatian/Croato-Serbian. The precise origin of this term is difficult to establish. Mass media reports discussed the establishment of 'ethnically clean territories' in Kosovo after 1981. At the time, the concept related to administrative and non-violent matters and referred mostly to the behaviour of Kosovo Albanians (Kosovars) towards the Serbian minority in the province.

The term derived its current meaning during the war in Bosnia and Herzegovina (1992–5). As military officers of the former Yugoslav People's Army had a preponderant role in all these events, the conclusion could be drawn that the concept has its origin in military vocabulary. The expression 'to clean the territory' is directed against enemies, and it is used mostly in the final phase of combat in order to take total control of the conquered territory.

Analysis of ethnic cleansing should not be limited to the specific case of former Yugoslavia. This policy can occur and have terrible consequences in all territories with mixed populations, especially in attempts to redefine frontiers and rights over given territories. There is a new logic of conflict that relies on violent actions against the enemy's civilian population on a large scale, rather than on war in the traditional sense, i.e. between armed forces. Examples of this logic and policy abound today (the extreme case being Rwanda in 1994).

It is important to underline that the policy of ethnic cleansing fundamentally represents a violation of **human rights** and international humanitarian law. Only when the means and methods of ethnic cleansing policies can be identified with genocidal acts, and when a combination of different elements implies the existence of intent to destroy a group as such, can such actions represent **genocide**. Ethnic cleansing lacks the precise legal definition that genocide has, although it has been widely used in General Assembly and Security Council Resolutions, documents of special *rapporteurs*, and the pamphlets of **non-governmental organisations**.

Some suggest that ethnic cleansing is merely a euphemism for genocide. There would seem, however, to be a significant difference between them.

The former seeks to 'cleanse' or 'purify' a territory of one ethnic group by use of terror, rape, and murder in order to convince the inhabitants to leave. The latter seeks to destroy the group, closing the borders to ensure that no one escapes. This observation should not be taken to imply that ethnic cleansing is not a barbaric international crime. It is most certainly punishable as a crime against humanity.

*See also:* **ethnicity; genocide; preventive diplomacy; safe haven; terrorism; war crime; wars of the third kind**

*Further reading:* Bell-Fialkoff, 1996; Cigar, 1995; Naimark, 2001; Pohl, 1999; Weine, 1999

## ETHNICITY

Terms such as 'ethnic groups' and 'ethnic conflict' have become quite common, although their meaning is ambiguous and vague. Most of the major armed conflicts in the world are internal conflicts, and most of them could plausibly be described as ethnic conflicts. In addition to violent ethnic movements, there are also many important non-violent ethnic movements, such as the Québécois independence movement in Canada. Political turbulence in Europe has also moved issues of ethnic and national identities to the forefront of political life. At one extreme, the former Soviet Union has split into over a dozen ethnically based states, and issues of nationhood and minority problems are emerging with unprecedented force. At the other extreme, the situation seems to be the opposite, as the **nation–states** of Western Europe are moving towards a closer economic, political, and possibly cultural integration. But here, too, national and ethnic identities have remained important. Many people fear the loss of their national or ethnic identity as a result of European integration, whereas others consider the possibilities for a pan-European identity to replace ethnic and national ones.

The word ethnicity is derived from the Greek *ethnos* (which in turn derived from the word *ethnikos*), meaning nation. It was used in this sense in English from the mid-fourteenth century until the mid-nineteenth century, when it gradually began to refer to racial characteristics. In the United States, 'ethnics' came to be used around the Second World War as a polite term referring to Jews, Italians, Irish, and other people considered inferior to the dominant group of British descent. In everyday language, the word ethnicity still has a ring of 'minority issues' and 'race relations'. In international relations, it refers to aspects of relationships between groups that consider themselves, and are regarded by others, as being culturally distinctive.

A few words must be said about the relationship between ethnicity and race. Whereas it used to be common to divide humanity into different races, modern genetics tends not to speak of races, for two main reasons. First, there has always been so much interbreeding between human populations that it would be meaningless to talk of fixed boundaries between races. Second, the distribution of hereditary physical traits does not follow clear boundaries. In other words, there is often greater variation within a racial group than there is systematic variation between two groups.

Ethnicity can assume many forms, and since ethnic ideologies tend to stress common descent among their members, the distinction between race and ethnicity is problematic. Ideas of race may or may not form part of ethnic ideologies and their presence or absence does not seem a decisive factor in interethnic relations.

The relationship between the terms ethnicity and nationality is nearly as complex as that between ethnicity and race. Like the words 'ethnic' and 'race', the word 'nation' has a long history, and has been used in a variety of different meanings in English. Like ethnic ideologies, **nationalism** stresses the cultural similarity of its adherents, and by implication, it draws boundaries *vis-à-vis* others, who thereby become outsiders. The distinguishing mark of nationalism is by definition its relationship to the state. A nationalist holds that political boundaries should be coterminous with cultural boundaries, whereas many ethnic groups do not demand command over a state. Although nationalism tends to be ethnic in character, this is not necessarily the case.

It should be noted that ethnic organisation and identity, rather than being primordial phenomena radically opposed to modernity and the modern state, are frequently reactions to processes of modernisation. When we talk of ethnicity, we indicate that groups and identities have developed in mutual contact rather than in isolation. But what is the nature of such groups?

The words 'ethnic group' have come to mean something like 'a people'. But what is a people? Does the population of Britain constitute a people, does it comprise several peoples, or does it form part of a Germanic, or an English-speaking, or a European people? Does this imply that ethnic groups do not necessarily have a distinctive culture? Can two groups be culturally identical and yet constitute two different ethnic groups? These are complicated questions. Contrary to a widespread commonsense view, cultural difference between two groups is not the decisive feature of ethnicity. Two distinctive groups, say, somewhere in New Guinea, may well have widely different languages, religious beliefs, and even technologies, but that does not entail that there is an ethnic relationship between them. For ethnicity to come about, the groups must entertain ideas of each other as being culturally different from themselves. Ethnicity is essentially an aspect of a relationship, not a property of an isolated group. Conversely, some groups may seem culturally similar, yet there can be a socially highly relevant (and even volatile) interethnic relationship between them. This would be the case of the relationship between Serbs and Croats following the break-up of Yugoslavia. There may also be considerable cultural variation within a group without ethnicity. Only in so far as cultural differences are perceived as being important, and are made politically relevant, do social relationships have an ethnic element.

Ethnicity is therefore an aspect of a relationship between agents who consider themselves as being culturally distinctive from members of other groups. It can thus also be defined as a social identity (based on a contrast *vis-à-vis* others) characterised by metaphoric or fictive kinship. There are four main types of ethnic groups.

1  *Urban ethnic minorities.* This category would include, among others, non-European immigrants in European cities and Hispanics in the United States, as well as migrants to industrial towns in Africa and elsewhere. Research on immigrants has focused on problems of adaptation, on ethnic discrimination from the host society, racism, and issues relating to identity management and cultural change. Although they have political interests, these ethnic groups rarely demand political independence or statehood, and they are usually integrated into a **capitalist** system of production and consumption.

2  *Indigenous peoples.* This word is a blanket term for aboriginal inhabitants of a territory, who are politically relatively powerless and who are only partially integrated into the dominant **nation-state**. Indigenous peoples are associated with a nonindustrial mode of production and a stateless political system.

3  *Proto-nations (ethnonationalist movements).* These groups, the most famous of ethnic groups in the news media, include Kurds, Sikhs, Palestinians, and Sri Lankan Tamils, and their number is growing. By definition, these groups have political leaders who claim that they are entitled to their own nation-state and should not be ruled by others. These groups, short of having a nation-state, may be said to have more substantial characteristics in common with nations than with either urban minorities or indigenous peoples. They are always territorially based, they are differentiated according to class and educational achievement, and they are large groups. In accordance with common terminology, these groups may be described as nations without a state.

4    *Ethnic groups in plural societies.* The term 'plural society' usually designates colonially created states with culturally heterogeneous populations. Typical plural societies would be Kenya, Indonesia, and Jamaica. The groups that make up the plural society, although they are compelled to participate in uniform political and economic systems, are regarded as (and regard themselves as) highly distinctive in other matters. In plural societies, **secession** is usually not an option, and ethnicity tends to be articulated as group competition. Most contemporary states could plausibly be considered plural ones.

*See also:* **diaspora; ethnic cleansing; irredentism; nation–state; nationalism; secession; self-determination**

*Further reading:* Guibernau and Jones, 1997; Hutchinson and Smith, 1996; Kurti and Langman, 1997; Nash, 1989; Oommen, 1997; Spinner, 1995

# EURO

On 1 January 1999, Austria, Belgium, Finland, France, Germany, Ireland, Italy, Luxembourg, the Netherlands, Portugal, and Spain formed the Economic and Monetary Union (EMU) and adopted a new currency, the euro, as their official trading currency.

The introduction of the euro is the most important integrating step since Europe began the unification process in the late 1950s. However, it is still a 'work-in-progress'. Not all of the countries in Western and Central Europe committed themselves to the EMU in 1999. Denmark and Britain opted out.

The first major development in the transition to the Economic and Monetary Union occurred on 11 December 1991. On that day, the national leaders of the European Community committed themselves to closer political and economic union by signing the Treaty on the **European Union** and the Treaty on Economic and Monetary Union. The agreement to adopt a single European currency came into force in November 1993 after being ratified by each of the participating states.

At the heart of the EMU is the European Central Bank (ECB). It replaces the European Monetary Institute as the core economic organisation in Europe. The ECB is responsible for the management of the foreign reserves of the member countries, interest rates, setting foreign exchange rates, and, perhaps most significantly, has the power to determine the value of the national currencies of Europe in relation to the euro. It is also responsible for the production of notes and coins.

Initially, the euro was only a trading currency. It could not be used to purchase consumer goods or to pay for services. On 1 January 2002, however, notes and coins became available and national currencies like the franc and the Deutschmark were gradually withdrawn from circulation. It is important to recognise, however, that the euro is legal tender in the entire 'euro zone', despite the fact that some countries are not members of the EMU. It is estimated, for example, that around 50 per cent of small and medium-sized companies in Britain have direct or indirect trade links with the European Union (EU) and use the euro as their preferred medium of exchange.

There are strict criteria for determining admittance to the EMU. The process relies, first on all, on favourable financial reports from the European Commission and the European Central Bank. There are also a number of 'convergence criteria' used by these institutions to determine suitability. The country seeking admission should have low inflation and low interest rates and may not have a national debt that is more than 60 per cent of the total value of its economy. The final say, however, lies with the European Parliament. Under these circumstances, it is difficult to see how countries such as Greece will ever make the cut. Indeed, it may well be the case that economic and monetary union will be something that only the larger economies of Europe will achieve and the long-term impact on the weaker economies of Europe is still unknown.

Advocates of the euro argue that a single, stable currency will improve Europe's competitiveness in the global marketplace by lowering transaction costs. Others believe that the euro will insulate Europe from the boom/bust cycle of the modern world economy and that the euro will have profound consequences for the place of Europe in world affairs because decisions by the European Central Bank will have a considerable influence on global financial flows. Thus far, however, the euro has managed to meet many of these expectations, having gained significant value against the other major currencies, including the dollar.

*See also:* **Bretton Woods; European Union; integration; regionalism**

*Further reading:* Chabot, 1998; De Grauwe, 1997; Kenen, 1995a; McNamara, 1999

# EUROPEAN UNION (EU) √

The name of the organisation for the growing number of member countries in Western Europe that have decided to cooperate across a wide variety of areas, ranging from a single market to foreign policy, and from mutual recognition of school diplomas to exchange of criminal records.

This cooperation takes various forms, officially referred to as the three pillars: the European Communities (EC, supranational), the Common Foreign and Security Policy (CFSP, intergovernmental), and cooperation in the fields of Justice and Home Affairs (JHA, intergovernmental).

The European Union as an umbrella organisation came into existence only in November 1993, after the ratification of the Maastricht Treaty. The EU now consists of 25 member states and remains in close high-level talks with Turkish officials regarding Turkey's full accession to the Union. Its original membership of six was gradually enlarged over time. Belgium, Germany, France, Italy, Luxembourg, and the Netherlands were the original member states. Denmark, the Republic of Ireland, and the United Kingdom joined in 1973. Greece became a member in 1981. Portugal and Spain were admitted in 1986, and the EU was enlarged in 1995 to include Austria, Finland, and Sweden. There is talk of the eventual admittance of Poland, Hungary, the Czech Republic, and Slovakia, and later perhaps others. European cooperation leading to the creation of the EU has evolved throughout the post-1945 era, marked by the signing of key treaties to promote further **integration**:

- *Treaty of Rome* (1958). This initial agreement established the basic principle of freedom of movement of goods, persons, services, and capital. The basic institutional mechanisms were created – the European Court of Justice, the Council of Ministers, the European Commission, and the European Parliament. It is more of a supranational constitution than an intergovernmental agreement as it confers enforceable legal obligations.
- *Single European Act* (1987). This is an effort to complete the integrated market by striving for harmonisation of regulations with respect to financial services, securities, insurance, telecommunications, as well as product safety and technical standards.
- *Maastricht Treaty* (1992). This treaty represents a deepening of integration, including monetary union and social policies such as working conditions (although forthcoming directives must be approved unanimously or by a qualified majority of members). The treaty was ratified by all member states although there were close calls in Denmark and France, and Britain claimed the right to opt out. Complete monetary union seems a remote possibility given the problems associated with the exchange rate mechanism (pegged currencies) and difficulties harmonising macroeconomic policies (member states must maintain specified debt/GDP, deficit/GDP, and inflation levels).

The key institutions of the EU are the Council of Ministers, the European Commission, the European Parliament, and the European

Court of Justice. The Council of Ministers (or simply Council) represents governments. The Council is composed of particular ministers: depending on the matter under discussion, either the ones responsible for specific policy areas (environment, transport, and treasury) or the foreign ministers for general affairs. The Council decides unanimously on major policy decisions as laid down in the treaty provisions, and in principle decides with a qualified majority on other matters. The Council always meets behind closed doors; only the outcome of the decision is published afterwards. In some cases it is not even clear which member states have supported or rejected which parts of the original Commission or European Parliament proposals. This secrecy is often thought to be one of the most undemocratic aspects of the European Union; Council members are effectively unaccountable to their national parliaments for whatever national position they claim to defend within Council meetings, and they can always blame other member states (without means of verification) for Council decisions out of line with national European policies.

The European Commission is the body with the formal and exclusive power to initiate all EU legislation, and is supposed to represent the interests of the Union as a whole, both in the political processes within the EU and in negotiations with the outside world. This means that it must take no instruction from any of the member states' governments; it is accountable only to the European Parliament and to the European Court. Also, it is the main body with a duty to look after correct implementation of the treaties and subsequent legislation. The Commission's members are nominated by their national governments and must be acceptable to all the government leaders of the member states. Small member states each have one commissioner, while the larger ones (Germany, France, Italy, Britain, Spain) each have two. That makes a total of 20 commissioners.

The European Parliament has 630 members who are elected directly by voters. It can veto budgets and has limited authority to amend legislation. Its powers have strengthened over time but remain limited.

The European Court of Justice can be compared to the Supreme Court of the United States. It has the task of interpreting the treaties or secondary EU legislation when disputes arise. This is a very important task, since final compromises reached within the Council are often deliberately vague to facilitate any agreement at all. Its rulings are binding for all courts of the member states, which have to set aside national law if it conflicts with European law. The case law of the Court can also be relied upon in national courts. Since the ratification of the Maastricht Treaty, the Court can also impose fines on member states that do not comply with its rulings. The European Court of Justice consists of 15 judges (one from each member state) and nine advocates–general who assist the Court by making an independent preliminary assessment of the case.

All EU legislation is concluded by some combination of the European Commission (which makes proposals and oversees the legislative process), the European Parliament, and the Council of Ministers (i.e. the representatives of the member states). The main types of legislation take the form of Regulations that are effective as law without any further action by member states, and Directives that are binding as to the result to be achieved, but they leave the member states with some discretion as to how to achieve it.

One of the looming issues facing the EU is whether it can forge a strong (EU) collective identity. Clearly, the continued influence of English as a second language will be an important factor, but so will the full adoption of an EU constitution. Although an EU constitution was adopted on 29 October 2004, both the Netherlands and French voters rejected ratification of the constitution, thus suspending plans for its full implementation.

*See also:* **euro; functionalism; integration; regional trade blocs**

*Further reading:* Bretherton and Vogler, 1999; Cowles and Smith, 2000; Dinan, 1999; Habermas, 1999; Kaldor, 2000; Nugent, 1994; Weiler, 2003; Westlake, 1994

## EXPLOITATION

This is among the most popular words used by students concerned about global inequality and what many of them perceive as the inherently exploitative behaviour of **multinational corporations** (MNCs) in the **Third World**. However, although the term often provides the user with a source of rhetorical righteousness, the word itself is almost meaningless in the absence of a rigorous account of the ways in which it is permissible and impermissible to benefit from others. That is because, in everyday usage, exploitation simply means taking unfair advantage of someone. But this of course begs the prior question of what 'unfair' means.

Within the Marxist tradition of thought, the concept of exploitation has a very specific meaning, and is linked to a particular **theory** of how **capitalism** works. Marx argued that all past civilised societies had a social class structure, founded economically on class control of the surplus product. Civilised societies, in this view, are all based on their technological ability to produce a surplus above the immediate needs of the physical reproduction of their workers. Marx argued that this social surplus has always been appropriated by a small minority of the population, thereby dividing the society into a class of producers and a class of appropriators of the social product.

Marx believed, for example, that ancient Greek and Roman societies generated most of their surplus product from slave labour. In this situation the slaves are the direct producers, and the slave owners the appropriators of the surplus product. Marx also believed that the surplus product of feudal European society stemmed from the labour of serfs who were bound to the land of their feudal lord. The serfs worked a certain number of days a week to cultivate the lord's land, thereby creating the surplus product that allowed the feudal lord to maintain soldiers and fortifications. In Marx's language, the appropriation of the surplus product by a narrow class is exploitation of the producing class. A class society is one in which a social surplus product is appropriated by one class through the exploitation of another.

The concept of exploitation in Marxism serves two different functions. First, it points to one of the two main reasons for criticising capitalism, the other being capitalism's tendency to inhibit the free development of the individual's creative powers. Second, it enters into an explanation of the class struggle, the implication being that the exploited tend to organise themselves against the exploiters. According to the traditional Marxist concept of exploitation, people are exploited if they work more hours than the labour time embodied in the goods that they can buy for their income.

It should be said that even when labour values are well defined, it would be very difficult to calculate them and hence very difficult to draw the exact dividing line between the exploited and the exploiters. The Marxist definition of exploitation has few supporters today for the simple reason that hardly anyone takes his theory of labour value very seriously. Moreover, even if one does accept that theory, we may ask whether the capitalist is robbing the worker and, if so, whether there is anything wrong in that. Marx argued that although capitalists do rob the workers, they also force the production of surplus–value and thus help to create what is to be deducted. In other words, if the capitalist manager were not there to organise production, there would be nobody who could steal the surplus, but nor would there be any surplus to steal. If the workers gain from being exploited by getting a part of the surplus which is made possible by the managerial talent of the capitalist, how can one complain about the capitalist appropriating the rest of the surplus?

If one is unconvinced about the scientific merits of Marxism in general and Marxist theories of exploitation in particular, then it follows that the term 'exploitation' should be used very carefully indeed. The facts of global inequality do not themselves justify the use of the term to describe the relationship between rich and poor, or between powerful and powerless actors on the global stage. This is not to say that the term cannot be used at all. It is merely to say that using the term properly depends on the justifications provided to label such relationships as unfair.

*See also:* **capitalism; distributive justice; imperialism; multinational corporation**

*Further reading:* Miller, 1999; Roemer, 1982

## EXTRATERRITORIALITY ✓

In **international law**, extraterritoriality refers to instances in which the jurisdiction and laws of one **sovereign** state extend over the territory of another, usually under a treaty granting such rights. In general, extraterritorial jurisdiction is most frequently exercised by consuls and **diplomats** in specific countries who, in addition to their ordinary consular duties, are vested with judicial **powers**. The term is also sometimes defined as the immunity from the laws of a state enjoyed by diplomatic representatives of other states. Such immunity has often been extended to armies in permitted transit and to warships. Extraterritorial rights may be surrendered by treaty, abolished by the annexation of the country granting extraterritorial rights to a country not granting such rights, or abolished by voluntary renunciation on the part of the state enjoying such rights.

Extraterritoriality is rooted in the concept of sovereignty, if only because it is traditionally considered a violation of it. In international law, sovereignty refers to a state's claim of exclusive jurisdiction over individuals or activities within its borders. Extraterritoriality therefore can be defined as a state's claim of jurisdiction over individuals or activities beyond its borders.

Extraterritorial claims can be differentiated into four types:

- *regional*: applying to individuals or activities within a specific area outside the territory of the state;
- *global*: applying to individuals or activities regardless of their location outside the territory of the state;
- *exclusive*: no other actor has jurisdiction over the individual or activity;
- *shared*: other actors may have some jurisdiction as well.

Beginning in the late eighteenth century and continuing well into the twentieth century, Western states claimed at least partial extraterritorial jurisdiction over their citizens in countries in Africa, Asia, the Middle East, and the Pacific. They believed that 'uncivilised' countries were not subject to the Christian law of nations and therefore were not sovereign. Christian states had a right and an obligation to protect their citizens in non-sovereign, non-Christian states. The development of the principle of **self-determination** made this conception of sovereignty increasingly untenable. Self-determination held that sovereignty was not a privilege of civilised states but a right of all states. In some cases, extraterritorial claims were renounced when countries became 'civilised'. In other cases, the West gave up its claims based purely on the right of self-determination. Today, regional extraterritoriality is dead. Legal reform in the affected countries and the rise of the principle of self-determination killed it. Shortly after the end of the Second World War, the principle of sovereignty based on exclusive territorial jurisdiction was extended to all countries, Christian and non-Christian.

It should be noted that the arrogance of many Europeans in equating civilisation with the particular civilisation of Europe was no less than that of the Chinese. Nor was the European belief that their religion was the one true faith any less dogmatic than that of the Muslim peoples with whom they came into contact. The standard of 'civilisation' on which the Europeans insisted did indeed lead to unjust treatment. However, the demand of Asian and African peoples for equality of rights in **international law** was one that they did not put forward until they had first absorbed ideas of the equal rights of states to sovereignty and of peoples to self-determination, which before their contact with Europe played little part in their experience.

*See also:* **imperialism; international law; international society; self-determination; sovereignty**

*Further reading:* Gong, 1984; Lang and Born, 1987; Neale and Stephens, 1988

# FAILED STATE

A nominally sovereign state that is no longer able to maintain itself as a viable political and economic unit. It is a state that has become ungovernable and lacks **legitimacy** in the eyes of the international community. In recent years states that have been referred to in this way include Cambodia, Haiti, Rwanda, and Sierra Leone.

To understand the precise character of a failed state, it is worth contrasting it with a successful or viable state that can maintain control of its territorial borders, provide a decent level of services such as health and education for its people, has a functioning infrastructure and economy, and is capable of maintaining law and **order**. Such a state is socially cohesive with a stable domestic political order.

Failed states have none of these qualities. They cannot provide basic needs or essential services for their citizens, they have no functioning infrastructure, and they are without a credible system of law and order. In some cases, **power** lies in the hands of criminals, warlords, armed gangs, or religious zealots. Others have been in the grip of civil war for many years. The most disturbing aspect of state failure is that it almost always involves the great suffering of civilians.

It would be a mistake to think that state failure is a wholly local event. On the contrary, it has regional and sometimes international implications. As **anarchy** takes hold, **refugees** flood across borders to escape the violence. Conflict will often spread into and destabilise neighbouring states. The civil war in Rwanda in the early 1990s, for example, undermined the already fragile stability of what was then called Zaire (now the Congo). Failed states can become a refuge for criminal gangs, drug dealers, and arms smugglers. Often an enormous humanitarian effort and very large sums of money are required to assist civilian populations. State failure is a problem for many states in the international system; it is not just a 'domestic' problem.

There are a number of causes of state failure. Some scholars identify its roots in the process of **decolonisation**. A key premise underlying decolonisation is that people flourish when they are able to govern themselves. But during the 1950s and 1960s, little thought was given to precisely who constituted 'the people', and few strategies were put in place by the exiting colonial powers to enable newly independent states to develop into mature, stable entities. The failure to deal with this issue has led to a number of civil wars of **self-determination**. To a certain extent, the **cold war** hid this problem from view. Aid flowed from the **superpowers** to the rulers of these states and helped to prop them up. Indeed, some of the rulers of these states did extremely well out of the cold war. However, the end of the cold war and the concomitant loss of **foreign aid** have exposed the real fragility of these states.

Another contributing factor associated with the end of the cold war is the problem of **democratisation**. Democratic forms of government stress the right of the citizens to participate in the decision-making process. Typically, autocratic states have an extremely tight grip on power. Stability is purchased through tyranny and terror. But the transition from autocracy to democracy often leaves the state without a clear understanding of who is in control. The opening up of a 'power vacuum' provides opportunities for disaffected groups to try to seize control of the government.

Two other factors need to be noted as well. The first is mismanagement and corruption. The second is the global capitalist system, since the heavily indebted nature of many of these weak states has considerably compromised their ability to develop.

While failed states are in a class of their own, it is important to recognise that there are many states (nearly all of them located in Sub-Saharan Africa) that are dangerously close to collapse. They have not quite degenerated into a state of chaos, but appear to be well on the way. What can be done about these states? A wide range of options is discussed in the literature, including the **containment** and **isolation** of such states, extra foreign aid, the delegation of some governmental authority to the **United Nations**, and even the reintroduction of the UN trusteeship system.

*See also:* **debt trap; decolonisation; democratisation; dependency; development; foreign aid; humanitarian intervention; modernisation theory; refugees; self-determination; structural adjustment programme; wars of the third kind; World Bank**

*Further reading:* Allen, 1999; Helman and Ratner, 1992/3; Reno, 2000; Zartman, 1995

## FEMINISM ⌄

A simple definition of feminism means the study of and movement for women not as objects but as subjects of knowledge. Until the 1980s, and despite the inroads of feminism in other social sciences, the role of gender (i.e. the relationship between sex and **power**) in the **theory** and practice of international relations was generally ignored. Today, this is no longer the case as a number of feminist thinkers have turned their critical sights on a field that has traditionally been gender-blind. Over the last decade, feminism has emerged as a key critical perspective within the study of international relations. The initial impetus of this critique was to challenge the fundamental biases of the discipline and to highlight the ways in which women were excluded from analyses of the state, international political economy, and international security. One can now distinguish between at least two main types of feminism in the study of international relations.

The first wave of feminist scholarship in the 1980s is now called *feminist empiricism*, in which international relations scholars have sought to reclaim women's hidden voices and to expose the multiplicity of roles that women play in sustaining global economic forces and state interactions. For example, women's participation and involvement facilitate tourism, colonialism, and economically powerful states' domination of weak states. The maintenance of the international political economy depends upon stable political and military relations among states. In turn, the creation of stable **diplomatic** and military communities has often been the responsibility of women (as wives, girlfriends, and prostitutes). Feminist empiricism exposes the role of women and demonstrates their importance in a wide variety of arenas. In case one might think that the role of women is marginal to the real business of the international economy, it should be noted that Philippine women working abroad as domestic servants annually contribute more to the Philippine economy than do the national sugar and mining industries.

A second focus of feminist research has been directed at deconstructing major discipline-defining texts and uncovering gender biases in the paradigmatic debates that have dominated the field since its inception in 1919. Sometimes referred to as *standpoint feminism*, this type of feminist scholarship argues for the construction of knowledge based on the material conditions of women's experiences, which give us a more complete picture of the world since those who are oppressed and discriminated against often have a better understanding of the sources of their oppression than their oppressors. Whilst feminist empiricism exposes the role of women in international relations, standpoint feminism alerts us to the ways in which the conventional study of international relations is itself gendered.

Despite the rise of feminism in the field, there remains a major imbalance between male and female academics in international relations, and many feminists attack the ways in which men's experiences are projected as if they represent some universal standpoint. According to standpoint feminists, the major Western intellectual traditions of **realist** and liberal thought have drawn from culturally defined notions of masculinity, emphasising the value of autonomy, independence, and power. Those traditions have formulated assumptions about interstate behaviour, security, progress, and economic growth in ways that allegedly perpetuate the marginalisation and invisibility of women.

Feminism is a rich, complicated, and often contradictory body of research in the study of international relations at the end of the twentieth century. In a broad sense, feminism is an umbrella term. It embraces a wide range of **critical theory** aimed at examining the role of gender in international relations. However, there is liberal feminism, radical feminism, Marxist feminism, post-Marxist or socialist feminism, **postmodernist** feminism, and the list continues. Given the commitment by all feminists to some kind of ethic based on equality between men and women, their work is sometimes equated with **idealism**, and they have themselves been criticised for ignoring men in their zeal to promote the emancipation of women. It remains to be seen how feminist scholarship will evolve to include a broader agenda of questions about gender in international relations theory and practice.

*See also:* **critical theory; postmodernism; theory; women in development**

*Further reading:* Enloe, 1990; Jones, 1996; Murphy, 1996; Peterson, 1992; Steans, 1997; Sylvester, 1994; Tickner, 1992, 1997

## FOREIGN AID ✓

There is a longstanding debate over the desirability and effectiveness of foreign aid from rich to poor states. Supporters of foreign aid programmes argue that aid is necessary to help capital-poor countries acquire new skills and technology. Foreign technical assistance spreads the benefits of scientific research, most of which is conducted by the wealthiest states in the world. In addition, government-to-government loans and **United Nations multilateral** assistance finance numerous **development** projects at lending rates below commercial levels. The largest lender, the **World Bank**, has followed a policy of giving seed money for major projects in order to attract private or local government investment for ventures that do not fit commercial criteria. Aid funds are often used to help establish leading sectors of the economy that can then, through links to less developed sectors, pull the development process along. Finally, former colonies argue that rich states have a moral obligation to assist the poor wherever the coloniser's industrial wealth was created with **Third World** resources. Even when the demand for restitution is difficult to justify, simple compassion calls for the rich to take some responsibility for relieving the burdens of global poverty.

Critics of foreign aid have put forward a number of reasons to explain why it has not been effective in promoting development. In the first place, the amounts are pitiful in light of the magnitude of the problem. Only a handful of states have managed to achieve the international standards declared by the United Nations, which hovers around 1 per cent of the gross domestic product (GDP) of advanced industrialised states. The United States, once the world leader in global aid, is now in fourth place after Japan, Germany, and France in terms of absolute amounts. Expressed as a percentage of its GDP, with 0.1 per cent of American GDP allocated to Overseas Development Assistance, the United States is close to the bottom of all industrialised donors. Furthermore, much of its foreign aid is in the form of military goods that contribute nothing to economic prosperity. More than half the amount of money in US foreign aid dispensed since the Second World War has been in the form of military aid. By supporting the power of the armed forces in many poorer states and encouraging the military to play an active political role, these security-assistance dollars have served to undermine democracy and economic development.

One reason for the extensive debate over aid is that so many diverse objectives drive its allocation, it is hard to evaluate how effective it is. While economic growth is clearly not the sole objective of foreign assistance, it is one of the few areas where empirical evidence permits evaluation. Growth is also important because without growth it is difficult, if not impossible, to achieve all the other goals – **security**, **human rights**, **democracy** – attributed to aid.

In many less developed countries, there is a negative correlation between aid flows and growth performance. Africa, for example, receives ten times more aid per capita than Latin America or East Asia and yet performs far worse by most or all economic measures. There are several explanations, but one point is clear. By removing a hard budget constraint, aid inflows to a country can impede the formation of a domestic consensus on the need for difficult economic reforms. Research suggests that countries with high inflation tend to implement more complete reforms and then enjoy higher average growth rates than countries that just muddle along at medium inflation rates. What happens is that aid flows are often cut off in countries with very high inflation rates but continue in countries with medium inflation rates. These aid flows protect countries from the full costs of bad economic policies, often preventing the onset of deeper problems and the important policy learning experience that is often critical to successful economic reform. Countries often have to 'hit bottom' to get a domestic consensus on the need for economic reforms. Of course, allowing countries to collapse economically is hardly an acceptable policy recommendation. To complicate the issue further, it is also important to note that in some cases aid has actually helped develop a consensus in favour of market reforms. For example, in Poland in 1989 the promise of foreign aid as something that the reform government could deliver was critical to its election and the undertaking of market reforms.

Both the timing and the role of aid flows in the implementation of policy reforms are still being widely debated. But what we do know is that financial aid to countries where there is no consensus at all in favour of reform has a negative impact.

How and why has so much aid continued to flow under such conditions? Conditionality, which is how aid is appropriated for the most part, is usually applied *ex ante*; that is, borrowing countries must meet certain conditions to be eligible for a loan and then must continue to meet those conditions along the way as aid is disbursed. But despite a marked increase in conditional lending in the past decade, and also an increase in the number of conditions on each loan, conditionality has not been particularly effective in attaining borrower compliance. The higher number of conditions actually seems to decrease borrower ownership of reforms. It creates a vicious cycle: weak compliance with conditions prompts donors to impose more conditions; increased conditions make it yet harder for the recipient to comply, thus increasing the incentive not to comply; and so on. On the donor side, meanwhile, the incentive structure rewards continued lending rather than halting financial flows in response to breaches in compliance. Ultimately, **multilateral** institutions are lending institutions, and they must lend to remain operational. So the average loan officer at the World Bank has a greater incentive to disburse loans on time than to enforce strict compliance from the recipients of those loans. As a result, many countries continue to receive loans even though they have bad records at both compliance and policy reform.

*See also:* **debt trap; dependency; development; distributive justice; failed state; foreign direct investment; International Monetary Fund; World Bank**

*Further reading:* Maren, 1997; Tarp, 2000; Tisch and Wallace, 1994

## FOREIGN DIRECT INVESTMENT (FDI) ✓

The transfer of capital, personnel, know-how, and technology from one country to another for the purpose of establishing or acquiring income-generating assets. There are two main types of FDI. The first is *fixed asset* investment, in which the investing company maintains a significant level of physical control over the asset (such as a manufacturing plant) during the life of the investment. The second is *portfolio* investment – the acquisition of shares and stocks located in foreign countries.

FDI is not a new phenomenon. Indeed, it was an important component in European colonialism. Yet over the last 30 years, levels of FDI in developed countries have increased dramatically. In 2006 foreign direct investment reached an all-time high of US$billion, while total cross-border flows of short- and long-term investment have more than doubled between 1995 and 2005. In addition, FDI spreads across a wide range of industries and firms. Traditional resource extraction firms have been joined in overseas locations by consumer-product firms, by manufacturing firms, and by companies in the service and information industries. Indeed, investment in primary sector industries (such as mining and oil) is a shrinking portion of foreign direct investment. When firms invest abroad, they do so for a variety of reasons: to gain access to resources or raw materials; to reduce costs; to expand markets; to follow their customers; or to compete with other firms.

Most FDI comes from companies based in the **OECD** region. Between 1960 and 1991, for example, over 85 per cent of all FDI came from the

United States, the United Kingdom, Japan, Germany, France, the Netherlands, and Canada. During the same period, however, the US share of FDI shrank from 65 per cent to around 16 per cent of the world total, while Japan's share increased from just 2 per cent to 21 per cent. This partly explains the debate during the 1980s concerning the relative decline of US **hegemony**. Since the 1970s, the **Third World**'s share of FDI has diminished. In 1994, for example, Africa received 1.4 per cent of global FDI, the Middle East and the transition economies of Eastern Europe received 1.6 per cent, and Latin America received 11 per cent. Asia, on the other hand, received around 20 per cent of global FDI, a figure that reflects the economic rise of the **newly industrialising countries** (NICs). Of course, since the Asian financial crisis of 1997–8 this figure has been significantly reduced.

FDI became a major issue during the 1970s, when the assets of a number of large American corporations were nationalised by left-wing governments. In the most famous case, Salvador Allende, the democratically elected President of Chile, nationalised the assets of ITT and Anaconda Copper. The fact that Allende was a socialist made the expropriation of US company assets a **cold war** foreign policy issue. The result was the overthrow and death of Allende by a military opposition (covertly supported by the United States) and the rise to **power** of Augusto Pinochet, a ruthless military dictator. Not surprisingly, both companies were immediately de-nationalised. One of the consequences of this and similar incidences elsewhere was the realisation among corporate CEOs that sound FDI needed high-quality **political risk** analysis.

There is a debate in the literature whether FDI is, in fact, a conduit for wealth extraction rather than for domestic **development**. Some observers argue that FDI creates jobs, increases the revenue and tax bases of the host government, facilitates the transfer of technology and human capital, and ultimately promotes development, economic growth, and prosperity. Opponents, on the other hand, argue that FDI serves to extract more national wealth than it contributes to the host country. They claim that FDI maintains the host country in a dependent situation. Second, it creates a skewed or uneven pattern of economic development. When the investment period comes to an end, for example, it can leave the local workforce in a precarious economic position. Third, to attract FDI, host countries increasingly compete with one another and can end up offering such favourable deals and incentives that they ultimately lose more revenue than they generate. Finally, there are environmental and health issues as well. For example, **multinational corporations** (MNCs) sometimes export heavy polluting technologies or 'dirty industries' that are highly regulated in the home country.

Despite the criticisms, FDI has grown into an important aspect of a host country's economic development plans and it seems likely to grow in the future. For example, in 2006 foreign direct investment in the developing world was more than US$325 billion. By contrast, official development flows in that year amounted to US$40 billion, and the entire **foreign aid** budget of the United States was only US$12 billion. Increasingly, therefore, contact between the industrialised world and the Third World is taking the form of foreign direct investment.

*See also:* **dependency; development; exploitation; foreign aid; multinational corporation; Third World**

*Further reading:* Bornschier *et al.*, 1984; Dicken, 1998; Dunning, 1993; Dyker, 1999

## FREE TRADE ✓

This concept refers to what is more accurately called open trade, or trade between countries based on the laws of comparative advantage. Comparative advantage is the low relative cost of a good compared with its relative cost in other countries. It is very important to understand what this means. 'Relative cost' means the cost of a good relative to other goods. It is this price ratio that is to be compared across countries. Comparative advantage, then, involves a double comparison, across both goods and countries, and that is critical to understanding it. In practice, every country has a comparative advantage in some goods.

The importance of the concept of comparative advantage is the economic **theory** that generates the laws of comparative advantage, first discovered by the political economist David Ricardo in the eighteenth century. The first law predicts what countries will do if given the opportunity, and the second law implies what countries should do:

- *The Positive Law of Comparative Advantage*: If permitted to trade, a country will export the goods in which it has a comparative advantage.
- *The Normative Law of Comparative Advantage*: If permitted to trade, a country will gain; i.e. the benefits of trade will exceed the costs.

One should note that the second law does not say that everybody gains from free trade. It says that there are costs due to trade, and then says that there are also benefits that are larger. Free trade is not an unambiguously good thing. Some people and firms lose from trade, and the case for free trade is only that other people and firms gain more. Consequently, if we are interested in increasing global economic growth, we are better off not restricting trade.

The direction of trade – whether a good is exported or imported – depends simply on whether its domestic price is above or below its world price. If it is below the world price, then the good will be exported. This will benefit the suppliers of the good, both the owners of the firms that produce it and the workers they employ. But it will harm domestic demanders of the good who will have to pay more for it, and these demanders include not only consumers, if it is a final good, but also other producers and their workers who use the good as an input. What advocates of free trade argue, however, is that the gains on the supply side of such a market are larger than the losses on the demand side, in the sense that the gainers could afford to compensate the losers and still remain better off.

If the domestic price of a good is higher than the world price, then the direction of trade will be the opposite. It will be imported. Here again there are winners and losers, but they are on opposite sides of the market from the other case. It is the demanders of imports who gain from their lower price, both consumers and firms buying them as inputs. And it is the suppliers, not of the imports themselves but of domestic goods that compete with them, who lose. Once again, advocates of free trade claim that the net effect is positive rather than negative. When trade follows the dictates of comparative relative prices, the gains outweigh the costs for both exports and imports. As prices move away from domestic market equilibrium towards their world levels, the losers cut their losses, reducing their quantities bought and sold, while the gainers take advantage of the opportunity by increasing quantities. It is these induced changes in quantities that generate the net gain.

In addition to promoting global growth and net wealth, supporters of free trade point to other benefits. First, it is argued that open trade fosters competition. If domestic firms are large enough to have market power to influence prices, then they will produce too little and charge too much, leading to inefficient consumer choices and reducing welfare. Trade undermines this market power by making large domestic firms compete with firms abroad. This forces them to behave more like perfect competitors, charging lower prices even though the firms themselves lose profits. Second, it is argued that trade promotes consumer choice, giving consumers access to many more varieties of goods than they could buy otherwise. Third, open trade relieves shortages of certain goods. Centrally planned economies have routinely had to combat smuggling more vigorously than is needed in market economies. Fourth, it is sometimes argued that free trade has a tendency to reduce wage differences between countries, which in turn can reduce the incentive to emigrate. Indeed, this was one of the goals of the North American Free Trade Agreement (NAFTA), which was expected to provide jobs and raise wages in Mexico sufficiently to draw Mexican workers away from the border with the United States and reduce their incentive to cross it.

In practice, however, the world is far from achieving the gains from free trade. Despite a great deal of rhetoric over the alleged **globalisation** of economic exchange, the world remains divided among national and regional markets, and the tendency is towards greater **regionalism** rather than a single global market for trade. Furthermore, it is very difficult in practice to measure the gains from open trade, whilst the losses are much easier to identify. The former are usually dispersed, whilst the latter are often concentrated among particular groups and firms.

For many **liberal internationalists**, however, the real importance of free trade is not the economic efficiencies stressed by political economists. The chief motive for liberalising world trade is peace. Many commentators argue that the **interdependence** of the world's economies is an important constraint on their going to war. Indeed, a major motivation for the founders of the post-1945 trading system was to prevent a recurrence of world war. By negotiating reductions in barriers to trade within Europe and in the larger world, countries would find it too costly to fight one another. Finally, free trade reduces the value of territorial control as a means to generate wealth, thus removing one of the traditional incentives for war among states.

*See also:* **Bretton Woods; embedded liberalism; interdependence; liberal internationalism; managed trade; newly industrialising countries; regional trade blocs; World Trade Organisation**

*Further reading:* Burtless *et al.*, 1998; Kaplan, 1996; Oxley, 1990; Roberts, 2000; Rosecrance, 1986

# FUNCTIONALISM

This concept must be understood in the context of the process of **integration** among states. Its theoretical application has been developed more extensively in Western Europe than elsewhere, in part because that part of the world has developed furthest along the path to integration. In the 1940s and early 1950s, functionalism was the proposed solution to the problem of how to bring states closer together to deal with issues that transcend territorial boundaries.

In the work of David Mitrany, one of the earliest pioneers in functional theory, a functional approach was presented as an alternative to political and constitutional forms of integration. After the failure of grand constitutional plans such as the **League of Nations** in the interwar period, functionalism represented a radically different form of international collaboration that would avoid an explicit concern with federal arrangements and their attendant legal and constitutional difficulties. Functionalism is the idea that international cooperation should begin by dealing with specific transnational problems (such as disease control) where there is some prospect of applying specialised technical knowledge and where the success of *ad hoc* functional arrangements will hopefully lead to further efforts to replicate the experience in an ever-widening process. In the early years after the Second World War, this expectation was raised by the recognition that governments faced a growing responsibility to provide welfare for their citizens, a responsibility that they could not fulfil in **isolation**.

Functionalism is also based on the hope that if governments begin to transfer functional responsibilities to international agencies with specific mandates to deal with issues over which there is a wide consensus regarding the need for cooperation, over time the principle of territorial and legal **sovereignty** will weaken. In the 1940s, the hope was that the interstate system could evolve into what was called a 'working peace system'. In some ways, functionalism is the economic and social equivalent to the contemporary concept of subsidiarity that is used in the context of European integration: the idea that political decisions should be taken at the lowest level of organisation most appropriate for those directly affected by them.

One can detect the influence of functional ideas in the development of organisations such as the World Health Organisation and the Universal Postal Union, and in areas such as civil aviation. Nonetheless, the concept as well as theories of integration associated with it have been criticised on three grounds.

First, it could be argued that the idea that it is possible both to separate technical from political issues and subordinate the latter to the former is somewhat naive. Second, although functionalism is often presented as a universal, non-political approach to international integration, it is in fact based on liberal utilitarian political values. Therefore it may be that the merits of functionalism are limited to those parts of the world that share the welfarist values that functionalism claims to promote. It is not clear that cultures and governments not infused with similar values can easily be drawn into the functionalist web of integration simply on the basis of its alleged benefits. Third, functionalism is based on an optimistic view that the benefits of technical cooperation will generate 'spillover' effects in other issue-areas. Early functionalist thinkers gave little thought to the actual processes of learning and adaptation that would be required to maintain the functional logic as it proceeded from less to more controversial issue-areas. Yet as the experience of the **European Union** demonstrates, spillover cannot be taken for granted, nor can the political and institutional design of integration be left to adapt organically to the technical requirements of particular issue-areas.

In the 1960s and 1970s, those inspired by functionalist ideas responded to such criticisms both by moderating their enthusiasm for global functionalism and by paying more attention to the problems of spillover. What became known as *neo-functionalism* was a more moderate conceptual tool for elaborating the process of integration in Western Europe. In particular, neo-functionalism is associated with the work of Ernst Haas. He acknowledged that the process of functionalism was easier to achieve in a regional context such as Western Europe, particularly in light of its history and shared democratic values in the post-1945 era. Unlike Mitrany, he admitted that it would be difficult either to separate technical from political issues or to avoid conflicts between states if the gains from collaboration were unequally distributed among them. Consequently, it is crucial to establish formal institutions that can impose and uphold agreements made by states. Such bodies have to enjoy some autonomy from national governments if they are to be effective, and the whole process cannot work unless states accept both the rule of law (hence encroachments of state sovereignty are difficult to reverse) and the principle of majoritarian decision-making.

In addition to these modifications, neo-functionalists inspired by Haas have paid a great deal of attention to the mechanics of and obstacles to spillover. They have examined issues such as socialisation and collaborative learning among political elites, emphasising that neo-functionalism (otherwise known as 'federalism by instalment') depends on the ability of political entrepreneurs and technical experts to apply consensual knowledge to the solution of common problems. Although many scholars of functionalism and neo-functionalism have become somewhat disenchanted with the project as progress towards integration in Western Europe slowed down considerably in the 1980s and 1990s, many of the ideas and theories associated with these concepts remain pertinent in the study of international collaboration.

*See also:* **European Union; idealism; integration; interdependence; non-governmental organisation; relative gains/absolute gains; sovereignty; theory**

*Further reading:* Ashworth and Long, 1999; Haas, 1964; Mitrany, 1975; Puchala, 1988

# GENOCIDE ✓

An endeavour to eradicate a people because of their nationality, race, **ethnicity**, or religion. Article 2 of the **United Nations** Convention of the Punishment and Prevention of the Crime of Genocide lists five genocidal acts:

1  killing members of the group;
2  causing serious bodily or mental harm to members of the group;
3  deliberately inflicting on the group conditions of life calculated to bring about its physical destruction in whole or in part;
4  imposing measures intended to prevent births within the group;
5  forcibly transferring children from the group to another group.

The term derives from the Greek word *genos*, which means race or tribe, and the Latin word *caedere*, which means to kill. It was officially coined in 1944, by Raphaël Lemkin, a French jurist living in the United States at the time. Unfortunately, like most concepts in the social sciences, the term suffers from overuse. Not all large-scale killings constitute genocide. What distinguishes genocide from other forms of killing is the scale and intentionality of the act. It occurs when a government or any other organised group deliberately sets out to destroy a particular group of human beings or undermine their ability to survive as a group. Thus forced sterilisation, mass rape, psychological and physical torture, deportation, resettlement, and ethnic cleansing may all be used as means to promote a policy of genocide even though none of them may constitute genocide *per se*.

While there have been instances of genocide throughout history, it took on two unique features in the twentieth century. First, the scale of genocide was unprecedented. At least 150 million people have been victims of genocide over the past 100 years. The second feature is the almost scientific and systematic quality of much of the slaughter, a feature that reached its most extreme manifestation during the Holocaust.

It is important to note an important anomaly in the definition of genocide given in the Convention. It does not consider the extermination of a political class as genocide. By this definition, the murder of some 1.7 million Cambodians by the Khmer Rouge in the mid-1970s does not qualify as a genocidal event because it was essentially class-oriented violence. However, most scholars agree that this is one of the starkest, most brutal, and systematic examples of genocide in modern history. Moreover, one of the unique features of the Khmer-sponsored genocide in Cambodia was that it was directed by Cambodians against Cambodians. In this, it resembles Stalin's purges during the 1950s.

What factors contribute to genocide? They range from ethnic **nationalism**, religious intolerance, and ideological confrontation to longstanding struggles for political **power**. In many cases, genocide is precipitated by a fear of 'the other', and the use of extreme stereotyping to dehumanise the enemy. Such feelings are exacerbated during hard economic times, civil wars, and periods of political instability.

Genocide, then, is the worst possible crime and is acknowledged as such by the international community. Indeed, for the first time since the Nuremberg Trials (1946), the international community appears to be serious about investigating, prosecuting, and punishing the perpetrators of genocide. The International Criminal Tribunal for the Former Yugoslavia (ICTY), for instance, has already investigated, prosecuted, and punished several tens of former military and state authorities, including Slobodan Milosevic, the former leader of Yugoslavia, who died in custody in March 2006. More important, **the International Criminal Court** (ICC), which entered into force in July 2002, recently issued several international arrest warrants against the leaders of militia groups in the Congo and Uganda.

Still, there is little guarantee that other states will fully cooperate with the ICC or the international community. The fact that genocide is taking place in the region of Darfur (2003–) and that the UN failed to act in a timely manner to stop the Rwandan genocide (1994) suggests that the political will of the international community remains unpredictable and lacklustre. By and large, **geopolitics** or the use of the veto in the Security Council to safeguard strategic interests, as well as state intransigence, continue to test the willingness of the international community to act accordingly. In many respects, the ability to stop genocide before it occurs and to punish it when it does take place is still constrained by the concept of **sovereignty**. The paradox is that while international criminal law seeks to punish offenders, it is **international law** that ultimately protects many of them.

*See also:* **ethnic cleansing; humanitarian intervention; war crime**

*Further reading:* Dobkowski and Wallimann, 1998; Kressel, 1996; Powers, 2003; Strozier and Flynn, 1998; Totten *et al.*, 1997

# GEOPOLITICS ✓

Geography has always played an important role in human affairs. It has shaped the identity, character, and history of **nation–states**; it has helped and hindered their social, political, and economic **development**; and it has played an important role in their international relations. Geopolitics is the study of the influence of geographical factors on state behaviour – how location, climate, natural resources, population, and physical terrain determine a state's foreign policy options and its position in the hierarchy of states.

The term 'geopolitics' was first coined by Rudolf Kjellén, a Swedish political scientist, in 1899. However, it only came into widespread use in the 1930s, when it was championed by a group of German political geographers and in particular the retired Major General Dr Karl Haushofer in the Department of Geography at the University of Munich. Haushofer's association through Rudolf Hess with Adolf Hitler brought the concept to the attention of the world when Hitler consolidated power for himself and the Nazi party in Germany during 1933. Numerous scholars in the West and in Russia, China, and Japan developed an interest in geopolitics as a science of statecraft, a method of thinking through the supposed significance of geographical factors in international relations. As a field of study, geopolitics was inspired by the work of two major nineteenth-century scholars: Alfred Thayer Mahan (1840–1914) and Sir Halford John Mackinder (1861–1947). However, one might also note the influence of the German pioneer of geopolitics, Friedrich Ratzel (1844–1904), and the French geographer Pierre Vidal de la Blache (1845–1918). Writing in the late nineteenth century, Mahan argued that naval **power** was the key to national power. A state that controlled the high seas (as Britain did at the time) could dominate international relations. The ability to achieve such control, however, was dependent on a large well-armed navy, long coastlines, and adequate port facilities. In 1919, Sir Halford Mackinder advanced a territorial counterpart to Mahan's thesis (which he repudiated in 1943). Referred to as the 'Heartland theory', Mackinder argued that the state that controlled the territory between Germany and Siberia could control the world. As Mackinder expressed it in a memorable phrase:

> Who rules Eastern Europe commands the Heartland
> Who rules the Heartland commands the World Island
> Who rules the World Island commands the World.

Despite its unfortunate association with Nazi Germany's foreign policy in the 1930s and 1940s (Hitler was obsessed with expanding Germany's 'living area' or *Lebensraum*), geopolitics is a serious field of inquiry. The various dimensions of geopolitics coalesce around the significance of the location of states on the world map. A state that is landlocked between two other states is likely to have very different foreign policy objectives from one that is surrounded by sea or other natural barriers. It has often been suggested, for example, that the **isolationist** tendencies in US foreign policy are directly related to its distance from Europe and that (prior to the invention of nuclear weapons) the Atlantic and the Pacific oceans provided it with a natural defence. This also accounts for the particular emphasis that the United States has placed on naval power over the last hundred years or so. In contrast, the location of Russia on the fringes of the West and its lack of secure borders help to explain its historically difficult relationship with the West.

For geopolitical analysts, there is also an important connection between location, wealth, and power. States that are located in areas with a temperate climate tend to be economically and militarily more powerful than other states. A wider variety of agricultural products can be grown, facilitating the extraction of natural resources. By the same token, those located around the equator or in the frigid areas of the planet tend to be economically underdeveloped and continually at the mercy of the environment.

Climate also impacts on the ability of a state to prosecute a war. The large number of French and German soldiers who froze to death whilst trying to conquer Russia in the nineteenth and twentieth centuries is an excellent example. In addition, climate affects terrain and this has an impact on warfare. Deserts, jungles, and mountain ranges require special training and equipment, and can either benefit an army or be the cause of spectacular military defeats. Thus location can have important strategic implications. Consider, for example, the obvious advantage a state that controls the headwaters of a large river system has over a downstream neighbour. Not only would the foreign policy objectives of each state vary according to their position along the river system, but it would also lead to very different strategic responses in the event of a military **crisis**.

At the heart of geopolitical analysis is a belief that states' economic and military capability, their position in the hierarchy of states, and how they relate to their neighbours are the consequence of geographical factors. In international relations, geography is destiny. But it is important not to fall into the trap of reducing a complex area of inquiry like international relations to a single factor. There are many ways of interpreting state behaviour – geopolitics is only one of them. Some scholars even argue that in the twenty-first century geopolitics is obsolete, superseded by 'chronopolitics'. The strategic value of the 'non-place' of speed has supplanted that of place as electronic communications and accelerated modes of transport have compressed time and space.

*See also:* **balance of power; realism**

*Further reading:* Braden and Shelley, 1998; Dodds and Atkinson, 2000; Gray, 2000; Hodder *et al.*, 1997; Kliot and Newman, 2000

## GLOBAL CIVIL SOCIETY ✓

Civil society refers to a public space where citizens and groups can engage in political activities independently of the state. It consists of diverse **non-governmental organisations** (NGOs) that are strong enough to counterbalance the state and, while not preventing the state from fulfilling its role as **peacekeeper** and arbitrator between major interests, can nevertheless prevent it from dominating the rest of society. Thus one of the benefits of a healthy civil society is that it reduces the **coercive power** of the state and helps it to become more responsive to the needs of its citizens. Developing a strong civil society is often seen as a strategy for overcoming political tyranny and is crucial to the whole process of **democratisation**. For example, one of the key aims of the Solidarity movement in Poland in the early 1980s was to develop organisations that were outside the control of the state.

The strongest civil societies exist in Western liberal–democratic states, in part because freedom of association and expression are necessary conditions for the existence of a civil society. Over the past two decades, however, a constant theme in the literature has been the withering away of civil society. Some observers blame the rise of corporatism, others the dominance of right-wing politics in most of the **OECD** world. But one of the greatest threats to civil society in the West is the growing tendency towards political apathy and the diminution of communal identity and political participation. As a counter to this, it has been suggested that more people need to get involved in voluntary associations and play an active role in the political life of their communities if civil society is to flourish.

If there is some debate about the future of civil society within a domestic context, this is also the case in international relations. The emergence of politically active, internationally oriented groups with highly developed networks and relationships, and an ability to pool resources and use sophisticated information and communications technology, has led to a blossoming literature on the subject of an emerging *global* civil society.

There are now many thousands of non-governmental organisations, political networks, single-issue groups, voluntary associations, and transnational social movements that stand largely outside the machinations of the state system, although some of them are also an important source of expertise and knowledge for states coping with global problems. The significance of these groups is as outlined below.

1 They form political communities and maintain a sense of solidarity among their ranks.
2 Many of them are organised on a global scale and they do not regard borders as an impediment to effective political action.
3 They do not regard the state as the only legitimate authority in the international arena.
4 They are mainly concerned with political issues that transcend territorial boundaries.
5 They generally promote a **cosmopolitan** ethical code that they would like to see all states accept and practise.

For some commentators, global civil society is part of the architecture of **globalisation** and, as such, provides new ways for individuals to think and act politically. It provides a space for marginal groups to have a political voice, it helps to create new collective identities, it increases the level of awareness of global problems, and fosters opportunities for new forms of **global governance**. What is more it reflects the evolution of international criminal justice, or the establishment of **international criminal courts**, which now ensure that individual perpetrators of gross **human rights** abuses will finally be held to account for their crimes.

There are two ongoing debates about the nature of and prospects for global civil society in the twenty-first century. First, there is no clear consensus about the appropriate relationship between global civil society and the forces of global **capitalism**. For example, some **NGOs** are extremely hostile to **multinational corporations** (MNCs) and see global civil society as a means to counter the forces of global capitalism, whilst others are more willing to work with states and MNCs in developing more humane and egalitarian forms of global governance. Second, the prospects for global civil society are unclear. There is an important debate in the literature on the scope and depth of an emerging global civil society. For example, whether individuals that live on opposite sides of the world and interact politically through advanced communications technology actually constitute part of a tangible self-sustaining community is at least an open question. Nonetheless, there is no doubt that those individuals who do seek a new kind of global politics will do so through the incipient institutions of global civil society. Ironically, how successful they will be is likely to depend on how seriously states respond to the challenges that they present.

*See also:* **global governance; International Criminal Court; multinational corporation; non-governmental organisation**

*Further reading:* Drainville, 1998; Falk, 1999; Kaldor, 1999; Keane, 2003; Lipschutz, 1992; Putnam, 2001

## GLOBAL GOVERNANCE ✓

The techniques, institutions, rules, norms, and legal arrangements used to manage relations between states and to facilitate cooperative action across various issue-areas. In the current international context, governance is carried out in the name of the global polity by both governmental and **non-governmental organisations**. This concept should not be confused with the term 'good governance' that is often used in some international organisations (particularly the **International Monetary Fund** and the **World Bank**) to promote a particular reform agenda for specific countries. Democracy, transparency, and market-friendly reforms are usually high on the list of that agenda.

Ever since the **Peace of Westphalia**, scholars have been concerned with the problem of governance. **Realists** have consistently argued that the most effective means of managing the international system is through the **balance of power**. In general, they do not believe that global governance can proceed much beyond the achievement of peace and stability among states. On the other hand, liberals have sought to foster global governance by developing elaborate institutional arrangements to promote cooperation between states. After early setbacks, such as the failure of the **League of Nations**, the liberal approach has made a spectacular comeback. It re-emerged after 1945 with the formation of the **United Nations** and the development of **regimes** to manage the global economy.

The recent surge of interest in global governance has received its impetus from three sources. The first is the end of the **cold war**. This increased the expectation that international institutions (particularly the **United Nations**) would play a more central role in the management of the international system. The second is the rise of **globalisation** and a new sense of 'globality' that pervades much contemporary thinking. For some observers, globalisation is itself a manifestation of global governance in so far as it compels states to conform to the competitive demands of a global market. The third source of renewed interest in the concept is the heightened awareness that our planet is bedevilled by problems that require a concerted and coordinated global approach. Contemporary debates about global governance revolve around the most appropriate location of authority and **power** within the context of a world experiencing both **integration** and fragmentation.

In very broad terms there are two competing attitudes towards the problem of global governance. On the one hand, many observers argue that it should be pursued in an incremental fashion, building on existing regimes and institutions that do not undermine the state as the key actor in international relations. On the other hand, there are those who claim that the state is an archaic institutional form in the twenty-first century, incapable of delivering the levels of governance required by a world facing environment problems, endemic poverty, resource scarcity, and unprecedented **population growth**. The issues are far too complex and difficult to be dealt with by a single state or even a coalition of states, and certainly not by a market interested only in economic growth. Consequently, the state should be subordinate to evolving supranational institutions whose power should increase at the expense of the **sovereign** state. Thus the concept of global governance is a contested one. It means different things to different people depending in large part on the theoretical framework that is used to define and evaluate the concept.

Furthermore, the concept of global governance is contested politically. For example, some conservatives argue that it is undermining the sovereignty of the state and that it represents an advanced stage along the road to global government. However, the prospect of such an event occurring any time in the near future is exceedingly remote. While it is true that states are looking for ways to manage the international system more effectively, there is little tangible evidence to suggest that they are willing to allow any supranational body to govern them directly. Moreover, sovereignty remains an important ideal for much of the world's population, particularly for groups seeking greater **self-determination**. For the foreseeable future global governance should be understood in terms of global management rather than global government.

Many writers on the left are also suspicious of global governance. They fear that global governance will reflect the values and interests of the rich and powerful states in the system at the expense of poor and weak states. In short, global governance is a highly politicised concept that raises fundamental questions about the proper locus of authority in international affairs, the accountability of global institutions, and the nature of international justice.

*See also:* **cosmopolitanism; European Union; Group of Eight; non-governmental organisation; regime; transnational social movements; United Nations**

*Further reading:* Diehl, 1997; Falk, 1995; Ferguson and Mansbach, 2004; Makinda, 2000; Rosenau, 1998; Thomas, 2000; Vayrynen, 1999

## GLOBAL WARMING ✓

Global climatic change due to increasing atmospheric concentrations of so-called 'greenhouse gases' (notably carbon dioxide and chlorofluorocarbons or CFCs) has dominated the environmental agenda since the mid-1980s and has engendered considerable international political debate. There is little doubt that over the past century human action has significantly increased the atmospheric concentration of several gases that are closely related to global temperature. These increased concentrations, which are set to continue to rise in the near future, are already affecting global climate, but our poor knowledge and understanding of the workings of the global heat balance make the present and future situation uncertain.

Global warming is closely connected with the impact of rises in greenhouse gases on the thin layer of ozone present in the stratosphere above the earth. Ozone absorbs incoming ultraviolet radiation from the sun, thus preventing the earth from overheating. In 1985 scientists discovered what soon became identified as a hole in the ozone layer over the Antarctic. Today, the hole is no longer confined to the Southern Hemisphere, since stratospheric ozone depletion has now been identified in the Northern Hemisphere and in the Arctic. Despite prompt international action to reduce chlorofluorocarbons, past emissions will continue to cause ozone depletion for decades to come because of the time lag between their production and release into the atmosphere and their damaging effects. Full recovery is not expected until about 2050 at the earliest. Meanwhile the increase in ultraviolet radiation reaching the earth's surface is compounded by the fact that greenhouse gases are transparent to incoming short-wave solar radiation even though they absorb re-radiated long-wave radiation from the earth's surface. Hence the term 'greenhouse'.

The **theory** relating increased atmospheric concentrations of greenhouse gases and global warming is strongly supported by evidence showing that changes in the atmospheric concentrations of greenhouse gases have fluctuated in close harmony with global temperature changes, indicating that the two are related. There is also evidence to suggest that the twentieth century is the warmest of the second millennium. Overall, the planet has warmed at the surface by about 0.6°C over the past century. In part, this reflects the operation of an enhanced greenhouse effect due to human pollution of the atmosphere.

It is important to note that the warming trend over the past century has not been continuous through either time or space. Two periods of relatively rapid warming (from the 1910s to the 1940s and again from the mid-1970s to the present) contrast with preceding periods which were respectively characterised by fairly unchanging (1860s to 1900s) and slightly declining (1940s to 1970s) temperature. Spatially, too, global warming has been discontinuous: the two hemispheres have not warmed and cooled in unison; moreover highly industrialised areas appear to be warming at a slower rate than less industrialised regions.

The formidable economic, social, and political challenges posed to the world's governments and other policymakers by impending global climatic change are unprecedented. Policy responses can be categorised broadly into those that aim to prevent change, and those that accept the changes and focus upon adapting to them. While the issue is a truly global one, since all greenhouse gas emissions affect climate regardless of their origin, the costs and benefits of measures to mitigate the effects of global warming are likely to spread unevenly across countries. The issue raises important questions of international equity since, at present, the major proportion of greenhouse gas emissions comes from the industrialised countries, which contain only about one-quarter of the world's population. **Third World** states have called for reductions in emissions from the industrialised countries to make more of the planet's capacity for assimilation of greenhouse gases available to those countries that are industrialising now, a plan which should be facilitated by transfers of finance and technology from the North to the South.

Most countries have accepted the need to make some effort to prevent global warming, or at least to slow its pace, by reducing greenhouse gas emissions. A contribution has been made in this respect by the Montreal Protocol, which was signed in 1987 and amended in 1990. Governments have committed themselves to reduce consumption and production of substances that deplete the stratospheric ozone layer, many of which also contribute directly to global warming. CFCs were due to be phased out by the year 2000. Most attention since then has been focused on carbon dioxide. In 1992, more than 150 states participated in the **United Nations** Framework Convention on Climate Change (the Earth Summit). They agreed to reduce emissions to earlier levels, in many cases the voluntary goal being a reduction of carbon dioxide emissions to 1990 levels.

An attempt to make agreed reductions legally binding was made in 1997 at the Kyoto Protocol, a follow-on to the original climate treaty, although the United States has now withdrawn from the Kyoto agreement. Kyoto also focused on a wider range of greenhouse gas emissions such as methane and nitrous oxide. The declared aim of the Protocol is to cut the combined emissions of greenhouse gases by about 5 per cent from their 1990 levels by 2008–12, specifying the amount each industrialised country must contribute towards this overall aim. Those countries with the highest carbon dioxide emissions, including the United States, Japan, the **European Union**, and most other European states, are expected to reduce their emissions by 6 to 8 per cent. In practice, individual country reductions can be greater or less than those agreed, since the Kyoto Protocol also officially sanctioned the idea of emissions trading between industrialised countries. Hence, if a state's emissions fall below its treaty limit, it can sell credit for its remaining allotment to another country to help the buyer meet its treaty obligation. In 2001, the Kyoto Protocol went into force. Among those opposed to the Protocol was the United States, which objected that the Protocol would cause undue damage to the American economy and that the developing countries needed to be held to the same standards as developed countries.

In the winter of 2007, the Intergovernmental Panel on Climate Change, a panel consisting of thousands of the leading scientists and authorities on global warming, issued its fourth report on climate change. It reaffirmed, among other things, that the carbon emissions released by humans were rapidly warming the earth's climate and that there was enough scientific certainty to warrant immediate action. Among their projections were a rise in global average temperature between 3–8 degrees Fahrenheit and a 7-23 inch rise in sea levels by the end of the twenty-first century. The findings coincide with recent pledges by US oil and gas companies and the US Congress to cap carbon emissions. Thus, while the evidence of the human impact on global warming is seemingly incontestable, the question that remains is whether the international community can effectively manage the future effects.

*See also:* **development; globalisation; sustainable development; tragedy of the commons**

*Further reading:* Drake, 2000; Houghton, 1997; Intergovernmental Panel on Climate Change Report, 2007; Paterson, 1996; Porter and Brown, 1991

# GLOBALISATION

A term that refers to the acceleration and intensification of mechanisms, processes, and activities that are allegedly promoting global **interdependence** and perhaps, ultimately, global political and economic **integration**. It is, therefore, a revolutionary concept, involving the *deterritorialisation* of social, political, economic, and cultural life. It would be a mistake, however, to view globalisation deterministically. Just as there are powerful forces of integration at work through the shrinkage of distance on a global scale, so there are forces of disintegration as well.

Globalisation has certain identifiable characteristics, although there is no consensus in the field about any of them! In the first place, it involves a growing consciousness of the world as a single place. This is reflected in phrases such as 'the global village' and 'the global economy'. Few places are more than a day's travel away and communication across territorial borders is now almost instantaneous. In 1980 there were about 1 million international travellers per day. In 2000 more than 3 million people crossed territorial borders as tourists each day. And in 2003, the WTO estimated that global tourism generated nearly US$693 billion.

Second, new information and communications technology has improved access to overseas markets and streamlined both the production and distribution of goods and the trade in foreign exchange. Third, human beings are becoming more and more dependent upon one another as problems such as **global warming**, the international drugs trade, and **terrorism** can only be managed through greater cooperation at a supranational level. Fourth, some observers argue that globalisation is erasing cultural differences. Sociologists, for example, like to talk about the *Coca-Colaisation* or *McDonaldisation* of global culture.

Finally, some observers claim that the **sovereign** state's capacity for independent political action is weakened by globalisation. This is especially true in the area of economic policy. The idea of a domestic economy hemmed in by well-defined borders and managed by the state is now obsolete. Today, domestic economic policy is subject to global market forces. The state has little effective influence or control over these forces. Any state that tries to exert its influence risks disinvestment, capital flight, and recession. In short, globalisation involves a radical transformation of existing economic and political structures in international relations. It involves an aspiration to think and act globally and an acknowledgement that humanity cannot effectively be ordered along geographical lines. To talk about globalisation, then, is not only to embark on a description of the present, but involves a comprehension of the forces shaping the future. In this sense it is a multifaceted, complex, and dynamic concept.

The causes of globalisation are many. Among the most important are liberal **capitalism** and the revolution in information and communications technologies. Liberal capitalism simply refers to the conjunction of liberal values (freedom, **human rights**, individualism, and democracy) with an economic system based on the market. This world view is widely held to have triumphed over communism and the idea of a planned economy, resulting in an international environment conducive to the free movement of capital and goods.

There is no agreement among scholars as to the origins of globalisation. It has been dated as far back as the dawn of Western civilisation. Some look to the origins of the modern state system for signs of globalisation, while others speak about the significance of the laying of the first transatlantic telegraph cable in the mid-nineteenth century. Nevertheless, what distinguishes globalisation today is the intensity and the speed at which these changes are occurring. This is easily demonstrated by the rapid increase in the number of non-governmental organisations. At the beginning of the twentieth century there were around 170 in existence. Today the figure stands at around 7,000. Interestingly, around 1980 the figure stood at close to 2,500. That represents a 100 per cent increase in 20 years. There is no doubt, then, that the 1980s were a crucial turning point in the history of this concept.

Evaluations of globalisation vary enormously. For some, it is a code word for American hegemony and the liberation of **multinational corporations** from effective control and regulation. This is a complaint which has accompanied the rise of 'anti-globalisation' movements in recent years. For others, it is a potential force for prosperity and greater equality through the expansion of capitalism. Some liberal activists have interpreted it as a vehicle for the promotion of universal human rights and world peace, while some cultural specialists view it as a pernicious force threatening the survival of local cultures and ways of life.

It is true that not everybody benefits from globalisation. To take full advantage of globalisation requires both capital and access to technology. Many states in the international system have neither. A large proportion of the world's population, for example, does not have access to the telephone. Being 'on the net' is not something which makes a lot of sense to those living in the poorest parts of the **Third World**. In other words, globalisation may not be global after all. At best, its spread and impact are uneven.

From the perspective of the **OECD** countries, there are many unresolved issues with respect to globalisation. Among them is its relationship to democracy. If globalisation is indeed weakening the ability of states to make autonomous economic and political decisions, then one might argue that globalisation is a dangerously anti-democratic force.

*See also:* **capitalism; clash of civilisations; end of history; global warming; multinational corporation; regionalism**

*Further reading:* Baylis and Smith, 1997; Holton, 1998; Hurrell and Woods, 1999; Kiely and Marfleet, 1998; O'Meara *et al.*, 2000; Scholte, 2000

## GREAT POWERS

For five centuries, the world's most powerful states – the Portuguese, Spanish, and Italians in the sixteenth century; the Swedes and the Danes in the seventeenth century; the British, French, and Germans in the eighteenth and nineteenth centuries; and, finally, the Americans and the Russians in the twentieth century – have assumed the mantle of great powers. Great powers, as the words suggest, are the most influential states in the international system at any one time. During the **cold war**, the United States and the Soviet Union called themselves **superpowers** in keeping with the enormous destructive capacity of their nuclear weapons and the global scope of their **national interests**.

With the dissolution of the Soviet Union, and the concomitant dismantling of the bipolar **balance of power**, we must reconsider what constitutes a great power in the twenty-first century. In the post-cold war world, Germany and Japan wield significant economic might, but they lack both the political will and the military potential for great power status.

After the collapse of the Berlin Wall in 1989, for a brief two years the Soviet Union adopted an internationalist role, and was seen by the Western countries as a partner in forging a new era in world politics. But that transitional period ended and the true post-cold war era began with the dissolution of the Soviet Union and the outbreak of the Bosnian **war** in 1992. With an economy smaller than that of Spain at present, it is difficult to see Russia emerging as a great power for many years, despite its continuing regional dominance in Central Asia. At the same time, China, with its vast economic potential and its rising military capability, will probably emerge in the coming decades as an influential force in global affairs.

The **European Union** (EU) in its current manifestation is seen by some as a halfway house, uncertain whether it can transform itself into a great power or will remain condemned to impotence. Many observers believe that the EU is at the crossroads. Its architects are no longer setting a premium on enlargement, or on strengthening its institutions and decision-making processes. Its leadership is feeble, and its central motor, the Franco-German relationship, is faltering. The issues surrounding the single European currency (the **euro**) are also deeply divisive.

At present, the United States is the only state with superpower capability in all spheres, but the role it plays today differs significantly from the role it played during the cold war. The United States no longer unilaterally dictates and implements global policies; rather it serves (albeit selectively and on its own terms) as a catalyst for **multilateral** action, as it did during the Gulf War in 1991 and more recently in Bosnia.

Domestic agendas now have a large impact on the foreign policy choices of all the great powers. This is a new, pervasive, and still imperfectly studied or understood phenomenon. In the absence of the kind of threat typified by the East–West confrontation of the post-1945 decades, foreign policy choices seem likely to be dictated by domestic concerns.

At the same time, the very definition of what constitutes a great power is a matter of some debate. It implies the existence of a club with some rule of membership. Traditionally, great powers were at the front rank in terms of military strength and were recognised to have certain rights and duties regarding international peace and **security**. Thus they have been accorded privileged status in organisations such as the **League of Nations** and the **United Nations**. They argued that they contributed to international **order** and stability not just by their sheer strength, but by pursuing particular policies *vis-à-vis* each other. Such policies include preservation of the balance of power, avoiding **crises** and controlling them when they do occur (rather than using them for unilateral advantage), and containing and limiting conflicts with one another.

Today, the appropriate criteria for membership of and performance within this particular club are unclear. The certainties of the bipolar world of the cold war have given way to the uncertainties of a unipolar world dominated, for the present, by the United States, or at least a world in which US policy decisions provide a major reference point against which others measure their decisions. It should be noted that there is also an ambivalent attitude towards the United States by many states, and feelings sometimes close to embarrassment that other major powers should be so dependent on the Americans. For example, Europe considers US engagement as a precondition to international order, yet many Europeans are also convinced that in today's world the United States cannot act as a lone ranger but must operate in concert with others. As the twenty-first century unfolds, it appears unlikely that the United States will be able to sustain its present lofty status. Other great powers will emerge, and it remains to be seen whether they will co-exist in ways that promote or undermine international order.

*See also:* **balance of power; concert of powers; European Union; Group of Eight; hegemonic stability theory; League of Nations; power; superpower**

*Further reading:* Bernstein and Munro, 1997; Garten, 1992; Joffe, 1998

## GROUP OF EIGHT (G8)

An intergovernmental organisation (IGO) comprising the world's leading industrial powers. Its members include the United States, Britain, France, Italy, Germany, Japan, Russia, and Canada. Russia is now a full member and the **European Union** participates in the annual summits. This has led commentators to speak about a G7½, a G8, and even a G8½. Certainly, the inclusion of Russia as a formal member means that G8 is now a more accurate name for this organisation.

The three main aims of the G7/G8 have remained relatively constant since the first summit in Rambouillet, France, in 1975. They are to provide global leadership on economic issues, to coordinate global economic policy among member countries, and to assist in the spread of liberal democracy and **capitalism**. Thus, it would be a mistake to think of the G7/G8 as an institution with a purely economic focus; it also has a strong political agenda. In addition, issues such as **terrorism**, the environment, crime, and regional **security** have been discussed over the years. More recently, a core concern has been to help Russia manage its transition to a market economy.

The G7 came into being in the early 1970s in response to a number of problems facing the world economy. After the Yom Kippur War, oil prices rose dramatically and many **OECD** states went into recession in 1974, suffering from escalating unemployment and inflation (a phenomenon known as *stagflation*). Moreover, the newly formed European Community underwent its first expansion to include Britain, the Republic of Ireland, and Denmark. Most important, however, was the dismantling of the **Bretton Woods** system, signalling the United States' refusal to support the fixed exchange rate currency system.

Unlike most other international governmental organisations, the G7/G8 does not have a high profile like the **United Nations** or the **World Trade Organisation**. It has no permanent secretariat and no physical infrastructure. Moreover, it is a very informal institution. Suggestions have been made to formalise the organisation but as yet there is no consensus on this question. Indeed, the member states agreed in Tokyo in 1993 to ensure that summit meetings remain as informal as possible.

G7/G8 summits are attended by heads of government, ministers for finance and foreign affairs, and personal representatives of the heads of government. They are designed to be open and to allow for frank and honest discussion about political and economic issues affecting the world economy. The inclusion of Japan ensures that the G7/G8 is not viewed as a wholly Atlantic institution. The organisation employs a consensus model of decision-making even though it is not always able to arrive at a consensus.

Although he did not take part in the summit, the former Soviet leader Mikhail Gorbachev met with G7 members for the first time in 1991. This historic event not only resolved the problems that had bedevilled the Strategic Arms Reduction Talks for a number of years, but it also paved the way for the full inclusion of Russia into the G7. In 1994 Russia was formally included in political discussions. However, the inclusion of Russia is more a feature of its old **cold war** status than its economic strength. After all, Russia's economy is weaker than that of Canada, the smallest of the G7 economies.

Perhaps the most familiar criticism of the G7/G8 is that it has never lived up to its expectations. According to some writers, it has failed to develop a coordinated set of economic policies to manage the global economy. The stock market crash of 1987 and the failure to reach agreement on how to cope with the Asian financial collapse of 1997–8 are often cited as examples of this failure. Nevertheless, the G7/G8 is likely to remain an important institution for **global governance** in the years to come.

*See also:* **Bretton Woods; concert of powers; global governance; great powers**

*Further reading:* Bayne and Putnam, 2000; Bergsten and Henning, 1996; Hajnal and Meikle, 1999; Kokotsis, 1999; Webb, 2000

# HEGEMONIC STABILITY THEORY ✓

The central idea behind hegemonic stability theory is that the world needs a single dominant state to create and enforce the rules of **free trade** among the most important members of the system. To be a **hegemon**, a state must have the capability to enforce the rules of the system, the will to do so, and a commitment to a system that is perceived as mutually beneficial to the major states. In turn, capability rests upon three attributes: a large, growing economy; dominance in a leading technological or economic sector; and political **power** backed up by military power. Over time, there is an uneven growth of power within the system as new technologies are developed. An unstable system will result if economic, technological, and other changes erode the international hierarchy and undermine the position of the dominant state. Pretenders to hegemonic control will emerge if the benefits of the system are viewed as unacceptably unfair.

The **theory** was developed in the 1970s and 1980s by American scholars from the **realist** tradition who identified the distribution of power among states as a central factor in explaining the openness and stability of the international economy. A powerful state with a technological advantage over other states will desire an open trading system as it seeks new export markets. Large states are less exposed to the international economy than small ones. A hegemonic state will allow other states to 'free ride' on the benefits that the hegemon provides to the international economy in the form of **public goods**. These are the kind of goods where exclusion of consumers is impossible and consumption of the good by one actor does not exhaust its availability for others. In international economic affairs an open trading system, well-defined property rights, common standards of measures including international money, consistent macroeconomic policies, proper action in case of economic **crisis**, and stable exchange rates are said to be public goods.

On the other hand, if power is more evenly distributed among states, they are less likely to support an open trading system. The less economically **developed** states will try to avoid the political danger of becoming vulnerable to pressure from others, whilst the state whose hegemony is in decline will fear a loss of power to its rivals and will find it hard to resist domestic pressures for protection from cheap imports.

Despite its attractive simplicity, the theory suffers from very few agreed-upon cases of hegemonic stability. Empirically, most scholars cite three instances of hegemonic stability: the Netherlands in the seventeenth century; Britain in the late nineteenth century; and the United States after 1945. To base a theory on only three case studies is problematic. The United States is a questionable case for two reasons. First, during the Great Depression, when the US had the ability to stabilise the system, it did not do so, even though stabilisation was certainly in its and the world's interest. Second, US hegemony has been fleeting. The high mark of US global economic hegemony was in the immediate decades after 1945. Since the 1960s, the US has actually declined in importance as Germany and Japan have eroded its dominance. How strong a case of hegemonic stability is the US if we can only point to roughly 27 years of economic dominance (1944–71)? One of the difficulties of evaluating hegemonic stability theory is the absence of agreed criteria for measuring hegemony. The theory was developed against a backdrop of a perceived decline of American hegemony and a dramatic rise in Japanese power. Since the end of the **cold war**, the collapse of the former Soviet Union and the prolonged recession in Japan have forced many scholars to re-evaluate their estimates of hegemonic decline.

In addition, the theory has given rise to an ongoing debate that has now transcended debates about hegemonic stability. The theory posits a direct causal link between the distribution of power and outcomes in the international economy. Liberal critics of the theory argue that this is far too simplistic. They claim that although a hegemon may be necessary to establish the institutions and regimes that facilitate free trade, these can be maintained despite changes in the distribution of power. If all states gain from an open world economy, they have a shared interest in cooperating to maintain institutions that promote collective benefits. Today, whilst particular concerns with the details of hegemonic stability theory have faded somewhat, the question of whether states are concerned with **relative gains/absolute gains** from cooperation remains a contentious issue in the field.

*See also:* **balance of power; free trade; great powers; hegemony; interdependence; public goods; realism; relative gains/absolute gains; superpower**

*Further reading:* Gilpin, 1981, 1994; Grunberg, 1990; Kennedy, 1987; Keohane, 1984; Kindleberger, 1973; Krasner, 1976; Strange, 1987

## HEGEMONY

*Hegemonia*, in the original Greek sense, means 'leadership'. In international relations, a hegemon is the 'leader' or 'leading state' of a group of states. But a 'group of states' presupposes relations between them. Indeed, leadership by necessity implies some degree of social **order** and collective organisation. The states which form the group are the units, of which the hegemonic state is but one, albeit the primary one. It is clear, therefore, that when we think about hegemony, we are thinking as much about interstate systems. Hegemony does not exist by itself, but is a unique political phenomenon that exists within a given interstate system, which is itself the product of specific historical and political circumstances.

Hegemony consists of the possession and command of a multifaceted set of **power** resources. More importantly, all hegemonic states share one common characteristic: they enjoy 'structural power'. It is this structural power that permits the hegemon to occupy a central position within its own system, and, if it so chooses, to play a leading role in it. Indeed, the ability to shape other states' preferences and interests is just as important as the hegemon's ability to command power resources, for the exercise of structural power makes it far less likely that the hegemon will have to mobilise its resources in a direct and **coercive** manner. This is also why only some states, with their rich endowment of human and natural resources, have at least the potential to become hegemons.

Hegemony, then, which in any case is backed by a preponderance of material power, may be sustained by a hegemonic transnational culture that legitimates the rules and norms of a hierarchical interstate system.

The way in which some scholars (particularly **critical theorists**) employ the concept of hegemony owes a great deal to the work of the Italian **communist** writer, Antonio Gramsci. Writing in the 1930s, Gramsci suggested that Marx was correct in arguing that the 'economic base' sets the limiting conditions for politics, ideology, and the state. But the underlying thrust of Gramsci's work is consistently away from simple forms of economic reductionism. What he centrally addressed was the complex nature of relations between structure and superstructure, which, he argued, could not be reduced to a reflection of economic conditions narrowly construed. His theoretical originality lay in the series of novel concepts that he used to expand and transform our understanding of politics.

Gramsci was greatly preoccupied with the character of state and civil society relations prevailing in relatively modern societies, especially **capitalist** democracies. He challenged the reductionist conception of the state as exclusively a class state, a mere instrument of ruling-class coercion and domination. He insisted on the educative role of the state, its significance in constructing **alliances** that could win support from different social strata, and the state's role in providing cultural and moral leadership. Although the economic structure may be, in the last instance, determinative, Gramsci gave much greater autonomy to the effects of the actual conduct of the struggle for leadership, across a wide front and on a variety of sites and institutions.

He argued that the role of the communist party was to engage and lead in a broad, multifaceted struggle for hegemony with the capitalist state. A shift in socialist political strategy was necessary, away from an outright frontal assault on the state to the winning of strategic positions on a number of fronts. Socialist struggle was conceived as a 'war of position' in the first instance against the forces of capitalist hegemony in civil society and culture.

Thus hegemony at a global level is not necessarily to be equated with material or military dominance (as in some forms of **realism**, particularly in the way that realists elaborate **hegemonic stability theory**); nor is it necessarily to be regarded as a desirable **public good** (as in some forms of **liberal internationalism**).

*See also:* **hegemonic stability theory; power; public goods; theory**

*Further reading:* Cox, 1981; Gill and Mittelman, 1997; Kupchan, 1998; Nye, 1990; Rapkin, 1990

## HISTORICAL SOCIOLOGY ✓

The sense that we are living in a rapidly changing world is widespread, but there is no agreement on what has actually changed, much less on how to understand these changes or where we are headed. Thus, for example, there is a lively debate as to whether the phenomena associated with **globalisation** are really new, or whether they date from the nineteenth century, the sixteenth century, or even earlier. To ask and answer such questions requires engaging in comparative and historical analysis.

To shed light on the direction and meaning of contemporary global transformations, a first necessary step is to isolate what is really new in the contemporary scene from phenomena that are constant or recurrent. We can only do this by comparing current global dynamics with those in past periods of fundamental systemic reorganisation. The most common (explicit or implicit) comparison that is made is between the present state of the world and the decades following the Second World War – the so-called Golden Age of **capitalism** and US **hegemony**. This comparison gives the (correct) impression of a fundamental shift in relations among states, between states and capital, and between states/capital and labour. Most especially, we sense a shift from a period of relatively predictable stability to a period of dizzying and unpredictable instability. This comparison alone may, however, be misleading. In addition, we would do well to compare the present not just to periods of relative stability, but to more analogous periods of instability and reorganisation of the modern world.

Over the past decade increasing attention has been paid to this kind of scholarship, which goes by the name of historical sociology. It explores the past – in particular, the way that societies change or reproduce – to help determine what future is socially possible.

Although the field of historical sociology is diverse, those historical sociologists whose concerns inevitably overlap with students of international relations share some common principles. In his excellent summary of their work, John Hobson argues that the figure of Max Weber looms large in the background. Drawing on Weber's work on the relationship between **war**, capitalism, and the state at the end of the nineteenth and in the early twentieth century, those whom Hobson calls Weberian historical sociologists provide some important methodological principles for students of war and global systemic change.

Among the most important principles, three stand out. First, it makes little sense to study international relations as if it were independent of domestic politics. Indeed, historical sociology is in part the attempt to explain just what were the historical conditions that gave rise to this distinction. Second, it also makes little sense to ignore the relationship between international politics and economics. The state itself is fundamentally Janus-faced. Its ability to generate loyalty from its citizens and extract resources from within its territorial boundaries in order to wage war with other states is intimately connected to its dominance over other actors in civil society. Third, and in direct contrast to realist theories of international relations, historical sociology has provided the study of international relations with very sophisticated analyses of the nature of **power**, especially state power. To give just one example, there is a crucial distinction in the literature between despotic and infrastructural power. The former refers to the capacity of the state to act without negotiating with other groups in society. The latter refers to the capacity of the state to penetrate society and to implement its policies and decisions through complex bureaucratic and administrative instruments. One of the key propositions to emerge from the field is that states with great infrastructural power find it much easier to adapt to change than do despotic states.

At present, the engagement between historical sociology and the formal study of international relations is proceeding slowly. Students of international relations are, perhaps understandably, averse to arguments claiming that our understanding of the present depends less on our knowledge of the daily newspaper than having a synoptic grasp of world history. Historical sociology is difficult work, demanding that we jettison many of our deeply held assumptions about our subject matter. Moreover, the body of **theory** arising from this field of study does not translate easily into recommendations for policy. Students wanting to engage with historical sociology may therefore have to abandon any direct interest in 'problem-solving', even though they will be rewarded with a more sophisticated knowledge-base of the historical sources of the problems themselves.

*See also:* **nation–state; theory; war; world–system theory**

*Further reading:* Hobson, 1998; Jarvis, 1995; Rosenberg, 1994; D. Smith, 1991; Teschke, 2003

# HUMAN RIGHTS

The term 'human rights' is strongly associated with the founding of the **United Nations** (UN) in 1945, and the adoption by the UN General Assembly of the Universal Declaration of Human Rights in 1948. It replaced the phrase 'natural rights', as well as the phrase 'the rights of Man', which was not universally understood to include the rights of women.

The origins of the concept can be traced back to ancient Greece and Rome, where it was linked to premodern natural law doctrines according to which human conduct should be judged according to the 'law of nature'. It was not until after the Middle Ages, however, that natural law doctrines became associated with liberal political theories about natural rights. In Graeco-Roman and medieval times, natural law doctrines taught the duties, as distinct from the rights, of 'Man'. Moreover, these doctrines often recognised the legitimacy of slavery and serfdom and therefore excluded the central ideas of human rights as they are understood today – the ideas of universal freedom and equality.

There are four basic characteristics of human rights. First, regardless of their ultimate origin or justification, human rights represent individual or group demands (usually the former) for the shaping and sharing of **power**, wealth, and other human goods. Second, human rights commonly refer to fundamental as distinct from non-essential claims or goods. In fact, some theorists go so far as to limit human rights to a single core right, or two – for example, the right to life or the right to equal freedom of opportunity. Third, most assertions of human rights are qualified by the limitation that the rights of any particular individual or group are properly restricted as much as is necessary to secure the comparable rights of others. Finally, if a right is determined to be a human right, it is understood to be universal in character, equally possessed by all human beings.

It is common to distinguish between three generations of human rights that succeeded each other historically. A first generation of *civil and political rights* derives from the seventeenth- and eighteenth-century revolutions in Britain, France, and the United States. Infused with the political philosophy of liberal individualism and the related economic and social doctrine of *laissez-faire*, these rights are conceived more in negative (freedoms from) than positive (rights to) terms. They are laid down in Articles 2–21 of the Universal Declaration of Human Rights, and include:

- freedom from gender, racial, and equivalent forms of discrimination;
- the right to life, liberty, and the security of the person;
- freedom from slavery or involuntary servitude;
- freedom from torture and from cruel, inhuman, or degrading treatment or punishment;
- freedom from arbitrary arrest, detention, or exile;
- the right to a fair and public trial;
- freedom from interference in privacy and correspondence;
- freedom of movement and residence;
- the right to asylum from persecution;
- freedom of thought, conscience, and religion;

- freedom of opinion and expression;
- freedom of peaceful assembly and association;
- the right to participate in government, directly or through free elections;
- the right to own property and the right not to be deprived of it arbitrarily.

One should note that it would be wrong to argue that such rights are merely negative ones. For example, the right to security of the person, to a fair and public trial, to asylum from persecution, and to free elections cannot be assured without some affirmative government action. What is constant in this first-generation conception, however, is the notion of liberty against the abuse and misuse of political authority.

A second generation of *economic, social, and cultural rights* finds its origins primarily in the socialist tradition. The rights in this category respond in large part to the abuses and misuses of **capitalist** development and what was claimed to be its underlying conception of individual liberty that tolerated the **exploitation** of working classes and colonial peoples. Historically, it is a counterpoint to the first generation of civil and political rights, with human rights conceived more in positive (rights to) than negative (freedoms from) terms, and requiring the intervention rather than the abstention of the state to promote equality. These positive rights are listed in Articles 22–7 of the Universal Declaration of Human Rights, and include:

- the right to social security;
- the right to work and to protection against unemployment;
- the right to rest and leisure, including periodic holidays with pay;
- the right to a standard of living adequate for the health and wellbeing of self and family;
- the right to education;
- the right to the protection of one's scientific, literary, and artistic production.

Finally, a third generation of *solidarity rights* is a product of both the rise and the decline of the **nation–state** in the last half of the twentieth century. Foreshadowed in Article 28 of the Universal Declaration of Human Rights, which proclaims that 'everyone is entitled to a social and international order in which the rights set forth in this Declaration can be fully realised', it appears so far to embrace six rights. Three of these reflect the emergence of **Third World nationalism** and its revolution of rising expectations, i.e. its demand for a global redistribution of power, wealth, and other important values: the right to political, economic, social, and cultural **self-determination**; the right to economic and social

**development**; and the right to participate in and benefit from 'the common heritage of mankind'. The other three third-generation rights – the right to peace, the right to a healthy and sustainable environment, and the right to humanitarian disaster relief – suggest the impotence or inefficiency of the nation-state in certain critical respects.

Over the past 50 years there has been a continuing debate over the priority that should be given to each type of human right. More recently, this debate has been overshadowed by a more fundamental divide between those who believe that it is still possible to talk about universal human rights, and others who hold that the identification and ranking of human rights depend on the customs and practices of particular cultures.

Primary responsibility for the promotion and protection of human rights under the UN Charter rests with the General Assembly and, under its authority, the Economic and Social Council (ECOSOC), the Commission on Human Rights, and the UN High Commissioner for Human Rights (UNHCHR). The UN Commission on Human Rights, an intergovernmental subsidiary body of ECOSOC established in 1947, serves as the UN's central policy organ in the human rights field. The High Commissioner for Human Rights, a post created by the General Assembly in 1993, is responsible for implementing and coordinating United Nations human rights programmes and projects, including overall supervision of the UN's Geneva-based Centre for Human Rights, a bureau of the UN Secretariat.

For the first 20 years of its existence (1947–66), the UN Commission on Human Rights concentrated its efforts on standard-setting (believing that generally it had no legal competence to deal with complaints about violations of human rights). Together with other UN bodies, it has drafted human rights standards and prepared a number of international human rights instruments. Among the most important of these have been the Universal Declaration of Human Rights (1948), the International Covenant on Economic, Social and Cultural Rights (1976), and the International Covenant on Civil and Political Rights together with its first Optional Protocol (1976). Collectively known as the International Bill of Human Rights, these three instruments serve as touchstones for interpreting the human rights provisions of the UN Charter. Also central have been the International Convention on the Elimination of All Forms of Racial Discrimination (1965), the Convention on the Elimination of All Forms of Discrimination against Women (1979), the Convention against Torture and Other Cruel, Inhuman or Degrading Treatment or Punishment (1984), and the Convention on the Rights of the Child (1989), each elaborating on provisions of the International Bill of Human Rights.

The Commission continues to perform this standard-setting role. From 1967, however, it was specifically authorised to deal with violations of human rights, and, since then, has set up mechanisms and procedures to investigate alleged violations of human rights and otherwise monitor compliance by states with international human rights law. Thus, much of the work of the Commission is now investigatory, evaluative, and advisory in character. On an *ad hoc* basis, it appoints special rapporteurs, special representatives, special committees, and other envoys to examine human rights situations and report back to the Commission. During the 1970s and 1980s, these fact-finding and implementation mechanisms and procedures became the focus of the Commission's attention. In the 1990s the Commission increasingly turned its attention to the need of states to overcome obstacles to the enjoyment of economic, social, and cultural rights, including the right to development and the right to an adequate standard of living. Increased attention has been paid also to the protection of the rights of minorities and indigenous peoples and to the protection of the rights of women and the rights of the child. Despite the proliferation of human rights laws, adherence to them remains a voluntary commitment on the part of nation-states.

*See also:* **cosmopolitanism; genocide; global civil society; human security; international law; torture; United Nations; war crime**

*Further reading:* Donnelly, 2007; Dunne and Wheeler, 1999; Forsythe, 2004; Ishay, 2004; Lukes, 1996; Rise *et al.*, 1999

## HUMAN SECURITY

The right to self-preservation is one of the most important modern concepts of realism in international relations. Thomas Hobbes, a seventeenth-century thinker, theorised that the right to self-preservation constituted a natural law, requiring a social compact between the citizen and state ruler. The individual's civil and political rights, in this sense, would be secured by the terms of the compact, but only if the individual consented to the unchecked power of the state ruler. Although later thinkers would seek to protect these rights against such power, Hobbes' state solution to domestic anarchy would eventually focus attention on the security of the state in the international realm.

As the modern state system evolved, states would stress the collectivisation of their security interests, or institutionalise **collective security**, which held that an unprovoked, aggressive attack against a member of an organisation would be considered an attack on all member states belonging to that international organisation (e.g. **League of Nations**, **UN**, **NATO**, and Warsaw Pact). Thus, while collective security emerged as the option for countering unruly state aggression, it left open the question of how best to promote the security of the individual, especially given the evolution of humanitarian law during the twentieth century (that featured the adoption of the Genocide Convention, Universal Declaration of Human Rights (1948) and the International Human Rights Covenants (1966)).

After the fall of the Soviet Union, the United Nations began to address this question in a concerted manner. In 1992, for instance, the United Nations Secretary-General Boutros Boutros-Ghali adopted the Agenda of Peace, which proposed sweeping human rights initiatives, including social and civic reconstruction in war-torn areas and a rapid deployment force. It was hoped that strong **human rights** initiatives would address the extreme poverty of **developing** states and the grave human rights abuses associated with **failed states**.

By the mid-1990s, many international officials began to take a harder look at the humanitarian dimensions of security. As the chief proponents of this new humanitarian agenda, Canada and Norway formed what came to be known as the Oslo–Ottawa axis. The primary objective of the **alliance** was to focus attention on human rights issues, including international humanitarian law, the protection of individuals from the effects of **war** and severe poverty and to demonstrate that the protection and development of humans was not only a moral issue, but a key priority of state and international security.

Accordingly, the term 'human security' first appeared in the 1994 Human Development Report, an annual publication of the United Nations Development Programme (UNDP). The report defines human security broadly as containing two main aspects: first, it means safety from chronic threats such as hunger, disease, and repression; and second, it concerns the protection from sudden and hurtful disruptions in the patterns of daily life, whether in homes, in jobs or in communities.

The report goes on to identify seven specific elements of human security:

- economic security (i.e. freedom from poverty);
- food security (access to food);
- health security (access to health care and protection from diseases);
- environmental security (protection from environmental pollution);
- personal security (physical safety from torture, war, and drug use);
- community security (survival of traditional cultures and **ethnic** groups);
- political security (protection against political oppression).

Canada managed to put the issue of human security up for debate at one of the UN Security Council meetings. Not long thereafter, the Canadian government commissioned a special panel to draft a report on Intervention and State **Sovereignty**. Inspired by the events of the Kosovo War (1999), in which the US elected to act militarily under the aegis of NATO, the panel was commissioned to investigate the legal obstacles to UN action, such as the duty of non-intervention, and **geopolitics**. In December 2001, the commission issued its report, which set forth the general parameters and guidelines for ensuring the security of civilians. Drawing on just war **theory** principles of the right of self-defence and legitimate cause, the report conceived the promotion of human security in terms of the responsibility to protect. Accordingly, when state and regional authorities failed to provide the necessary basic security against a systematic attack on the civilian population (crimes against humanity), the duty to protect would rise to the international level.

It is important to note here the distinction between human security and human development. Whilst human development refers to long-term social, economic, and cultural programmes such as education and health care, human security represents the exigencies of saving the lives of those threatened by severe crises. In this respect, it could be said that human security focuses on the political and moral risks of protecting disaffected and abused peoples, while calling attention to the need for greater moral accountability, especially as this relates to the preventive role of the **International Criminal Court**.

Despite the growing importance of implementing human security, however, many human rights scholars have argued that human security remains a fuzzy concept. The looming issue is whether scholars and policymakers can articulate a clearly defined set of parameters or policy applications of human security. Certainly, a more precise meaning is needed to facilitate its application to developing states, especially where social deprivation, drought and famine are concerned. However, this should by no means diminish the rapid evolution and general applicability of the concept of human security.

*See also:* **coercion; ethnic cleansing; genocide; global governance; human rights; International Criminal Court; security; United Nations; war**

*Further reading*: Human Security Report, 2006; Nef, 1999; Paris, 2001; Suhrke 1999

## HUMANITARIAN INTERVENTION ✓

Much has been written on the subject of humanitarian intervention in the 1990s. The word 'intervention' describes the exercise of public authority by one state in the territory of another without the consent of the latter. Intervention is thus more than mere 'interference' in the internal affairs of another state. The term *dictatorial interference* most accurately captures the **coercive** elements of intervention. Humanitarian intervention refers to (forcible) action by one state or a group of states in the territory of another state without the consent of the latter, undertaken on humanitarian grounds or in order to restore constitutional governance. It usually involves military force, but it need not. In short, the intervention is undertaken by one state or group of states on behalf of citizens in another state, often against their own government. Humanitarian intervention must be distinguished from humanitarian aid, whose delivery requires the consent of the receiving government. Humanitarian aid is consistent with state sovereignty. Humanitarian intervention is not.

Up to 1990, it was nearly universally agreed that humanitarian intervention is unlawful. It is expressly forbidden in the **United Nations** Charter (Article 2 (4)(7)) precisely because it undermines state sovereignty. The principle of sovereignty is the basis of **international law** and the United Nations. Unless states agree to respect the territorial integrity and political independence of other states, it is difficult to see how they can co-exist as equals in the formal terms of international law. However, justice is often the price to be paid for achieving **order** in international relations. In the absence of any normative justification for state sovereignty, it can function as a shield behind which states may systematically abuse the **human rights** of their own people.

During the **cold war**, it was possible to identify interventions whose motives and outcomes were, in part, humanitarian. Many observers cite Vietnam's invasion of Kampuchea/Cambodia in December 1978 as a classic instance of humanitarian intervention that brought an end to the **genocidal** rule of Pol Pot. But this and other instances of humanitarian intervention were never justified as such by the intervening state. Instead, and consistent with international law, the justification was that of self-defence.

After the cold war ended in 1989, the consensus over the illegality of humanitarian intervention began to crumble in the face of massive violations of human rights that were occurring in Yugoslavia and numerous African states. Public opinion in the United States and much of Western Europe demanded that governments do something to bring an end to what appeared to be a growing list of internal conflicts. Since traditional **peacekeeping** missions were often ineffective, many observers argued that the time had come to enlarge the scope of legitimate use of force to include humanitarian intervention. There are, however, three key problems with this argument whose solution continues to elude the international community.

First, although it is true that humanitarian intervention undermines state sovereignty, the relationship is a complex one. The word 'intervention' implies that the act is designed to influence the conduct of the internal affairs of a state, and not to annex or to take it over. Hitler's invasion of Poland in 1939 was a case not of intervention but **war**; European colonialism in Asia and Africa was not intervention, nor even war, but conquest. The line between intervention on the one hand and conquest on the other is not always easy to draw, nor is it fixed and stable. However, intervention, in contrast to war and conquest, involves influencing the internal affairs of a state in a specific direction without either taking it over or seeking to defeat it in a military confrontation. Precisely because intervention is not conquest, acts of humanitarian intervention are supposed to be short-lived. As a result, humanitarian intervention by itself cannot resolve the fundamental social and political root causes of conflicts.

Second, who are the appropriate agents to properly engage in humanitarian intervention? There is not one single instance of humanitarian intervention where the motive to intervene was not one of a number of goals. It is impossible to imagine that states would (or should) always place humanitarian concerns ahead of the **national interest**. This being the case, they will always choose to intervene in some places rather than others. For example, in Central Africa, the **great powers** did not see it as part of their responsibility (nor of their interests) to use force to prevent the 1994 Rwandan genocide, nor – later – to separate **refugees** from the military and political elements in the Zairean and Tanzanian camps, nor – in 1996 – to help humanitarian agencies rescue hundreds of thousands of refugees scattered in the rainforest during the Zairean civil conflict. Yet in 1999, the United States and its **NATO** allies did believe that humanitarian intervention was justified in Kosovo. Given the inevitable mixed motives of the great powers, humanitarian intervention is unlikely ever to be implemented in a consistent manner. One response to this problem is to argue in favour of the United Nations as the appropriate agent of humanitarian intervention. Another response is to contend that a humanitarian council, independent of the UN, and with no veto powers, be established. This way, the **geopolitical** interests of UN Security Council members would no longer impede efforts to intervene on humanitarian grounds.

Finally, humanitarian intervention is intended to address what is regarded as a violation of human rights. Since the views on the latter are culturally conditioned, no definition of humanitarian intervention can be culturally neutral. In the seventeenth century many Christian writers thought that European states had a duty to intervene in the internal affairs of other countries to end such practices as human sacrifice and cannibalism. They also thought that saving souls was a humanitarian act, and that a society that denied the freedom to propagate Christianity or that harassed missionaries merited humanitarian intervention. Today, the human rights abuses that generate calls for humanitarian intervention tend to exclude slow death through poverty, malnutrition, and economic and political mismanagement. By and large our conception of humanitarian intervention is distinctly political in nature and centred on the state. Distress, suffering, and death become a matter of humanitarian intervention only when they are caused by the breakdown of the state or by an outrageous abuse of its power.

In short, the concept of humanitarian intervention is often associated with benign **cosmopolitan** objectives. In recent years, international policymakers have sought to devise broad moral and ethical guidelines to ensure that the international community will be able and willing to respond appropriately to humanitarian emergencies. Moreover, under the leadership of the former UN Secretary-General, Kofi Annan, UN reform appears underway, which would further facilitate such responses, though by no means guarantee international action.

*See also:* **CNN factor; English School; human rights; human security; international law; legitimacy; peacekeeping; peace of Westphalia; United Nations**

*Further reading:* Ayoob, 2002; Holzgrefe and Keohane, 2003; Oudraat, 2000; Phillips and Cady, 1995; Roach, 2005b; Tsagourias, 2000; Wheeler, 2000; Woodhouse and Ramsbotham, 1996

## IDEALISM

Idealism allegedly dominated the study of international relations from the end of the First World War until the late 1930s. Sometimes referred to as *utopianism*, idealism is in fact a variant of **liberal internationalism**. Notable liberal idealists are Immanuel Kant, Richard Cobden, John Hobson, Norman Angell, Alfred Zimmern, and Woodrow Wilson.

The term is not a flattering one. Idealists are out of touch with current thinking, they put moral principles before practical or prudential considerations, and are naïve about the world around them. They are futurists who seek a perfect world. It is not surprising, then, that it was the self-proclaimed **realists** who coined the term to describe the liberal internationalism of the interwar years. Whether it deserves such a label is debatable. Recent research indicates that the idealist thinkers of the period were not as 'other-worldly' as many realists suggested. Yet, the label has stuck and continues to be used both by realists in their ongoing debate with liberals, and by theorists writing on the interwar years.

Idealism came to prominence in reaction to the carnage of the First World War. Most intellectuals and policymakers of the day pointed the finger at the *Realpolitik* of the European **great powers** and set themselves the task of abolishing war as an instrument of statecraft. Philanthropists such as Andrew Carnegie donated money to study the problem, peace groups formed, universities began to teach international relations, and many intellectuals began to try to educate people about the benefits of developing an internationalist orientation. Indeed, the birth of international relations as a separate discipline coincided with these developments. However, the best summary of the thinking of the period is to be found in Woodrow Wilson's 'Fourteen Points', a set of principles that he took with him to the Versailles Peace Conference in December 1918. This document not only provided an outline for the settlement of the First World War, it was also the basis for the establishment of the League of Nations.

Generally speaking, the idealists shared a belief in progress and were of the view that the procedures of parliamentary democracy and deliberation under the rule of law could be firmly established in international **diplomacy**. This is why they placed so much importance on the **League of Nations** and on strengthening **international law**.

A central characteristic of idealism is the belief that what unites human beings is more important than what divides them. The idealists rejected **communitarian** and realist arguments that the state is itself a source of moral value for human beings. Instead, they defended a **cosmopolitan** ethics and sought to educate individuals about the need to reform the international system. Interwar idealism was as much a political movement as an intellectual one. Alfred Zimmern, for example, regarded his professorial chair at Oxford University as a platform 'for the preaching of international relations'.

Idealism fell into disrepute with the collapse of the League of Nations and the outbreak of the Second World War in 1939. Although the idealists had sought to use the League system to replace European *Realpolitik*, in fact it simply became a forum that reflected the competing **national interests** of the great powers of the day. From an intellectual perspective, however, it was the critique of E. H. Carr, a British Marxist, that completely undermined its credibility. In his famous text entitled *The Twenty Years Crisis* (1946), Carr argued that the aspirations of the idealists (whom he disparaged as utopians) were only to be expected in a new field of study where the desire for change and the dictates of the moment overshadowed all else. Only with disillusionment and failure do scholars become more circumspect and clear-headed about the nature and purpose of their subject matter. Carr refers to this attitude as realist because such a view does not shy away from a hard, ruthless analysis of reality. Furthermore, he suggested that idealism was an expression of the political philosophy of the satisfied great powers. It was simply the product of a particular set of social, political, and historical circumstances rather than a timeless moral code devoted to universal ends. When it came to a concrete political problem, it could not find an absolute and disinterested standard for the conduct of international politics. The idealists were also naïve about the role of **power** in international relations. Not all states had, according to Carr, an interest in peace. Those who dominated the international system were more likely to pursue peace because it was in their interests to maintain the international status quo. Contrary to the belief of the idealists, then, there was no natural harmony of interests among states.

Since the outbreak of war in 1939, idealism has been regarded as an example of both policy failure and theoretical naïveté in international relations. However, the tide seems to be turning. There is now much more acceptance of liberal thinking in international relations than there was during the **cold war**, and a number of scholars are also revising some of the conventional wisdom about 'idealist' thinking in the 1920s and 1930s.

*See also:* **communitarianism; cosmopolitanism; disarmament; international law; League of Nations; liberal internationalism; perpetual peace; realism**

*Further reading:* Carr, 1946; Crawford, 2000; Kober, 1990; Long and Wilson, 1995; Schmidt, 1998

## IMAGINED COMMUNITY

This concept is the brainchild of one of the most original students of **nationalism**, Benedict Anderson. In his well-known book *Imagined Communities: Reflections on the Origin and Spread of Nationalism* (1991), Anderson is particularly interested in how people come to believe that, as individuals, they are members of a particular nation that is entitled to **sovereignty** over a piece of territory and can feel so loyal to their nation that they are prepared to die in its defence.

Anderson focuses on the historical process of collective imagination that he believes to be constitutive of nationhood. The nation is imagined as both limited and sovereign. It is imagined because the members of the nation never know most of their fellow members. It is imagined as limited because no nation sees itself as coterminous with humanity. Anderson examines three paradoxes of nationalism in some depth:

1  the objective modernity of nations in the eyes of historians versus their subjective antiquity in the eyes of nationalists;
2  the formal universality of nationality as a sociocultural concept versus the particularity of its manifestation;
3  the political power of nationalism versus its philosophical povert.

Anderson argues that nationalism has to be understood not in relation to self-consciously held political ideologies, but in relation to the large cultural systems that preceded it. Nationalism arose at a time when three other cultural conceptions of identity were decreasing in importance. First, there were changes in religion. Nationalism represented a secular transformation of fatality into continuity, magical contingency into worldly meaning. The unselfconscious coherence of religion declined after the Middle Ages because of the explorations of the non-European world and the gradual demotion of the sacred language itself. Older communities lost confidence in the unique sacredness of their language (the idea that a particular script offered privileged access to sacred ontological truth). Second, there were changes in the dynastic realm. In feudal forms of imagination, states were defined by 'high centres' – borders were porous and indistinct. With the decline of the legitimacy of the sacral monarchy in the seventeenth century, however, people began to question the belief that society was naturally organised around 'high centres' such as Rome. Third, and here Anderson is most original, he argues that we must take into account the feudal conception of time, in which cosmology and history were indistinguishable. It was changes in the conception of time that made it possible to 'think' the nation. The pre-modern era is characterised by a conception of *simultaneity-along-time* in which time is marked by 'pre-figuring and fulfilment'. This is gradually replaced by the conception of *simultaneity-across-time*, in which time is measured by clocks and calendars. The idea of a sociological entity moving calendrically through time is a precise analogue of the idea of the nation, which also is conceived as a solid community moving steadily through history.

The decline of old ideas set the stage for a new form of collective cultural consciousness. The reason it took the form of nationalism is due to the fortuitous interaction between capitalism, a new technology of communication (print), and the fatality of linguistic diversity. Capitalism was important because the expansion of the book market contributed to the revolutionary vernacularisation of languages. This was given further impetus by the mass production of Bibles during the Reformation and the spread of particular vernaculars as instruments of administrative centralisation. In turn, printed languages laid the foundation for national consciousness by creating unified fields of exchange and communication. In combination, print capitalism created the possibility for nationalism by providing a medium for the new representations of time and space.

In short, by treating nationalism as a response to epochal change, and by examining the material and cultural conditions for the possibility of the nation as an imagined community, Benedict Anderson's work is essential reading for students of nationalism. Thinking of the nation in this way raises interesting questions about whether new forms of communication in the twenty-first century are shaping the imagination of alternatives to the nation. Anderson himself is somewhat sceptical. He points to the emergence of long-distance nationalism by members of ethnic minorities in the West who can take advantage of new technology (such as e-mail) to intensify their sense of belonging to imaginary homelands far away from the state in which they live. It remains to be seen whether contemporary spatio-temporal accelerations enhance or retard nationalism in the twenty-first century. Either way, Anderson's contribution to the study of international relations remains his examination of the impact of such accelerations 300 years ago.

*See also:* **capitalism; globalisation; nation–state; nationalism**

*Further reading:* Anderson, B., 1991, 1998; Chatterjee, 1994; A. Smith, 1991; Ullock, 1996

## IMPERIALISM

A policy aimed at conquering or controlling foreign people and territory. The essence of an imperial state is that it seeks to derive a benefit of some sort from those states and peoples unable to defend themselves against its superior military and/or economic force. This benefit may take the form of **power**, prestige, strategic advantage, cheap labour, natural resources, or access to new markets. Imperial states have achieved their goals in a number of ways. The most common method is through conquest and occupation, but the transportation of settlers and missionaries as well as market domination have also played a part in maintaining effective control over an empire.

There have been empires throughout history. The Egyptians, Assyrians, Babylonians, Romans, and the Mongols all sustained great empires. But it is the period of European expansion from the late fifteenth century onward that is now most often associated with the term. It is customary to divide European imperialism into two phases. Spain, Portugal, Britain, France, and Holland made up the first wave from about 1500, pursuing broadly **mercantilist** economic policies.

The second wave, sometimes referred to as the *new imperialism*, began during the 1870s and finally ended in 1945. It was led by Britain, which by the late 1800s was competing with emerging **great powers** such as Germany and the United States. How would Britain keep up in a rapidly changing world? Many felt that the answer rested in imperialism or the practice of gaining colonies for new markets and resources. Soon countries such as France, Japan, and the United States began to establish their own colonies, which became a source of pride as well as economic benefit. Many Europeans felt that they had some obligation to bring their 'superior' culture to their colonies. Christian missionaries travelled across Africa and Asia to spread their religious beliefs.

One of the first targets for the new imperialism was Africa, whose countries were too weak to stop a European army. The 'scramble for Africa' began when Henry Stanley claimed the Congo River Valley for Belgium. France then claimed Algeria and built the Suez Canal. In response, Britain took over Egypt to control the Canal, which was crucial to its shipping routes to Asia. France then colonised Tunisia and Morocco, whilst the Italians, not to be left out, took Libya. By the early 1900s most of Africa was taken over by European colonists.

Like Africa, South Asia was soon dominated by the new imperialism of the era. Britain considered India, already conquered earlier, as 'the jewel in the crown', supplying the home country with valuable spices and raw materials. In East Asia, China refused access to foreigners, but the British made large profits by smuggling addictive opium into the country. In contrast to China, Japan was forced to accept European and American influence, which it took full advantage of in order to launch its own imperial policies in Southeast Asia and the Pacific. Although Latin and South America were not generally colonised by countries other than Spain, many of their economies were dominated by the United States and Europe.

There are five main competing theories of imperialism:

- A number of *conservative* writers argued that imperialism was necessary to preserve the existing social **order** in the imperial states, so that their internal social conflicts could be contained and channelled abroad. This was the view of figures such as Cecil Rhodes and Rudyard Kipling.

- For *liberals* such as John Hobson and Norman Angell, the increasing concentration of wealth within imperial states led to underconsumption for the masses. Overseas expansion was a way to reduce costs of production and to secure new consumer markets. Imperialism was a policy choice; it was not inevitable. An imperial state could solve the problem of underconsumption by increasing the income levels of the masses through legislation or by transferring income from the rich to the poor.

- For *Marxists*, the liberal explanation is largely correct, but its prescription is not, since the state represents the interests of capital rather than labour. According to Lenin's famous argument, imperialism represents the final stage of **capitalism**. He argued that the First World War was the culmination of the competition among capitalist states for new markets and investment opportunities.

- *Realists* such as Hans Morgenthau argued that imperialism is primarily a manifestation of the **balance of power**, and that it is part of the process by which states try to achieve a favourable change in the status quo. The main purpose of imperialism is to decrease the political and strategic vulnerability of the state. The trouble with Lenin's argument according to this school of thought is that not all capitalist states have been imperialist, and not all imperialist states have been capitalist!

- Finally, there are a range of *social-psychological* **theories** inspired by the work of Joseph Schumpeter, who argued that imperialism was 'an objectless disposition on the part of the state to unlimited forcible expansion'. Such a disposition was a form of learned behaviour that was institutionalised in the imperial state by a 'warrior class'. Although the latter was created because of a legitimate need for the state to defend itself, the warrior class relied on imperialism to perpetuate its existence.

The second wave of imperialist activity declined rapidly after the First World War. It received renewed impetus with the rise of Nazism in Germany, but by the end of 1945 it was clear that an anti-colonial spirit prevailed among the international community. Both the United States and the Soviet Union were fundamentally opposed to colonialism and staunchly defended the **self-determination** of peoples. Europe could no longer sustain the economic costs of its far-flung empires and the newly formed **United Nations**, in response to growing unrest from **nationalist** movements in the colonies, began to promote **decolonisation**. Consequently, Britain ceded control of India and Pakistan in 1947, Burma in 1948, Ghana and Malaya in 1957, and Zimbabwe in 1980. In all, 49 countries were granted independence by Britain. The Dutch relinquished control of Indonesia in 1949. Portugal, the last European colonial power in

Africa, granted independence to its colonies in 1974 and 1975. The French grudgingly left Indo-China in 1954 and Algeria in 1962 after bloody fighting with independence movements in both colonies.

Despite international condemnation of European colonialism, vestiges of it remain. In some cases, the colony has decided to retain its status, primarily for economic reasons. Bermuda, for example, is still officially a part of the British Empire. In other cases, the struggle for independence continues to be the defining characteristic of the relationship. The Melanesians, for example, have struggled against French domination since the early 1980s. Moreover, a number of writers have argued that the United States and the Soviet Union were themselves imperialist, even though they opposed colonialism. Accordingly, during the **cold war** the *Pax Britannica* was replaced by the *Pax Americana* and the *Pax Sovietica*.

Imperialism has been a permanent feature of world history. Despite the end of colonialism and the cold war, new forms of imperialism will undoubtedly appear. Whether they will be as malevolent as those of the past is something that cannot, as yet, be determined.

*See also:* **capitalism; decolonisation; dependency; exploitation; Marxism; self-determination**

*Further reading:* Brewer, 1980; Doyle, 1986; Hobson, 1965; Lenin, 1968; Snyder, 1991

# INTEGRATION

A concept that came to prominence in the 1950s, initially as a description of changes in Europe's political and economic architecture. Scholars quickly realised that what was taking place within Western Europe had important implications for international relations generally, and for international relations theory. Drawing on sociological theories of **functionalism**, writers such as David Mitrany, Karl Deutsch, and Ernst Haas made important contributions to the study of integration in international relations and laid the intellectual foundations for the study of **interdependence** in the 1970s.

Integration can best be understood as a process. It involves (a) a movement towards increased cooperation between states; (b) a gradual transfer of authority to supranational institutions; (c) a gradual homogenisation of values; and (d) the coming into being of a **global civil society** and with it, the construction of new forms of political community. The most advanced state of integration would be one where states were either federated on a global scale or allowed to atrophy altogether in favour of a global or world government. How far the international system is from this point is a measure of how far integration has progressed.

There are two levels of integration at work in international relations today. The first is system-level integration. This refers to a process whereby states transfer some degree of political, economic, and legal decision-making power to supranational institutions on a global scale. This is designed to improve the quality of domestic and **global governance**, to streamline decision-making, and provide a basis for collective action. Some scholars regard the **United Nations** as a good example of system-level integration despite the fact that the UN remains accountable to, and an instrument of, states.

The second level is regional integration. This is where a number of states within close proximity to one another join together to form a federal political and economic union. The **European Union** (EU) is an example of regional integration.

Integration is not a new phenomenon. Before the twentieth century, however, integration was generally accomplished either by colonisation or by **war**. Since the time of the **League of Nations**, however, integration has been managed consensually. This is not to say that consensus has always been reached. The European experience since the late 1950s indicates how difficult a task it has been to achieve consensus on matters of principle. Indeed, the future of system-level and regional integration is, to a large extent, dependent on the success of the European Union. But not all European voters want a United States of Europe and there are states that still do not want to join. For example, the first Danish referendum dealing with entry into the EU failed and the second referendum only just managed to get more than the required number of votes. Also, an increasing number of German and French voters are voicing their opposition to further integration.

European integration is a child of the cold war. The initial impetus came from the Marshall Plan and the special circumstances surrounding the reconstruction of Europe. Now that the cold war has ended, some observers are forecasting a return to a more **anarchical** Europe. But there are wider issues confronting integration than what is happening in Europe. First, even if the process continues there, it is not clear what it might mean for the states of Africa, Asia, and Latin America. Thus far, attempts at integration have not met with much success. Moreover, in many of these areas the overarching trend is towards disintegration rather than integration. The situation in West and Sub-Saharan Africa is the starkest example of this trend. Second, while integration may make governance easier for elites, it also makes states more vulnerable to external forces. Workers are finding it increasingly difficult to compete in the new global labour market and this is likely to have consequences for governments. Also, protectionism is far from dead and buried. As economies begin to go into recession, governments will be pressured 'from below' to protect the national economy. This will probably slow down the pace of both systemic and regional integration.

*See also:* **European Union; functionalism; interdependence; liberal internationalism; regionalism**

*Further reading:* Axtmann, 1997; Butler, 1997; Dinan, 1999; Williams, 2000

## INTERDEPENDENCE

The condition of a relationship between two parties in which the costs of breaking their relations or of reducing their exchanges are roughly equal for each of them. In the study of international relations, interdependence between states has two dimensions: *sensitivity* and *vulnerability*. Sensitivity refers to the degree to which states are sensitive to changes taking place in another state. One way to measure this dimension is to examine whether changes in particular areas (for example, rates of inflation or unemployment) vary in similar fashion across territorial boundaries. Vulnerability refers to the distribution of costs incurred as states react to such changes. Thus two states may be equally sensitive to oil price rises but they may not be equally vulnerable. One of them might find it easier than the other to switch to alternative supplies of energy, thereby reducing its **dependence** on oil.

As a concept, interdependence began to be examined in earnest in the early 1970s. According to some scholars, three major changes were taking place in international relations. First, states were becoming increasingly interdependent across a variety of issue-areas, from consumer goods to security. Second, the decision-making capacity of states *vis-à-vis* the global economy was weakening. Third, the more interconnected states were becoming, the more vulnerable they were to disruptions and events in other parts of the globe. As evidence of these changes, interdependence **theorists** pointed to significant increases in transnational capital flows and technology transfers, the rise of **multinational corporations**, the thawing of relations between the **superpowers**, the growing importance of international institutions (both governmental and non-governmental), and the growing permeability of borders. Moreover, issues such as **human rights**, poverty, **development**, the environment, and energy politics had forced their way onto the foreign policy agenda of states. To many theorists of interdependence, the crude **power** politics of the **cold war** years appeared to be giving way to a more cooperative and rule-governed world. It is important to understand that the theorists of interdependence were not just talking about increased interconnectedness in a variety of issue-areas. The shift was also qualitative. The world was changing. The **realist** view that states were independently pursuing their **national interests** did not seem to present an accurate picture of the way states acted under conditions of what Robert Keohane and Joseph Nye called 'complex interdependence'.

For Keohane and Nye, complex interdependence challenged realism in at least three ways. First, realists focused only on interstate relations, but transgovernmental and transnational activity significantly affected states and weakened their capacity to act autonomously in international relations. There was nothing within the realist paradigm that could account for this important shift. Instead, Keohane and Nye stressed multiple channels of communication (interstate, transgovernmental, and transnational). Second, realists argued that there was a hierarchy of issues among states and distinguished between the 'high politics' of **security** and the 'low politics' of trade. Keohane and Nye argued that this distinction was obsolete. Finally, in an era of complex interdependence, Keohane and Nye argued that military force was becoming less usable and less important as a policy option.

Initially, the interdependence literature looked like displacing realism as the dominant framework of analysis. But this expectation was short-lived. A number of scholars argued that the literature contained a simplistic reading of realism. More importantly, the literature blurred the crucial distinction between sensitivity and vulnerability. For realists, the latter was more important than the former. After all, 'asymmetrical interdependence' was just another phrase for the inequality of power among states. Since there was no causal link between changes in sensitivity and vulnerability in the international system, it was premature to predict any qualitative change in international relations. In particular, Kenneth Waltz (1979) argued that many scholars of interdependence exaggerated its likely impact on the structure of the international system.

Despite these and other criticisms, the research on interdependence in the early 1970s had an important impact on the field. Not only did it help to revive the flagging fortunes of **liberal internationalism**, it also anticipated many of the changes that would be associated with **globalisation** in the 1980s and 1990s.

*See also:* **anarchy; foreign direct investment; free trade; integration; liberal internationalism; power; realism**

*Further reading:* Barry Jones and Willetts, 1984; Clemens, 1998; Kenen, 1995b; Keohane and Nye, 2000; Waltz, 1979

## INTERNATIONAL CRIMINAL COURT (ICC)

The International Criminal Court (ICC) was established in 1998 and entered into force on 1 July 2002. Of the many important precedents of the ICC, there are two that deserve attention: the Nuremberg Trials or the International Military Charter (1946), and the International Criminal Tribunals, more particularly the International Criminal Tribunal for the Former Yugoslavia (ICTY) and the International Criminal Tribunal for Rwanda (ICTR). The ICTY Statute, for instance, contains new elements of crimes against humanity, which would later be incorporated into the ICC Statute. Unlike the **international criminal tribunals**, however, the ICC is a permanent court, which, having been established under treaty law rather than under the Chapter VII powers of the **UN** Charter (where **ethnic cleansing** was determined to constitute a breach in international peace and security), can exercise jurisdiction over perpetrators of gross **human rights** abuses. More precisely, the ICC can exercise jurisdiction over perpetrators whose crimes have been committed within the territorial boundaries of a state party to the ICC Statute.

The ICC, therefore, has at least four identifiable aims: (1) to ensure that the worst perpetrators are held individually accountable for their crimes; (2) to serve as a court of last resort that can investigate, prosecute, and punish the perpetrators of **genocide**, crimes against humanity, and **war crimes**; (3) to assist national judiciaries in investigating and prosecuting the worst perpetrators, which also means allowing states prima facie to investigate and prosecute the perpetrators of these crimes; and finally, (4) to help promote international peace and security by having its effectiveness to deter future would-be perpetrators. Each one of these aims is to be realised and practised within the framework principle of complementarity. The complementarity principle holds that the states will be allowed prima facie to investigate and prosecute, but that the ICC Prosecutor may intervene in the national judiciary's affairs , should the state prove unwilling or unable to investigate and/or prosecute.

In addition to the office of the Prosecutor, there are four other principal organs of the ICC: the judicial chambers of the ICC (the Pre-Trial , Trial, and Appeals), the Office of the Prosecutor, Registry, and Assembly of States Parties (the legislative organ). Together, these organs are designed to maintain the Court's independence from the UN Security Council, and to ensure that the legal standards of impartiality and accountability are effectively upheld. One of the issues that was discussed at the Rome

Conference (that resulted in the establishment of the ICC) was whether the UN Security Council or the ICC Prosecutor should be able to determine when certain acts of aggression had occurred. The negotiators failed to reach an agreement on a solution or compromise to this problem. Instead, they elected to hold open-ended sessions or meetings to discuss the future elements and comprehensive definition of the crime of aggression.

However, ICC officials and state delegates did agree that the Prosecutor should have the right to initiate an investigation (*proprio motu*). This would prove important for two reasons: it would provide the Prosecutor with an added measure of independence and encourage the Prosecutor to assume a potentially assertive role in pressuring states to hand over suspected perpetrators. It is worth mentioning here that Luis Moreno-Ocampo, the first and current ICC Prosecutor, has already issued several indictments and arrest warrants for rebel leaders in Uganda and the Congo including Thomas Lubanga (the first person to be officially put on trial by the ICC), and Joseph Kony. He has also announced that his Office has gathered enough evidence to indict several high-ranking Sudanese officials, including Ahmad Muhammad Harun.

Despite these promising signs, however, the ICC Prosecutor remains dependent on the voluntary cooperation of states. If states choose not to comply with the ICC's demands, the ICC, which lacks an effective enforcement mechanism, will need to rely on three factors or measures: (1) the willingness of other states and the UN to pressure the non-compliant state; (2) the cost of and damage to the non-compliant state's reputation; and/or (3) the Security Council's willingness to impose **coercive diplomatic** measures on any state that fails to comply with the demands of the ICC. Given the lack of an enforcement mechanism, *Realpolitik* or power politics is certain to test and shape the Court's credibility, and its effectiveness in getting the worst perpetrators to stand trial.

Another important and much publicised issue facing the ICC is US opposition. The United States, for instance, has claimed that the jurisdiction over its military personnel would allow the ICC to pass legal judgement on matters related to national security decisions; and that certain vengeful states will file bogus claims with the ICC, thereby politicising the Court. In this context, the US has sought special exemption status of its military through the NATO Status of Forces Agreements (SOFAs) aimed at protecting US soldiers, sailors, and airmen stationed overseas. In addition, the US has objected that the Court's automatic jurisdiction over nationals of non-state parties would violate international treaty law. According to this claim, the ICC could exercise jurisdiction over individuals of non-state parties only when the non-state party consented to the authority of ICC jurisdiction on a case by case basis.

When the 9/11 attacks occurred, US Congressional and Executive opposition took a dramatic turn for the worse. Now, the **war on terror** became, by extension, a virtual war on the Court. A key domestic piece of this virtual war was the American Servicemembers Protection Act (ASPA), a bill passed by the US Senate in December of 2001, stipulating special legal protection for its own servicepersons from unlawful detainment overseas. On 6 May 2002, the Bush administration officially withdrew the US signature from the Rome Treaty, and in the following days, pledged to veto the UN mandate that would extend the date of maintaining peacekeeping operations in Bosnia. To address the growing US threat of withdrawal, the Security Council held a special meeting. The result was the adoption of Security Council resolution 1422, granting a special 12-month exemption to all military personnel of non-states parties. At this time, the Bush administration also adopted a text from the Article 98 Bilateral Immunity Agreements, which called for the immunity of all American citizens from ICC jurisdiction.

Despite US opposition, however, the ICC has managed to develop without US support. Interestingly, the United States has recently signalled its support of the ICC's accusations against the perpetrators of the genocide in the Darfur region. These events have given rise to two important issues: whether the United States will, in the future, begin to work with, or at least cooperate with the ICC regarding matters related to peace and security; and whether the ICC's assertive role in global politics will help to promote international peace and security via a credible global deterrent effect. Such issues remain open-ended, however, and will undoubtedly require further analysis.

*See also:* **ethnic cleansing; genocide; global civil society; global governance; human security; international criminal tribunals; sovereignty; United Nations; war**

*Further reading:* Bassiouni, 2000; Broomhall, 2004; Danner, 2003; Lee, 1999; Roach, 2006; Schabas, 2006; Sewall and Kaysen, 2000; Weller, 2002

## INTERNATIONAL CRIMINAL TRIBUNALS

International criminal tribunals are *ad hoc* criminal courts designed to investigate, prosecute, and punish the perpetrators of gross **human rights** abuses. Unlike the **International Criminal Court**, which is a permanent standing court, international criminal tribunals are temporary courts established under Chapter VII of the **UN** Charter. In 1993, for instance, the UN Security Council declared that the unlawful detentions and mass killings in Bosnia–Herzegovina constituted a breach in international peace and security (the same rationale would later be invoked, albeit somewhat differently, to create the International Criminal Tribunal for Rwanda (ICTR) in 1994). As such, the International Criminal tribunal for the Former Yugoslavia (ICTY) represented a novel mechanism for promoting peace and security. And although some would argue that it provided an excuse, or weak alternative to the more stringent demand for military intervention to stop the war, it eventually received strong financial backing and international support. More importantly, the ICTY seemed to overcome the problem of victor's justice, in which criminal justice served the political interests of only the most powerful states (the Allied Powers in the case of the Nuremberg Trials). In doing so, it nonetheless provided a prosecutorial mechanism that operated independently of the UN Security Council, while establishing the practice of concurrent jurisdiction whereby the ICC Prosecutor and national judiciary would work together to investigate and prosecute the perpetrators of gross human rights abuses.

Accordingly, the ICTY Statute, which sets forth the Office of the Prosecutor, Judiciary (a chamber of judges and appeals chamber), and Registry contains 34 articles, three of which encode the the elements of **war crimes**, crimes against humanity and **genocide**. As such, it consists of three aims: (1) to empower the prosecutor to investigate the core crimes of genocide, crimes against humanity, and **war crimes**; (2) to focus on the individualisation of guilt of the perpetrators; and (3) to establish an historical record for the purposes of promoting national reconciliation.

Whether or not the ICTY has succeeded in promoting national reconciliation remains an open-ended issue, however. In fact, it is fair to say that many Serbs continue to see the ICTY as biased against the Serbs. Some, for instance, have even argued that the ICTY Prosecution showed a willingness to ally itself with Western interests, notably **NATO**, in order to punish the Serbs. Highlighting this claim was the decision by Louise Arbour, the Chief Prosecutor of the ICTY, to indict Milosevic on 27 May 1999 at the height of the Kosovo War. In light of this looming perception of bias, there are two general challenges or problem areas that need to be considered.

First, international criminal tribunals require a substantial budget to achieve their aims of investigating and prosecuting the perpetrators of violence. The ICTR, for instance, continues to lack the necessary resources to prosecute many of the perpetrators. Currently, it faces the daunting task of trying several thousands of offenders of gross human rights atrocities. The ICTY, in comparison, is currently running a total operating budget of nearly $700 million, as of April 2006. But the large sum has not alleviated concerns of the high cost of holding trials, and the attendant need to get defendants to enter guilty pleas in return for lighter sentences. In short, because international criminal tribunals operate on a temporary and/or indefinite time basis, it is imperative that they operate efficiently within given budgetary, time constraints.

Second, *ad hoc* international criminal courts expose the complications arising from the exercise of the Chapter VII powers of the UN Charter. Indeed, it is quite possible that the permanent members of the Security Council would never adopt a resolution that would allow the generals of these member states to be investigated and prosecuted by an international court. From this standpoint, it follows that the permanent member states of the Security Council will likely use their power to block the prosecution of any of their own military personnel stationed overseas.

Given these factors, there remains the important question regarding the strategic effect of international criminal tribunals. How should they, for instance, complement truth commissions, or the investigative panels charged with the task of documenting atrocities and establishing a historical record? Should they be expected to use the evidence gathered from these commissions in order to prosecute and punish relevant targeted perpetrators? What needs to be stressed here is that truth commissions are non-prosecutorial, which is to say that they do not hold criminal proceedings to punish perpetrators of gross human rights atrocities. In the case of the South Africa Truth and Reconciliation Commission (TRC) (1996), authorities granted amnesty to the accused perpetrators in exchange for public testimony. The TRC's aim here was clear: it wished to promote forgiveness and national healing.

But it is also true that many truth commissions remain weak, or have been unsuccessful in promoting national healing (e.g. Guatemala). This trend does not mean that new international criminal tribunals, such as the International Criminal Tribunal for East Timor, will fail to complement the work of commissions. If anything such tribunals are likely to provide the necessary assistance to poorly funded national courts, which lack the funds and **legitimacy** to hold impartial and effective prosecutorial proceedings.

*See also:* **ethnic cleansing; genocide; human rights; human security; International Criminal Court; security; United Nations; war**

*Further reading:* Kerr, 2004; Ratner and Abrams, 2001; Roper and Barria, 2006; Simonovic, 1999

# INTERNATIONAL LAW ✓

There are two kinds of international law: private and public. The former is concerned with the resolution of international disputes between individuals and companies, while the latter governs relations between states. It includes such things as claims to territory, use of the sea, **arms control**, and **human rights**.

All states have a supreme law-making body. The international community, however, has no equivalent authority. Instead, *treaties* are the principal means by which states establish legal obligations binding on each other. Since there are more and more activities that require international cooperation, treaties have proliferated and now deal with an enormous variety of subjects. There are two main types of treaties. A bilateral treaty is concluded between two states whereas a **multilateral** treaty is concluded by more than two states. The most significant treaties are multilateral treaties concluded between all the states of the world.

Each state has its own constitutional practices regulating the treaty-making **power** of its government. For example, in the United States the Constitution controls treaty-making power. The President can make treaties, which become binding only with the agreement of two-thirds of the US Senate. International agreements that are not treaties, otherwise known as executive agreements, can be made by the President alone without the consent of the Senate and in recent years have become much more numerous than treaties.

There is no uniform procedure for the conclusion of a treaty, but generally the process involves a series of stages including negotiation, consent to be bound, ratification, and entry into force. Parties to the treaty may limit their commitment to certain aspects of the treaty through Reservations or may vary their obligations through Protocols.

*Customary* international law is the second most important source of international law. It is formed by the common practices of states, which over a period of time become accepted as legally binding. Some practices carried out by a few states only attain the status of regional customary international law whilst other practices that are common to the vast majority of states attain the status of worldwide customary law.

Until fairly recently, customary international law was the principal means by which international law was developed, but it has proved too slow to accommodate the rapidly changing nature of international law. Today the multilateral treaty has overtaken it. Furthermore, the increase in the number of states from the small 'club of twenty' that existed after the First World War to today's 190 or so, has made it difficult to prove the consensus of practice needed to establish customary international law.

However, some of the current law of the sea owes its development to the common practices of states, indicating that customary international law is still very important.

Customary international law is based on two factors. The first is a constant and uniform practice. It is necessary to prove that a large number of relatively strong states are involved in the practice and that it has been in use for a significant period of time. The second factor is the acceptance by states that the practice is legally binding. Some states may be bound by customary international law, even if they protest, where the vast majority of states have consented to it. For example, during the years of apartheid, the South African government used to protest that its racial policies did not breach international law, even though the international community considered those policies illegal.

The third main source of international law is **United Nations** *Resolutions*. Passed by the General Assembly as recommendations in the first instance, they may create international legal obligations by influencing the formation of customary international law and lead to the creation of multilateral treaties dealing with the issues raised by the Resolution. Some Resolutions are so important they receive the honorary title of Declaration. This is a formal instrument suitable for rare occasions when principles of great and lasting importance are being enunciated, such as the Declaration of Human Rights. Because Declarations are still only UN Resolutions, they cannot be made legally binding, even though there is a strong expectation that states will abide by their provisions.

The most important aspect of international law is that it cannot be enforced in the same way as domestic law. There is no international police force and states cannot be compelled to perform their legal obligations since there is no higher authority than the states themselves. The main ways in which international law is enforced between states are **reciprocity** and legal responsibility. States abide by their legal obligations because they want other states to do the same. A good example is **diplomatic** immunity. In addition, most states abide by international law most of the time because they want to be seen as law-abiding and legally responsible.

The vast majority of legal disputes between states are resolved through a combination of negotiation, mediation, and conciliation. The international community does have a weak judicial procedure to arbitrate disputes in the form of the International Court of Justice (ICJ). It has 15 judges who are chosen to represent the different geographical areas of the world. Its function is to decide disputes submitted to it by states and to give advisory opinions on international legal matters submitted to it by international organisations. Only states can take cases before the Court.

Individuals, groups, or non-governmental actors are prevented from taking complaints, although states can take complaints on their behalf, providing the rights which have been infringed are also the rights of the state. States cannot be forced to appear before the Court but will usually have signed a treaty which obliges them to do so, or have accepted the jurisdiction of the Court in a declaration. The role of the ICJ has not been without criticism. Many states have criticised the Court for declining to take a strong role in international legal affairs. The Court has tended to be conservative and to favour the established legal rights of the more powerful states. Like the United Nations, it relies on states taking into account world public order rather than their own **national interests** when deciding to abide by international law and the Court's decisions.

*See also:* **extraterritoriality; humanitarian intervention; International Criminal Court; international society; just war; reciprocity; United Nations; war crime**

*Further reading:* Franck, 1990; Higgins, 1995; Malanczuk, 1997; Shaw, 1997

# INTERNATIONAL MONETARY FUND (IMF)

The Great Depression of the 1930s had an enormous impact on the advanced industrialised states. In the United States and Europe agricultural prices fell, unemployment skyrocketed, banks closed leaving people penniless, factories stood idle, and international trade collapsed. Indeed, the onset of the Depression was one of the main reasons why so many ordinary Germans were willing to follow Hitler into **war** in 1939.

At the same time, the outbreak of war in Europe proved to be a key factor in the United States' economic recovery. Increases in the level of production needed to fight the war stimulated economic growth, put people back to work, and money into circulation. One of the important questions confronting American policymakers, however, was how to maintain the new level of economic activity after the war. Would the international economy dramatically slow down again? Would high tariffs continue to be a feature of the international economic landscape? Would high levels of unemployment return?

The purpose of the **Bretton Woods** Conference was primarily to ensure that these things did not happen. The 1944 Conference had two main goals: to stabilise the value of money and to promote international trade. Along with the **World Bank**, the International Monetary Fund (IMF) was created to facilitate both these goals. Article 1 of the IMF's Charter states that its purpose is to:

- promote international monetary cooperation;
- facilitate the expansion and balanced growth of international trade;
- promote and maintain high levels of employment;
- promote exchange stability and avoid competitive exchange rate depreciation;
- eliminate foreign exchange restrictions;
- offer resources to countries to correct maladjustments in their balance of payments without resorting to measures destructive of national or international prosperity;
- shorten the duration and lessen the degree of disequilibrium in the international balance of payments of its members.

The original mandate of the IMF was achieved primarily by linking the world's currencies to the American dollar. Members were required to fix the value of their currencies in relation to the dollar. Changes beyond 1 per cent had to be discussed with the other members of the Fund and agreed to by them. Investors, manufacturers, and states benefited enormously from what was called the *par value* system. Not only did it give them a clear idea of the actual value of different currencies, it also helped to bring a degree of predictability to the international economy. The par value system lasted until the early 1970s, when the US decided it could no longer afford to allow countries to convert their US dollars into gold.

It is customary to talk about the collapse of the Bretton Woods system in the early 1970s. This is not quite correct. In fact, the IMF survived because the need for monetary stability became more crucial in the absence of fixed exchange rates. Nonetheless, the role of the IMF has changed since the 1970s. True, it continues to promote monetary stability and trade, but increasingly its role is to assist countries that are in the midst of financial **crisis**. Indeed, it has become something of an economic crisis management institution. It offers financial and technical assistance to countries experiencing monetary problems and remains a lender of last resort. This gives the IMF enormous power to determine the economic fate of countries experiencing balance-of-payment problems. If, for example, a member country has continuing economic problems, the IMF will initiate **structural adjustment programmes** (SAPs). These macroeconomic reforms can include debt reduction strategies, privatisation policies, and cuts in public spending. Unfortunately, these strategies generally impact on the poor most severely. It is for this reason that SAPs are regarded as particularly iniquitous by some observers.

Today, the IMF has more critics than friends. Some economists suggest that the world economy would function better without it, and that many of its SAPs exacerbate crises rather than alleviate them. Others suggest that while it is an imperfect institution, it is better at maintaining economic stability than many governments. Whatever the truth, there is little evidence to suggest that the IMF is heading for the institutional scrap-heap. There have been muted calls for a new Bretton Woods Conference, but this message has not yet filtered up to policymakers and government officials. At the same time, it is hard to imagine how the global economy could function effectively without some institutional guidance. The challenge is to ensure that a balance is struck between good economic management and human needs. In striking this balance, the IMF appears to have a long way to go.

*See also:* **beggar-thy-neighbour policies; Bretton Woods; capital controls; capitalism; embedded liberalism; structural adjustment programme**

*Further reading:* Danaher, 1994; Helleiner, 1996; McQuillan, 1999; Sharufk, 1999

## INTERNATIONAL POLITICAL ECONOMY

One of the fastest growing sub-fields in international relations has been the international political economy (IPE). Broadly speaking, IPE refers to the study of the interaction of trade, finance, and the state; and how states respond politically to the (shock) effects of the global market. One of the key features of the international political economy is the global security architecture or the network of economic and political institutions designed to promote free trade and capital flows. Within this framework, many issues are addressed, including intellectual property rights, issues of **human rights** protection and promotion, unfair trading practices, the North–South divide, and environmental problems.

In the study of the international political economy, one encounters three general distinctive perspectives: economic nationalism, liberalism, and Marxism.

*Economic **nationalism*** (or neo-**mercantilism**) remains largely synonymous with mercantilism, or the accumulation of bullion or wealth to aggrandise state power. More generally, it refers to the zero-sum relationship between wealth and state power (one person's loss is another's gain). Alexander Hamilton, the first Secretary of Finance for the United States, theorised that state power was based on accrued wealth and needed investitures to build and maintain a strong army or national defence system. Hamilton believed that such wealth needed to be centralised in the form of strong financial institutions, since this would ensure an efficient financial system. From the late seventeenth century to mid-twentieth century, such accumulation would represent high volume production. Robert Reich, for instance, has argued that mass production reached a crystallising point in the United States in the 1950s: when there was a so-called national contract among labour, management, and the public. Although **globalisation** or global competition would ultimately undermine the benefits of this contract, the resurgence of economic nationalism in East Asia has renewed attention to the zero-sum equation of political and economic state power, particularly as this relates to the export-led financial growth of the technological software products of many East Asian countries (e.g. Malaysia, Singapore, and South Korea).

*Liberalism*, in contrast, focuses on the following positive-sum process of the economy: the accumulated or aggregate benefits of free markets and trade. As one of the principal architects of economic liberalism, Adam Smith argued that a free market was based on the maximum allocation of resources or the unhindered exchange between buyer and seller (*laissez faire*). Thus, if the seller and buyer were allowed to trade freely on the market, then the market would yield an optimal price for goods and services. In the early to mid-1800s, David Ricardo applied Smith's theory to the international level. He argued that states needed to specialise in the production of goods in order to gain what he called a comparative advantage. His theory held that when each state manufactured and sold the goods that they produced most efficiently, all states would be made better off. It should be noted here that comparative advantage still holds true today, albeit in a far more complex manner.

Lastly, **Marxism** focuses on the social inequalities and oppression generated by the privatisation of capital or the private ownership of the means of production (property, equipment). As such, Marxism explains the dynamics of the market in terms of class conflict, between the middle class (bourgeoisie) and working class (proletariat), as well as the effects of exchange controls and unfair labour practices. Here, Karl Marx was able to show how these practices resulted in what he called surplus value: the added wealth gained from under-employment or unpaid wages for overtime (work hours that were not covered in the worker's contract). It was Marx's idea, however, that the workers would ultimately unite to overthrow the oppressive laws of **capitalism**.

It is important to note, then, that these three perspectives have evolved over time. In the twentieth century, for instance, the stock market crash (1929) ushered in a new era of Keynesian economics, in which the state assumed a far more prominent role in regulating flows of capital and providing for the social welfare of its citizens. Here, John Maynard Keynes theorised that strong regulatory mechanisms and state investment could maintain and stimulate economic growth, thus enabling the capitalist system to overcome the debilitating effects of economic **crises**. Eventually, this formula would reach the international level, in the form of the **Bretton Woods** system. In this context, Keynes was responsible for helping to devise the system of cash or liquidity reserves of the **International Monetary Fund (IMF)** whose aim was to allow financially troubled countries to receive short-term loans that could reduce the international shock effects associated with domestic financial crises.

Since its establishment, however, the Bretton Woods system has had a controversial impact on the world economy. Whilst growth has rapidly increased, the social and human effects of the free market system has become a central issue of international economic stability. The conversion from fixed exchange rates (all currencies were pegged to the dollar) to floating ones in 1973 would subsequently result in growing uncertainty and instability within the system. Recent financial collapses in East Asia (1997), Russia (1998), and Mexico (1994) have all stressed the increasing volatility and interconnectedness of the global financial system; whilst protests against the **WTO** in Seattle and Rome continue to call attention to unfair trading practices.

*See also:* **communism; dependency; digital divide; globalisation; hegemony; historical sociology; liberalism; Marxism; nationalism; theory; world system theory**

*Further reading*: Gill, 1997; Gilpin, 1987; Rupert and Solomon, 2005; Strange, 1987

## INTERNATIONAL SOCIETY ✓

The concept of a society in social **theory** has generally presupposed notions of cultural cohesion and social **integration** associated with national societies. Consequently, the idea that relations among states may take place within the context of an international society appears somewhat strange. Nonetheless, a number of scholars associated with what has become known as the English School have developed a rich body of scholarship based on this idea.

The concept refers to a group of states that share certain common interests or values, and who participate in the maintenance of international institutions. In the past it was possible to point to a shared civilisation among states that facilitated communication and cooperation among them. For example, one could argue that Western Christendom in the sixteenth and seventeenth centuries, or perhaps European political culture in the eighteenth and nineteenth centuries, restrained states from pursuing their self-interests in a totally **anarchical** environment. Most scholars trace the origins of contemporary international society to Europe, and in particular the 1648 **Peace of Westphalia** that generated the constitutive rules of interstate co-existence. Today's international society encompasses the globe, raising the question of whether the religious and cultural diversity of contemporary international relations renders the concept redundant as a tool of analysis. Members of the English School suggest that this is not the case, since the rules of contemporary international society continue to play an important role in sustaining international order. **International law** continues to affirm and reinforce the primacy of the states system. It specifies the minimum conditions of co-existence among states, and regulates the terms of cooperation among them in a variety of different issue-areas.

The term 'international society' is important in drawing our attention to two fundamental aspects of international relations. First, it suggests that attempts to construct a rigid dichotomy between domestic politics (the site of hierarchy, **order**, and perhaps justice) and international relations (anarchy, absence of order, the site of **power** politics) are doomed to fail. In so far as international relations are rule-governed in the sense that rules are not mere expressions of power but also help to restrain that power, the **realist** approach is fundamentally flawed. Second, it suggests that the sources of state conduct cannot be deduced solely on the basis of observable and measurable factors. The term 'international society' implies that relations among states are infused with normative significance. States relate to one another in the context of claims about rights and obligations rather than mere struggles for power.

Both these aspects of international relations raise a number of interesting questions. If international relations cannot be understood adequately simply as a manifestation of power politics (realism), is it therefore unnecessary to radically transform the international order to achieve global peace and justice (as some **critical theorists** and **cosmopolitans** claim)? Whose interests are served by the rules of co-existence among states? Are those rules capable of adaptation in the interests of individuals, or are they designed to protect states alone? Is international society a concept that is applicable across the globe, or is its scope confined to particular states and regions?

Although it is impossible to answer these questions in any definitive manner, the range of answers continue to be at the heart of contemporary debates in the field. For some scholars, the concept of international society adds little to our understanding of international relations. The rules of co-existence may be expressed neatly in constitutional charters, and international institutions may flourish, but in the end international relations remains a realm in which a 'logic of consequences' prevails over a 'logic of appropriateness'.

International society is not a static concept. Its strength varies over time and space. During the height of the **cold war**, when international relations appeared to be the site of a dangerous ideological struggle over the terms of international order, evidence of a society of states was weak. In the months following the end of the cold war, it re-emerged as a powerful element in facilitating collective action to reverse Iraq's invasion of Kuwait.

Finally, some scholars suggest that the concept is analytically obsolete. In an era of **globalisation**, we need to explore the possibility of international relations taking place within a broader global society in which states are but one of a number of important actors shaping the world. Moreover, even if the element of international society can be said to contribute to international order, it is hostile to ideas of cosmopolitan justice. If the latter is to be achieved at all, it is not enough that states tolerate one another; they need to participate in a broader common project that begins to tackle common problems, such as those presented through environmental degradation and human inequality.

*See also:* **anarchy; constructivism; cosmopolitanism; diplomacy; international law; just war; realism**

*Further reading:* Bull, 1995; Buzan, 2004; Dunne, 1998; Griffiths, 1992; Shaw, 1994

# IRREDENTISM

This term is derived from the Italian phrase *terra irredentia*, meaning 'unredeemed land'. It was first used to refer to Italian-speaking areas under Austrian and Swiss rule during the second half of the nineteenth century. Following its unification, Italy fought a number of **wars** in order to annex those territories (Trente, Dalmatia, Trieste, and Fiume). Irredentism can be defined as a territorial claim made by one state to areas under the **sovereign** authority of another state. It is related to, but different from, the term **secession**, which refers to attempts by a national minority to break away from an existing state to form one of its own. Although secession is not the same as irredentism, they are closely related. A state may openly try to annex a territory from another state; however, a minority may demand that the land it inhabits be separated from the state to which it currently belongs and be united with another state. A good example is the case of Kurdistan, a region composed of Kurds presently living in Iraq, Iran, Syria, and Turkey.

Irredentism is strongly connected with the most aggressive aspects of modern **nationalism**. However, even before the emergence of nationalist ideologies, many states attempted to justify **imperialism** by using the argument of redeeming territory or liberating their brethren. For example, the justification for the Crusades was to redeem the Holy Land and to liberate fellow Christians from the dominance of Muslims. Irredentism is motivated by two aims: (1) the drive to expand, to increase **power**, and/or wealth; and (2) affinity for kith and kin. As such, the pursuit of irredentist goals is often violent, and has been the source of numerous wars in the twentieth century. Examples include Argentina's claims against Britain over the Falklands/Malvinas islands and the Republic of Ireland's former commitment (prior to the Good Friday Agreement) to a united Ireland.

Although irredentism is often justified in terms of helping **ethnic** minorities and liberating them from the state in which they presently live, there are two reasons why irredentist claims often do not improve but instead worsen their status and conditions. First, they may contribute to a self-fulfilling prophecy for both the minority and the state in which it resides. The government subject to irredentist claims may further discriminate against a minority, perceiving it as a threat to national **security**. It may adopt oppressive policies to discourage the minority from endorsing irredentist goals, which in turn may be regarded by the leaders of the minority as evidence that they can no longer live under the domination of an alien state. Since irredentist movements are rarely successful, minorities can end up worse off than they were before the conflict. Second, what is central in many irredentist movements is territory rather than people, in which case the latter become mere pawns in the irredentist game. The irredentist state is not really concerned with the well-being of the group. Often, it just uses it to destabilise its opponent, as Iraq did prior to its invasion of Kuwait in August 1990.

Since the end of the Second World War, and particularly after the end of the **cold war**, irredentism has been experiencing a paradox. On the one hand **international law** is hostile to irredentism. The more recent the international documents, the more explicit they are in condemning and banning irredentist aspirations and actions. The **United Nations** Charter emphasises respect for territorial borders and state **sovereignty**, as does the Organisation of African Unity (OAU), the Organisation of American States (OAS), and the Helsinki Final Act (1975) with regard to Europe.

On the other hand, the breakdown of cold war regional arrangements in Eastern Europe, East Asia, Africa, and the Middle East inevitably brings to the fore the need to redefine political boundaries. In the last years of the twentieth century irredentist conflicts re-emerged in a vast area stretching from the Northern Balkans to the Spratly and Kurile Islands in the South Pacific. Many governments of the states in this huge geographic area are confronted with political and economic instability, a rebirth of ethnic nationalism, and a pressure for **democratisation**. In addition, the **legitimacy** of existing borders is increasingly being challenged.

In this context, it is important that the international community (particularly the United States, the United Nations, and regional security organisations) responds to the problem of irredentism in a proactive rather than reactive fashion. Whilst irredentist predispositions can never be fully suppressed, the intensity of irredentist conflicts can be reduced by an adherence to some fundamental concepts of political pluralism within states and a greater regard and respect for minority rights. Since ethnic nationalism is unlikely to disappear in the near future, we need to develop mechanisms, methods, and strategies to manage irredentist conflicts.

*See also:* **democratisation; extraterritoriality; nationalism; secession; sovereignty; United Nations**

*Further reading:* Carment and James, 1995; Chazan, 1991; Heraclides, 1990; Horowitz, 1992; Midlarsky, 1992

## ISOLATIONISM

A political strategy committed to minimal **diplomatic** participation in the international system. The fundamental idea behind isolationism is that a state will be more secure and less prone to external interference if it limits its contact with other states.

Four factors make it possible for a state to pursue such a course of action. First, either it must already be relatively free from the threat of invasion or so powerful that it does not need to form **alliances** in order to defend itself. In such circumstances, it may believe that withdrawing from the international system, fortifying its borders, and pursuing separate **development** makes good strategic sense. Second, an isolationist state needs to be economically self-sufficient. It must have adequate goods and services, resources, and population to enable it to survive its self-imposed diplomatic isolation. Third, isolationism requires either political consensus or strong authoritarian rule to withstand domestic challenges to its foreign policy. Finally, **geopolitical** considerations are important. A state that is geographically remote or surrounded by a mountain range, ocean, or desert is in a significantly better position to pursue isolationism than one that is land-locked.

Although a number of states have pursued a deliberate policy of isolationism at various times over the past 200 years (including Japan and Ethiopia), the most famous example is the United States. American isolationism was first spelled out by President George Washington in his

'Farewell Address' in 1797. He argued that America should 'steer clear of permanent alliances with any portion of the foreign world'. Specifically, he had Europe in mind. Washington believed that American involvement in European diplomacy would undermine American democracy and threaten the liberty it had fought so hard to achieve.

American isolationism was primarily a political stance – a refusal to join alliances or to commit US forces abroad on behalf of another state. It was a response to the war-prone character of Europe and was geared to consolidating American independence. In short, it was a policy of survival during a period of nation-building. Yet it was never very consistently applied. First, the United States was an **imperial power**. Not only did it extend its power south to Florida and the Gulf of Mexico and westward to the Pacific, but it also acquired overseas territories in the Pacific and the Caribbean. Moreover, the Monroe Doctrine of 1823 declared Latin America off-limits to Europe. This effectively meant that the southern part of the continent, including the Caribbean, became part of an American sphere of influence. Second, while successive administrations preached isolationism during the nineteenth century, they continued to pursue commercial ties with Europe, believing that economic interaction could be kept separate from political interaction.

Isolationism ended with the US involvement in the First World War and the 1918–19 intervention against the Russian Bolsheviks. After the Versailles settlement of 1919, however, the United States once again returned to its official policy of isolation. It was not until the United States entered the Second World War some 20 years later that it adopted a more internationalist foreign policy orientation. Yet the desire to retreat from world affairs continues to inform foreign policy debate in the United States. Indeed, the tension between isolationism and internationalism is an enduring source of controversy in American diplomacy and it is likely to remain one for many years to come.

*See also:* **cold war; containment; hegemonic stability theory; hegemony; liberal internationalism**

*Further reading:* Nordlinger, 1996

## JIHAD

Jihad refers to the duty to defend Islam against state aggression. It remains one of the most widely invoked principles of Sharia (Islamic law), and is generally associated with aggressive wars and, in its most extreme manner, the militancy of terrorist groups. It is important to note that sharia or Islamic law consists of the legal codes, principles and rules derived from the teachings of the Prophet Mohammed (the Sunna text, Koran, and Hadith) in the seventh century AD. Most Arab (Islamic) states and Islamic states have adopted sharia in the form of sharia appeals courts (criminal legal system), including Sudan, Saudi Arabia, Yemen, and Pakistan. In essence, Sharia represents a path towards spiritual fulfilment, that is, the pursuit of various spiritual and practical goals, including the protection of faith, life, intellect, lineage, property, and the elimination of corruption. When jihad is invoked, it is meant to preserve and promote the Islamic community or *ummah*, where everyday life is structured by five pillars of Islam: the teachings of Mohammed in the Sunna text and Hadith, prayer, pilgrimage to Mecca, fasting, and Zakat Tax (or alms giving that is typically 2.5 per cent of one's income).

Jihad consists of two levels of meaning. On the most personal level, it expresses the personal and spiritual struggle for fulfilment of Muslims; whilst on the state (or political) level, it reflects the radical, military struggle against Western hegemony or Western occupation of the Arab world. When jihad is invoked as a military struggle against the infidels of the West, there is often the tendency to prioritise this latter level. For many Islamic scholars, however, this type of invocation more often than not obscures and misrepresents the Muslim's personal spiritual fulfilment. Nonetheless, it is possible to view the military aspects of jihad as a strictly strategic feature of preserving the values of Islam, in which Islamic justice requires inner jihad to guide the conduct of the affairs of the state.

It is important to stress that militaristic jihad often reflects a rigid and oftentimes uncompromising interpretation of Islam. Islamic scholars from the medieval period (the *ulema*), for instance, distinguished between *Dar al-Islam*, referring to the lands occupied by Muslims, and *Dar al-harb*, representing the land or territory occupied by non–Muslims, in order to study the threat of war and aggression against non–Muslims. Compared to the **clash of civilisations** thesis in international relations, this rigid distinction between *Dar al-harb* and *Dar al-Islam* leaves little, if any, room for long-term cooperation.

Accordingly, many modern Islamic scholars argue that the traditional distinction between *Dar al-harb* and *Dar al-Islam* ignores Mohammed's emphasis on the realm of *Dar al-sulh* (the making of **alliances**). Mohammed, it could be said, saw treaty making as the supreme safeguard against war, or the threat of unlawful invasion by the infidels into Arab lands. In this sense, it could be said that jihad remains consistent with the provisions of self-defense encoded in Article 51 of the **UN** Charter (self-defence as the pretext for authorising the use of force).

Still, this legal overlap has not diminished the collective efforts to interpret jihad in an aggressive or proactive manner. Indeed, more have become willing to wage a global jihad whose purpose is to combat the aggressor globally, whether this means driving out US military forces in Iraq or the Israeli troops from the West Bank. Al Qaeda is perhaps the most notorious group to have invoked a global jihad. Their aim is twofold: to drive out the US occupying forces in Iraq and other areas; and to reclaim **sovereign** control of Arab lands. The success of the 9/11 attacks against the World Trade Center and the Pentagon have shown that Al Qaeda's tactics remain difficult to detect, much less gauge. And while for many, such suicide attacks against the civilian population constitute crimes against humanity, for a small number they serve the purpose of preserving and promoting the Islamic faith.

Today, the military agenda of jihadist Islamic groups represents what many refer to as Political Islam or Islamism (Islamic fundamentalism): when the Islamic faith is politicised for the purposes of mobilising support to drive out the infidel from Arab lands. In this way, it demonstrates how the Koran has served the political interests of some extremist groups, such as Al Qaeda, and the Islamic Jihad. Still, one cannot entirely ignore the troubling paradox: that Western military occupation and cultural **imperialism** remain key sources of political mobilisation for such groups, even though extremism violates, at least for many Muslims, the spirit and integrity of jihad.

*See also:* **Arab League; clash of civilisations; international law; sovereignty; terrorism; war**

*Further reading:* Esposito, 2002; Kamali, 2002; Lewis, 2003; Mamdani, 2004; Mazrui, 1997

## JUST WAR

Can the use of violence through **war** ever be justified? Throughout history, conventions and agreements about acceptable conduct have carefully circumscribed the waging of war. These rules have been codified in **international law**. They are expressed philosophically in the just-war tradition and practically in the United Nations Charter and the findings of the Nuremberg **war crimes** tribunal. The rules are not always followed, but most states have affirmed them as prudent and reasonable moral standards that provide appropriate criteria for judgement. A fundamental premise underlies the just-war tradition: the unchanging nature of humankind, in which good and evil co-exist. All human beings commit immoral acts during their lives. These acts include killing other human beings. Because of this unfortunate propensity, it has been necessary for individuals and states to defend themselves from aggression. This requirement, in turn, has led to the development of rules of conduct – the principles of just war.

The principles of just war are usually divided into two sections. The first, *jus ad bellum*, refers to the justice of deciding to participate in a war. The second, *jus in bello*, refers to the rules of morality which govern the way any war may be conducted.

## PRINCIPLES OF JUST WAR

### *Jus ad bellum* (just recourse to war):

Just cause

Legitimate authority

Just intentions

Public declaration (of causes and intents)

Proportionality (more good than evil results)

Last resort

Reasonable hope of success

### *Jus in bello* (just conduct in war):

Discrimination (non–combatant immunity)

Proportionality (amount and type of force used)

Each of these main principles merits elaboration.

### *Just cause*
Just cause means having right on your side. In general, just cause focuses on the principle of self-defence against unjustified aggressive actions. Self-defence is the only just cause formally recognised in modern international law. This principle is also the basis of **collective security**, according to which other states are justified in coming to the aid of a state that has been subject to aggression from another state.

### *Legitimate authority*
Legitimate authority refers to the lawfully constituted government of a **sovereign state**. Only the primary authority of the state has the power to commit its citizens to **war**.

### Just intentions

St Thomas Aquinas, who based just-war **theory** upon natural law, first articulated this element of *jus ad bellum* in Western thought at length. Revenge is not a morally acceptable basis for conducting war. The war must be prosecuted with reluctance, restraint, and a willingness to accept peace when the objectives that justified the war in the first place have been achieved. Although classified under the *jus ad bellum* section of the principles, just intentions have even greater significance for the individual soldier in the conduct of war, philosophically underlying the rules of war that protect noncombatants and require acceptance of surrender and humane treatment of prisoners of war.

Aquinas also developed the theory of double effect. This theory was originally formulated to reconcile an evil (killing) with a good (resisting aggression). So long as the killing itself was not desired, but was merely an unavoidable consequence of achieving the lawful objective, it was permitted. Later, double effect was extended to permit military actions which, while justified in themselves by necessity and the other principles of just war, caused collateral harm to civilians and their property. It is now a rationale for violating the principle of noncombatant immunity. The principle has many safeguards, including that the evil effects not be intended, that all reasonable efforts be made to achieve the desired military goal without the undesired noncombatant effects, and that the good achieved outweigh the evil that incidentally occurs.

### Public declaration

The purpose of this requirement is to state clearly the *casus belli* and the terms under which peace might be restored. It also serves to inform a state's citizenry of the cause which requires resort to arms and the ensuing risk to life and limb of those who will participate in the conflict.

### Proportionality

In terms of *jus ad bellum*, or justification for going to war, proportionality means having a reasonable relationship between the goals and objectives to be achieved and the means being used to achieve them.

### Last resort

This principle recognises the destructive consequences of war and insists that it be avoided if at all possible, consistent with the legitimate interests of the state. It means that negotiations, compromise, economic **sanctions**, appeals to higher authority (the **United Nations**, for example), and the like must be pursued to redress grievances, if possible, before resort to war is justified.

### Reasonable hope of success

The state must not squander the lives and property of its citizens in a hopeless effort.

In addition to these criteria for evaluating arguments for going to war, the just-war tradition contains two crucial principles for evaluating the ways in which states fight once war has begun, namely discrimination and proportionality.

### Discrimination

The basic principle here is that noncombatants should be immune from attack. Noncombatants have traditionally been divided into two groups, based on class and function. The class of noncombatants refers to persons who have been defined as not acceptable as military targets, including medical personnel and clergy, whether in uniform or not, infants and small children (normally all children), the aged, wounded, or sick, and those otherwise helpless to protect themselves. Those who are noncombatants by function include farmers, merchants, and others not directly involved in the war effort. Among civilians, those who make war decisions or produce war materials are generally considered as direct contributors to the war effort and, thus, are combatants. Those who perform services or produce goods necessary for living are noncombatants, even though military personnel may use their services or goods.

### Proportionality

Just as proportionality is one of the *jus ad bellum* principles, so does moral proportionality apply to the means by which war is waged. With respect to *jus in bello*, proportionality means that the amount and type of force used must be such that the unjust consequences do not exceed the legitimate objectives.

Over time, the just-war tradition has evolved from a set of principles designed to cover relations between Christian princes to more secular versions that rest ultimately on a consensus among states that their continued independence should not be overturned by force of arms. In recent years there has been a growing interest in debating the merits and practicality of just-war principles. Debate has focused on the following questions: Is it possible to justify nuclear war when the policy of nuclear **deterrence** contravenes the principles of discrimination and proportionality? How realistic are just-war criteria under the pressures of modern conventional war? How can the principles of just-war theory be adapted to cover instances of **humanitarian intervention**? The continued relevance of the tradition depends on its ability to adapt to changes in the practice of war in the twenty-first century and beyond.

*See also:* **deterrence; humanitarian intervention; international law; international society; legitimacy; Peace of Westphalia; pre-emption; United Nations; war; war crimes**

*Further reading:* Davidson, 1983; Gorry, 2000; Johnson, 1984; Walzer, 1992

## LEAGUE OF NATIONS

The League of Nations (LON) was the predecessor to the **United Nations**. It represented a major attempt by the **great powers** after the First World War (1914–18) to institutionalise a system of **collective security**, and its founding Covenant was formulated as part of the Treaty of Versailles (1919). The first meeting was held in Geneva in 1920, with 42 states represented. Over the next 26 years, a total of 63 states were represented at one time or another. The last meeting was held in 1946, at the end of which the League was formally replaced by the United Nations which promptly moved its headquarters to New York, reflecting not only the status of the United States but also disillusionment with the performance of the League.

Like the United Nations, the League consisted of an Assembly, a Council, and a Secretariat. The Assembly, consisting of every member state, convened annually in Geneva. The Council was composed of several permanent members (France, Britain, Italy, Japan, and later Germany and the Soviet Union) and some non-permanent members elected by the Assembly. It met more often than the Assembly to consider political disputes and to focus on the reduction of armaments. Its decisions had to be unanimous. The Secretariat, the administrative branch of the League, consisted of a Secretary-General and a staff of 500 people. Several other organisations were associated with the League such as the World Court and the International Labour Organisation.

To some extent, the League was an extension of liberal, parliamentary practice to international relations. It was based on the idea that political compromise arrived at by open discussion was the best means to promote political stability, an idea deeply held by one of the main architects of the League, US President Woodrow Wilson. Like so many international organisations, the League was also designed in light of the alleged lessons of the First World War, of which three were particularly important. First, in 1914 Germany had crossed the border into France and Belgium. It was believed that in future **wars** it would be easy to decide who was the aggressor, a decision that was meant to trigger a range of collective countermeasures, ranging from **diplomatic** boycotts to the imposition of **sanctions** and ultimately war. Second, the system for the prevention of conflicts rested on the assumption that war could be prevented by the application of reason based on legal principles. The idea that power could be subordinated to law was a common assumption among many **idealists** of the interwar period. Third, the speed of political developments in 1914 led to the implementation of several mechanisms of delay to slow down unilateral decision-making in a **crisis**. Only after a period of three months subsequent to bringing a dispute to the Council was resort to war legal. It was assumed that such time limits would be respected. The failure of the League to deter or punish aggression by Italy, Japan, and ultimately Germany in the 1930s reflected some fundamental flaws in the design of the League.

It should be noted that the League was never fully representative of the international community. The United States Senate did not ratify the treaties and did not become a member of the League. South Africa and Liberia were the only African states. The Soviet Union was not invited to Versailles, and did not join the League until 1934. Few South American states were represented, and only China, Japan, and Thailand represented Asia. Germany was missing from the start in light of its alleged responsibility for the First World War. Because the League was primarily a European body, the number of states that were able to carry out any police action against an aggressor was effectively limited to France and Britain. Without their consent, of course, no decision was likely to be carried out, and France in particular was determined to use the League to **contain** Germany in Europe.

The ultimate failure of the League to maintain international peace and **security** was a product of its limited membership, its preservation of a territorial settlement that humiliated Germany, and its faith in the willingness of great powers to subordinate their short-term **national interests** to the preservation of international peace. Confronted with the rise of fascism in Italy, Germany, and Japan in the 1930s – a powerful bloc of states that glorified war and embarked on a sustained rearmament programme to achieve their aim to reconfigure the global **balance of power** in their favour – the League was impotent. Indeed, it was established during a period in which powerful states continued to rely on war as a means of resolving conflict, and when new forms of **nationalism** not only undermined some European empires (Austria–Hungary, Turkey) but also justified new patterns of **imperial** domination. In light of the rapid shifts in power that were taking place in the first half of the twentieth century, combined with the diplomatic isolation of the United States and the Soviet Union, it is hardly surprising that the League participated in rather than prevented the decline of Europe.

Despite its sorry record, the League did achieve some successes in disputes among small states (for example, between Greece and Bulgaria in 1925 and between Poland and Lithuania in 1927). During its brief history, it considered more than 60 cases ranging from technical legal disputes to major cases of armed conflict. It was successful in bringing half of them to a peaceful conclusion, even if they only involved minor states and on issues where a legal approach could be applied. It should also be remembered that the League was responsible for overseeing the first stages of **decolonisation** in disposing certain territories that had been colonies of Germany and Turkey before the First World War. Territories were awarded to other League members in the form of mandates, and were given different degrees of political independence in accordance with their geographic situation and stage of economic **development**.

*See also:* **collective security; decolonisation; idealism; United Nations**

*Further reading:* Gill, 1996; Knock, 1995; Walters, 1986

## LEGITIMACY

Legitimacy in international relations generally refers to the right to exercise moral and political authority. Political institutions that play a key role in promoting **human rights** and **security** tend to enjoy a high degree of legitimacy. The **EU**, it could be said, enjoys a high political standing, as do legal institutions like the **International Criminal Court**, because of the strong perception of their impartiality and fairness. In this sense, legitimacy derives from the perception of the public authority's right to rule and exercise jurisdiction over an issue and/or territorial boundaries.

As one of the principal thinkers of legitimacy, Max Weber, an early twentieth-century social scientist, theorised that legitimacy derived from the state's monopoly on the use of force. Domination in this sense was a type of authority whose legitimacy represented the bureaucratic administration of affairs and the binding juridical power of the state. As such, the bureaucracy and juridical courts provided the legitimate mechanisms for enacting and upholding the state law. But the question that arises is why citizens willingly abide by the decisions of the state even if this means supplying the unchecked power of the state to enforce its rules and decisions that violate the personal liberties of citzens. The question, however, becomes more problematic at the international level, where there is no single centralised government to regulate the affairs of the international realm.

During the 1990s, international legal scholars addressed this question by focusing on the functional aspects of legitimacy. Thomas Franck, for instance, argues that legitimacy is **functional** when states desire to be recognised as a member of a community in which they learn to abide by the rules of the club in order to secure its benefits of membership. States, in this sense, are no different from individuals who fulfill their daily routines: they learn to conform to the rules and to impose self-constraints on their own behaviour. This self-enforcement mechanism, in Franck's view, explains why state leaders voluntarily comply with international rules, since states can ill afford to ignore the consequences of non-compliance, such as disrepute and isolation.

On the other hand, rules and institutions are not simply legitimate because of the desire and interest to abide by the rules of the system. If this were the case, then legitimacy would be based on the strict submission to the rules, with little if any attention paid to the (democratic) capacity to shape these rules. Thus, one could argue that the desire to conform to rules is not sufficient to validate the rules. Values must be taken into account. Only when values can shape the law can one begin to identify with these rules as legitimate. Thus, on the one hand, legitimacy provides an external standard for assessing the ways of correcting deviations from the rules. On the other hand, legitimacy remains a problematic concept since conformity to the law does not directly confer legitimacy, but is the product of one's ability to shape the legal rules.

Nonetheless, when one chooses the rules that will govern behaviour, one, in turn, learns to identify with these rules. Christian Reus-Smit (2004), for instance, argues that legitimacy is a historical and evolutionary concept whose meaning and significance can be explained in terms of the emergence of new moral standards such as women's and children's rights.

One of the problems associated with promoting the legitimacy of new humanitarian norms, however, is that legal principles may not support legitimate, moral objectives such as stopping **genocide**. Legal scholars and political scientists refer to this condition as the critical gap between legitimacy and legality. Here it is argued that legal principles have become outdated or inconsistent with the legitimate need to stop and prevent cases of genocide or severe humanitarian emergencies. The Independent Commission on the Kosovo War (2000), for instance, which investigated this issue and the surrounding events of the Kosovo War, concluded that the intervention of Kosovo was 'legitimate yet illegal'. It recommended among other things that the international community draw up a set of moral guidelines to resolve the inconsistency. Clearly, when a legitimate cause arises, the international community will need to find ways of removing the legal obstacle to legitimate international action. This is one reason why legitimacy has become such a crucial, albeit contestable concept in international relations.

*See also:* **Bush doctrine; European Union; genocide; human rights; sovereignty; United Nations**

*Further reading:* Coicaud, 2002; Falk, 2004; Franck, 1990; Reus-Smit, 2004; Weber, 1971

## LEVELS OF ANALYSIS

Facts do not speak for themselves; they must be interpreted. If we are to move beyond a recounting of the events to an interpretation of them, we need **theory**. Theories may be based on different levels of analysis and on different assumptions about the nature of international relations. The most common taxonomy in the field refers to three levels of analysis – international, domestic, and individual. On what level should analysis focus? In one sense, the answer is a given for the study of international relations. The forum is the international arena in which states are the core actors. Yet the state is not necessarily the appropriate level at which to focus analysis. The behaviour of states in the international arena may be best explained as the outcome of domestic political processes among groups or institutions within states, or by the behaviour of specific individuals within those groups or institutions.

One possibility for theory is to focus exclusively on the *international political system*. Such an approach presumes that domestic politics can be safely ignored in explaining state behaviour. For example, **realists** tend to focus on changes in the **balance of power** among states as a property of the system's **anarchic** structure. A second possibility for a theory of international relations is to treat the behaviour of states as the consequence of *domestic politics*, the behaviours of domestic interest groups or domestic political institutions. States are the nominal actors in the international system, but national behaviour is determined by the action and interaction of bureaucracies and legislatures, political parties, business and union lobbies, and other advocacy groups. Finally, the behaviour of states in international affairs can be treated as the consequence of the *actions and interactions of individuals*, such as heads of state. In this conception of international relations, national behaviour may reflect either the particular choices of powerful individuals or the collective consequences of numerous individual choices. In either case, however, understanding how states behave in international affairs requires attention to individual interests, habits of thought, or world views.

There is no consensus among scholars over the most appropriate level of analysis. This can be easily illustrated by a brief overview of debates about the causes of war. Some scholars argue that the underlying causes of **war** can be found in the structure of **power** and **alliances** in the international system or in the way that structure changes over time. Others trace the roots of war to political, economic, social, and psychological factors internal to the state. Some liberal theorists argue that liberal democratic states are inherently peaceful whereas authoritarian states are more warlike. Some radical scholars argue that war results from the tendencies of **capitalist** states to expand in search of external markets, investment opportunities, and raw materials. War has also been traced to attempts by political leaders to solve their internal political problems through the adoption of hostile foreign policies, on the assumption that external conflict will promote internal harmony. Some theorists argue that war results from **misperception**, the effects of stress on **crisis** decision-making, bureaucratic rigidities, and other flaws in the decision-making process which prevent the selection of those policies that are most likely to advance the **national interest**. Others insist that decisions for war are based on very careful cost–benefit calculations incorporating interests, constraints, and uncertainties.

There are good reasons to pay attention to the levels of analysis. They help to orient our questions and suggest the most appropriate type of evidence to explore. Despite the absence of a consensus in the field about the priority that should be given to different levels, and indeed whether or not they can be clearly distinguished from each other, the choice may vary depending on the particular issue under examination. For example, focusing on particular individuals to explain the course of events may be appropriate under some conditions. When political institutions are unstable, young, in crisis, or collapsed, leaders are able to provide powerful influences. George Washington and Vladimir Lenin had a great impact on international relations in part because they were leaders in the early years of the United States and the former Soviet Union. Adolf Hitler and Mikhail Gorbachev are important in part because their states were in economic crisis when they came to power. Beyond these pragmatic considerations, however, the so-called 'level-of-analysis problem' in the study of international relations remains a lively focus of theoretical debate and controversy.

*See also:* **anarchy; constructivism; democratic peace; misperception; theory; war**

*Further reading:* Evans *et al.*, 1993; Singer, 1969; Waltz, 1959; Wendt, 1987

## LIBERAL INTERNATIONALISM ✓

Although some realists condemned it as a form of **idealism** in the late 1930s and just after the Second World War, liberal internationalism became the focus of renewed attention at the end of the twentieth century. At least for a short time in the early 1990s, particularly after the Gulf War and the collapse of the Soviet Union as well as **communism**, it seemed to many that the dream of world **order** – most often associated with the statecraft of President Woodrow Wilson during and after the First World War – had a chance of being realised. Some of the optimism of that period has since disappeared, and it is becoming clear that liberal internationalism faces many theoretical and practical challenges.

Liberal internationalism is essentially a project to transform international relations so that they conform to models of peace, freedom, and prosperity allegedly enjoyed within constitutional liberal democracies such as the United States. Indeed, at least in terms of political rhetoric, the United States has been the leader in promoting liberal internationalism of one kind or another in the twentieth century.

Whilst such a project envisages a wide variety of ways to achieve its lofty goals, three stand out as particularly worthy of note. First, *commercial* liberalism promotes the idea of **free trade** and commerce across state borders on the assumption that economic **interdependence** among states will reduce incentives to use force and raise the cost of doing so. According to this variety of liberal internationalism, the territorial divisions between states need not cause conflict if territorial control becomes dissociated from political **power**. So in addition to providing economic benefits, free trade is seen as a means of uniting people and perhaps attenuating their political loyalties to the **nation–state**.

If commercial liberalism operates at a transnational level, what is often referred to as *republican* liberalism is directed at the relationship between states and their citizens. Republican liberalism endorses the spread of democracy among states so that governments will be accountable to their citizens and find it difficult to pursue policies that promote the sectional interests of economic and military elites. Over the past ten years there has been an extensive debate on the extent to which democracies are more peaceful than non–democratic states and the reasons behind the alleged link between the domestic character of states and their foreign policies.

Finally, what is called *regulatory* or *institutional* liberalism operates at the level of the international political structure. At this level liberal internationalism stands in contrast to the realist insistence that the structural **anarchy** of the international political system must always subordinate collective interests to **national interests**. Many liberal internationalists believe that it is possible to promote the rule of law and develop international institutions and practices that moderate the **security dilemma** among states.

It should be noted that liberal internationalism is fundamentally reformist rather than revolutionary. It seeks not to transform the basic structure of the states system, but rather to moderate those elements that realists have identified as the fundamental causes of **war**.

At the beginning of the twenty-first century, liberal internationalism faces many challenges, among which the following three are the most daunting.

First, it is clear that the three main types of liberal internationalism do not necessarily support one another; in fact they are often contradictory. For example, in an era of **globalisation**, how can states represent and be accountable to their citizens when they must adapt their macroeconomic policies to the constraints of global **capitalism**? Moreover, it remains unclear whether commercial liberalism promotes or impedes republican liberalism. For example, the pace of **democratisation** does not match the speed with which Russia has embraced capitalism. Indeed, one can think of numerous countries that have managed to embrace capitalism without democracy, China being the most outstanding example.

Second, not all liberal internationalist values can be enjoyed simultaneously. Peace, individual freedom, and the rule of law may coexist within some liberal democratic states, but the domestic analogy breaks down at the international level. This confronts liberal internationalists with some intractable dilemmas, not least of which is how to reform a world that contains a mixture of liberal and non-liberal states. Should the latter be accommodated or **coerced**? How should the United States deal with **human rights** abuses in China? Should it hope for gradual reform in China or link further trade to internal reform?

Third, there is a powerful tension between liberal **cosmopolitanism** and liberal internationalism. The former is based on the subordination of the state to the liberal value of individual autonomy and freedom. In theory, liberals have always viewed the state with suspicion. In contrast, liberal internationalism tends to take the state for granted. In so far as liberal internationalists promote the rule of law among states, this contradicts their ethical goal of promoting individual freedom. For example, liberal internationalists are often divided on the issue of **humanitarian intervention**. On the one hand, they are sympathetic to the idea that state **sovereignty** should not be absolute, and that a state's claim to represent its citizens is not legitimate if it systematically abuses their human rights. On the other hand, they are wary of sanctioning the use of military force by outside parties on behalf of individuals who are being oppressed by their own government. Humanitarian intervention undermines the rule of **international law**, and can provide opportunities for powerful states to advance their own national interests by invoking liberal ideals. Similarly, liberal internationalists are divided on the issue of **self-determination**. On the one hand, they are sympathetic to the idea of self-government. On the other hand, they are wary of endorsing a principle that in practice often subordinates the individual to the interests of the nation.

In response to these dilemmas, liberal internationalism either places its faith in the idea of historical progress to overcome the challenges confronting it, or it mutates in a more radical, cosmopolitan direction. The problem with the first stance is a tendency towards complacency, whilst the latter stance is vulnerable to realist accusations of idealism. In the end, however, being called an idealist may be a small price to pay for sticking to one's ethical principles!

*See also:* **appeasement; collective security; cosmopolitanism; democratic peace; democratisation; embedded liberalism; end of history; humanitarian intervention; idealism; interdependence; perpetual peace; realism; relative gains/absolute gains; security dilemma; self-determination**

*Further reading:* Burchill, 1996; Deudney and Ikenberry, 1999; Franceschet, 1999; Hoffmann, 1998; Matthew and Zacher, 1995

## LOOSE NUKES

Nuclear material that has been stolen from installations and military bases in the former Soviet Union and offered for sale on the black market. This material includes warheads, weapons components, and fissile material such as highly enriched uranium (HEU) and weapons-grade plutonium. The implications of 'loose nukes' are quite terrifying, particularly if they fell into the hands of **terrorist** organisations because this would automatically give them enormous political leverage. It would also be extremely difficult to predict when and where such devices might be used. Indeed, some analysts believe that loose nukes pose a very real danger to Western **security** and that much more needs to be done to deal with the problem than has been achieved thus far.

The theft of nuclear material is not a new problem, but it has become acute since the end of the **cold war** and the collapse of the former Soviet Union. There are at least five interrelated dimensions to the problem.

1    Since 1990, economic conditions in Russia have become extremely harsh. There has been a chronic shortage of basic commodities such as

food and clothing. Essential services such as water, electricity, and heating have been intermittent at best, and millions of workers have gone unpaid for months at a time. It is estimated that there are more than 100,000 individuals working in Russia's nuclear industry. In such a desperate environment, it is not difficult to understand why some individuals might turn to nuclear smuggling as a way of staying alive.

2    Criminal organisations within Russia have been lured by the opportunity of making large sums of money. There are well over 5,000 such organisations operating in Russia today. Moreover, because the nuclear industry is spread over hundreds of thousands of square kilometres, policing is a massive problem. Security is generally poor and the guards at sensitive installations are often not properly trained. Their low morale and depressed economic conditions make them prime targets for criminal gangs.

3    The ease with which nuclear materials can be smuggled out of Russia and the ex-Soviet republics whose borders are poorly guarded makes smuggling a relatively simple operation for well-organised groups.

4    The fracturing of the former Soviet Union into autonomous republics has meant that there is no central authority to oversee the security of many nuclear sites.

5    It should not be forgotten that such a trade exists because there is an international market for this material. **Rogue states** such as Iraq, terrorist groups, and criminal organisations in Europe, the Middle East, and elsewhere have often advertised their willingness to purchase high-grade fissile material and weapons components.

It is difficult to determine the extent of the problem. Most of the information is anecdotal and hard to verify. Officials within Russia's nuclear industry have consistently argued that a black market in nuclear materials does not exist. On the other hand, Western experts have suggested that such a market has been thriving since the early 1990s. A number of smugglers and intermediaries have been arrested in Germany, the Czech Republic, Turkey, and elsewhere in Europe. In 1994, half a kilogram of nuclear weapons-grade material was discovered at Munich Airport. In the same year, German police arrested a known criminal for possession of 5.6 grams of plutonium. These and other incidents certainly demonstrate that such a trade exists, but they do not tell us how pervasive it is. According to some estimates, there are more than 140 metric tons of plutonium and 1,000 metric tons of HEU stored at various sites across Russia. Even if a small portion of this material managed to fall into the wrong hands, it would represent a considerable danger to the international community.

There is no simple solution to the problem of loose nukes in the twenty-first century. If Russia is unwilling to admit that a problem exists, then it is difficult for countries in Europe and elsewhere to deal with the issue. A number of options have been put forward, however. The building of a stronger relationship with Russia, training specialists to police borders, and long-term management strategies for dealing with fissile material are some of the most obvious ones.

*See also:* **arms control; arms trade; nuclear proliferation; rogue state; terrorism**

*Further reading:* Allison, 1996; Cameron, 1999; Lee, 1998

## MANAGED TRADE

Managed trade is sometimes referred to as strategic trade policy. It became popular in the 1980s, particularly in the United States, from where there emerged a number of proposals to abandon the **multilateral** trading system and begin managing trade from Washington. A move towards managed trade – substituting government intervention and market–share goals for market forces and multilateral rules – would represent a change in policy for the United States, which since the end of the Second World War has been a leading advocate of liberalising international trade. The argument that the United States should adopt managed trade always involved Japan and frequently boiled down to no more than the following: Japan, which managed its trade, was doing very well economically, so managed trade must work. The advocates of managed trade tended to overlook Japan's high savings rate, long working week, low illiteracy rate, and relatively modest government spending. Since the prolonged recession in Japan throughout the 1990s, the dangers of moving further towards a managed trading system have receded somewhat, but they have not entirely disappeared.

The **theory** of managed trade suggests that if the government commits itself to subsidise its companies, foreign competitors can be driven out of international markets. Governments can ensure the longrun viability of domestic companies by subsidising the sunk costs of setting up large operations with spare capacity. Should the foreigners contest the market, domestic corporations would undercut their prices by increasing volume and achieving lower unit costs.

Another argument for managed trade is based on the assumption that there are key sectors of the economy that are supposed to have links with other sectors. Loss of key sectors is supposed to produce a ripple effect, as related sectors contract. Conversely, when key sectors are nurtured and permitted to grow, they allegedly create benefits throughout the economy, as related sectors grow. The decline of certain elements of the US electronics industry, especially televisions, VCRs, and semiconductors, is usually cited in support of the key sectors theory. Perhaps the best-known argument for the existence of key sectors comes from the deindustrialisation or 'manufacturing matters' school of thought. It is argued that the United States needs to maintain a strong manufacturing sector if it is going to develop a strong services sector. The problem with this argument is that productivity growth in US manufacturing was very high in the 1980s and 1990s and manufacturing's share of the US gross national product has remained roughly constant for several decades.

It remains arguable that Japan's economic success in the postwar era has been the result of managed trade and the influence of the Japanese Ministry of International Trade and Industry (MITI). Although some industries supported by MITI, such as semiconductors, have succeeded, other MITI projects have failed. For example, the aluminium-smelting industry, which MITI nurtured, has practically disappeared from Japan. In addition, some of Japan's greatest commercial successes are firms that entered new markets even though MITI tried to hold them back. Honda and Sony are good examples. It is therefore not clear whether Japan's economic growth occurred as a result of or in spite of MITI.

Opponents of managed trade argue that it is little more than an income-support programme for politically well-organised, protection-seeking interests. Not surprisingly, Japan is the object of most proposals for managed trade. Americans tend to associate bilateral trade deficits with unfair trade practices; however, in a multilateral trading system there is no reason for bilateral trade figures to balance out. Why should the US demand for imported automobiles exactly equal South Korea's demand for imported aircraft? Another widespread belief – typically manifested in rhetoric about level playing fields – is that the United States is experiencing bilateral trade deficits because its markets are open to foreign competition, whereas other countries' markets are closed to US competition. Opponents of managed trade believe that the US trade deficit is the result of macroeconomic conditions and policies, not unfair trade practices. The low US savings rate and its recent tendency to spend more than it earns have produced a large influx of capital, a correspondingly large trade deficit, and a number of bilateral trade deficits. Finally, opponents doubt that policymakers would be able to make the correct and sometimes tough decisions by acting on the basis of economic evidence, not politics. The large amount of information that governments would need before being able to operate managed trade makes chances of its success highly remote.

In short, managed trade is a sophisticated argument for protection. In theory, the government is led to subsidise large domestic corporations in pursuit of gaining large profits from its trading partners. One consequence of this subsidy competition is that the targeted markets are more likely to be closed to small and medium-sized economies. If the latter pursue an aggressive strategic trade policy, there is a distinct possibility of triggering reactions from their major trading partners. For trade dependent economies, ease of access to other markets is essential.

*See also:* **beggar-thy-neighbour policies; Bretton Woods; embedded liberalism; free trade; interdependence; mercantilism; multilateralism; newly industrialising countries; World Trade Organisation**

*Further reading:* Krugman, 1986; Prestowitz, 1988; Tyson, 1992

## MARXISM

Marxism is an ideology that derives from Karl Marx's (1818–83) critique of **capitalism**. Marx's theoretical approach is dialectical in nature, which is to say that it is based on the cognitive and material struggle to overcome the social contradictions of the accumulation of wealth. Here Marx reformulated George Friedrich Hegel's dialectic (*Aufhebung*) by demonstrating how alienation was rooted in the material conditions of the workers' lives. By this account, the appropriation of labour through private property became an essential condition of the workers' consciousness. Thus, for Marx, the purpose was not simply to interpret society, but, as he famously stated in the *German Ideology*, 'to change it'.

To this day, this motto remains one of the central ideas underlying historical materialism. According to Marx, historical materialism is a complex process referring to the multiple ways that social and economic relations have evolved through various modes of production (i.e. feudalism, capitalism, and socialism). Driving this evolutionary process was class conflict and the attendant opposition between ideas and social practices. In the context of capitalism, such conflict reflected the antagonisms between labour and capital, in which the bourgeoisie used its ownership of the means of production (property, capital, interest, and rent) to force the worker to work without due compensation. Marx referred to this social condition as surplus value. In *Capital*, for instance, Marx showed how surplus value was generated from the false exchange of the value of commodities and how the price of commodities failed to represent the actual value of labour power.

The wide acceptance of his systematic critique of capitalism, especially during the late part of the nineteenth century and early part of the twentieth century, would serve as the basis for a new socialist orthodoxy: an orthodox Marxism that was both reductionist and scientific. By the early 1920s, however, some Marxist thinkers would return to Hegel's holism or notion of totality, to challenge the reductionism of Marxism. Western Marxism, as the reformist movement would come to be known, highlighted the contributions of Georg Lukacs, Karl Korsch, and Antonio Gramsci. Most notably, Lukacs argued that orthodox Marxism had relied on the inert immediacy of facts to validate its laws and concepts. To rectify this problem, one had to relate these facts to a broader, more dynamic understanding of society as a whole. In the same vein, Gramsci contended that the dialectical interplay of culture and economics played an important role in the workers' revolutionary movement. In time, their ideas would have a profound influence on the writing of the Frankfurt School **theory** during the 1930s, which some have referred to as a second stage of Marxism.

Marxism of course would also play a key role in shaping the political landscape of the twentieth century. Vladimir Lenin's rise to power in 1917 marked, in many ways, the pinnacle of Marxist-Leninism. In interpreting Marxism, Lenin formulated his thesis of **imperialism** which treated imperialism as the final stage of capitalism. Under Lenin's thesis, there were four main tenets: (1) the most powerful **nation-states** had divided the world into areas of colonial or territorial possession; (2) financial or lending capital had led to the rapid overseas expansion or the monopolisation of overseas resources; (3) cheap labour was now sought overseas to generate greater profits; and (4) a world-wide revolution would result from the continuing global expansion of capitalism and colonialism.

Like Marx, however, Lenin underestimated the resilience of the state to accommodate the needs of the workers. Both Marx and Lenin, for instance, assumed that the state would wither under the pressure of the revolution, and that national differences would dissolve in the process. As history would reveal, though, the withering of national cultures and the state has not taken place. More importantly, the Soviet Union would become an oppressive, authoritarian state, one that resorted to capitalist measures (incentives) such as wage differentials to grow its state-controlled economy. Its demise in 1991 would nonetheless signify the emergence of one **superpower**, the United States, prompting debate as to whether Marxism was still relevant.

Whilst it is true that the fall of the Soviet Union diminished much of the prominence of Marxism, it has not eliminated Marxism as an important source of thinking in IR. Marxism, which has had a profound impact on international relations theory, particularly in the developing world with the works of Raul Prebish, Gunthur Franck, Fernando Cardoso, and Immanuel Wallerstein (**world–system theory**), continues to play an important role in defining the underlying issues of **feminism** and **critical theory** in IR. More recently, on a practical level, the rise of Hugo Chávez, the socialist populist leader of Venezuela, and other Latin American countries such as Brazil and Ecuador, illustrate the continued importance of Marxist concepts (social inequality and oppression) for opposing global capitalism and Western imperialism. What this should suggest is that as long as capitalism remains dominant, so too will Marxism remain an influential source of ideas for opposing the effects of global capitalism.

*See also:* **communism; dependency; digital divide; international political economy; world–system theory**

*Further reading:* Brown, 1992b; Kolakowski, 1978; Marx, 1976; Tucker, 1978; Wallerstein, 1979

## MERCANTILISM

Mercantilism is often seen as one of three approaches to the **theory** and practice of **international political economy**. The first is *laissez-faire* liberalism, which advocates **free trade** and minimal state intervention in both the domestic and the international economy. The second perspective seeks to understand the workings of the global **capitalist** system in order to demonstrate its inherently **exploitative** nature. There are different versions of this general approach, but all share a **Marxist** heritage. The best-known of these is **world–system theory**. The third perspective is mercantilism. Sometimes referred to as *economic nationalism*, it is the oldest of the three perspectives. It was the dominant economic philosophy of European states from the fifteenth century to the late seventeenth century. Since that time, it has gone through a number of manifestations and continues to be an important economic alternative to both liberalism and Marxism.

Essentially, mercantilism is an economic philosophy that believes that economic management should be part of the state's pursuit of its **national interests** defined in terms of wealth, power, and prestige. Francis Bacon, an early defender of this philosophy, wrote that there was a direct line 'from shipping to Indies, from Indies to treasure, and from treasure to greatness'. Consequently, mercantilists are not interested in improving the quality of life of humanity or fostering mutual cooperation among states in the international system. Their primary goal is the maximisation of **power** and they see economic activity as a vehicle for achieving this end.

In order to achieve 'greatness' through 'treasure', mercantilist states typically do two things. First, they orient their domestic economy so as to produce a favourable balance of trade. Their goal is to produce goods for export while at the same time keeping imports low. Second, they will gear their industries to producing value-added products from cheap imported raw material. Thus, mercantilist states tend to discourage agricultural production in favour of manufacturing, impose high import duties on foreign-made products, and offer subsidies to domestic industries. They are also notorious for pursuing **beggar-thy-neighbour** policies. Mercantilist states, then, are highly interventionist.

One should distinguish between *benign* or *defensive* mercantilism and *malevolent* and *aggressive* mercantilism. The former is designed to protect a state's core values and safeguard its autonomy in the face of the internationalisation of production. The other variant (popular in the 1930s) wages economic warfare against other states in order to triumph over them.

In theory if not in practice, mercantilism fell into disrepute towards the end of the eighteenth century. One reason for this was the publication of Adam Smith's *Wealth of Nations* (1776). This rightly famous liberal text set out explicitly to demonstrate that mercantilism was flawed. Among other criticisms of mercantilism, Smith suggested that it was inefficient for a state to produce a product that could be produced more cheaply elsewhere. Later this would become the basis for David Ricardo's theory of comparative advantage and the doctrine of free trade. It would be a mistake to think that mercantilism is dead and buried, however. Protectionist and neo-mercantilist policies continue to be a part of the economic thinking of some states.

*See also:* **free trade; international political economy; managed trade; world-system theory**

*Further reading:* Gilpin, 1987; Magnusson, 1995; Ricardo, 1996

## MERCENARY

Traditionally, the ultimate symbol of **sovereignty** is a state's ability to monopolise the means of violence; i.e. to raise, maintain, and use military forces. While there have always been exceptions, the evolution of the international system over the centuries has been such that military conflict has been conducted using state-raised forces.

However, in the post-**cold war** era, national military forces are waning; both numbers of personnel and sales of weapons have declined significantly. Yet although the total number of **wars** has dropped in recent years, in certain areas of the world fierce conflicts still continue.

In many countries, ruling authorities – or those seeking authority – try to impose **order** any way they can. Some have sought intervention by outside states. But the **great powers** are reluctant, seeing no vital interest to be served by sending their troops to other countries to try to quell an **ethnic** or **nationalist** conflict like Bosnia, or for a **humanitarian intervention** as in Somalia or Rwanda.

Some states have sought intervention by **United Nations peacekeeping** forces. Given the difficulties of gaining consent by warring factions and the reluctance of troop-contributing states to provide forces and funding, this is often not a realistic option. Thus it is not surprising that many governments are turning to the private sector in search of services traditionally provided by the public sector.

Specifically, the past few years have seen increased prominence given to the re-emergence of mercenary organisations working for profit. The modern twist, however, is that rather than being ragtag bands of adventurers, paramilitary forces, or individuals recruited clandestinely by governments to work in specific covert operations, modern mercenary firms are corporate. Instead of organising clandestinely, they now operate out of office suites, have public affairs staff and web sites, and offer marketing literature.

Traditionally, mercenaries have been defined as non-nationals hired to take direct part in armed conflicts. The primary motivation is monetary gain rather than loyalty to a **nation–state**. Although most notoriously associated with the colonial days of Africa, mercenaries have been used in virtually every corner of the globe. They have existed since war began. During the Middle Ages (1100–1500) mercenaries were frequently used. During this period many rulers hired trained professional soldiers to protect their fledgling states.

It is important to distinguish between four different types of mercenary. The first type comprises those traditional mercenaries whose primary motivations are profit or adventure. The second type comprises small military groups that work for a host government and provide **security** for a specific region. A third type can be identified as transnational ideological groups, those compelled by ideology or religion to train and fight in foreign areas. For example, some Islamic fundamentalists carry out what they believe to be God's will by travelling to aid struggling Islamic fighters in different countries, as was the case during the former Soviet Union's occupation of Afghanistan. Finally, the most recent development is the organisation of mercenaries into firms with internal structures similar to those of **multinational corporations**. Whereas paid soldiers of the previous three groups fall under the jurisdiction, at least in principle, of domestic or international customary law, employees of international business corporations answer only to the firm. The important distinction here is that such firms are bound by the terms of a business contract and not necessarily those of **international law**.

Perhaps the most successful and highly publicised mercenary firms are Executive Outcomes (based in South Africa) and Sandline International (London). They are both private sector firms that either offer military training and services or provide actual combatants for use in conflict.

Do mercenary firms have a positive or negative impact on international security and stability? Some **human rights** groups believe that, under current domestic and international law, mercenaries lack accountability. Hired soldiers are often flown into designated areas on private, company-owned helicopters and similarly airlifted out of a region once the operation is finished. Mercenaries conveniently bypass the legal customs procedures of passports and visas, preventing smaller states from keeping identifiable records of those who have entered or exited the country.

On the other hand, it could be asked if other states are not going to step in to contribute to **multilateral** peacekeeping or peacemaking forces, why shouldn't a government hire a private force able to keep order?

Often, mercenaries construct or impose an equilibrium in a region by eliminating or suppressing the opposition. Stopping the violence, however, does not necessarily solve the underlying problems that caused fighting to erupt in the first place. Based on the evidence to date, corporate mercenary firms are an inadequate means of long-term conflict resolution because they leave a region just as vulnerable to disruption and chaos as when they arrived. When firms leave, repressed or newly formed opposition groups revert to violence. Mercenary companies, in effect, become a temporary means of propping up the existing order but do nothing to address underlying causes of unrest and violence. While this may be a valid criticism of the long-term benefits of military intervention by a mercenary group, it is not a valid criticism of the specific group. After all, they are hired precisely for their military services. Instead of banning mercenaries entirely, supporters of the mercenary trade encourage similar regulatory standards as those for states that seek the services of private security firms.

It can be argued, at least with respect to some mercenary organisations, that their attempts to train national military forces cannot be any worse than what states already do. In fact, one might argue that it is the modern, state-centred form of military service which is the most destructive. It is the period since the French Revolution when military service came to be associated exclusively with **nationalism** that has encompassed the most destructive wars in history.

In the end, the future of conflict resolution rests on the actions of the international community. In 1989, the **United Nations** drafted the International Convention Against the Recruitment, Use, Financing, and Training of Mercenaries. The Convention needs ratification by 22 countries to enter into force. Australia recently became the twelfth state to sign. However, signatories such as Angola and Zaire, which hire mercenaries, show that the Convention alone will not end the use of private armed forces.

Given the historical longevity of mercenaries, it seems foolish to try to prohibit them. It has been suggested that to bring transparency to mercenary activities, an international register for such firms should be established. The model is the UN Register of Conventional Arms, which compiles declarations by both importers and exporters of conventional arms, thus permitting cross-checking. A similar register could be created for private military advisory firms which would contain declarations by the importers – the states or groups employing such firms – and the exporters – the firms themselves. If a firm withheld data on the grounds that it was proprietary, it could be released by the employer.

Lastly, in order to allay fears about human rights violations, and as a condition for operating outside the borders of the state in which they are headquartered, mercenary firms should be required to abide by the relevant human rights instruments, i.e. Geneva Protocols, rules of war, and customary international humanitarian law. Documented violations would be cause for penalties such as fines and suspension. If an employee of a firm was found guilty of committing crimes against humanity or war crimes, which have long been defined by international treaty, he or she could be tried before a court that would have the power to try individuals. Such a permanent international court may be established in the next few years. This would be especially important if such firms were employed by regional groups or even by the United Nations itself.

*See also:* **failed state; peacekeeping; war; war crime; wars of the third kind**

*Further reading:* Arnold, 1999; Fowler, 2000; Musah and Fayemi, 1999; Shearer, 1998

# MERCOSUR

For many decades, South American countries have remained dependent upon US imports and goods and services. In the 1960s and 1970s, import substitution policies or investment in the domestic manufacturing sector, which aimed to promote economic independence, became an important alternative to export-led growth. Despite some of the gains of import substitution, many South American countries continued to experience economic and political turmoil. In an effort to address these problems, Argentina and Brazil entered into what became known as the Argentine–Brazil Economic Integration Program (ABEIP). The aim of the agreement was twofold: to promote free trade between these countries; and to help facilitate the fledgling democratic regimes of these countries.

In 1990, presidents Carlos Menem of Argentina and Fernando Collor de Mello of Brazil agreed to press forward with more ambitious plans of economic integration in the Southern Cone of America. On 26 March 1991, Brazil, Argentina, Paraguay, and Uruguay (Chile declined to join the treaty) signed the Treaty of Asuncion, which established the Mercado Comun del Sur or Mercado Comun do Sul (Mercosur). The treaty not only represented the commitment of these countries towards economic integration; it also reflected the increasing **multilateral** trading among these countries, as well as the desire to compete and cooperate with other economic regional organisations, notably the North American Free Trade Agreement (NAFTA) and the European Community (now the **European Union**). The treaty also adopted a programme that would decrease the number of exempted imports from tariffs.

As a **regional trading bloc**, Mercosur consists of three stages of formation: (1) the establishment of a new open market area; (2) the adoption of a Customs Union (1995); and (3) the creation of a common market to rival the European Union. Its Customs Union, for instance, has helped to significantly reduce tariffs in these countries and to increase exports to EU countries and the United States. Institutionally, then, the founders of Mercosur adopted the following principal political instruments:

- internal liberalisation of trade;
- common external tariffs;
- the implementation of a Council of the Common Market Group;
- the establishment of 24 special protocols including capital goods and automobiles;
- the creation of a Council of the Common Market.

One of the weaknesses of Mercosur, however, is that its political institutional mechanisms remain inadequate to facilitate the full integration of its markets. Whereas the EU, for instance, consists of a Commission (Executive), Parliament, and Court of Justice, Mercosur is comprised of the Council of Heads of State. As such, Mercosur, while able to coordinate the financial policies, remains fairly limited with regards to promoting further political cohesion and economic integration. Although the emergence of new left of centre populist governments has significantly challenged the terms of free trade and Customs Union of Mercosur, it is not clear if opposition to US **hegemony**, especially the policies of non-Mercosur countries such as Venezuela and Ecuador, will limit the economic growth envisioned by Mercosur. Nonetheless, while Mercosur has yet to achieve the integrative framework of the EU, it has initiated some economic integration that has, to a large extent, promoted democratic rule in the Southern Cone countries.

*See also:* **European Union; international political economy; managed trade; NAFTA; regional trade blocs; regionalism**

*Further reading:* Manzetti, 1994; Preusse, 2001; Roett, 1999

# MISPERCEPTION

The body of literature on this concept is inspired by the work of psychologists who have studied the way in which individuals acquire information, organise that information into a set of coherent beliefs, and then adapt those beliefs as new information arrives and evidence changes. Our perceptions shape the way we understand and interpret our environment, and our subjective perceptions often differ from reality. We often see what we expect to see or what we want to see. This proposition has inspired a number of scholars to examine how perceptions and misperceptions affect foreign policy decisions. They have looked at the nature of misperception and its impact on particular areas of foreign policy (particularly nuclear **deterrence** strategy and during periods of **crisis**).

There are a number of ways in which political leaders and decision-makers often misperceive the conduct of others. Most attention has been paid to three main types of misperception.

First, it is common to misperceive the values that adversaries place on achieving their objectives. There are numerous examples in history of political leaders either underestimating or exaggerating the difficulty of deterring other states from particular policies. Examples of the former include the misperceptions of political leaders in Britain during the years of **appeasement** *vis-à-vis* Germany prior to the outbreak of the Second World War, and the misperceptions of successive American decision-makers during the Vietnam conflict. In the 1930s the British government underestimated the degree to which Hitler could be dissuaded from going to war, and in the 1960s the United States failed to realise the degree to which North Vietnam valued unification with the South. On the other hand, there is evidence to suggest that Western leaders exaggerated the difficulties of deterring President Milosevic from his attempts to create a Greater Serbia in the 1990s. One could also argue that Saddam Hussein would not have invaded Kuwait in 1990 had he correctly perceived the reaction by the international community.

A second common form of misperception arises from the widespread belief that other states have available alternatives to the policies they are implementing. This is a common misperception of the most powerful states in the international system. For example, the pressures felt by Japan in 1941 (when it attacked Pearl Harbor) and by China in 1951 (when it became directly involved in the Korean War) illustrate why some states feel they must act in ways that are likely to lead to war. Japan and China perceived the alternative to fighting not as maintaining the status quo but as permitting a drastic erosion of the positions they had established.

A third form of misperception is based on the assumption that one's own behaviour is more transparent and understandable to others than it really is. Many American policymakers during the **cold war** often expressed surprise when confronted with the idea that the Soviet Union could be legitimately worried about the size and composition of the US nuclear arsenal. They found it difficult to comprehend how the Soviet Union could fail to recognise the benign motivations of American nuclear strategy.

There are a number of reasons why misperception occurs. Some of these are based on well-known psychological factors; others are derived from inappropriate belief systems. Among the former are cognitive overconfidence, the common propensity to avoid cognitive dissonance, and what is called defensive avoidance.

Cognitive *overconfidence* refers to the ways in which we often exaggerate our understanding of our environment. Cognitive *dissonance* is the tendency to assimilate new information to our pre-existing beliefs rather than the other way round. Defensive *avoidance* refers to the common psychological tendency to refuse to perceive and understand extremely threatening stimuli. All these sources of misperception may be more influential during periods of extreme stress, and much of the relevant literature examines how they manifest themselves during particular crises in international relations.

*See also:* **crisis; deterrence; levels of analysis**

*Further reading:* Jervis, 1976; Jervis *et al.*, 1985; May, 1973; Stein, 1982; Zerubavel, 1993

# MODERNISATION THEORY

**Development** economics is one of the most unsettled fields of international relations. It is awash with a profusion of competing **theories** of the causes of underdevelopment and swarming with even more approaches to development policy. Modernisation theory is one such approach that was developed by some European and American social scientists to explain the process of transformation from traditional to modern societies. Traditional societies were defined as those characterised by small villages, subsistence agriculture, simple social structures, and particularistic forms of behaviour. Modern societies were defined as those characterised by cities and towns, commercial agriculture, industry, complex social structures, and universalistic forms of behaviour. Modernisation scholars believed that the transition to modernity, the condition of being modern, would recapitulate the European experience. It was supposed that the former colonies would undergo the same developmental processes that European states had experienced, and would end up looking much like them.

The best-known particular theory of economic modernisation was developed by American economist W. Rostow (1960). Rostow described five stages of growth which he then used to explain the major discontinuities of economic development as they affected the now-industrialised states. The strength of Rostow's theory is how deeply rooted it is in the *economic* history of the rich countries. The major weakness is the assumption that the poor countries are poor simply because they 'took off' later than the rich countries (or because they have yet to take off).

Rostow identifies a pre-industrial stage which he labels traditional society. The first step on the road to development is to meet the preconditions for take-off. This involves enough modernisation of agriculture to feed a growing population of non-farmers; some infrastructure in the form of roads, canals, or railroads; and the growing influence and **power** of a group willing and able to lead the country into industrialisation. Once the preconditions are met, the country is ready for take-off. Savings of 10–15 per cent of gross domestic product (GDP) will be regularly invested in one or more manufacturing industries. This is the point at which self-sustaining growth begins. The leading industry brings other industries along through both forward and backward linkages. For example, Swedish timber exports grew rapidly in the 1860s. This provided investment opportunities in the logging and sawmilling industries. Growth then occurred in the sawblade industry (a backward linkage) and the wood-products industries such as furniture (forward linkages). Note that some industries might not have sufficient linkages to propel an economy into take-off. Jamaica's bauxite exports go from the mines to the harbour without any linkages to the local economy other than the mining jobs.

The next stage broadens the economic base of the growing economy. Rostow switches his metaphor at this stage and calls it the drive to maturity. More forward and backward linkages occur. A cacao exporter starts to export chocolate bars and to manufacture the agricultural machinery used on the cacao plantations. Sweden's wood-product exports broaden to include matches while the use of hydroelectric power for remote sawmills is the first step in the development of an electrical industry. The final stage, the age of high mass consumption, starts when rising wages lead to the increased consumption of new consumer goods.

Modernisation theory suggests that development will proceed naturally once an economy has achieved the preconditions for take-off (or the preconditions for **capitalism** in the **Marxian** version). The development process could be accelerated by relatively small amounts of **foreign aid** targeted to countries on the verge of take-off. Rostow thought (in 1960) that US$4 billion (about US$25 billion in today's dollars) could push the entire underdeveloped world into take-off mode.

This way of understanding modernisation assumes that all states would, over time, pass through a single, universal process of state formation. Further, it assumes that the original European states had reached the end of the process. The end point towards which all non-European states were supposedly evolving, albeit at different rates, was the industrialised, **democratised**, urbanised, bureaucratised, and culturally cohesive **nation-states** of Europe. Such a view is, first of all, ahistorical; that is, it sees the creation of the state as a universal, inevitable process rather than as a result of historical conditions and actions. Second, such a view is ideological in two ways. First, it hides from view, and implicitly justifies, the often violent processes through which Europeans imposed the state in non-European areas. Second, it considers the state's positive features as a gift of a modern, rational European civilisation to the non-European world, and its negative features as the result of the inability of non-European peoples to live up to advanced European standards. Again, the result is to justify a European global **order** that either eliminates or co-opts non-European ways of life, transforming them so that they reinforce the global order.

*See also:* **dependency; development; foreign aid; historical sociology; imperialism; newly industrialising countries; world-system theory**

*Further reading:* Binder, 1971; Black, 1966; Huntington, 1968; Rostow, 1960; Tilly, 1990

# MULTILATERALISM

This term refers to three characteristics or principles underlying relations among states or groups of states and other actors in specific issue areas (particularly trade). The principles are non-discrimination, indivisibility, and diffuse reciprocity.

*Non-discrimination* means that states should carry out their treaty obligations without any contingencies or exceptions based on **alliances**, or on the idiosyncrasies of the circumstances at hand, or on the degree to which **national interests** are perceived to be at stake. The most often cited example of such non-discrimination is the obligation of states to extend Most Favoured Nation (MFN) status to all other states in the trading regime governed by the General Agreement on Tariffs and Trade (GATT) and its successor, the **World Trade Organisation** (WTO).

Next comes the principle of *indivisibility*. In the context of military cooperation, for example, states are required to meet their commitments to all other states in a **collective security** agreement. For multilateral **security** regimes, this refers to the requirement that peace be regarded as indivisible for and by each signatory to the collective security treaty.

Finally, the principle of *diffuse reciprocity* means that continuity in the application of the principles of non-discrimination and indivisibility is an essential ingredient of multilateral arrangements. Episodic, 'single-shot' instances of interstate cooperation within the context of otherwise individually competitive or hostile relations among states do not qualify as multilateral. Instead, joint participation has to take place over an extended period of time and so comes to be predicated upon, and the basis for, anticipations about the longer-run functioning of the collective agreement. In other words, states extend what is sometimes called 'the shadow of the future'. Iterated or repeated instances of cooperation in a multilateral setting can promote diffuse reciprocity among states and help to transform their sense of self-interest.

The end of the **cold war** and the growing **integration** of the world economy through unprecedented movements of capital, people, and information have sparked new interest in multilateralism as an organisational form in international relations and the global political economy. States, non-governmental actors, firms, and other transnational actors are responding to a panoply of new and old problems on the global agenda. In the economic and environmental spheres, for example, the existence of organisations such as the WTO and an array of transnational environmental networks all suggest that the shift towards market liberalisation and global integration will be attended by important forms of multilateral regulation, management, and political lobbying.

Multilateralism, then, is a particular way of bringing together international actors to support cooperation, incorporating principles of non-discrimination, diffuse reciprocity, and generalised institutional structures. Today, there is much debate over the prospects for multilateralism. First, although it is often argued that multilateral forms of cooperation provided the basis for the expansion of global trade in the second half of the twentieth century, today regional trade arrangements are proliferating. It remains to be seen to what extent **regionalism** and multilateralism undermine or reinforce each other. Second, multilateral cooperation is uneven across the world. For example, it is more common within and between North America and Western Europe than among states in the Asia-Pacific region. The lack of political multilateralism in the Asia-Pacific region is, in part, due to the fact that the United States did not introduce multilateral norms and institutions to the region in the immediate postwar era in the same way that it did in Europe.

*See also:* **beggar-thy-neighbour policies; Bretton Woods; cold war; embedded liberalism; managed trade; reciprocity; regime; regionalism; unilateralism; World Trade Organisationm**

*Further reading:* Gill, 1997; Ruggie, 1989; Schechter, 1998; Sewell, 2000; Wilkinson, 2000

## MULTINATIONAL CORPORATION (MNC)

Sometimes called multinational enterprises (MNEs) or transnational corporations (TNCs), these are powerful actors that carry out commercial activities for profit in more than one country. Increasingly, they view the world as a single economic entity and their impact on the global economy is immense. Indeed, there is almost no area of human life that is not influenced in some way by these giant firms. For example, the largest 500 corporations control more than two-thirds of world trade, much of which takes place between their own subsidiary firms. Moreover, the largest 100 corporations are estimated to account for about one-third of global **foreign direct investment** (FDI). Although there are more than 53,000 MNCs worldwide (and approximately 450,000 affiliate and subsidiary firms), most of the top 500 corporations have their headquarters in **OECD** member states.

The term 'multinational corporation' is misleading in a couple of ways. First, it implies a level of internationalisation of management and stock ownership that does not exist. Second, most MNC activity takes place within the territorial borders of the **sovereign** state and not between 'nations'. A more satisfactory designation would probably be 'global business enterprise'.

MNCs are not new. For example, the Hudson Bay Company and the British East India Company began operating during the first wave of colonial expansion over 300 years ago. Of course, the character of MNCs has changed dramatically since then. The Industrial Revolution, advances in technology and communications, and new management techniques have been particularly important. For example, in the early 1900s Henry Ford's new production-line methods enabled him to vastly increase the number of automobiles he could manufacture in a single year. By 1911, he had constructed an assembly plant in Europe and established Ford as a major player in the emerging worldwide automobile industry.

While multinational corporations have a long history, it was not until the **Bretton Woods** Conference (1944) laid the foundation for an international economic **order** based on the principles of **free trade** that they began to expand their commercial activities on a grand scale. This had a lot to do with the position of the United States in the post-1945 order, and especially the strength of the American dollar.

MNCs are, without doubt, the most controversial of all non-state actors. In the eyes of many critics they are predators, accused of toppling elected governments, **exploiting** underdeveloped countries, engaging in illegal activities, ignoring **human rights**, and wilfully damaging the environment. There is certainly ample evidence to support some of these accusations. During the 1970s, for example, ITT and Anaconda Copper (with the help of the CIA) were accused of overthrowing the democratically elected socialist government of Salvador Allende in order to retrieve their nationalised assets. Union Carbide's factory in Bhopal, India caused the death of nearly 4,000 people and injured almost half a million. Royal Dutch Shell was one of very few MNCs to remain in South Africa during the apartheid years, despite calls from the international community and some **non-governmental organisations** to abandon its commercial interests there. Moreover, the Ok Tedi mine in New Guinea, operated by BHP, has done significant environmental damage to the Fly River system and irretrievably altered the lives of the local inhabitants.

At the same time, defenders of multinational corporations portray them as engines of progress, innovative in research and development, a modernising force in international relations, and the best hope for overcoming the chronic underdevelopment and poverty in the **Third World**.

It is difficult to evaluate these positions. Much depends on the ideological predisposition of the critic. With the exception of the **newly industrialising countries** (NICs), there has been little discernible improvement in the living standards of people in the Third World. Indeed, there is evidence to suggest that global inequality is growing significantly. True, many MNCs operating in the Third World have set up hospitals, schools, and other valuable infrastructure. Some of them also provide employment, professional training, health care, and educational opportunities for their employees. But it is equally true that others impact heavily on the local culture, employ child labour, damage the environment, and often engage in corrupt practices. Nonetheless, there is some indication that multinational corporations are beginning to realise that they must act more responsibly in the communities in which they operate, and that it is in their own interest to do so. In so far as the search for new markets and consumers is becoming more important for multinational corporations than extracting resources, it is not in their interest to place their reputations at risk by engaging in practices that could besmirch their global image.

*See also:* **exploitation; foreign direct investment; free trade; globalisation; imperialism**

*Further reading:* Barnet and Cavanagh, 1994; Doremus *et al.*, 1998; Falk, 1999; Korten, 1995; Schwartz and Gibb, 1999; Stopford, 2000

## MUTUALLY ASSURED DESTRUCTION (MAD)

A relationship between two states in which each can destroy the other's society even after absorbing an all-out attack (or *first strike*) by the other state. In short, each state has an *invulnerable second-strike* capability. MAD is closely associated with the concept of **deterrence**. As explained elsewhere in this book, deterrence refers to the ability of a state to persuade its enemy not to attack because the enemy would then suffer unacceptable losses. But deterrence cannot succeed unless two conditions are present. First, the threat of retaliation has to be credible. Second, a state must have the capability to retaliate once it is attacked. The central question for policymakers during the **cold war** was how to ensure that these conditions were achieved.

Broadly speaking, there were two competing approaches. *Nuclear utilisation theory* (NUT) sought not only to use nuclear weapons to deter the former Soviet Union, but also to develop such weapons into a war-fighting instrument. According to defenders of NUT, a nuclear war could be limited to a specific theatre and not necessarily degenerate into a global nuclear war. They also suggested that it might be possible to win a such a war. The alternative to NUT, and the one that eventually came to dominate US nuclear thinking, was *mutually assured destruction* (MAD).

MAD evolved over a number of years, but its implementation is usually associated with Robert McNamara, John F. Kennedy's Secretary of Defence in the early 1960s. McNamara tried to determine what level of damage the United States would have to inflict on the Soviet Union to be sure that the latter would not contemplate a first, or pre-emptive, strike against the United States and its allies in Western Europe. He believed that the US would need as few as 400 nuclear weapons to destroy one-third of the Soviet population and over two-thirds of its industrial infrastructure. Out of these calculations, McNamara developed the doctrine of 'assured destruction'. MAD is an extension of this logic and can be defined as a condition where it is not possible to attack another state without being devastated in return. The necessity for an invulnerable second-strike capability explains why submarines were so important to the US defence system during the cold war. They were extremely difficult to destroy in an opening attack and since each submarine could carry 20 or more nuclear missiles, they provided an invulnerable second-strike capability. With such a capability, the Soviets would know that even if they launched a successful first strike against land-based nuclear weapons, they would suffer unacceptable levels of damage from other sources. The value of MAD, then, is that it delivers a stalemate. During the cold war the **superpowers** were often compared to two scorpions in a bottle.

Debates about the stability of MAD have been going on since the 1960s. Some writers argue that MAD is exceedingly dangerous and fails to take the arms race into account, especially the development of new weapons technologies. This argument was first made in the early 1980s when the Reagan administration began to talk about developing an anti-ballistic missile system (ABM). A system such as the 'star wars' programme could conceivably protect its possessor against retaliation, making it possible to start and 'win' a nuclear war. In the last few years this debate has intensified, with Russia and China voicing their anger over US attempts to build an effective missile shield directed against nuclear **rogue states**. The second debate has been whether or not MAD actually kept the cold war from turning into a hot war. John Mueller, for example, argues that the existence of nuclear weapons had little to do with the lack of open warfare between the superpowers. Among other things, the memory of the carnage of two conventional world wars was enough to ensure that policymakers in the United States and the Soviet Union worked tirelessly to keep the cold war from exploding into a hot war.

There is no doubt that the end of the cold war has altered nuclear thinking dramatically. With a reduction in the number of nuclear weapons, the signing of a range of treaties, and the new spirit of cooperation between the **great powers**, the primary concern for policymakers today is that **weapons of mass destruction** may fall into the hands of **terrorists** and rogue states. In this context, traditional theories of deterrence are no longer applicable in quite the same way as they were at the height of the cold war.

See also: **arms control; cold war; deterrence; nuclear proliferation; weapons of mass destruction**

Further reading: Cimbala, 1998; Freedman, 1981; Mueller, 1996; Paul et al., 1998

## NATION-STATE

Nations and states may seem identical, but they are not. States govern people in a territory with boundaries. They have laws, taxes, officials, currencies, postal services, police, and (usually) armies. They wage **war**, negotiate treaties, put people in prison, and regulate life in thousands of ways. They claim **sovereignty** within their territory. By contrast, nations are groups of people claiming common bonds like language, culture, and historical identity. Some groups claiming to be nations have a state of their own, like the French, Dutch, Egyptians, and Japanese. Others want a state but do not have one: Tibetans, Chechnyans, and Palestinians, for example. Others do not want statehood but claim and enjoy some autonomy. The Karen claim to be a nation trapped within the state of Burma/Myanmar. The Sioux are a nation within the boundaries of the United States. Each of these nations has its own special territory, rights, laws, and culture, but not statehood. Some imagined nations are larger than states or cross state boundaries. The Arab nation embraces more than a dozen states, while the nation of the Kurds takes in large areas of four states.

Some people assume that states are fixed and permanently established across most of the globe. But in fact states are in flux. State boundaries are often changed – by war, negotiation, arbitration, or even by the sale of territory for money (Russia sold Alaska to the United States, for example). A few states have endured, but others may be here today and gone tomorrow. In recent years, a number of states have disappeared – Czechoslovakia, East Germany, North and South Yemen, and of course the Union of Soviet Socialist Republics.

Diplomatic **recognition** confers legitimacy on a new state (or on the government of a state) but sometimes there is a lack of consensus within the international community. For example, the Palestinian people are largely under the jurisdiction of other states, although they are seen by the majority of the international community as having strong claims to independent statehood. Other nations claiming the right to independent statehood fail to win backing and are dismissed as frivolous or illegitimate (such as Kosovo). When the **United Nations** was founded, it was composed of just 51 member states. Today there are 192. The great majority of today's members were then either colonies (as in most of

213

Africa) or parts of other states (such as those that emerged after the collapse of the Soviet Union).

The classical nation-states in Northern and Western Europe evolved within the boundaries of existing territorial states. They were part of the European state system that took on a recognisable shape with the **Peace of Westphalia** in 1648. By contrast, the 'belated' nations – beginning with Italy and Germany – followed a different course, one that was also typical for the formation of nation-states in Central and Eastern Europe; here the formation of the state followed the trail blazed by an anticipatory national consciousness. The difference between these two paths (from state to nation *versus* from nation to state) is reflected in the backgrounds of the actors who formed the vanguard of nation and state builders. In the former case, they were lawyers, diplomats, and military officers who belonged to the king's administrative staff and together constructed a state bureaucracy. In the latter case, it was writers, historians, scholars, and intellectuals who laid the groundwork for the subsequent **diplomatic** and military unification of the state. After the Second World War, a third generation of very different nation-states emerged from the process of **decolonisation**, primarily in Africa and Asia. Often these states, which were founded within the frontiers established by the former colonial **regimes**, acquired sovereignty before the imported forms of state organisation could take root in a national identity that transcended tribal differences. In these cases, artificial states had first to be filled by a process of nation-building. Finally, with the collapse of the Soviet Empire, the trend towards the formation of independent nation-states in Eastern and Southern Europe has followed the path of more or less violent **secessions**. In the socially and economically precarious situation in which these countries found themselves, the old ethnonational slogans had the power to mobilise distraught populations for independence.

The nation-state at one time represented a response to the historical challenge of finding a functional equivalent for the early modern form of social **integration** that was in the process of disintegrating. Today we are confronting an analogous challenge. The **globalisation** of commerce and communication, of economic production and finance, of the spread of technology and weapons, and above all of ecological and military risks, poses problems that can no longer be solved within the framework of nation-states or by the traditional method of agreements between sovereign states. If current trends continue, the progressive undermining of national sovereignty may necessitate the founding and expansion of political institutions on the supranational level.

Some observers believe that the role of the nation-state has been reduced to that of a municipality within the global capitalist system, responsible for providing the necessary infrastructure and services to attract capital investment. However, this is much too simplistic. Societies also demand identity, and the nation-state has sometimes been successful in providing this where other identities have been weak. It can therefore play an important part in expressing to the outside world a unique identity associated with a particular locality. The nation-state is less successful in those situations where the population is fragmented between several large groups who do not wish to surrender portions of their different identities in order to produce a national identity. Malaysia, Indonesia, and Yugoslavia are just a few particularly good contemporary examples. In these cases, the national ideology for various reasons fails to assimilate large sections of the population, causing an ongoing crisis of belief within the society that is generally responded to with the use of (sometimes violent) **coercion** by the apparatus of the state and by the dominant group.

The cultural effects of accelerating globalisation have brought with them disintegrating factors that tend towards the atomisation of societies, and towards the breakdown of older social, political, and cultural units, including that of the nuclear family unit. This tendency is most pronounced in the economically advanced nation-states of the West, and has tended to reduce the authority, importance, and relevance of the nation-state as an institution.

Alongside this atomisation within societies, especially Western societies, has come a seemingly contradictory tendency towards **regionalism**. The surrender of many of the economic functions of nation-states to regional entities has been a feature of this latest round of globalisation. Perhaps more significant has been the growth of global cities and their increasing independence from the nation-state to which they ostensibly belong. New York, London, and Tokyo have been identified as being global cities of the first order, whilst Los Angeles, Frankfurt, Zurich, Paris, Sydney, and Singapore, among a dozen or so others, can be considered second-order global cities. The relationship of these global cities to national governments is changing, especially in critical areas such as monetary policy, interest rates, commercial treaties, and immigration.

The development of global cities has been accompanied by the growth of territory that has become peripheral from the major social and economic processes, and which cuts across the boundaries of rich and poor countries. Whilst including much of what was known as the **Third World** and the countries of the former **communist** bloc, this peripheral economic wilderness now includes large regions within the developed countries themselves.

However, it should be remembered that controlling population movements has become a key function of the modern nation-state, and keeping the poor immobile has become a principal concern, especially for those wealthy regions of the world that do not want their cities 'flooded' with people – usually unskilled – for whom their economy has no useful purpose.

In the next century we may witness the further decay of the nation-state as the all-powerful and sole centre of power, and with that we will see the further growth of non-state organisations, and the concentration of actual power within the global cities. Some of these organisations stand above the state – for example, the **European Union**. Others are of a completely different kind, such as international bodies and **multinational corporations**. What they all have in common is that they either assume some of the functions of the nation-state or manage to escape its control. Being either much larger than states or without geographical borders, they are better positioned to take advantage of recent developments in transportation and communications. The result is that their power seems to be growing while that of the nation-state declines.

*See also:* **capitalism; European Union; failed state; globalisation; historical sociology; imagined community; nationalism; non-governmental organisations; Peace of Westphalia; regionalism; secession**

*Further reading:* Barkin and Cronin, 1994; Van Creveld, 1999; Jackson and James, 1993

## NATIONAL INTEREST  ✓

Of all the concepts covered in this book, this one is the most vague and therefore easily used and abused, particularly by politicians. To claim that a particular foreign policy is in the national interest imparts a degree of authority and legitimacy to that policy. Although the concept attracted a great deal of scholarly attention soon after the Second World War, particularly in the United States, this is no longer the case today.

Still, this is not a concept we can just dismiss as mere rhetoric. Without an accepted notion of the national interest, those who are called upon to evaluate their leaders' performance have no helpful criteria by which to do so. The concept is usually used in two related ways. On the one hand, the word *interest* implies a need that has, by some standard of justification, attained the status of an acceptable claim on behalf of the state. On the other hand, the national interest is also used to describe and support particular policies. The problem is how to determine the criteria that can establish a correspondence between the national interest expressed as a principle and the sorts of policies by which it is advanced.

In formal terms, one can identify two attributes of such policies. The first is one of *inclusiveness*, according to which the policies should concern the country as a whole, or at least a sufficiently substantial subset of its membership to transcend the specific interests of particular groups. In contrast, the second attribute is one of *exclusiveness*. The national interest does not necessarily include the interests of groups outside the state, although it may do so. Given these attributes, what criteria link the concept to specific policies? Those who tackle this question do so in one of three ways.

First, one may simply equate the national interest with the policies of those officially responsible for the conduct of foreign policy. The national interest is what decision-makers at the highest levels of government say it is. They are the best judges of various policy trade-offs, therefore the national interest is something to be dispassionately defined and defended by those who possess the appropriate expertise and authority to speak for the whole country. The difficulty with this elitist approach is that it does not help in distinguishing a good foreign policy from a bad one. For according to this argument, as long as the government pursues what it deems to be general societal objectives and does so for long enough, it can never act contrary to the national interest.

A second approach, closely identified with the **realist** school of thought, conceives of the national interest in terms of some basic assumptions about the nature of international relations and the motivations of states. These include the idea that **anarchy** makes **security** the paramount foreign policy concern of states. Security, in turn, requires the acquisition and rational management of **power** (which can never be wholly divorced from military force), and only policies conducted in this spirit can serve the national interest. Of course, this approach depends on the truth of the underlying assumptions. At the risk of oversimplifying a very complex debate, there are at least two problems with this approach. First, it often suffers from the resort to tautology in that interest is often defined in terms of power, and power in terms of interest. It is not very helpful to say that nations must seek power *because* they seek power! Second, there is an important tension between free will and determinism in the realist approach. For if international relations are indeed determined by a struggle for power, it should not be necessary to exhort leaders to abide by the national interest as defined by realists. If it is necessary to do so, the alleged constraints of anarchy cannot be invoked as the basis for identifying the national interest.

In complete contrast, a third approach to the national interest suggests that the rules for its identification are given by tenets of the political process that have an independent normative value – those of democratic procedure. In other words, the national interest can best be identified when it resolves itself into a verifiable expression of the nation's preferences. On the assumption that a nation's interests cannot be more accurately expressed by some external observer than by the standards of the nation itself, this approach undermines both elitist and realist views. In the absence of democratically aggregated and expressed judgements on the matter, the link between foreign policy and the national interest cannot be known. This does not mean that non-democratic countries lack a national interest – merely that we cannot know what it is if it is not defined by democratic procedures.

*See also:* **security; power; realism**

*Further reading:* Chafetz *et al.*, 1999; Finnemore, 1996; Krasner, 1978; Trubowitz, 1998

## NATIONALISM

Despite the importance of nationalism, there is a lack of consensus about what it is and why it has maintained such a firm hold over so much of the world's population. Any examination of nationalism must be preceded by some kind of definition of what constitutes a nation. This question is complicated by the manner in which people often use the terms nation, state, and country interchangeably. The last two terms refer to political entities. The first is a term used to describe a group of people who may or may not live in the same state or country. The difference is conveyed in the German by the words *Staatsangehörigheit* (citizenship) and *Nationalität* (nationality). A person can be of German *Nationalität* without being a German citizen.

Definitions of nation or nationality rely either upon objective or subjective criteria, or on some combination of the two. Most objective definitions of nationality rely on the commonality of some particular trait among members of a group. Shared language, religion, **ethnicity** (common descent), and culture have all been used as criteria for defining nations. A casual examination of the history of national differentiation indicates that these factors often reinforce each other in the determination of a nationality. Certain nationalities, such as the Croats, are now defined as distinct from Serbs almost exclusively on the basis of religious differences. Likewise, Urdu-speaking Pakistanis are distinguished from Hindi-speaking Indians largely because of religion.

In other cases, however, a shared religion seems a less accurate method for drawing the boundaries of a nationality. The German nation, for example, is divided mainly among Protestants and Catholics. Conversely, the inhabitants of France and Italy, though both overwhelmingly Catholic, belong to two different nationalities.

One of the most frequently used of all the objective marks of nationality is a common language. Indeed, a shared language has been a very powerful factor in national unification. Yet this definition, too, is fraught with difficulties. For one thing, what we today call national languages are, to one degree or another, artificial constructs. This is certainly true in the case of many of the languages of east-central Europe and of the non-European world. For example, the Serb philologist Vuk Karadzic modelled modern Serbo-Croatian out of the so-called Stokavian dialect in the early nineteenth century; this was part of a self-conscious attempt at uniting the Southern Slavs (Yugoslavs) into one nation.

Other national languages have been created for **imperial** purposes. The various languages of central Asia (e.g. Uzbek, Kyrgyz, and Khazak) did not exist until they were conjured out of local dialects by Soviet linguists during the 1920s. The languages were then used as evidence to support Soviet claims of the existence of several nations in Central Asia, which was then divided into separate Soviet Socialist Republics as part of a divide-and-rule strategy.

Even in cases where a popular vernacular becomes a national language, this transformation typically happens after the foundation of a **nation-state**. For example, French became a national language only after the creation of a French nation-state. In 1789, only about half of the population in the Kingdom of France spoke French. To the nationalist Revolutionaries, making French the common language of the nation was of the utmost importance. The same could be said of German, Italian, Hungarian, and other modern European languages. A common vernacular language of administration, state education, and military command was an important tool in the extension of the modern state's bureaucratic control. Thus, national languages are largely the creation of modern nation-states, not the other way around.

It seems, therefore, that pre-existing common linguistic or religious attributes may not be absolute indicators of a nation. Ethnicity or common descent are other possible criteria for national boundary drawing. These were especially popular during the late nineteenth and early twentieth centuries and blended with that era's fascination with racial pseudo-science. To the modern student, however, ethnicity seems a much less compelling criterion. The people of the various Mediterranean nations, for example, are plainly the product of centuries of inter-ethnic marriages. Likewise, the American, Mexican, or British nations are made up of people of many different ethnic backgrounds.

Hence, while objective traits can be useful as very rough criteria for defining the existence of a nation, they are not enough. Indeed, a nation may be a very subjective entity. Many students of nationalism are eventually led to the (almost tautological) conclusion that people belong to a certain nation if they *feel* that they belong to it.

As an ideology, nationalism is the claim that people belonging to a particular group called a nation should inhabit a particular area and control a state of their own. Such a definition points to nationalism as a method of drawing boundaries among people. Whether nationalism is viewed as an ideology or a state of mind, one can still ask, why did so many people abandon earlier, universalist ideologies (e.g. Christianity) and non-national self-identifications (e.g. occupation or social status)?

Some trace the roots of nationalism to the Reformation. The Reformation itself was important in the development of proto-nationalist feeling, especially when considered in light of the revolution in printing and the subsequent surge in publications in various vernaculars (as opposed to the universalist Latin), which weakened the church hierarchy as interpreters of the Bible and laid the groundwork for the establishment of the nation. While the print revolution may have sown the seeds of national self-consciousness, most people continued to identify themselves by their religious affiliation rather than their nationality.

Most students of nationalism draw a causal link between the changes underway in Europe during the end of the eighteenth century and the development of nationalism during that same period. As people left their villages and farms for the growing cities, they also left behind many of their previous attachments and were receptive to new ones. The great social and economic changes underway during the late eighteenth century were accompanied by change in political thought, as liberalism began to compete effectively against the ideas of the divine right of kings and absolutism. The American War of Independence, for example, was both a manifestation of the idea of national **self-determination** and an assertion of radical liberal principles. The American nationality was defined by the belief in a set of liberal propositions which, the Americans believed, applied not only to themselves but also to all humankind. Similarly, English nationalism as it developed during the eighteenth and nineteenth centuries maintained its roots in the idea of individual liberty.

The growth of the centralised state as well as the fascination with vernacular languages fostered the growth of nationalism. The modern state needed to promote a common language among its subjects. Public (i.e. state-run) schools emerged at precisely the time when nationalism was growing. The state used its schools to teach a common national (i.e. enforced) language, partly to reinforce a sense of loyalty to the state, but also to facilitate state functions, such as tax collection and military conscription. The extraction of revenues from the population and the formation of vast military organisations for territorial aggrandisement drove the evolution of the modern state system in Europe. The subsequent emergence of nationalist ideology is closely connected to this process. As direct rule expanded throughout Europe, the welfare, culture, and daily routines of ordinary Europeans came to depend on which state they happened to reside in. Internally, states undertook to impose national languages, national educational systems, national military service, and much more. Externally, they began to control movement across frontiers, to use tariffs and customs as instruments of economic policy, and to treat foreigners as distinctive kinds of people deserving limited rights and close surveillance. As a result, two mutually reinforcing forms of nationalism emerged: one refers to the mobilisation of populations that do not have their own state around a claim to political independence; the other to the mobilisation of the population of an existing state around a strong identification with that state. Besides these aspects of the growth of the modern state, it is no accident that the participation of the masses in politics coincided with the age of nationalism. As politics became more democratic and monarchs lost the last vestiges of their previous **legitimacy**, rulers needed something new upon which to base their **power**.

Both liberalism and nationalism shared a healthy loathing of dynastic absolutism and of the censorship and oppression that it brought, linking their fates closely together through the eighteenth and early nineteenth centuries. The Revolutionary and Napoleonic Wars, however, succeeded in destroying many aspects of individualism and liberalism that had existed in nationalism. Beginning in the mid-nineteenth century, the history of nationalism on the continent of Europe would be dominated by increasingly anti-liberal, or anti-individualistic, themes. The emerging nations of Europe became acquainted with nationalism not as a vehicle of individual liberty but as an adoration of collective power.

In much of Western Europe the geographic boundaries of the nation-state had preceded the building of the nation itself. For example, there was a Kingdom of France before there was a French nation. In Central and Eastern Europe the situation was completely reversed. In these areas nations were born before nation-states. Much of east–central Europe was controlled by four great multinational empires, namely the German, Russian, Habsburg, and Ottoman. Many of the people who inhabited these empires had no historical state with which they might identify. For the peoples living in Central and Eastern Europe, the liberal aspirations of nationalism were submerged while the goal of building a nation-state became paramount. The development of nationalism in Asia, and later in

Africa, was greatly influenced by the growing role of European powers in those areas. It is, in fact, in Asia and Africa where nationalism developed last and where many of its worst manifestations are today in evidence.

The role of nationalism in international relations is ambiguous. On the one hand, nationalism provides a justification for dividing humanity on the basis of territory. On the other hand, since many territorial boundaries were determined prior to the rise of nationalism (particularly in Asia, the Middle East, and Africa), the principle of national self-determination is deeply subversive of contemporary **international law** based on state **sovereignty**. There are no signs that this paradox is about to come to an end in the foreseeable future.

*See also:* **communitarianism; cosmopolitanism; diaspora; ethnicity; imagined community; irredentism; nation-state; secession; self-determination; sovereignty**

*Further reading:* Gellner, 1983; Greenfeld, 1992; Hobsbawm, 1991; Mayall, 1989; A. Smith, 1995

## NEWLY INDUSTRIALISING COUNTRIES (NICS)

A group of countries in East Asia that has achieved remarkably high rates of growth over the past 40 years. Often referred to as the 'Asian tigers' or the 'four dragons', Hong Kong, Singapore, South Korea, and Taiwan have demonstrated that it is possible for some former **Third World** economies to develop into economic and industrial giants. There is some debate about which other countries potentially belong in this category, but candidates include Brunei, China, India, Malaysia, the Philippines, and Thailand in Asia, and Mexico and Brazil in Latin America.

From the early 1970s until the Asian financial **crisis** in 1997, the 'Asian tigers' consistently made the list of the top 17 trading states. By the late 1990s, they controlled about 15 per cent of world trade in manufactured goods and had become leading investors of capital in the region and elsewhere. Moreover, Hong Kong and Singapore are now the largest container ports in the world. Hong Kong is one of the largest foreign investors in the world and Taiwan has become a world leader in micro-electronic research and development.

These are remarkable statistics and it is not surprising that prior to the Asian financial crisis of 1997–8, intergovernmental organisations such as the **International Monetary Fund** (IMF) and the **World Bank** promoted the Asian NICs as a **development** model for other Third World countries.

The reason for the success of the Asian NICs is hotly debated. Some writers have pointed to the long-term impact of the Korean and the

Vietnam Wars. It has been suggested, for example, that the US$8 billion in American aid to the region between 1953 and 1969 played a crucial role in the development of these four economies. They also enjoyed a privileged access to markets in Japan and the United States where there existed a high demand for low-cost consumer goods. Others have looked at the economic strategies employed by national governments.

Generally speaking, two strategies have been promoted. The first, known as *import-substitution industrialisation* (ISI), tries to persuade local industries and subsidiaries of **multinational corporations** to set up and manufacture for domestic consumption. High tariffs are put in place to protect these industries during their infancy. The other approach involves *export-oriented* development. This strategy targets a range of industries that governments believe can successfully compete in the world marketplace. These industries are given subsidies and preferential treatment by governments. For the Asian NICs, their lack of raw materials made it difficult to pursue a policy of ISI. Other factors have also played their part, including high rates of saving, close corporate relationships between government and business, a commitment to education, strong authoritarian governments, and the strict control of labour unions. Perhaps the most common explanation during the 1980s was that the tigers were carried along in the slipstream of the Japanese economic miracle. It is also not insignificant that both South Korea and Taiwan were once colonies of Japan. However, the flagging Japanese economy and its reduction in overseas investment during the early 1990s failed to impact on the tiger economies. Moreover, the NICs themselves became powerful capital investors during this period. **Foreign direct investment** (FDI) by Hong Kong, for example, has outstripped that of Japan for almost a decade. This suggests that no single explanation is likely to suffice.

The rise of the NICs has challenged the **dependency** model of Third World underdevelopment, which assumes an intimate relationship between the core and the periphery. The Third World provides the core with raw materials and other primary products at low prices, while the core sells capital, technology, and value-added goods back to the periphery at much higher prices, repatriating the profits and interest payments to the core. The result is the permanent impoverishment of the Third World. Yet the Asian NICs have shown that it is possible to break free of this relationship. South Korea, for example, is now a member of the **Organisation for Economic Cooperation and Development** (OECD). What this suggests is that it is no longer possible to treat the Third World as a single entity with a common bond in a subservient relationship to the countries of the core. The transition of the Asian NICs to the status of first world economies requires far more nuanced **theoretical** treatments than the dependency model is capable of generating.

*See also:* **dependency; development; free trade; regionalism; Third World**

*Further reading:* Garran, 1998; Haggard, 1990; Milner, 1998; Vogel, 1991

## NON-GOVERNMENTAL ORGANISATION (NGO) ✓

One of the most prominent features of contemporary international relations is the growth in the number of non-governmental organisations (NGOs). Increased interconnectedness, partly associated with improvements in communications technology and transport, has given rise to literally thousands of specialised organisations, agencies, and groups. They are made up of private individuals, both paid and unpaid, and are committed to a vast range of issues, including protection of the environment, improving the level of basic needs in the **Third World**, stopping **human rights** abuses, delivering food and medicine to warzones, advancing religious beliefs, and promoting the cause of women (see **women in development**). What stands out about these organisations is that they establish intricate networks and links between individuals across the globe.

Conventional wisdom is that these entities are peripheral to the study of international relations. It is hard to accept this view, however. Many NGOs are a force to be reckoned with. They have huge memberships, budgets, and the **power** to influence and shape government policy. Treating them as a marginal feature of international relations undermines the possibility of fully understanding their impact.

Despite being a key concept in the lexicon of international relations, there is little scholarly agreement concerning the criteria for determining which organisations should be classed as NGOs and which should not. For some writers, any transnational organisation that has not been established by a state is an NGO. Humanitarian and aid organisations, human rights groups, lobby groups, environmentalists, professional associations, new social movements, **multinational corporations**, **terrorist** and criminal organisations, and ethnic and religious groups all qualify as NGOs on this account. Others use the term to refer to a much narrower range of organisations. An NGO is any transnational actor that is not motivated by profit, does not advocate violence, accepts the principle of non-interference in the domestic affairs of states, and works closely with the **United Nations** and its agencies. Here, the term is limited mainly to humanitarian organisations. Thus it is a notoriously imprecise concept.

One way of making sense of this terminological imprecision is to distinguish between the motives of different NGOs, particularly those that have universalist and non-partisan aspirations, and those that are motivated primarily by self-interest. The Red Cross, Amnesty International, the Salvation Army, OXFAM, Care, Greenpeace, and *Médecins sans Frontières* fit into the former category. Their broad goal is the betterment of humanity as a whole. Multinational corporations and many private organisations fit into the latter group.

A great deal has been written about the impact of NGOs on international relations. Three points are worth noting in this regard. First, while NGOs are autonomous actors, many work closely with intergovernmental organisations (IGOs) that have been formed by states to advance their interests. The United Nations is the most notable IGO. The **International Monetary Fund** (IMF), the **Organisation of Petroleum Exporting Countries** (OPEC), the **European Union** (EU), and the **North Atlantic Treaty Organisation** (NATO) are also important examples. In each of these cases, the members are states, not private individuals.

The policy networks between IGOs and NGOs are particularly strong in the areas of human rights and **development**. Many NGOs have expertise in the provision and delivery of aid and humanitarian relief and the collection and analysis of data, while the IGOs can finance NGO activities. For example, almost half of *Médecins sans Frontières*'s budget comes from national governments. Moreover, NGOs are often politically neutral and this means that they can move into warzones, liaise with the warring factions, and provide help to the civilian population. This is something that states cannot easily accomplish without violating the principle of non-intervention. All this makes NGOs very useful to states. Indeed, IGOs are increasingly taking advantage of the unique position of NGOs. It is worth noting, for example, that between 1990 and 1994 the proportion of European **foreign aid** dispersed through NGOs increased from 42 per cent to 67 per cent.

At the same time, some NGOs exert significant influence over other NGOs. Oil companies such as Shell and Exxon, for example, have to deal with Greenpeace activists. Similarly, the anti-smoking lobby around the world has gone a long way to bring the tobacco companies to account for their marketing practices. NGOs do this by lobbying politicians, exposing bad practices through the media, and organising mass rallies.

Second, some scholars argue that NGOs have become such a significant part of the international landscape that a **global civil society** is emerging. As individuals interact at the international level, they become more **cosmopolitan** in their outlook and less attached to the **sovereign** state.

Can we conclude from this that NGOs are eroding the power of the state? Not really. While there are literally thousands of NGOs operating around the world, globally speaking they represent a rather small number of individuals. If a nascent global civil society is occurring, it is one populated by elites and specialists.

Third, the growth of NGOs highlights the growing significance of 'people power' in international relations. This has come about mainly because states have failed to respond to the immediate social, political, environmental, and health needs of individuals. Nowhere was this better demonstrated than at the Fourth World Conference on Women, held in Beijing in 1995. At that time, tens of thousands of women from NGOs around the world came together to discuss a range of issues specifically affecting women. There is no evidence to suggest that this trend of growing involvement by NGOs in contemporary international relations is waning.

*See also:* **global civil society; United Nations; women in development**

*Further reading:* Clark, 1995; Risse-Kappen, 1995; Ronit and Schneider, 2000

## NON-TARIFF BARRIER (NTB)

Until the 1980s, the main instrument for states to restrict imports from other states and to protect domestic industries was the tariff. A tariff is a tax imposed on goods imported from outside the country that is not imposed on similar goods from within the country. Import tariffs may be levied on an *ad valorem* basis, i.e. as a certain percentage of the estimated market value of the imported item. Alternatively, they may be levied on a specific basis, i.e. as a fixed amount per unit imported. Tariffs (sometimes called duties) may be imposed mainly to raise revenues because they are relatively cheap and easy taxes for a small or poorly organised government to collect. In developed industrial states they allow domestic producers of the good in question an artificial competitive advantage over their foreign competitors, usually at the expense of domestic consumers of the product. Domestic producers enjoy higher prices, a bigger market share, and higher profits.

Since the 1980s, and in light of the substantial progress made in lowering tariffs through successive rounds of negotiations under the 1947 General Agreement on Tariffs and Trade (GATT), states have developed a host of non-tariff barriers (NTBs) to achieve the same goals as tariffs. Import tariffs levied on industrial products by the major industrial countries were reduced from a weighted average of about 50 per cent of product value in 1947 to around 5 per cent by the end of the twentieth century.

Many NTBs are now regulated by the successor to GATT, the **World Trade Organisation** (WTO). Whilst NTBs vary enormously across the international system, there are four main types.

First, trade may be limited by the imposition or negotiation of various *quantitative* restrictions (QRs), such as quotas. These are usually regarded as more onerous than tariffs because of the more limited flexibility that they permit in trade and because they place greater limits on the extent to which foreign and domestic sellers can compete. In 1962 several major textile-trading countries established a temporary agreement regulating trade in cotton textiles in an attempt to protect their domestic industries. In 1973 the agreement was succeeded by the Multi-Fibres Agreement (MFA), enlarging its coverage to include wool and synthetic fibres. Another example of quantitative restrictions is the use of voluntary export restraints (VERs), which were predominantly imposed by the United States and the **European Union** against Japan and **newly industrialised countries** (NICs) in order to protect certain domestic sectors, particularly textiles, cars, and hightechnology industries. They essentially involve a bilateral agreement where the quantity and type of goods to be traded are fixed according to the requirements of the importing country.

Second, trade may be restricted by domestic *product regulations* demanded by governments. Some of these may not be explicitly targeted at international trade but they may affect the costs or feasibility of trade. Most obvious are the many regulations, standards, and other measures that restrict the form that a good may take or the manner in which it may be produced for sale in the domestic market. Such rules may be intended to protect the public safety or health, or they may only seek to ensure compatibility of products that must be used in combination.

Third, governments may use *subsidies* to protect particular industries. Although the WTO bans subsidies provided directly for exports, it is far more difficult to regulate subsidies for overall production of a particular good or service. Subsidies that are not specific to particular firms or industries, and subsidies for research and development, regional **development** and for adaptation to environmental regulation are not regulated at the international level.

Fourth, states may *dump* exports on overseas markets. Dumping is the export of a good for an unfairly low price, defined either as below the price on the exporter's home market or as below some definition of cost. The World Trade Organisation permits anti-dumping import duties equal to the dumping margin – the difference between the actual and the 'fair' market price.

The use of NTBs has been the subject of much discussion in recent years. Two questions have dominated the debate. First, to what extent have NTBs replaced tariffs in restricting international trade? This is difficult to measure, since so many NTBs are hidden from view by their very nature. In many cases, even the identification of a non-tariff barrier is subjective; what is an NTB to one person is a legitimate activity to another. Second, are they necessarily to be condemned and brought under international regulation? Again, the literature is divided between those who see all NTBs as constraints on the evolution towards a **free trade** system, and others who believe that states have a legitimate reason to use them to protect their basic **national interests**. In any case, the debate is sure to remain high on the academic and diplomatic agenda, particularly at the highest levels of the World Trade Organisation, whose mission has been complicated enormously by the new protectionism in international trade.

*See also:* **beggar-thy-neighbour policies; Bretton Woods; free trade; managed trade; multilateralism; regional trade blocs; World Trade Organisation**

*Further reading:* Finger, 1993; McKinney, 1994; Milner, 1988; Ruggie, 1994

## NORTH ATLANTIC TREATY ORGANISATION (NATO)

NATO is sometimes referred to as the Atlantic Alliance. Established in 1949 (its headquarters are in Brussels), NATO is charged with protecting the security of Western Europe. More specifically, its mandate is to safeguard the freedom and security of its members, to maintain stability within the Euro-Atlantic area, to manage and prevent international **crises**, to act as a consultative forum on European security issues and, finally, to uphold the values of the **United Nations** and promote democracy, **human rights**, and **international law**. Essentially, it is a collective defence organisation that regards a military attack on any one of its member countries as an attack on all of them.

The original treaty to set up NATO was signed in Washington on 4 April 1949 and came into force in August of the same year. Twelve states signed the treaty, including the United States, Canada, the United Kingdom, France, the Benelux countries, Italy, Norway, Iceland, Denmark, and Portugal. Since then, NATO's membership has expanded to include Turkey (1952), Greece (1952), Germany (1955), Spain (1982), the Czech Republic (1997), Poland (1997), and Hungary (1997).

NATO was set up not only to deter an attack on Europe by the Soviet Union, but also to allay West European fears of a revival of German militarism. The 1949 treaty committed the United States to a permanent role in European security affairs, a dramatic change of policy that ran counter to the traditional US concern to avoid 'entangling alliances'. Initially, Congress allocated US$1.3 billion to establish NATO and this sum rose considerably after the Korean War broke out in 1950.

By the end of 1949, the **alliance** partners had established a permanent command structure for the organisation. In 1952, under General Dwight D. Eisenhower, NATO held its first joint military exercises. In its early years, NATO planners were primarily concerned with building up a well-equipped fighting force. It was not until after Germany became a full member in 1955 that NATO developed into a highly structured and unified defence force. It was also Germany's membership that prompted the Soviet Union to form the Warsaw Pact later that year.

NATO has an extremely complex organisational structure and it is not possible to do justice to this complexity here. Briefly, NATO includes civilian, military, and military command strands. The North Atlantic Council has overall control of NATO and is made up of representatives from each of the member states. The civilian wing is headed by a European, while the military wing is under US control.

During the **cold war**, NATO was never far from controversy. In the early years, problems arose over the use of nuclear weapons to deter a Soviet attack. In the mid-1960s, France withdrew its troops from NATO control, as it was concerned about the sincerity of US claims that it would use nuclear weapons to deter a Soviet attack on Europe. NATO also attracted strong resentment from peace activists and environmentalists concerned over the potential for a nuclear **war** in Europe.

More recently, the collapse of the Soviet Union and the demise of the Warsaw Pact have raised questions about the relevance of the organisation in a vastly changed European security environment. Chief among these are concerns about the future role of the United States, the role of NATO in so-called 'out-of-area' operations (such as its involvement in Yugoslavia), and whether it should be enlarged to include more states from Central and Eastern Europe.

However, despite the end of the cold war, Russia remains the major concern for NATO planners. There are those who suggest that an expanded NATO will lead to a new configuration of **power** in Europe and this will have a destabilising effect on Russia. At present, there are few signs of such an eventuality. Moreover, through such groupings as the Euro-Atlantic Partnership Council (EAPC) and the Planning and Review Process (PARP), new structures have been developed to maintain a dialogue with Russia. In the future, the greatest threat to NATO arises from the growing defence cooperation among European states (particularly France and Germany) and ongoing doubts about the commitment of the United States to the defence of Europe.

*See also:* **alliance; cold war; collective security; deterrence**

*Further reading:* Bebler, 1999; Heller, 1992; Sandler and Harley, 1999; Yost, 1999

## NUCLEAR PROLIFERATION

In May 1998, India and Pakistan engaged in a series of nuclear tests, raising the possibility of escalation in the pace of nuclear proliferation around the world. Nuclear proliferation refers to the spread of nuclear weapons to states that did not possess them prior to 1968, when the Nuclear Non-Proliferation Treaty (NPT) was signed. Until the Indian and Pakistani nuclear detonations, international efforts to arrest the spread of nuclear arms in the 1990s seemed to be enjoying some success. The rate of nuclear proliferation appeared to be slowing down, the geographic scope of proliferation was shrinking, and de-nuclearisation was achieved in 1996 in parts of the former Soviet Union. Three post-Soviet states with nuclear weapons left on their territory – Belarus, Kazakhstan, and Ukraine – cooperated in the removal of those weapons to Russia and joined the Nuclear Non-Proliferation Treaty (NPT) as non-nuclear-weapon states. Today, Russia is the only Soviet successor state with nuclear weapons. The indefinite extension of the NPT itself in May 1995 showed that the norm of non-proliferation had become more deeply entrenched in international affairs than ever before.

At the same time, there exist powerful countervailing trends that could place recent non-proliferation achievements at risk and even threaten to rupture the painstakingly built non-proliferation **regime**. Among these, the danger of **loose nukes** or weapons-usable materials from the former Soviet Union is rightly regarded as the most serious cause of concern.

Before the end of the **cold war** and the collapse of the Soviet Union, a total of eight states possessed nuclear weapons. Five of these were formally declared nuclear weapons states according to the NPT: the United States, the Soviet Union, Britain, France, and China. In addition to India and Pakistan, it was also known that Israel had a covert nuclear weapons development programme. On the other hand, there were a large number of states that probably could have produced nuclear weapons but which had not done so. In the 1980s Argentina, Brazil, Romania, and Taiwan all took steps of one type or another to pursue nuclear arms but backed away or renounced their acquisition. South Africa – which had secretly acquired a six-weapon undeclared nuclear arsenal in the late 1970s – actually eliminated the weapons it possessed in 1991.

There are three main reasons why there was not more proliferation than actually took place during the cold war. First, each of the two

**superpowers** provided **security** guarantees to its allies. There was no need for Germany and Japan to develop nuclear weapons under the nuclear umbrella of the United States. Second, despite the arms race (sometimes known as *vertical* proliferation) between the Soviet Union and the United States, they had a common interest in maintaining, as far as possible, their control over *horizontal* proliferation. Finally, many states signed the most important piece of international legislation on this issue, the NPT, in 1968. This is a unique treaty in that, unlike every other treaty that is based on the notion of **sovereign** equality, the NPT formally distinguishes between states that do, and those that do not, possess nuclear weapons. The formal inequality built into the NPT has been a source of controversy ever since, notwithstanding its longevity and relative success.

In the years to come, it is unlikely that many states will join India and Pakistan in developing nuclear weapons. Iran, Iraq, Libya, and North Korea remain states of significant proliferation concern. It is possible that Algeria also bears watching because of violent internal conflict and questionable nuclear technology cooperation with China. In addition, in late 1997 there were reports of Syrian efforts to acquire nuclear research installations from Russia. However, there have been continued efforts to improve verification procedures by the International Atomic Energy Authority (IAEA), although the failure of the United States Congress to ratify the 1996 Comprehensive Test Ban Treaty (CTBT) in 1999 represents a significant step backwards in the evolution of a robust non-proliferation regime. Moreover, after the Iranian government declared on 10 May 2005 that it would restart its production of enriched uranium at its Isfahan plant, the IAEA has assumed an informative, albeit somewhat ineffectual role in the ensuing tensions between Iran's nuclear intentions and US demands.

There is some debate over how much we should be concerned with the spread of nuclear weapons. If **mutually assured destruction** (MAD) helped to keep the cold war cold, why shouldn't other nuclear-armed states be deterred from going to war with one another? There are two problems with this view. First, it assumes that MAD did promote stability between the superpowers during the cold war, whereas it could be argued that there were plenty of other reasons why the superpowers did not go to war with each other. Second, there are technological problems of control. Nuclear weapons in the United States and the former Soviet Union were equipped with elaborate devices to control access to the weapons. It is unclear if the same command-and-control procedures would apply in states such as North Korea, Iraq, and Syria.

*See also:* **arms control; arms trade; cold war; deterrence; loose nukes; mutually assured destruction; rogue state; weapons of mass destruction**

*Further reading:* Dunn, 1991; Howlett, 1999; Reiss, 1995; Sagan and Waltz, 1995

## ORDER

A stable pattern of relations among international actors that sustains a set of common goals or purposes. Order should not be confused with peace or justice. For order to exist, two conditions must be present. First, the actors must tacitly agree to abide by certain uniform practices that preserve the international system as a whole. Second, armed conflict must not be so pervasive as to undermine the integrity of the system.

Since the seventeenth century, the main actors in the international system have been independent **sovereign** states. Under conditions of **anarchy**, maintaining order has been a particularly difficult **theoretical** and practical problem. Some **realists** argue that the **balance of power**, **diplomacy**, and the formation of **alliances** provide the best methods of maintaining order. **Liberal internationalists** defend a much greater role for international institutions in developing mutually accepted norms and rules of conduct. Many **critical theorists** offer a more radical solution to the problem of order. They seek to transcend the current international system altogether, arguing that what is called order is little more than institutionalised injustice. Order, then, is a contested concept, with little scholarly consensus concerning what constitutes order, how it is best maintained, how it relates to justice, and whether the present international system can and should be transcended.

No scholar has more thoroughly analysed the concept of order than Hedley Bull. He distinguishes between three levels of order discernible in international relations. At the most abstract level, *order in social life* refers to the basic arrangements of a society that allow it to sustain fundamental goals such as **security** against violence and the protection of private property. *International order* is a pattern of activity that sustains the elementary goals of the society of states. According to Bull, there are four such goals: the preservation of **international society** itself; the independence of member states; peace and stability; and the development of norms and rules of international conduct such as the laws of **war**. The third level is *world order*. This is order among all of humanity. For Bull, states are not the only way in which human beings can order themselves. It is possible that the state system will one day be transcended. Indeed, Bull argues that international order is a transient form of order. Because individuals are the basic unit of social life, world order is of more fundamental value. International order has only instrumental value. Despite acknowledging the tension that exists between international order and world order, critics are right to point out how dismissive Bull is (at least in his early work) of world order projects. He argues that the existing state system affords better prospects for achieving world order than any form of world government. Moreover, although deeply interested in the normative dimensions of international society, especially the relationship between order and justice, Bull himself never articulated a vision of a just world order beyond the existing state system.

These different kinds of order highlight an underlying tension between order and justice. It is quite possible to have patterned relationships between actors that sustain an unjust order. And many writers have argued that this is precisely the problem with the contemporary international order. Other commentators (including Hedley Bull) argue that order must always take priority over justice because it is a precondition for the realisation of all other values. Yet many scholars disagree with this: without some standard of justice, any order is likely to be both unstable and unjust. There is no obvious resolution to this dichotomy between order and justice, at least not while the sovereign state continues to occupy centre stage in the international system. However, there are signs that the sovereign state may be faltering. **Globalisation** and the rise of transnational problems such as **global warming** and **terrorism** present enormous challenges both to the integrity of the state and to international order; these will have important implications for the order–justice debate.

*See also:* **anarchy; balance of power; critical theory; distributive justice; liberal internationalism; realism**

*Further reading:* Bull, 1995; Cox and Sinclair, 1996; Holsti, 1991; Paul and Hall, 1999; Rengger, 2000; Slaughter, 2004

## ORGANISATION FOR ECONOMIC COOPERATION AND DEVELOPMENT (OECD)

Often referred to as a 'rich man's club', the OECD is an intergovernmental organisation that serves the interests of the world's most developed economies. The OECD currently has 29 member states. They are Australia, Austria, Belgium, Canada, the Czech Republic, Denmark, Finland, France, Germany, Great Britain, Greece, Hungary, Iceland, Ireland, Italy, Japan, South Korea, Luxembourg, Mexico, the Netherlands, New Zealand, Norway, Poland, Portugal, Spain, Sweden, Switzerland, Turkey, and the United States.

The organisation came into being in 1961 to replace the Organisation for European Economic Cooperation (OEEC). In a famous speech at Harvard University on 5 June 1947, US Secretary of State George Marshall put forward a plan to rehabilitate Europe's war-torn economies. He argued that it was not for the Americans to dictate to the Europeans how the aid should be spent and the OEEC was formed to distribute the aid. The OEEC came into being in 1948 with a request for US$28 billion. Congress eventually approved a four-year **foreign aid** package of over US$13 billion.

The OEEC was remarkably successful in achieving its recovery aims. By the mid-1950s, trade between the West European states had doubled and they had achieved several successive years of economic growth. Although its value as a coordinating body was widely acknowledged, the organisation began to lose its sense of purpose after the aid ceased in 1952. By 1960, the member states sought the admission of the United States and Canada in a bid to strengthen transatlantic economic ties. This precipitated a change of name from the OEEC to the OECD and a new, more international policy orientation.

Located in Paris, the OECD has an annual budget of about US$200 million. Its organisational structure is quite straightforward. The Council is the main decision-making body of the organisation that oversees various policy committees that are made up of representatives from the member states. A Secretariat supports the activities of the committees. The official languages are English and French.

The goals of the OECD are spelled out in Article 1 of the Convention signed in Paris on 14 December 1960. They are:

1   To achieve the highest sustainable economic growth and employment and a rising standard of living in member countries, while maintaining financial stability, and thus to contribute to the world economy.
2   To contribute to sound economic expansion in member as well as non-member countries in the process of economic **development**.
3   To contribute to the expansion of world trade on a **multilateral**, non-discriminatory basis in accordance with international obligations.

Thus the OECD provides an important forum for its members to coordinate their economic policies, exchange ideas, establish trade and other agreements, and facilitate links between member and non-member states.

While its primary focus is the economic welfare of its members, in more recent years the OECD has begun to involve itself in a much broader range of social, political, and cultural issues. High on the agenda at present are issues relating to biotechnology, emerging and transitional economies, transnational crime, environment, energy, and the information society. The OECD also maintains strong links with other international agencies, including the **International Monetary Fund**, the International Atomic Energy Agency, the **World Bank**, the **World Trade Organisation**, and the Council of Europe.

Underpinning the organisation is a commitment to democracy and to the market economy. It is staunchly anti-protectionist and promotes the free flow of goods and services around the globe. Membership is conditional on acceptance of these principles. Over the last 40 years, only nine states have been admitted to the organisation: Japan (1964), Finland (1969), Australia (1971), New Zealand (1973), Mexico (1994), the Czech Republic (1995), Hungary (1996), Poland (1996), and South Korea (1996).

*See also:* **free trade; global governance; Group of Eight (G8)**

*Further reading:* Blair, 1993; Lawrence, 1996

## ORGANISATION FOR SECURITY AND COOPERATION IN EUROPE (OSCE)

The origins of the OSCE may be found in Soviet proposals beginning in the mid-1950s to hold an all-European conference to resolve the 'German question' and to ratify the postwar status quo in Europe. Talks did not begin until 1973 in Helsinki under the auspices of the Conference on Security and Cooperation in Europe (CSCE), the informal forerunner to the OSCE. Thirty-five delegations were present, including the United States, the Soviet Union, Canada, and all the European states except Albania. The negotiations continued until 1975.

The main issues were divided into three substantive 'baskets'. Basket I concerned **security**, focusing primarily on a set of principles to govern relations among states. It also included specific confidence-building measures (CBMs) – military provisions intended to provide assurances to potential enemies that a country is not preparing to launch a surprise attack. Basket II issues concerned cooperation in areas of economics, science and technology, and the environment. Basket III issues concerned cooperation in humanitarian areas, including human contacts, travel and tourism, information and cultural exchanges, and education. This basket also covered many **human rights** issues, especially the freer movement of peoples, ideas, and information across national boundaries.

The concluding stage of the initial CSCE was a summit conference of heads of state of all 35 countries, at which the Final Act was signed. It contains the *Decalogue*, ten principles that the member states believed should govern interstate relations:

1 **sovereign** equality of states;
2 refraining from the threat or use of force;
3 inviolability of frontiers;
4 territorial integrity of states;
5 peaceful settlement of disputes;
6 non-intervention in internal affairs;
7 respect for human rights and fundamental freedoms;
8 **self-determination** of peoples;
9 cooperation among states;
10 fulfilment of obligations under **international law.**

These ten principles created the normative structure that has undergirded the CSCE and the OSCE ever since. The elaboration of these principles has fostered the normative core for a Eurasian security **regime**. Of particular importance was the provision allowing for the peaceful negotiated change of borders, advocated by the Federal Republic of Germany. During the **cold war**, however, there was a contradiction between Western states' insistence on respect for human rights and most **communist** states' argument that CSCE efforts to promote human rights constituted intervention in their internal affairs.

With the end of the cold war, however, a new consensus has emerged. When member states freely accept certain principles – including those in the Decalogue – this effectively gives other members limited rights of involvement in their internal affairs in order to uphold those norms. This applies to issues such as intrusive inspection to verify compliance with CBMs, and provisions for human and minority rights. The Helsinki Decalogue has evolved in such a way as to weaken the absolute nature of state sovereignty to a far greater degree than was envisaged when the Final Act was signed in 1975.

Following a summit meeting in November 1990, the CSCE evolved into a formal international organisation. Before this date, the CSCE had functioned as a series of conferences, moving from site to site without a permanent headquarters. After 1990, it established a Secretariat in Vienna, a Conflict Prevention Centre in Vienna, an Office for Free Elections (subsequently renamed the Office for Democratic Institutions and Human Rights) in Warsaw, and a Parliamentary Assembly made up of parliamentarians from all member states. In 1994 the CSCE was renamed the Organisation for Security and Cooperation in Europe and declared itself to be a regional security organisation under Chapter VIII of the **UN** Charter. By 1998, the OSCE had an annual budget of US$180 million, most of which was allocated to the OSCE missions and projects in the former Yugoslavia. The entire staff amounted to about 250 people. The United States contributes approximately 10 per cent of the general budget. Today, the OSCE has 55 member states.

The OSCE engages in four main activities:

1   assisting **democratisation** in Europe;
2   **preventive diplomacy**;
3   conflict resolution;
4   post-conflict **security** building.

The democratisation aspect of the OSCE's mandate was evident in its missions to Estonia and Latvia in the early 1990s. Here the organisation addressed basic issues, such as citizenship and language laws, as well as school curricula, migration, and dialogue between different **ethnic** communities in an effort to reduce tension between the national majority and both countries' Russian minority population. The preventive diplomacy aspect was especially apparent in the OSCE's early-warning and early-intervention activities in Ukraine. The OSCE has engaged in conflict resolution by assisting in the negotiation of ceasefires between warring parties. Furthermore, it has monitored **peacekeeping** forces and other bilateral or **multilateral** arrangements. Post-conflict security building entails verifying **disarmament** agreements, establishing links between domestic organisations and foreign donors, assisting in the return of **refugees**, and supervising elections. These have been among the principal tasks undertaken by the OSCE in Bosnia, Croatia, Kosovo, and Albania over the last decade.

The OSCE is still at an early stage in its evolution, so it is difficult to judge its effectiveness in maintaining peace and security in Europe. On the one hand, it remains a very small organisation confronting enormous challenges such as the violent collapse of Yugoslavia and difficult issues dividing the successor states of the former Soviet Union. On the other hand, it currently draws upon a wider membership – extending from Vancouver to Vladivostok – than do the **North Atlantic Treaty Organisation** (NATO) and the **European Union** (EU). It is also the only organisation that confronts the links between different dimensions of peace and security in Europe, unlike NATO or the EU. Thus far the OSCE has compiled a record of modest success in preventing the outbreak or reignition of violent conflicts and contributing to security building in the aftermath of conflicts. The two greatest attributes of the OSCE are its proven ability to strengthen democratic institutions in societies undergoing transition and its capacity to respond rapidly to **crises**. Unfortunately, there has also been disappointment in its failure thus far to resolve underlying conflicts in those regions that experienced violence in the early post-cold war years.

*See also:* **cold war; democratisation; European Union; North Atlantic Treaty Organisation; peace-building; peacekeeping; preventive diplomacy; regime**

*Further reading:* Bothe *et al.*, 1997; Hyde-Price, 1991; Lehne, 1991; Maresca, 1985

## ORGANISATION OF PETROLEUM EXPORTING COUNTRIES (OPEC)

The Organisation of Petroleum Exporting Countries (OPEC) is probably the best-known example of an international cartel, even though the diamond trade is more successfully controlled. A cartel is a national or international organisation of producers who act in concert to fix prices, limit supply, divide markets, or set quotas. The cartel seeks maximum profits by driving out competition and by limiting production in times of oversupply. Cartels are usually criticised for eliminating the price benefits of competition. Their defenders argue that they distribute risks, stabilise markets, and protect weak members. Cartels often fail because member firms or states deviate from the rules of the cartel to serve their own interests.

OPEC was formed at a conference held in Baghdad in September 1960. There were five original members: Iran, Iraq, Kuwait, Saudi Arabia, and Venezuela. Between 1960 and 1975 the organisation expanded to 13 members with the addition of Qatar, Indonesia, Libya, United Arab Emirates, Algeria, Nigeria, Ecuador, and Gabon. Currently, OPEC consists of 11 member states (Ecuador dropped out in 1992 and Gabon withdrew in 1995), of which Saudi Arabia is the most powerful.

OPEC was set up to help unify and coordinate members' petroleum policies and to safeguard their interests. Among other activities, OPEC holds regular meetings of national oil ministers to discuss prices and, since the early 1980s, to set production quotas. OPEC also provides some financial assistance to developing countries through its OPEC Fund for International Development (founded in 1976), and conducts research on such topics as energy finance, technology, and relevant economic issues. The countries that make up OPEC produce about 40 per cent of the world's oil and hold more than 77 per cent of the world's proven oil reserves. OPEC also contains most of the world's excess oil production capacity.

It should be noted that OPEC did not establish the oil cartel. It simply took over an existing one. Before 1960, the 'seven sisters' (seven major oil companies including BP, Esso, Shell, Gulf, and Mobil) controlled the price of oil. They worked together as an organised cartel controlling exploration, production, transportation, marketing, and refining. During the 1960s, OPEC was unable to sustain the high oil prices of the 1950s. There were deep divisions between member states, and they often refused to respect quota resolutions. For example, Kuwait had a very low production rate so it demanded high quotas. On the other hand, Venezuela had a very high production rate that was being sold very cheaply, hence it demanded low quotas to increase the price of oil. By 1970 OPEC was merely a group of weak partners that depended heavily on income from oil, but could not create a cohesive policy.

In the early 1970s, however, the situation changed. In 1969 the American-backed Libyan government was overthrown by a military regime led by Colonel Gaddafi. He stopped the high production of Libyan oil. Moreover, Libya stopped trading with the major oil companies. Other countries followed the Libyan example. More importantly, the 1973 Arab–Israeli War finally led to an agreement among OPEC member states to reduce oil exports to countries that supported Israel. In 1973 exports were reduced by 50 per cent. In addition the price of oil rocketed, contributing to the widespread recession of the 1970s that also damaged the economies of non-oil-exporting states in the **Third World**.

OPEC began to lose control of the price of oil in the late 1970s. For instance, responding to the oil shocks of the era, states began to conserve energy and use it more efficiently. Moreover they began to rely upon alternative energy sources. In Japan the share of oil in total primary energy consumption fell by 23 per cent between 1973 and 1996, while the share of natural gas and nuclear energy increased by more than 10 and 14 per cent respectively. Recently, international environmental initiatives to cut carbon emissions and control **global warming** have accelerated this trend.

An expanding global oil supply has also reduced OPEC's **power**. During the 1970s, the OPEC countries took control of their oil industries and nationalised the foreign oil companies' operations on their soil. Deprived of the opportunity to invest in most of the OPEC countries, the major oil companies looked for opportunities in states such as Norway and the United Kingdom. As a result, OPEC's oil now accounts for only 26 per cent of the world's energy requirements outside the former Soviet Union and the United States, compared with 56 per cent 20 years ago. Oil ventures in the Central Asian states of the former Soviet Union will glut the world market even further.

Recent technological innovations have also played a role in increasing oil stocks. The expense and risk associated with finding and developing oil in difficult places has been sharply reduced, as has the time it takes for oil to be brought on-stream and produced. The revolution in oil technology has significantly expanded output among non-OPEC producers, most notably in the North Sea, the US side of the Gulf of Mexico, and off the coast of West Africa.

There is perhaps no better indicator of how much times have changed than the differing impacts of the two wars in the Persian Gulf. The Iranian **crisis** in 1979 and the Iran–Iraq war in 1980 created an oil shortage that proved to be a financial windfall for OPEC. But the aftershocks from the 1991 Gulf War have emerged as a mixed blessing. On the one hand, **sanctions** imposed on Iraq for the past decade have kept a major producer off the market. On the other hand, the war and its aftermath led to financial difficulties for both Kuwait and Saudi Arabia in spite of the latter's financial gain from the Iraqi embargo. Saudi oil replaced Iraq's oil market share by almost 80 per cent, in effect doubling its income. However, the extravagant spending and lavish subsidies bestowed on Kuwaiti and Saudi citizens, together with weapons purchases from the United States, have helped to drain their coffers.

Nonetheless, the future is not entirely bleak for OPEC. According to recent forecasts, global primary energy demand is expected to climb 40 per cent by the year 2010, with fossil fuels still accounting for nearly 90 per cent of that consumption. Asian countries alone will account for 44 per cent of that increased demand, and present OPEC with a potential market opportunity. Also, whilst many states have reduced their dependence on oil imports, the United States has increased its reliance on oil from the Middle East.

*See also:* **global warming; Third World**

*Further reading:* Adelman, 1995; Chalabi, 1989; Claes, 2000; Drollas and Greenman, 1989; Yergin, 1993

## PEACE-BUILDING

Peace-building is a relatively new concept that has risen to prominence in the 1990s. It arose in response both to the spread of civil **wars** in the **Third World** as well as the attempt by the former **United Nations** (UN) Secretary-General, Boutros Boutros-Ghali, to develop more wideranging measures than the traditional forms of UN **peacekeeping** to deal with them. Most of these recent conflicts are internal in nature. All of them result in widespread personal suffering and social and political dislocation.

Peace-building means action to identify and support structures that will tend to strengthen and solidify peace in order to avoid a relapse into conflict. As **preventive diplomacy** aims to prevent the outbreak of a conflict, so peace-building starts during the course of a conflict to prevent its recurrence. Only sustained, cooperative work on the underlying economic, social, cultural, and humanitarian problems can place an achieved peace on a durable foundation. Unless there is reconstruction and development in the aftermath of conflict, there can be little expectation that peace will endure.

Peace-building is a matter for countries at all stages **of development**. For countries emerging from conflict, peace-building offers the chance to establish new institutions, social, political, and judicial, which can give impetus to development. Land reform and other measures of social justice can be undertaken. Countries in transition can use peace-building measures as a chance to put their national systems on the path of **sustainable development**.

The most immediate task for peace-building is to alleviate the effects of war on the population. Food aid, support for health and hygiene systems, the clearance of mines, and logistical support to essential organisations in the field represent the first peace-building tasks. At this stage too, it is essential that efforts to address immediate needs be undertaken in ways that promote, rather than compromise, long-term development objectives. As food is provided, there must be concentration on restoring food production capacities. In conjunction with the delivery of relief supplies, attention should be given to road construction, restoration and improvement of port facilities, and the establishment of regional stocks and distribution centres.

So what is the promise and what are the essential ingredients of peace-building?

- It should be aimed at channelling the energy generated by conflict in constructive, non-violent rather than destructive and violent directions. Its aim is not to eliminate conflict but to generate positive change (which may be relatively spontaneous or directed).
- Normal sociopolitical processes (incremental changes through time) can transform conflicts by the parties acting alone, by expert third parties acting together and/or by judicious advocacy and political intervention. Peace-building usually incorporates a wide cross-section of political decision-makers, citizens, aid and development agencies, religious organisations, and social movements. Too often in the past, conflict transformation has been seen largely as a political problem. It has to be cast as a social and economic problem as well if sustainable structural change is to occur.

- Peace-building can take place at any stage of the escalatory cycle. If preventive diplomacy does not take place at the first sign of trouble and problems remain unaddressed, then transformational processes, in the early stages of an evolving conflict, may take the form of early warning and the application of suitable preventive measures. As the conflict escalates (especially if it turns violent), transformation may depend on some kind of **crisis** management or intervention. Later it may require conciliation, mediation, negotiation, arbitration, and collaborative problem-solving processes. Finally, of course, conflict transformation involves reconstruction and reconciliation.

Peace-building strategies are all those processes that seek to address the underlying causes of violent conflicts and crises to ensure that they will not recur. They are aimed at meeting basic needs for **security** and **order**, shelter, food, and clothing. Peace-building is what most societies do spontaneously – namely develop effective national and international rule-making **regimes**, dispute resolution mechanisms, and cooperative arrangements to meet basic economic, social, cultural, and humanitarian needs and to facilitate effective citizenship.

Peace-building occurs at all levels – in the community, nationally, and internationally. For example, putting in place **arms control** regimes and increasing numbers of confidence-building mechanisms are all attempts to ensure that national and international transactions are cooperative and peaceful. So are in-country initiatives that are aimed at reducing gaps between the rich and the poor, extending basic **human rights** between all peoples, and building sustainable development processes. There are six basic elements in a reconstructive, post-conflict, peace-building strategy:

- jump-starting the national economy;
- decentralised, community-based investments;
- repairing key transport and communications networks;
- demining (where relevant and linked to other priority investments);
- demobilisation and retraining of ex-combatants;
- reintegration of displaced populations.

Peace-building is a complementary process to peacekeeping. Conflict resolution requires effort at a number of levels. Whereas peacekeeping involves military forces provided by third parties in an attempt to contain or prevent violence, peace-building involves the physical, social, and structural initiatives that can help provide reconstruction and rehabilitation. Most United Nations peacekeeping operations now entail peace-building in some measure.

*See also:* **development; failed state; humanitarian intervention; Organisation for Security and Cooperation in Europe; peacekeeping; peace studies; preventive diplomacy; security; structural violence; sustainable development; United Nations; wars of the third kind**

*Further reading:* Banks, 1987; Boulding, 1995; Boutros-Ghali, 1992; Evans, 1993; Ryan, 1995

## PEACEKEEPING

In 1998 the **United Nations** (UN) marked half a century of peacekeeping. International peacekeeping has undergone a number of transformations since its establishment. While peacekeeping itself was not originally spelled out in the UN Charter, it has become a prominent vocation for the international organisation. Much of the effort in traditional peacekeeping has focused on the use of lightly armed troops providing a buffer zone between belligerent parties.

Initially, the authors of the UN Charter believed that peace enforcement was the best means to ensure the maintenance of international **order**. However, this hope was dashed with the marginalisation of the UN during the **cold war**. The development of peacekeeping evolved due to a series of compromises and an ability to adapt each mission to the particular circumstances facing it in the field. Nonetheless, during the cold war the progress of peacekeeping was characterised by a number of principles that have defined the rules that each UN peacekeeping deployment must follow. Three of these are particularly crucial: the rule of *consent*, the necessity of *impartiality*, and the adherence to the principle of the use of force only in *self-defence*.

Not only is consent required from the host government of the state where peacekeepers are to be deployed, but consent of all local warring parties must be secured if there is to be any hope of establishing a working relationship with the parties to a conflict. The perception of state **sovereignty** as supreme within the framework of the UN system has dictated that consent must be given in order to legitimise the presence of an international force within a state's boundaries. The principle of consent is one of the main dividing lines between peace enforcement (defined in Chapter VII of the UN Charter), and peacekeeping (authorised under the terms of Chapter VI of the Charter).

Another characteristic that is essential is the perception of unbiased deployment of peacekeepers. Peacekeeping entails a third party acting in the capacity of an impartial referee to assist in the settlement of a dispute between two or more parties. The credibility of the entire force can be brought into question if it is perceived as being biased in favour of one of the warring sides. Peacekeeping operations are not meant to prejudge the solution of controversial questions, and they are not meant to change the political balance affecting efforts to settle the conflict.

Finally, a key element that distinguishes an enforcement mission from a traditional peacekeeping operation is the use of force. In a peacekeeping mission, soldiers are not allowed to use force except in self-defence.

Peacekeeping operations are normally set up by the Security Council, which decides the operation's size, its timeframe, and its mandate. Since the UN has no military or civilian police force of its own, member states decide whether to participate in a mission, and if so, what personnel and equipment they are willing to offer. Military and civilian personnel in peacekeeping operations remain members of their own national establishments but serve under the operational control of the UN, and they are expected to conduct themselves in accordance with the exclusively international character of their mission. They usually wear blue berets or helmets and the UN insignia to identify themselves as UN peacekeepers.

Between 1948 and 2007, there have been 61 peacekeeping operations, 36 of which were set up in the years between 1988 and 1998. When the cold war ended in the late 1980s, the rising number of civil **wars** combined with greater cooperation among the five permanent members of the UN Security Council, led to a rapid increase in peacekeeping operations. In 1990, the UN budget for peacekeeping was less than US$0.5 billion. By 2007 this had increased to almost US$5.5 billion, putting the total estimated cost for all peacekeeping operations between 1948-2007 at approximately US$41.75 billion. Some scholars distinguish between first-generation and second-generation peacekeeping operations. First-generation peacekeeping operations were usually set up to deal with conflicts between states, and part of their rationale was to preclude direct intervention by either the United States or the Soviet Union. For this reason non-permanent members of the Security Council provided most of the personnel. Since the cold war, second-generation peacekeeping missions have been sent into wars that are civil rather than interstate, and the scope of their mandate has expanded to include: delivering humanitarian assistance; organising and monitoring elections; disarming and demobilising former fighters; and training civilian police. Of the 32 operations launched by the UN in the 1990s, 13 were deployed in Africa.

Since the mid-1990s there has been a general decline in both the cost and number of peacekeeping operations. The UN now has less than one-sixth the number of peacekeepers deployed in its peak year of 1993. Whereas nearly 80,000 peacekeepers were deployed in 1993, by the year 2000 fewer than 15,000 were on active duty. The United States accounts for less than 5 per cent of UN forces. By 1997 the cost of UN peacekeeping had fallen to less than US$1 billion, although member states still owe the United Nations more than that sum in current and back peacekeeping dues. After the failure of UN peacekeeping missions in Somalia, Yugoslavia, and Rwanda in the mid-1990s, the UN is far more cautious about sending peacekeeping troops than it was after the Gulf War in 1991.

So far, the more modest UN peacekeeping operations of the late 1990s have managed to get by despite the substantial sums of money owed by member states and the United States in particular. But this is about to change. Led by Washington, the United Nations is once again expanding its involvement in the world's peacekeeping operations. To start with, there is Kosovo. With full US support, the UN is charged with running the civilian administration of this war-ravaged country – a task that goes well beyond anything it has been asked to do previously. The UN is also engaged in East Timor, providing security and administrative support as this new state recovers from the devastation of its struggle for independence from Indonesia. The UN never comes cheap – and the increasing demands being placed on it can only be met if member countries provide the financial resources that are required to mount increasingly complex peacekeeping operations.

*See also:* **cold war; humanitarian intervention; international law; mercenary; peace-building; preventive diplomacy; safe haven; sovereignty; United Nations; wars of the third kind**

*Further reading:* Berdal, 1993; Coulon, 1998; Durch, 2000; Goulding, 1993; Jett, 2000; Shawcross, 2000

## PEACE OF WESTPHALIA

A term given to the political settlement that ended the Thirty Years War (1618–48). From the late sixteenth century onwards, Central Europe went through a period of intense religious turmoil. This was particularly acute in Germany, where Lutherans, Calvinists, and Zwinglians challenged the right of the Holy Roman Empire (then under the control of the Habsburgs of Austria) to determine their religious fate.

The **war** began when the Archbishop of Prague destroyed a number of Protestant churches. In response, and after appeals to the Holy Roman Emperor had failed to settle the issue, Bohemian Protestants stormed the Emperor's palace, threw two of his ministers out of a window, deposed the Catholic King, and placed Frederick, Elector of the Palatinate, in **power**. This part of the war ended after Johan Tserclaes, Count of Tilly, defeated Frederick at the Battle of the White Mountain some years later.

But this defeat did not put an end to the enmity between Catholics and Protestants. On the contrary, the defeat of the Bohemians hammered home the very real danger to Protestantism in other parts of Europe. In successive attempts, the Danes (1625–9) and the Swedes (1630–4) battled against the Catholic Emperor but failed to overcome his vastly superior forces. It was not until the French joined the Swedes in 1635 that the tide began to turn against the Holy Roman Empire. By this time, the war had lost much of its religious character. The French entered the war in 1635, concerned with the growth of church power in Central Europe. For them, it was not so much a religious struggle against the Holy Roman Empire as a political struggle for power in Europe.

The combined power of the French and the Swedes was enough to overcome the Holy Roman Empire. In 1644, and after a number of French-Swedish victories, negotiations to settle the conflict began. Eventually, on 24 October 1648, the Treaty of Westphalia was signed in Münster and Osnabrück. The war had been one of the bloodiest conflicts in European history. It left Europe in ruins and reduced the population of Germany by almost one-half. Towns and villages vanished, property was destroyed, plague and disease were rampant, demobilised **mercenaries** and soldiers turned to robbery, and there was a general decline in European culture. It took almost 200 years for Germany to recover from the effects of the Thirty Years War. In essence, the war brought the Middle Ages to a close and undermined the power of the Holy Roman Empire in Europe.

The treaty itself is one of the most remarkable documents in European history (the full text can be found at http://www.tufts.edu/ departments/ fletcher/multi/texts/historical/westphalia.txt). Among other things, it details the return of territory won during the various battles, absolves the warring parties of wrong-doing, removes impediments to trade, commerce, communications, and movement, and prescribes the manner in which the armies would be disbanded and prisoners set free. The Treaty recognised the **sovereignty** of the German states, the Swiss Confederation, and the Netherlands whilst the French and the Swedes made significant territorial gains. Moreover, as a consequence of the Treaty, France became the dominant state in Europe.

Far more significant, however, is that the Treaty is often credited with establishing the legal basis for the modern state system. Not all scholars agree on this. Some see the modern state emerging much earlier, others much later. But there is no doubt that the Peace of Westphalia is an important turning point in European politics and in world history. The Treaty established two core principles. The first was *rex est imperator in regno suo*. Literally, it means that the king is sovereign within his own domain and not subject to the political will of anyone else. The settlement recognised the absolute power of rulers and linked this personal or dynastic rule to a specific territory. The second principle was *cuius regio, eius religio*. This principle confers upon the king the power to determine which religion is practised in his realm. It was a principle that prohibited interference in the internal affairs of other states on religious grounds, and it remains important today in providing the basis for **international law**. ⌄

*See also:* **international law; nation–state; sovereignty**

*Further reading:* Asch, 1997; Caporaso, 2000; Gutmann, 1988; Krasner, 1993; Parker, 1997

## PEACE STUDIES

Only in the second half of the twentieth century has peace studies been institutionalised as a distinct field of study in the academy and as a body of knowledge and applied skills that can be used in many spheres of our personal, social, and political lives. In academia, however, scholars still struggle for the recognition of peace studies as a distinct field of interdisciplinary or multidisciplinary study. At the same time, one cannot ignore the relationship between the study and practice of peace studies and related fields of inquiry such as psychology, sociology, communication, security studies, international relations, and foreign policy. But whether peace studies is treated as a multidisciplinary field of inquiry or as a new credible profession, its emergence needs to be situated in a historical context.

The study of **war** and peace dates backs to ancient times. Most historical overviews on the origins of peace studies, however, especially those that focus on the international arena, stress the impact of the two world wars and their aftermath. The horror, suffering, and destruction that resulted from the wars led to a search for alternatives to **realism** – the dominant paradigm of international relations. This search triggered ongoing debates on the origins, nature, and dynamics of conflict and cooperation that dominate the study of international relations to the present day.

Although the literature on the evolution of peace research and peace studies mentions the impact of the two world wars, its primary focus tends to be on the impact of the Second World War. This is partially because the suffering of civilians during that conflict reached numbers like never before. According to some estimates, while military deaths were roughly the same in both wars (nearly 17 million), civilian deaths in the Second World War were seven times greater than in the First World War and have been estimated at 35 million. Another reason for dealing primarily with the impact of the Second World War on the debates about conflict and cooperation involves the claim of some scholars that the Second World War really began when the First World War ended with a problematic resolution reflected in the Treaty of Versailles in 1919.

Yet, despite some questioning of the **power** politics paradigm that dominated the study of world politics during the period mid-1940s to mid-1960s, no serious alternatives were in sight; during those decades, the primary emphasis was on the study of war and its causes. Peace for the most part remained an abstract concept, defined merely as the absence of war. Many scholars in the social sciences argued that war as a problem has a scientific solution. Thus they employed quantitative measures to examine the origins of wars and their consequences, stressing the need for such studies (and scholars) to remain value-neutral.

Since the 1960s, there have been a number of crucial turning points that have had a significant effect on the development of the field of peace studies. These turning points include:

- the 1960s, especially the peace movement opposing the Vietnam War;
- the rise of the nuclear freeze movement and other **disarmament** campaigns at various stages of the **cold war**;
- the end of the cold war and the collapse of the Eastern bloc.

The field of peace studies was originally conceived as a critical field of study that would constitute a viable alternative to more traditional fields of study and practice. Peace researchers stressed the potential of peace studies to trigger systems change, that is, to transform social and political structures in ways that would make them more responsive to basic human needs. In order to move in that direction, many scholars in the field believe that peace studies must become a tool for networking, coalition-building, and political mobilisation at the grassroots level to promote political change grounded in the principles of equality and social and economic justice. The move away from conventional approaches to the theory and practice of peace studies requires more than simply adding new perspectives to the existing body of literature. Peace studies is a transformative project which seeks to construct alternative accounts of social and political realities and therefore takes place simultaneously in the domains of theory, research, practice, and activism.

*See also:* **cold war; cosmopolitanism; idealism; peace-building; security; structural violence; war**

*Further reading:* Elias and Turpin, 1994; Kegley and Raymond, 1999; Rogers and Ramsbotham, 1999; Whittaker, 1999

## PERPETUAL PEACE

A condition of lasting peace within the international system. The concept does not simply mean that it is possible to abolish **war** forever, it also implies that it is possible for human beings to achieve a just world **order** in which war will be unnecessary. The two ideas go together. Of course, there has never been a time when perpetual peace has prevailed. Consequently, the elaboration of these ideas has usually taken the form of *peace projects*; that is, plans to bring about perpetual peace. Their authors have included such thinkers as Dante Alighieri, Erasmus, King George of Bohemia, the Abbé de Saint Pierre, Jean-Jacques Rousseau, and (most famously) Immanuel Kant.

It was during the eighteenth-century Enlightenment era that peace projects were seriously discussed in Europe. Two themes dominate the intellectual thinking of the period – a commitment to human progress combined with a strong belief in the moral perfectibility of humankind. Taken together, these ideas formed the basis for a powerful evolutionary philosophy based on reason. Despite the apparent progress of the arts and sciences, the problem of war remained the major stumbling block to the creation of a better world. Most of the writers of the period were also reacting to the pessimism of political thinkers such as Thomas Hobbes, who argued that peace could only be a temporary condition sustained by the **balance of power**. Kant described Hobbes and other **realists** of the era as 'sorry comforters'.

Without doubt, Immanuel Kant was the greatest of the Enlightenment thinkers who took up the problem of reconciling the **anarchy** of the international system with the need to bring about perpetual peace. According to Kant, war was a source of evil and moral corruption. The frequency of war meant that the rights and freedoms of individuals were continually threatened by aggressive states. Moreover, states could not perfect their own constitutions while they were concerned with the prospect of being invaded by other states. But like Hobbes before him, Kant regarded war as the natural state of humanity. Consequently, a way had to be found in which states could co-exist in harmony. In Kant's view, it was the duty of all individuals and states to bring about the abolition of war by embarking on a progressive goal towards perpetual peace.

His most impressive attempt at coming to grips with the problem is contained in an essay entitled *Perpetual Peace: A Philosophical Sketch* (1796). It is not his only work on the topic, but it is certainly the best-known. The aim of the essay is to determine the conditions of a lasting peace by showing how states could become part of a global **cosmopolitan** community without creating a single world government, a prospect that Kant described as 'soulless despotism'.

The first part of the essay is devoted to what Kant calls the *preliminary articles*. These articles are a set of prohibitive laws, the purpose of which is to change the attitude of states towards each other. They include such things as gradually abolishing standing armies, not incurring debts in relation to external affairs, and undertaking not to interfere with the constitutions of other states. Accompanying these articles is a second set of *definitive articles* which offer a framework by which a lasting peace can be secured. They include a demand that all states develop a republican constitution, set up of a federation of free states, and establish a general rule of universal hospitality and free passage.

Kant was well aware of the role of **power** in international affairs. However, there are two reasons why he believed that his plan would succeed. The first is that states will eventually become morally, economically, and demographically exhausted from making war upon each other. After numerous imperfect attempts to achieve peace, therefore, states will eventually form a successful and lasting coalition. The second reason is that, for Kant, 'moral right' is all-pervasive. Even tyrants invoke the law from time to time and the most expedient kings and princes are not completely without principles. The problem is how to persuade such leaders to change their behaviour. Public education and free speech are crucial elements. After all, it is the ordinary citizen who feels the effects of war most acutely. In the end, human beings would slowly and painfully emerge from their political immaturity and see that the only alternative to perpetual peace is, in Kant's words, 'the peace of the graveyard'. In the final analysis, Kant holds firmly to the view that enlightened self-interest is the key to bringing about a world federation and the eventual abolition of war.

Of course, the concept of perpetual peace is still looked upon with disdain by realist scholars. According to them, it is a naïve and even dangerous idea because attempts to institutionalise it are likely to have tragic consequences. They point to the failure of the **League of Nations** and outbreak of the Second World War as evidence. One of the more interesting **communitarian** critics of the concept of perpetual peace is Hegel, a nineteenth-century German philosopher. According to Hegel, the most fundamental cause of war lies in the peculiar nature of the state, whose autonomy protects and represents the communal identity of its inhabitants. A people are a product of a particular *milieu*, they have a history, common language, customs, passions, and particular social and political rules. Their identity cannot encompass all of humankind. For Hegel, war arises out of a conflict between opposing ways of life. Even when states cooperate, they always have their own goals and interests in mind. Treaties and **alliances** can be made, but they last only as long as they serve the welfare of the contracting parties.

*See also:* **anarchy; collective security; democratic peace; end of history; global governance; idealism; liberal internationalism; peace studies; realism**

*Further reading:* Bohman and Lutz-Bachman, 1997; Brown, 1992a; Hurrell, 1990; Reiss, 1991; Spegele, 2001

## POLITICAL RISK

Human beings live with risk all their lives. They risk their happiness in relationships, their property if they live in certain locations, their health if they smoke, and their money if they gamble. Indeed, Ulrich Beck has recently argued that risk is becoming the organising principle of late modern society.

Scholars began to take the idea of risk seriously during the Renaissance, when mathematicians (and addicted gamblers) sought to unlock the mysteries of dice throwing. Out of these early inquiries grew the theory of probability – the mathematical heart of the concept of risk. The word 'risk' derives from the Italian verb *risicare*, meaning to dare. The proverb *chi non risica, non rosica* neatly incorporates this meaning and translates into the familiar English phrase 'nothing ventured, nothing gained'.

Risk refers to the possibility that an unintended harm such as injury, loss of income, or damage may occur by undertaking a certain course of action. The unintended harm may not eventuate, however. Risk assessment is the attempt to determine the likelihood that future outcomes will be different from those experienced in the past and the present.

Risk does not mean a complete lack of control over the future. For this reason, it is often contrasted with chance. The latter implies that the future is entirely contingent. Risk implies the possibility of management and the mitigation of pure chance. There are two main ways that this can be accomplished. The first is through *scenario planning*, which requires a detailed assessment of all the available evidence and a range of strategies put in place to deal with possible future losses. The second, and by far the most common tactic, is to take out an *insurance policy*. Companies investing in foreign countries often use both approaches.

Political risk analysis, which is sometimes referred to as *country* risk or **sovereign** risk analysis, falls into the first category. It is an example of an applied social science. More accurately, it is that point where international relations meets international business. Briefly stated, political risk analysis assumes that political forces may affect the expected performance of an investment or the viability of an intended one. Political risk analysis is a useful planning tool and one that, under conditions of **globalisation**, is becoming more and more necessary to protect investors from incurring heavy losses, especially in volatile offshore locations.

It used to be the case that political risk analysis was concerned with determining the extent to which expropriation, governmental change, **war**, and regulatory changes might affect a particular overseas investment. This was particularly the case during the 1960s and 1970s when a spate of ideologically motivated expropriations took place. In Chile, for example, the holdings of ITT and Anaconda Copper were nationalised by the incoming socialist government. Political risk was also seen to be something quite different from economic risk, which was concerned with currency problems, increases in taxation, the non-convertibility of funds, runaway inflation, domestic price controls, and fluctuations in share prices. Today, however, the distinction between political and economic risk is far less clear. After all, markets are political entities. They are maintained by governments and have consequences that affect the polity as a whole. Consequently, the gamut of political risk analysis has dramatically broadened and now includes economic concerns such as those listed above, kidnapping, **terrorism**, theft of intellectual property, **human rights** issues, environmental damage, civil disturbance, piracy, regional instability, employee theft and embezzlement, property damage, corruption, regulatory and policy changes, cultural issues, breach of contract, and human resource issues. The primary concern of political risk analysis, then, is to understand how the social, political, cultural, and economic environment affects a company's investment opportunities and to use that information as a forecasting tool in order to manage future risk.

Like most applied social sciences, political risk analysis has gone through a methodological shift. During the 1960s and 1970s, analysts sought to develop quantitative models of political risk assessment based on rational choice and probability **theory**. Today, analysts use both quantitative and qualitative techniques. Some analysts have devised sophisticated rating systems that they apply to countries; others investigate past behaviour patterns; still others seek information from knowledgeable individuals. There is no consensus as to a preferred approach.

A typical risk assessment will begin by looking at the character of a country's political system, the performance of the economy, how other companies have fared in the same sector, the prospects for political and regulatory change, the relationship between the government and the governed, and so on. It will then evaluate the data and offer a range of recommendations. It is important to understand that a political risk assessment is continually evolving and that monitoring the assessment over time is an important part of the whole process.

A political risk assessment is of little use unless it is implemented. There is some evidence to suggest that many corporate CEOs commission them, but fail to act upon the information once they receive it. Yet implementation of a risk management strategy is a crucial component of any sound business or investment plan. There are numerous cases where companies have paid a high price because they failed in this regard. One way that a company can minimise risk, especially in a global context, is to take out an insurance policy. The United States government has set up the Overseas Private Investment Corporation (OPIC) precisely for this reason. Also, the **World Bank** started up the Multilateral Investment Guarantee Agency (MIGA) in 1988 to bring a degree of confidence to investment in projects in the **Third World**.

Although the concept of political risk has gone largely unnoticed in the field of international politics, every policymaker, strategic analyst, and security adviser is implicitly a risk assessor. Indeed, it is hard to imagine a military intervention, trade agreement, or a humanitarian relief effort that does not involve foreign policymakers in determining levels of risk and how best to manage them.

*See also:* **globalisation; multinational corporation; Third World**

*Further reading:* Beck, 1992; Bernstein, 1998; Moran, 1998; Vertzberger, 1998

## POPULATION GROWTH

At the beginning of 1992, the earth supported about 5.4 billion people, a dramatic rise since 1900, when it contained about 1.6 billion people. In 2006, the world population reached 6.5 billion people and is projected to surpass 9 billion in 2050.

Each day, the world's human population increases by about 250,000 people, or more than 90 million each year. This annual increase is approximately equal to the population of Mexico. The rate at which the human population is growing can be illustrated by how little even catastrophic natural disasters slow it down. For example, in June 1990 an earthquake in Iran killed an estimated 40,000 people. Within six hours, new births worldwide replaced the number of people lost from this immense tragedy.

Population growth is due not simply to an increase in births but to the excess of births over deaths. Improvements in public health and medicine around the world propel population growth by enabling people to live longer. The growth feeds itself as greater numbers of young women survive to childbearing age and start to have children.

These advances are causing the world's population to double at a much faster rate than ever before. In the year 1000, the human population grew at a rate so slow that, had it continued, the world population would not have doubled for 575 years. By 1825, the doubling time had decreased to about 100 years. Today, the world's population doubles every 35 to 40 years.

But the growth rate varies greatly from country to country. In the richer, industrialised states such as the United States, Canada, Japan, and the countries of Western Europe, population growth averages 0.2 per cent per year. Germany and Hungary have rates that are sometimes less than zero, meaning that their populations are declining. In the developing nations, however, population growth is much higher. The highest growth rates occur in Africa and in Arab states on the Persian Gulf.

Although population growth rates expressed in percentages may seem insignificant, the difference between a worldwide 1 per cent rate of growth and a 3 per cent rate is the difference between adding 54 million people and adding 200 million people each year. A sustained worldwide growth rate of 3.7 per cent, for example, would cause the earth's population to double in only 20 years.

Many economists and social planners believe that economic **development** is the key to slowing population growth. In poor countries, where many people farm for a living, there is an economic advantage to having several children who can help with the work and provide for the parents in old age. When societies become economically and technologically advanced, however, modern agricultural techniques enable the production of the same amount of food using the labour of fewer people. In such societies, large families are unnecessary and may be costly. As a result, family size drops. This so-called demographic transition has helped to reduce the growth of populations in the wealthier, industrialised countries.

Unfortunately, a rapidly expanding population can by itself prevent a developing country from improving its economy. Its people can become poorer when its population growth outstrips its economic growth. Kenya, for instance, with a 1992 population of 24 million, will have 48 million people in 2012 if the current population growth rate continues. Few experts believe that Kenya's economic circumstances can improve sufficiently during that time to provide adequately for so many people. Kenya may be doomed to worsening poverty unless it can limit its population growth.

The human population is expanding in many regions simply because people lack awareness of birth control or the ability to limit the size of their families. In other cases, people in developing countries who want to limit the growth of their families lack access to contraception. Family planning methods are simply not available in large sections of the world. But attempts to slow population growth confront more than economic or educational problems. Human reproduction is a matter of great religious and cultural importance as well. The religious teachings of many people prohibit or discourage contraception. And some cultures traditionally value large families as a sign of prestige and **power**.

The problem of uncontrolled population growth prompted the government of China in 1955 to restrict families to only one child. China is one of the most densely populated countries in the world. It has the largest population, at more than 1 billion people. China's 9.6 million square kilometres (3.7 million square miles) gives it a population density of about 119 people per square kilometre (309 people per square mile). But because the land is not all habitable, the density in some places is much higher than these figures suggest.

By comparison, the United States, whose 300 million people live on a land area approximately equivalent to that of China, has a population density of only 30 people per square kilometre (70 people per square mile).

Experts say that China's population control programme has not been a clear success. The government's rules are modified for special groups within the larger population. Also, families often desire male children, a wish that in practice may lead to the killing of female newborns or simply a disregard for governmental restrictions. Thus, there are more births than officially allowed in order to produce males. In the 1990s, despite many years' experience with the policy, the population of China was still increasing by about 1.4 per cent annually. At this rate, China's population will double in about 50 years.

One of the problems of having an increasing world population is the difficulty of feeding everyone. As many as 13 million people die every year from malnutrition and starvation, despite the fact that global food production continues to increase and total world food supplies are adequate. Of course, there are complex political and economic factors that lead to poverty and hunger in various regions. But some scientists fear that current demands for agricultural resources already exceed the earth's capacity to supply the population on a continuing basis. From 1950 until 1984, world agricultural production nearly tripled. In the mid-1980s, however, world agricultural production began to level off, and, in certain places, production declined.

Loss of farmland is a major cause of the decline in agricultural production. Usable farmland is lost for many reasons, but the major causes are erosion and salinisation. Erosion occurs when wind and water rob land of its nutrient-rich soil. Salinisation is the accumulation of salts in the soil, a problem common in regions where irrigation is used. Finally, as cities grow, they take over land once available for agriculture. The result of all these factors is that less and less land must feed more and more people. Dwindling farmland is not the only problem, however. Across the entire globe, overpopulation continues to deplete croplands, fisheries, water resources, and energy supplies. Some scientists fear that uncontrolled population growth will thus produce dangerous conflicts among states and regions over access to the earth's natural resources.

*See also:* **development; failed state; Third World**

*Further reading:* Cohen, J., 1995; Evans, 1998; Homer-Dixon and Blitt, 1998; Kaplan, 2000; Livi–Bacci and Ipsen, 1997; Milwertz, 1996; Parnwell, 1993

## POSTMODERNISM ✓

A distinctive approach to the study of international relations that emerged (in this field, at least) in the 1980s. It is characterised by three main themes.

First, postmodernists are hostile towards claims to universal or absolute truth. They reject the idea of an external reality independent of our perceptions and the language we use to express those perceptions, and therefore they claim to undermine the traditional distinction between **theory** and practice. Postmodernists argue that all truth–claims are based on *metanarratives*, or background worldviews, according to which particular claims to truth or value are legitimated or rejected. The abiding postmodern hostility to these paradigms is summed up in the classic definition of postmodernism as 'incredulity towards metanarratives'. In particular, we should be wary of the claims of the dominant metanarratives of modernity, the competing accounts of universal human nature, knowledge and historical progress that constitute the various streams of the Enlightenment project, notably those of **realism**, liberalism, **Marxism**, and modern scientific methods. Postmodernists claim that such metanarratives purporting to legitimate bodies of knowledge or ethical and political systems are not themselves legitimated by any further foundation. Rather, they stand alone as separate and distinct *discourses* talking across one another. When they come into conflict there is no way to adjudicate among them.

Second, postmodernists seek to unmask putatively emancipatory grand narratives as oppressive. Particular liberations have given birth to new forms of 'caging'. Liberalism has emancipated us from feudalism only to deliver us to **capitalism**. Marxism has merely replaced capitalism with Stalinism. Modern science has neglected and marginalised premodern forms of human knowledge. The conception of the metanarrative excludes, as its shadow, a conception of the 'other' that does not fit that particular category. The excluded other can then be legitimately oppressed. Indeed, truth itself is a mask for **power**.

Third, in so far as postmodernism does turn out to have a distinctive ethical position of its own, it might be summed up as 'respect for difference'. We should be wary of any large-scale programmes of liberation. Rather than revolution, our focus should be resistance at a local specific level. We should turn away from universalist understandings and principles towards a heightened respect for and fostering of otherness.

In order to understand postmodernity, one must understand the historical and intellectual outline of the modern worldview that postmodernists seek to subvert. The Cartesian notion 'I think therefore I am' asserts that the rational, doubting individual thinking self must exist. Newton's discovery of the predictable mechanistic physical universe became the context for individuals rationally and objectively to discover and control their destiny. It is argued that modernity presupposed and promoted optimistic progress based on individualistic, objective truth in a universe that can be conquered and controlled.

In the study of international relations, scholars inspired by postmodernism draw our attention to the ways in which knowledge and power are inextricably connected in the **theory** and practice of international relations. They sometimes describe themselves as self-imposed exiles on the margin of the academic discipline of IR, constantly probing its conditions of possibility and the limits to its allegedly authoritative knowledge-claims. For them, orthodox students of international relations are forever in search of some elusive ideal (order, stability, freedom, equality), some philosophically pure foundation from which to account for and recommend reforms to the practice of statecraft. They also engage in projects of disciplinary 'deconstruction'. The goal is to expose the strategies by which particular discourses of power/knowledge in the field construct oppositional conceptual hierarchies (such as order/**anarchy**, inside/outside) and repress dissent by appealing to allegedly objective characteristics of the world.

The reception to this work has been mixed. On the one hand, many (mostly younger) scholars have welcomed the participation of postmodernist-inspired critiques of epistemological orthodoxies. What unites post-positivist critics (whether they call themselves postmodernist or not) is a shared frustration with the way in which 'the discipline' adjudicates what is to count as proper theory on the basis of narrow metatheoretical criteria overly indebted to the philosophy of the natural sciences. On the other hand, its critics accuse it of being little more than a trendy manifestation of cognitive and ethical relativism. For example, the postmodernist critique of modern reason would seem to exclude it from participating in any renewal of normative arguments about a just world order. By reducing truth and ethics to power, the postmodern deconstruction of realism ends up by reaffirming the view that power cannot be controlled to serve emancipatory human interests, assuming that they exist of course.

*See also:* **cosmopolitanism; critical theory; power; realism; theory**

*Further reading:* Ashley and Walker, 1990; Cochran, 1995b; George, 1994; Jarvis, 2000; Lyotard, 1984; Smith, 1999

## POWER

At its simplest, power in interstate relations may be defined as a state's ability to control, or at least influence, other states or the outcome of events. Two dimensions are important, internal and external. The *internal* dimension corresponds to the dictionary definition of power as a capacity for action. A state is powerful to the extent that it is insulated from outside influence or **coercion** in the formulation and implementation of policy. A common synonym for the internal dimension of power is autonomy. The *external* dimension corresponds to the dictionary definition of power as a capacity to control the behaviour of others; to enforce compliance. Such influence need not be actively exercised; it need only be acknowledged by others, implicitly or explicitly, to be effective. It also need not be exercised with conscious intent; the behaviour of others can be influenced simply as a by-product of powerful acts (or potential acts).

Most scholars focus on power as a means, the strength or capacity that provides the ability to influence the behaviour of other actors in accordance with one's own objectives. At the national level, this influence is based on relations between state A and another actor B with A seeking to influence B to act in A's interest by doing x, by continuing to do x, or by not doing x. Some governments may seek power for its own sake. But for most, power, like money, is instrumental, to be used primarily for achieving or defending other goals, which could include prestige, territory, or **security**. To achieve these ends, state A can use various techniques of influence, ranging from persuasion or the offering of rewards to threats or the actual use of force.

From this standpoint, the use of a state's power is a simple relational exercise. However, there are subtle characteristics of power that render its use more art than science. Moreover, relationships among the elements of national power as well as the context in which they are to be used to further a state's **national interests** are seldom clear-cut propositions. All this means that in the end, power defies any attempts at rigorous, scientific assessment.

National power is contextual in that it can be evaluated only in terms of all the power 'elements' (such as military capability, economic resources, and population size), and only in relation to another player or players and the situation in which power is being exercised. A state may appear powerful because it possesses many military assets, but the assets may be inadequate against those of a potential enemy or inappropriate to the nature of the conflict. The question should always be: power over whom, and with respect to what?

Power is historically linked with military capacity. Nevertheless, one element of power alone cannot determine national power. Part of the problem stems from the fact that the term *power* has taken on the meaning of both the capacity to do something and the actual exercise of the capacity. And yet a state's ability to convert potential power into operational power is based on many considerations, not the least of which is the political and psychological interrelationship of such factors as government effectiveness and national unity. In this context, the elements of national power, no matter how defined, can be separated only artificially. Together, they constitute the resources for the attainment of national objectives and goals.

Closely allied to all this is the fact that national power is dynamic, not static. No particular power factor or relationship is immune to change. Over the last century, in particular, rapid changes in military technologies have accelerated this dynamism. The United States's explosion of a nuclear device instantly transformed its power position, the nature of **war**, and the very conduct of international relations. A war or revolution can have an equally sudden effect on power. The two world wars devastated Europe, facilitated the rise of the United States and the Soviet Union, and set the **developing** world on a road to **decolonisation**, thereby dismantling in less than 50 years a system that had been in existence for over three centuries. Economic growth can also quickly change a state's power position, as was the case with Japan and Germany after 1945. In addition, the discovery of new resources, or their depletion, can alter the **balance of power**. Certainly **OPEC**'s control over a diminishing supply of oil, coupled with its effectiveness as a cartel, caused a dramatic shift in power relations after 1973.

Such shifts are not always so immediately discernible. Power is what people believe it is until it is exercised. Reputation for power, in other words, confers power regardless of whether that power is real or not. At the same time, there are examples throughout history of states that continued to trade on past reputations, only to see them shattered by a single event.

Evaluation of national power is difficult. The basic problem, as we have seen, is that all the elements of power are often interrelated. In other words, like all strategic endeavours, more art than science is involved in the evaluation of where one state stands in relation to the power of other **regional** and global actors.

In addition to thinking about power as a relationship between actors, one should also bear in mind an important distinction between *relative* power and *structural* power. The latter confers the power to decide how things will be done, the power to shape frameworks within which states relate to one another, relate to people, or relate to corporate enterprises. The relative power of each party in a relationship is more, or less, if one party is also determining the surrounding structure of the relationship. Analytically, one can distinguish between four separate but related structures of power in international relations:

- the *knowledge structure* refers to the power to influence the ideas of others;
- the *financial structure* refers to the power to restrict or facilitate their access to credit;
- the *security structure* shapes their prospects for security;
- the *production structure* affects their chances of a better life as producers and as consumers.

In studying power as a relationship between states and other actors, it is important to bear in mind the role of structural power in shaping the terms of the relationship itself. For example, many scholars have argued that although the power of the United States appeared to be declining relative to other states during the second half of the twentieth century, it possesses vast resources of structural power that continue to sustain its **hegemonic** position in the international system.

*See also:* **hegemony; political risk; realism; relative gains/absolute gains; security**

*Further reading:* Lukes, 1974; Nye, 1990; Strange, 1996; Sullivan, 1990

## PRE-EMPTION

Pre-emption constitutes one of the central tenets of the **Bush doctrine**. In international relations, pre-emption or preventive **war** refers to a state's willingness and ability to attack another state that poses an imminent threat to its national **security**. The rationale for pre-emption dates back to ancient times. One of the first documented cases can be found in Thucydides' *Peloponnesian War*, notably the Athenian generals' decision to invade the island of Melos in the fifth century BC. Here, the Athenian generals reasoned that the extension of Athenian rule was necessary to preserve the safety, **order**, and justice of Melian society against the potential occupation by Sparta. The Melians, however, objected that the real danger lay in turning 'uncertainties into realities' and that the Athenians' decision was based on an unjustified extension of Athenian military power. Yet, the generals rationalised that invading Melos was in the best interests of both Athens and Melos. For not only would it preserve the democratic values of Melos, it would pre-empt the anticipated takeover by Sparta.

Such an idea has been re-enacted on many occasions in the modern era. During the **cold war** era, pre-emption played an important role, albeit in a strictly military sense. In particular, it represented the first-strike capability of the **superpower:** the US's ability to use nuclear arms to destroy a Soviet city. During the 1950s, the US's first-strike capacity remained unequalled, which is to say that the US relied on its first-strike ability to deter the Soviet Union from attacking the US. However, by the 1960s the Soviet Union's first-strike capacity would rival the US's, resulting in the condition known as **mutually assured destruction** or **MAD**.

Whilst any nuclear pre-emptive strike strictly remains an option of the very last resort, states have used conventional military tactics to stage pre-emptive strikes and attacks. For Israel, pre-emption has, in many cases, become a matter of state survival at the expense of Arab state security. Two of the most well-known pre-emptive Israeli attacks occurred in 1967, when the neighbouring states of Jordan, Syria, and Egypt were perceived to be amassing their military forces along the Israeli border, and in 1981, when Israel launched an attack on Iraq's nuclear plant in Osirak. The attack in 1967 (the Seven Days War), however, had the effect of increasing tensions dramatically between Israel and its Arab neighbours to the south east and north. Despite the Camp David Accords (1978) and the Oslo Peace Accords (1993), tensions continue to remain high between Arab states and Israel.

During the post-9/11 era, pre-emption has assumed a central role in the Bush doctrine. Under this doctrine, pre-emption represents an aggressive plan of action or military tactic for conducting the global **war on terror**. According to the Bush administration, the US can ill-afford to wait for a **terrorist** threat to materialise fully before attacking. In order to avert the consequences of a terrorist attack, it must first strike at the terrorists and any state(s) harbouring them. The Bush administration has already invoked this rationale to justify its invasion of Iraq in 2003, by rationalising that Saddam Hussein's prior use of chemical gas against his own people demonstrated his potential willingness to use **weapons of mass destruction** against others. The aim of pre-emption, in this context, was to eliminate the potential threat posed by Saddam's purported supply of weapons of mass destruction; first by deposing Saddam, then by installing a new democratic government that would help to safeguard the country from future threats to its safety and freedom.

It is important to note how pre-emption challenges two of the following long-standing tenets of **realism** in US foreign policy: (1) the need to exercise self-restraint and prudence in the pursuit of its goals; and (2) the necessity of engaging actively in **diplomacy** in order to resolve policy differences. For realists, the state's exercise of self-restraint arises from imperfect information at the international level. Because one country is liable to misinterpret the intentions of another, and vice versa, there remains the ever present possibility of war; hence the need for diplomacy. The problem of gathering sufficient evidence thus exposes the difficult consequences of pre-emption. Many, for instance, have argued that it creates more uncertainty than it eliminates, thereby exacerbating the very tensions that it seeks to diminish.

It is not surprising, then, that pre-emption has been labelled as an extremely risky strategy. Not only does it serve to generate seemingly uncontrollable circumstances; it also challenges **international law**, in particular, the principle of self-defence encoded in Article 51 of the **UN** Charter. In effect, pre-emption blurs the line between self-defence and the actions of the aggressor, making it difficult, if not self-defeating, to justify the policy. It should also be stressed that preemption, as suggested by the Bush doctrine, constitutes the need for absolute security. Yet absolute security, for many, can only lead to its opposite condition: absolute insecurity. One therefore needs to be cautious with how one justifies pre-emption, since the concept introduces more risk and uncertainty than it tries to eliminate or control.

*See also:* **Bush doctrine; coercion; security; sovereignty; unilateralism; war; war on terror; weapons of mass destruction**

*Further reading:* Dolan, 2005; Ikenberry, 2002; Spence, 2005; Thucydides, 1954

# PREVENTIVE DIPLOMACY

The main focus of preventive diplomacy is to identify and respond to brewing conflicts in order to prevent the outbreak of violence. Supporters of preventive diplomacy believe that conflicts are easier to resolve before they become violent. Once a violent conflict has erupted, it is extremely difficult to bring it to an end. In the meantime, lives have been lost, new waves of hatred have been created, and enormous damage has been inflicted. On the other hand, some scholars argue that conflicts may not be ripe for resolution until a 'hurting stalemate' has set in, when the situation has become intolerable to both sides and appears likely to become very costly. When a hurting stalemate is eventually reached, by definition both parties have suffered great losses and have become desperate to compromise. Agreements that might have been unacceptable previously may appear more palatable when compared to the pain the parties are suffering or expect to endure in the future. Typically it takes considerable time – often years – before parties to intense conflicts reach a hurting stalemate. In the interim, they all lose a great deal.

Preventive diplomacy offers the possibility of avoiding much of the pain and suffering associated with violent conflict and the hurting stalemate that so often follows violence. Potential third parties (such as states or international organisations) can be most effective when they recognise that a much earlier point of intervention may be available. Before a conflict turns violent, the issues in the dispute are fewer and less complex, and conflicting parties are not highly mobilised, polarised, and armed. Significant bloodshed has not occurred, and thus a sense of victimisation and a desire for vengeance are not intense. The parties have not begun to demonise and stereotype each other, moderate leaders still maintain control over extremist tendencies, and the parties are not so committed to victory that compromise involves loss of face.

However, a difficulty in applying preventive diplomacy is that very often only a very narrow window of opportunity exists during which parties may intervene to prevent the outbreak of violence. At early stages in a conflict, the gravity of the situation may not be recognised so that no stimulus to intervene arises. Furthermore, premature intervention may actually create a self-fulfilling prophecy and even stimulate conflict in the minds of disputing parties. Early interventions that are insensitive to local conditions, the needs and interests of the parties, and the nature of their conflict may also widen rather than narrow differences between the parties. For example, if outside parties and international institutions appear to legitimise **nationalist** claims for **self-determination** at the outset of a conflict, they may also legitimise extremist propaganda and undermine existing political authorities. At the same time, if outside parties wait too long, the threshold of violence may be crossed before preventive diplomacy can be engaged. Once that threshold is crossed, any opportunity to resolve the conflict may be seriously delayed or lost altogether. Timing the engagement of preventive diplomacy is thus an extremely critical, yet elusive, factor in the process of conflict resolution.

Preventive diplomacy first requires attention to 'early warning' to detect situations that might lead to violent conflict. Protests, demonstrations, and riots may provide such early warning signals, as may repressive actions by governments to suppress dissent. Parties to disputes may themselves report threats to the peace that they have witnessed or experienced. These warnings usually appear in the midst of conflicts between states or within them. Among the most prominent warnings of an incipient conflict are irredentist appeals to **secede** and unify with another state, threats to expand an ongoing conflict into neighbouring states, sporadic guerrilla action by radicalised minority group members against state institutions or their representatives, and indications of potential unauthorised external intervention in ongoing internal conflicts.

Early warning is not enough to trigger an appropriate response, however. There must also be a capability to distinguish warnings of real conflicts from false alarms. The problem for preventive diplomacy is often not the inability to identify potential trouble spots but, rather, one of understanding such situations well enough to forecast which ones are likely to explode and when. However good their intentions, states and **multilateral** organisations may antagonise important constituencies by too many cries of 'wolf' when no violence takes place. They may also alienate parties if they try to intervene prematurely in situations that do not seem to justify early outside intervention. And they may exhaust both their willpower and their limited resources by trying to intervene in more conflicts than they can handle at any one time.

Once the incipient **crisis** has been recognised, the next and often more difficult problem is to get the parties to enter into direct negotiations among themselves or get outsiders to intervene. Early warning does not necessarily make for easy response. Preventive diplomacy may take many forms, such as verbal **diplomatic** protests and denunciations, imposing **sanctions**, active monitoring and verification of agreements, **peacekeeping**, providing good offers, and other forms of third-party mediation.

*See also:* **crisis; diplomacy; Organisation for Security and Cooperation in Europe; peace-building; peacekeeping; United Nations; wars of the third kind**

*Further reading:* George and Holl, 1997; Lake and Rothchild, 1998; Lund, 1995

## PRISONERS' DILEMMA

A particular example within game **theory**, which demonstrates how and why a rational selection of strategies may be less profitable than a non-rational selection in certain situations. Before describing this game and its application to international relations, it is important to have a basic understanding of game theory in general. Game theory is a formal mathematical method used to study decision-making in situations of conflict or bargaining, in which it is assumed that each player will seek his or her maximum advantage under conditions of rationality. Players may be individuals, or groups such as states. The framework of game theory consists of the players, a statement of their values in quantified form, the rules and the pay-offs for each combination of moves. The result of any game may be *determinate* (i.e. one solution is logical as an outcome, given conditions of complete rationality) or *indeterminate* (i.e. no single logical outcome is obvious). Game theory usually concentrates on two-player games, as calculations and statements of strategies rapidly increase in complexity with games of more than two players.

The values that players attach to possible outcomes of the game must be quantified, in order to allow the calculation of optimal strategies and the pay-offs of the various outcomes. A strategy is a set of contingency instructions concerning moves in the game, designed to cope with all possible moves, or combinations of moves, of the opponent. The rules of the game state all the relevant conditions under which the game is played, such as which player moves first or whether moves are simultaneous; how moves are communicated; what information is available to each player concerning the opponent's values and strategies; whether threats can be made binding; and whether and to what extent side-payments are permitted (these are payments made by one player to the other outside the formal structure of rewards and penalties of the game itself, such as a bribe). Games may be *zero-sum* (where the pay-offs to the players add to zero: what one loses, the other wins), or *non-zero-sum* (where certain outcomes are possible which give both players advantages or disadvantages, compared to other outcomes).

The type of game known as Prisoners' Dilemma is a non-zero-sum game. The scenario involves two prisoners who are suspected of jointly committing a crime, but neither has yet confessed. They are held in separate cells, unable to communicate with each other. Each prisoner is told that: (1) if neither confesses both will go free; (2) if both confess they will both be imprisoned; and (3) if only one confesses, turning state's evidence against the other, that one will be positively rewarded while the other will serve a longer prison term.

Since each prisoner is better off confessing, given the action of the other (the reward is better than just going free, and the short prison term is better than the long one), the normal outcome in the absence of cooperation between the prisoners is for both to confess. Both could be better off than that equilibrium, however, if they could somehow agree to cooperate and neither confess. Unfortunately for them, such cooperation is bound to be difficult since both have an incentive to break any agreement by confessing.

The lesson of this game for students of international relations is that cooperation among states will be difficult to achieve in the absence of communication and of ways to enforce agreements. Three possible strategies to overcome such difficulties are widely discussed in the literature.

First, the expectation that players will fail to cooperate assumes that the game is played only once. However, if the game is repeated with the same players, and assuming that they value future absolute gains from cooperation, it is possible that they will learn to achieve a mutually beneficial outcome by employing a 'tit-for-tat' strategy. This prescribes that a state initially cooperates and thereafter mimics another state's moves – cooperating or defecting. Over time, the other state may become convinced that the first state will cooperate if it does.

Second, some scholars argue that the creation of powerful international institutions or **regimes** helps states to cooperate, even though they co-exist in an international political system characterised by structural **anarchy**.

Third, it may be argued that the degree to which the system confronts states with dilemmas modelled in the above scenario is often exaggerated. There are some major problems in reducing real-life situations to the form of a game, including the quantification of preferences (i.e. the degree to which states are motivated by the pursuit of **relative** or **absolute gains** through cooperation), the complications introduced by third parties or coalitions, and the general distinction between the complications of actual situations and the formal rigour of game theory.

*See also:* **anarchy; arms control; beggar-thy-neighbour policies; regime; relative gains/absolute gains**

*Further reading:* Axelrod, 1984; Axelrod and Keohane, 1985; Conybeare, 1984; Jervis, 1988; Schelling, 1984; Snidal, 1985

# PUBLIC GOODS

It is widely acknowledged that the marketplace is the most efficient way of producing private goods. But the market relies on a set of goods that it cannot itself provide: property rights, predictability, safety, and so on. These goods often need to be provided by non-market or modified market mechanisms. In addition, people need both public and private goods, whether or not they engage in market transactions – peace is a case in point. Public goods are recognised as having benefits that cannot easily be confined to a single buyer or set of buyers. Yet once they are provided, many can enjoy them for free. Street names are an example; a clean environment is another. Without a mechanism for collective action, these goods can be underproduced. A stricter definition relies on a judgement of how the good is consumed: if no one can be barred from consuming the good, then it is *non-excludable*. If it can be consumed by many without becoming depleted, then it is *non-rival* in consumption. Pure public goods, which are rare, have both these attributes, while impure public goods possess them to a lesser degree, or possess a combination of them.

Looking at education can help us understand why public goods are difficult to produce in proper quantities. Suppose there are many illiterate people and many eager employers. A person's first employer would be the one to shoulder the burden of educating her. But why should that first employer pay all the costs, while future employers will reap the benefits for free? This prospect might discourage employers from paying the cost to educate their workforce. The solution is for all employers to pool resources to jointly finance education or at least to bridge the gap between the benefits that education brings to individuals – for which they could pay – and the extra benefits that employers jointly get. But since non-employers benefit as well, the whole community is usually brought into this effort.

This, in a simplified form, is the dilemma of providing public goods. And with **globalisation**, the externalities – the extra costs and benefits – are increasingly borne by people in other countries. Indeed, issues that have traditionally been merely national are now global because they are beyond the grasp of any single state.

In the study of international relations, **realists** argue that the supply of public goods depends upon the existence of a single leader. In international economic affairs, for example, an open trading system, well-defined property rights, common standards of measures including international money, consistent macroeconomic policies, proper action in case of economic **crises**, and stable exchange rates, are said to be public goods. The public goods analysis of **international political economy** gained prominence parallel to the ascent of **regime** analysis. Regimes, international institutions, and the decision-making procedures that led to them have been considered to serve the interest of all countries. However, in the absence of external enforcement, realists argue that countries are reluctant to negotiate international regimes since all actors have an incentive to free-ride.

In theory, the probability that public goods (including those constituting a **liberal international** economic **order**) will not be provided is high if the number of actors is large. One way to solve the problem is to introduce selective incentives. If a private good is unavoidably linked to the public good, the latter may result as a by-product. Alternatively, a small group of cooperating actors, or joint leaders, can replace a **hegemon**, thus jointly providing international public goods. Openness, therefore, can arise or be maintained in the absence of a hegemon.

*See also:* **globalisation; hegemonic stability theory; hegemony; regime; relative gains/absolute gains**

*Further reading:* Conybeare, 1984; Gowa, 1989; Hardin, 1982; Olson, 1971

# REALISM √

The name given to a particular theoretical approach to the study of international relations. According to its proponents, realism has been around for a very long time. Some scholars trace its intellectual origins all the way back to Thucydides, the chronicler of the Peloponnesian **wars**. Thucydides argued that the cause of the war between the Athenians and the Spartans (around 420 BC) was an increase in Athenian military **power** and the insecurity that it created among the Spartans. In making this and other observations about state behaviour, Thucydides is said to have begun one of the main traditions of thinking about international relations. Niccolo Machiavelli, Thomas Hobbes, and Max Weber are also regarded as seminal thinkers in this intellectual tradition, although it is quite possible to find statements by a large number of past philosophers, theologians, historians, and political commentators that might be called realist. It is important to recognise, however, that none of these early writers actually thought of himself as a realist. Thus while the origins of realism may lie in the writings of these early thinkers, its formulation as a theoretical approach to the study of international relations is a relatively recent development beginning in the late 1930s and early 1940s.

E. H. Carr and Hans J. Morgenthau are crucial figures in that development. They were among the first scholars to use the term 'realism' and to elaborate its fundamental assumptions by contrast with the allegedly **idealistic** study of international relations that prevailed during the interwar period. They claimed that there was no natural harmony of interests among states and that it was foolish and even dangerous to hope that the struggle for power among states could be tamed by **international law**, **democratisation**, and international commerce. For both these writers, the failure of idealistic students as well as some diplomats to understand these basic points was part of the reason why the **League of**

**Nations** failed to stop the outbreak of the Second World War and why Hitler nearly succeeded in conquering Europe.

Whatever their other differences, and there are many, all realists share a common premise; that the realm of interstate behaviour is sufficient unto itself for the purposes of explanation and normative justification. Realism conjures up a grim image of international politics. Within the territorial boundaries of the formally **sovereign** state, politics is an activity of potential moral progress through the social construction of constitutional government. Beyond the exclusionary borders of its sovereign presence, politics is essentially the realm of survival rather than progress. Necessity, not freedom, is the appropriate or realistic starting-point for understanding international relations. A precarious form of **order** through the **balance of power**, not **cosmopolitan** justice, is the best we can hope for in the international **anarchy**: a realm of continual struggles for power and **security** among states. Thus, realism contains both descriptive and prescriptive insights about international relations.

Realists are great lovers of history. According to them, history teaches us that war and conflict are the norm in international relations. Proposals for **perpetual peace** simply fly in the face of history and fail to take into account the fact that human nature is fundamentally flawed. It is this hard-nosed and uncompromising view of international relations that has led to realists being referred to as conservatives and pessimists.

Despite its dominance throughout the post-1945 era, realism has been the subject of endless criticism and elaboration, much of it from those sympathetic to some of its fundamental assumptions. For example, many scholars were unhappy with the terminological imprecision in Morgenthau's understanding of realism. He used the term 'power' in so many ways that it was impossible to understand precisely what he meant by the term. In the 1960s and 1970s other scholars thought that realism needed to be modified to account for the increase in the level of institutional and economic **interdependence** among states. But perhaps the most significant criticism of early, or what is called classical, realism relates to its postulate that wars start because human beings are evil by nature. If this is the case, then how is it that peace and cooperation occur from time to time? Overcoming this problem is one of the key characteristics of *neorealism*. Kenneth Waltz, its leading exponent, argues that realism does not need this postulate. Instead, he argues that anarchy is a crucial structural feature of the international system. Wars occur as a result of this structure rather than as a result of particular defects in human nature.

Waltz may have rescued realism from some of its critics, but his new structuralist version became the focal point of a critique that was far broader in scope than anything the discipline had known previously. Critics attacked the scientific pretensions of neorealism, its defence of **cold war** bipolarity in sustaining international order, and its marginalisation of ethical questions.

Today, some scholars are asking whether realism still has any relevance in an allegedly shrinking and **globalising** world where intrastate violence seems to have taken the place of interstate war. Only time will tell. But realism does have an extraordinary capacity for adaptation and modification. Those who are hopeful of its demise, therefore, are likely to be in for a long wait to see their ambitions fulfilled.

*See also:* **anarchy; balance of power; communitarianism; constructivism; end of history; idealism; interdependence; national interest; power; theory**

*Further reading:* Donnelly, 2000; Griffiths, 1995; Guzzini, 1998; Keohane, 1986b; Mastanduno, 1999; Waltz, 1959, 1979

## RECIPROCITY

To reciprocate means to give and take on a mutual basis. Reciprocity is therefore the quality of a relationship in which the parties engage in the mutual exchange of goods, services, or other aspects of the relationship. In the study of international relations, reciprocity is usually discussed in the context of **international law** and trade relations between states.

In discussions of international law, reciprocity is often presented as the reason why states abide by rules without the need for some set of institutions to enforce the rules through the threat or use of **coercion**.

This claim assumes that the major problem undermining compliance with international law is the absence of trust among states. However, the long-term advantages of observing international law may be greater than the short-term advantages of violating it. As long as most states respond in good faith to each other's compliance with agreements, then a virtual cycle of 'tit for tat' behaviour may evolve. Reciprocity can then promote a stable international environment in which those states that choose to violate international law may be excluded from the society of states.

In the context of trade relations among states, reciprocity is a key concept in the study of **regimes**. It is often claimed to be one reason for the willingness of states to engage in and abide by trade agreements, particularly those that facilitate the expansion of **free trade** in the global economy. For example, reciprocity gives exporters an incentive to lobby for liberalisation in international trade. Without reciprocity, the costs of protection are concentrated in import-competing industries, while the benefits of liberalisation are diffuse. In contrast, a reciprocal trade agreement yields foreign liberalisation, the benefits of which are concentrated in export industries. In the United States, the advantages of reciprocal trade agreements with other states have enhanced the power of the American President to negotiate specific reciprocal trade agreements with other states. To obtain concentrated benefits for exporters, Congress delegates trade negotiation authority to the President, who has the sole **power** to negotiate with foreign governments, and whose preferences generally favour more trade liberalisation. Exporter lobbying for reciprocal agreements causes legislators' preferences to shift in favour of greater liberalisation. This encourages further delegation of authority to the President.

It should not be assumed that reciprocity is always a good thing. One should distinguish between *negative* and *balanced* reciprocity. The former refers to the mutual exchange of harms rather than benefits. Think of the reciprocal escalation of arms spending by the **superpowers** during the **cold war**. The latter term refers to the exchange of equally valued benefits among states. One should also bear in mind an important distinction between *direct* and *indirect* or *diffuse* reciprocity. The former refers to reciprocal agreements between particular states. The latter refers to **multilateral** agreements between groups of states. Such agreements may benefit each member of the group in the long run, but the costs and benefits may not be equally distributed at any given time. The degree to which direct reciprocal agreements complement or compete with diffuse or indirect agreements remains a key issue in the debate between supporters of **regionalism** and multilateralism in the study of contemporary international trade.

*See also:* **beggar-thy-neighbour policies; international law; multilateralism; prisoners' dilemma; regime**

*Further reading:* Becker, 1986; Gilligan, 1997; Keohane, 1986b; Rhodes, 1993

# RECOGNITION

Membership in the international system depends on the general recognition by other states of a government's **sovereignty** within its territory. Such recognition is extended formally through the establishment of **diplomatic** relations and by membership in the **United Nations** (UN). It does not necessarily imply that a government has popular support but only that it (usually) controls the state's territory and agrees to assume its obligations in the international system – to accept internationally recognised borders, to assume the international debts of the previous government, and to refrain from interfering in other states' internal affairs. In other words, the act of recognition establishes the status of a political entity in **international society**. That status provides the new state with formal equality in the context of **international law**: it is able to join international organisations, and its representatives are entitled to all the benefits of diplomatic immunity.

Since 1945 recognition has taken place primarily in the context of **decolonisation**. However, since the end of the **cold war**, recognition has played an important role in the dissolution of states that have fragmented as **nationalism** has re-emerged as a potent force in international relations. The process has been surprisingly peaceful in some cases (for example, the former Czechoslovakia and the former Soviet Union) and extremely violent in others, particularly Yugoslavia.

There is no collective agreed practice, in law or politics, to guide state recognition. It is a **unilateral** decision rather than a collective one, and as yet there are no universal criteria for recognition. Some states are explicit in the criteria they use (for example, Britain) whilst others such as the United States prefer greater flexibility in determining whether to accord recognition. The British tend to rely on the effectiveness of control over a particular territory exercised by a fledgling state, but this preference is not shared by all states. For example, in 1967 five states (Gabon, Ivory Coast, Zambia, Haiti, and Tanzania) recognised Biafra's claim to independence from Nigeria. By 1970 Biafra acknowledged that it had not managed to establish such independence, leading to the withdrawal of recognition by the other African states. The advantage of the British position is that it signifies neither approval nor support of the new state. In contrast, the United States uses diplomatic recognition as an instrument of its foreign policy. Thus it recognised the State of Israel within a day of that country's unilateral declaration of independence in May 1948, but it refused to extend recognition to the People's Republic of China until 1979.

Since the late 1970s, although the United States has moved closer to the British position on recognition, there remains a lack of consensus in the international community over the conditions for recognising new states or for withdrawing recognition from existing states. This became clear during the early 1990s in the context of the wars in Yugoslavia. In 1991 Germany argued that it would unilaterally recognise Slovenia and Croatia at the end of the year. Britain argued that such recognition was premature in light of the ongoing war with the nominal Federal Republic of Yugoslavia. There were powerful arguments on both sides of the issue. Germany argued that recognition would send a clear message to the Serbian government that its aggression could not continue without transforming a civil war into an interstate conflict. On the other hand, in the absence of any commitment to assist Croatia militarily, it remained unclear why Serbia would heed the message. Ultimately, Germany succeeded in prevailing over dissenting voices in the **European Union**, but there is little evidence that recognition had any effect over the conflicts that continued throughout the first half of the 1990s.

The issue was again raised in 1999 during the conflict between Serbia and the Yugoslav Republic of Kosovo. This time the United States mobilised its **NATO** allies to bomb Serbia because of its repression of the Kosovars, but the United States refused to countenance Kosovo as an independent state. It argued that such recognition could lead to further fragmentation in the region, although it was difficult for many observers to see how Kosovo and Serbia could remain part of a single state after the war.

In short, the acts of recognition as well as the withdrawal of recognition remain political acts. They vary from state to state, and a particular state can use different criteria over time depending on its interpretation of the national interest. Whilst recognition provides a state with important privileges that come with membership of an exclusive club, it is not accompanied by any guarantees. The wars in Yugoslavia provide another good example of this lesson. When conflict broke out in Bosnia in 1992, the existing (Muslim) government was widely recognised by the international community. It was of little help in preventing the de facto partition of Bosnia three years later.

*See also:* **diplomacy; humanitarian intervention; international law; self-determination; sovereignty**

*Further reading:* Chimkin, 1992; Krasner, 1999; Peterson, 1997

## REFUGEES

According to conventional usage, a refugee is someone seeking refuge from danger. In international relations, the legal definition is more restrictive. As defined by the 1951 Convention relating to the Status of Refugees, refugees are individuals who, owing to a well-founded fear of being persecuted for reasons of race, religion, nationality, membership of a particular social group or political opinion, are outside the country of their nationality and are unable or, owing to such fear, unwilling to avail themselves of the protection of that country. Refugees are therefore people who need the protection of a foreign state. Asylum-seekers are people who apply to that state to have their refugee status recognised. Refugees may enter a state legally or illegally, individually or as part of a mass movement.

They may eventually return home, settle indefinitely in the country of asylum, or resettle in a state that accepts refugees from other countries.

International concern to assist refugees began in earnest after the First World War. The first High Commissioner for Refugees was appointed in 1921, specifically to assist Russians uprooted by **war** and revolution. Over the next 20 years there were several attempts to protect refugees, including the establishment of the International Force for Refugees (1930), the Intergovernmental Committee on Refugees (1938), and the **United Nations** Relief and Rehabilitation Administration (1943). Each new organisation received a larger mandate than its predecessor. At the end of the Second World War, an International Refugee Organisation was established to return or resettle the thousands of refugees created by the war in Europe. Although it helped to stabilise the region, its task remained incomplete when the United Nations began discussions to establish the United Nations High Commission for Refugees (UNHCR) as part of a broader attempt to promote a formal, **multilateral** approach to the problem.

The mandate of the UNHCR is to implement the landmark 1951 Convention. Although it is a creation of Western states, the UNHCR is a humanitarian organisation, whose mission is to protect and promote the rights of refugees. Under the Convention, these rights include freedom of religion (Article 4), access to courts (Article 16), access to employment (Article 17), access to education (Article 22), public benefits (Article 23), and freedom of movement (Article 26). As far as possible, states are obliged to grant refugees the same rights as citizens. Despite the humanitarian basis for this legislation, states continue to have the choice to limit the scope of certain rights, and retain the authority to implement their obligations through their own legal processes. Indeed, the wording of the legal definition places a large burden of proof on refugees to demonstrate that their fear is in fact well founded.

Patterns of refugee movements have varied a great deal in the second half of the twentieth century. In the 1940s, refugees from war-torn Europe were the focus of attention. In the 1950s, as tension between liberal **capitalist** states and the **communist** bloc increased, accepting refugees from the East became a useful propaganda tool for Western states, demonstrating the superiority of political systems based on individual **human rights**. Since the definition involved persecution, granting the status to people fleeing communist **regimes** reflected badly on the entire communist system. From the 1960s onwards, the flow of refugees increased from **Third World** states. In addition to changing patterns of refugee movements, there has been a sustained increase in the numbers of refugees. In 1980, there were about 6 million refugees and 2 million internally displaced persons worldwide. At the start of 2006, there were nearly 21 million refugees, an increase of six percent from 2005. It should be noted that the vast majority of these people are not going to Western countries. At most, only about 10 per cent claim asylum in industrialised states.

The problem of refugees can be expected to increase in the twenty-first century. There are two main reasons. First, the conditions that generate refugees are unlikely to disappear in the foreseeable future. Patterns of demographic change are very uneven. Rapid **population growth** is confined to developing states, who are also confronting huge economic and political challenges as inequality continues to grow between rich and poor. The post-**cold war** era has also been characterised by the spread of civil wars in which civilians have been the explicit target of **ethnic cleansing**, sometimes as a deliberate policy of their own governments. The forced migration of people is often a deliberate strategy, as has been dramatically illustrated in Yugoslavia and East Timor over the last decade. In such circumstances, many states face the possibility of sudden, massive influxes of refugees. Second, despite the humanitarian sympathy for refugees in most Western states, this is tempered by ongoing concerns over unemployment and economic insecurity. Consequently, Western states are unlikely to subordinate their perceived **national interests** to humanitarian impulses. As more states restrict their refugee intake, it becomes harder for particular states *not* to follow the trend. If one state's laws are more generous than its neighbours' are, asylum-seekers will naturally favour it over other countries in the region. Germany provides a good example. Prior to unification, West Germany included a clause in its Constitution giving refugees the automatic right to asylum, which is more than the UNHCR Convention orders. Consequently, it received more applications for asylum than any other state in Europe (over half a million in 1992 alone). Germany removed this right from its Constitution in 1993.

The UNHCR is under great pressure as a result of these trends. On the one hand, its mandate is expanding to focus on forced displacement of people within as well as between states, and it is also at the forefront of repatriation efforts as well as the provision of humanitarian assistance to war-affected populations. Worldwide, refugees now constitute only 50 per cent of UNHCR's beneficiaries. At the same time, it is dependent on voluntary financial contributions to carry out existing and new programmes. The sum required for UNHCR operations has risen from around US$550 million in 1990 to over US$1.45 billion in 2006. Under the new UNHCR mandate of 1993, the UNHCR has continued to seek what it calls three durable solutions: (1) voluntary repatriation by the refugees; (2) local settlement in the host country; and (3) third party resettlement, administered by either a third state or the United Nations.

*See also:* **cold war; diaspora; ethnic cleansing; safe haven; United Nations; wars of the third kind**

*Further reading:* Loescher, 1992, 1993; Plaut, 1995; Richmond, 1994; UNHCR, 2000

## REGIME ✓

Regimes are sets of principles, procedures, norms, or rules that govern particular issue areas within international relations. Regimes are important because they facilitate some form of **global governance** in an **anarchical** realm. They reflect the fact that states often have converging interests and are willing to cooperate to achieve certain outcomes. As a consequence, some scholars believe that regimes play a significant role in reducing the level of international conflict between states and facilitating cooperation at the international level.

Regimes can take the form of conventions, international agreements, treaties, or international institutions. They can be found in a variety of issue areas, including economics, the environment, policing, transport, **security**, communications, **human rights**, **arms control**, even copyright and patents. Indeed, they exist in most issue areas where states have similar interests. The **World Trade Organisation** (WTO), the **United Nations** Convention on the Law of the Sea (UNCLOS), and the Chemical Weapons Convention (CWC) are all examples of firmly established regimes.

A regime can be bilateral, **multilateral**, **regional**, or global in scope. It can also be formal and highly institutionalised or quite loose and informal. The WTO is a good example of a formal and institutionalised regime, while UNCLOS and the CWC have fewer institutional structures underpinning them. Yet they are similar in the sense that each requires compliance from states. States that have accepted the conditions set out by the regime are under an obligation to act according to its principles.

The notion of convergence is crucial to understanding the character of regimes. Regimes presuppose that states have similar interests across a range of issues and that these interests can best be served by coordinated action. In other words, regimes provide a regulatory framework for states that facilitates a semblance of global governance. Imagine, for example, the difficulty in getting mail to someone on the other side of the world without a formal agreement governing the distribution of mail. Think for a moment about the chaos in the skies if there were no rules or procedures regulating airline traffic. Who would risk overseas flights under such circumstances?

Some scholars have argued that regimes function best when power is concentrated in the hands of a preponderant state. Hegemonic stability theory suggests that the presence of a hegemon makes it possible (and easier) to enforce rules and norms across an issue area. The role of the United States in putting in place an open trading system in the aftermath of the Second World War is often cited as an example of the importance of power in determining the success of regimes.

Since the 1970s, **theoretical** inquiry into regimes has developed into a growth industry. Today, there are at least three main divisions within contemporary regime theory:

- *Realist theories* stress the role of power in generating cooperation between states.
- *Interest-based theories* highlight the value of regimes in promoting the common interests of states.
- *Knowledge-based theories* focus primarily on the way that ideas and norms shape perceptions of international problems and the role of regimes in this process.

Despite the differences of emphasis in these approaches, all agree that regimes are an important source of stability in the international arena, particularly as states increasingly confront problems that do not respect territorial boundaries and require international cooperation.

*See also:* **anarchy; constructivism; global governance; hegemonic stability theory; international society; realism**

*Further reading:* Aggarwal, 1998; Crawford, 1996; Hasenclever *et al.*, 1997; Krasner, 1982; Strange, 1982

## REGIONAL TRADE BLOCS

The rapid growth of regional trading relationships in Europe, Asia, and Latin America has raised policy concerns about their impact on excluded countries and on the global trading system. Some observers worry that the **multilateral** system may be fracturing into discriminatory regional blocs. Others are hopeful that regional agreements will instead become building-blocks for further global trade liberalisation. This is certainly not the first time in history that **regionalism** has been popular. There were widespread attempts at regional trading arrangements in the 1960s which largely failed. But before that, in the 1930s, there was a major fragmentation of the world trading system into competing blocs.

There is little point in trying to identify the earliest regional trading arrangement in history. For as long as there have been **nation-states** with trade policies, they have discriminated in favour of some valued neighbours and against others. Regional trading arrangements have at times played major roles in political history. For example, the German *Zollverein*, the customs union that was formed among 18 small states in 1834, was a step on the way to the creation of Germany later in the century. This precedent has not been lost on those Europeans who today wish to turn the **European Union** into a single state.

It is somewhat easier to identify the historical origins of the obverse of regional trade blocs: the principle of non-discriminatory trade policies. The principle goes under the name of *most-favoured nation* (MFN) policies. The United Kingdom adopted non-discrimination as its trade policy early in the nineteenth century, when it undertook unilateral trade liberalisation in 1846 through the famous repealing of the Corn Laws. The principle of non-discrimination began to spread to other countries with the Anglo-French commercial treaty of 1860.

The principle says that when a country extends trade concessions to one partner, it must extend them to all. Nineteenth-century negotiators hoped that the procedure would eliminate a potentially harmful incentive that would otherwise hamper negotiations. That is, those who negotiated early had an incentive to withhold concessions, for fear that a partner who entered negotiations at a later stage would get a better bargain, from which the early partner would be excluded. As it turned out in the late nineteenth century, the system based on the non-discrimination principle worked well and helped to reduce tariffs among an ever-growing number of countries.

After the First World War, strenuous efforts of Britain and the **League of Nations** to reinstate the MFN clause as the basis of trading arrangements were unsuccessful. The world divided into separate blocs such as the British Commonwealth, Central Europe, and others. The victorious allies who planned the world economic system after 1945, particularly the United States, believed that the discriminatory trade practices in the 1930s had contributed to the collapse of world trade and in turn to the Great Depression. Accordingly, the MFN principle was built into the postwar trading system in the form of Article I of the General Agreement on Tariffs and Trade (GATT). The United States opposed discriminatory tariff policies, such as the British Commonwealth preferences, at the time of the GATT's founding. It soon dropped its opposition to preferences, however, in the context of European

**integration**. The Americans considered the political desirability of peaceful European integration to be important enough to warrant an exception to the MFN principle.

Between 1990 and 1994, the GATT was informed of 33 regional trading arrangements, nearly a third of all deals since 1948. The surge in regional trading arrangements over the last 20 years constitutes a break with preceding postwar history. Previous regional agreements had been neither so numerous, nor so successful, as those of recent years. Perhaps most important, where the United States once tended to oppose them, choosing to emphasise multilateral liberalisation through the GATT instead, now the United States is at the forefront of some of the largest regional initiatives. Some observers are concerned that the world is dividing into three continental trading blocs, one in the Americas centred on the United States, one in Europe centred on the European Union, and one in Pacific Asia centred on Japan.

Formal regional trading agreements can cover a spectrum of arrangements, from small margins of preference in tariffs to full-scale economic integration. Five levels can be distinguished: preferential trade arrangements, free trade areas, customs unions, common markets, and economic unions. The loosest type of arrangement is the granting of partial *preferences* to a set of trading partners. If the concessions are **reciprocal**, we may apply the term preferential trade arrangement (PTA) to describe the club of countries covered. If the members of a *preferential trade arrangement* go so far as to eliminate all tariffs and quantitative import restrictions among themselves (100 per cent preferences), then they form a *free trade area* (FTA). Typically, they retain varying levels of tariffs and other barriers against the products of nonmembers. The next level of integration occurs when the members of an FTA go beyond removing trade barriers among themselves and set a common level of trade barriers *vis-à-vis* outsiders. This at a minimum entails a common external tariff. A full *customs union* would also harmonise quantitative restrictions, export subsidies, and other trade distortions. Indeed, it would set all trade policy for its members as a unified whole. It would, for example, engage in any future trade negotiations with other countries with a single voice.

Beyond the free exchange of goods and services among members, a *common market* entails the free movement of factors of production, namely labour and capital. Going beyond the free movement of goods, services, and factors, *economic union* involves harmonising national economic policies, including typically taxes and a common currency. The decision of the European Community to change its name to the European Union in 1994 represented a determination to proceed to this higher stage of

**integration**. The full unification of economic policies typically would in turn require political federation.

*See also:* **beggar-thy-neighbour policies; Bretton Woods; European Union; free trade; multilateralism; non-tariff barriers; reciprocity; regionalism; World Trade Organisation**

*Further reading:* Bhalla and Bhalla, 1997; Frankel, 1997; Geiger and Kennedy, 1996; Ito and Krueger, 1997; Mason and Turay, 1994; Ohmae, 1995

## REGIONALISM

This term refers to intensifying political and/or economic processes of cooperation among states and other actors in particular geographic regions, although it is most often discussed in the context of trade flows. At least since the beginning of the 1980s, the world economy has become more and more tripolar, with more than 85 per cent of world trade concentrated in three regions: East Asia, Western Europe, and North America. At the same time, these are also areas in which attempts to engage in some regional **integration** have taken place. The deepening and the expansion of the European economic integration, increasing **interdependence** among three North American countries (US, Canada, Mexico) as well as the transformation of the Association of Southeast Asian Nations (ASEAN) into a more economy-oriented association since the 1980s are examples of this. In contrast, other regions have been successively losing their share of the world market, so that at the end of the twentieth century they represent approximately one-tenth of the world trade volume.

Essentially, a region is a spatial concept. It is defined by a combination of geographical proximity, density of interactions, shared institutional frameworks, and common cultural identities. Regions can be identified empirically by relying on data on mutual interactions such as trade flows, similarities of actor attributes, and shared values and experiences. But one should also bear in mind that regions are dynamic entities. They are not so much measurable building-blocks of the international **order** as spatially defined cultural, economic, and political constructions whose nature and functions are transformed over time.

The term 'regionalism' captures these dynamic aspects of regional cooperation defined as the growth of social and economic interaction and of regional identity and consciousness. Regionalism results from the increasing flow of goods, people, and ideas within a spatial entity which thus becomes more integrated and cohesive. Regionalism can develop 'from below' (i.e. from the decisions by companies to invest and by people to move within a region) or 'from above' (i.e. from political, state-based efforts to create cohesive regional units and common policies for them).

Practically everyone writing today on regionalism argues that it is growing strongly in almost every part of the world. This trend, sometimes depicted as the 'second coming' of regionalism (the first one took place in the 1960s), has been explained by several, often disparate, factors. The alleged decline of US material **hegemony**, the end of the **cold war**, the rise of the Asia-Pacific region, and the export-led reorientation of **development** strategies in the **Third World** have all fostered a more decentralised international system. This has, in turn, enhanced the autonomy of regions and their dominant actors. The standard arguments on the rise of regionalism mention, at a minimum, the establishment of the North American Free Trade Agreement (NAFTA), the deepening integration in the **European Union**, and the growing economic interdependence in East Asia. Regional cooperation may also be promoted as a counterweight to the uneven globalisation of the world economy. Finally, regionalism may be a reaction against dominant states that try to coopt local actors by granting special privileges to them.

The main debate about regionalism is whether it is leading to a more polarised or a more cooperative world economy and world order. While the proliferation of regional trade agreements has raised concerns about their implications for the multilateral trading system, most observers argue that these two systems have not been contradictory. However, the relationship between regionalism and a multilateral system is a complex one, and it is becoming more complex as the number and the scope of regional initiatives increase. Ensuring that regionalism and **multilateralism** grow together (*open* regionalism) – and not apart (*closed* regionalism) – is perhaps the most urgent issue facing trade policymakers today.

Well-structured regional integration arrangements may be helpful to the strengthening of an open world economy for three main reasons. First, regional arrangements can enhance the awareness of interdependence between trading partners, thereby enhancing the acceptance of international rules on the part of national governments and interest groups. Second, regional arrangements in general face similar challenges to those faced by the multilateral trading system. Therefore, the problems and solutions experienced during regional negotiations will be useful in overcoming similar difficulties that arise in the multilateral processes. Finally, increasing inter-regional cooperation mechanisms can serve as a building-block for the strengthening of multilateralism. The stronger the cooperation among the three major traders of the world economy (Asia, Europe, and North America), the more likely it is for the world economy to be integrated globally, rather than be fragmented into several **regional trade blocs**. Thus there can be a mutually supportive relationship between multilateralism and regionalism.

*See also:* **foreign direct investment; free trade; globalisation; regional trade blocs; World Trade Organisation**

*Further reading:* Coleman and Underhill, 1998; Fawcett and Hurrell, 1995; Gamble and Payne, 1996; Katzenstein, 1996b; Mittelman, 1996

## RELATIVE GAINS/ABSOLUTE GAINS

What are the main obstacles to international cooperation among states? For some scholars, the obstacles can be traced to the concern by national policymakers that even if all states gain from cooperation (an increase in absolute gains), some will do so more than others thereby enhancing their **power**. In short, states are primarily concerned with the distribution of gains from cooperation (or relative gains). For other scholars, such concerns are less important than the possibility that particular states will defect from cooperative arrangements to enhance their own interests, regardless of the distribution of gains from international cooperation. In international relations theory, the debate is usually framed as taking place between neorealists and neoliberal institutionalists.

Neorealism and neoliberal institutionalism are the dominant **theories** of international relations within mainstream North American international relations scholarship. Much of the debate in the field has been articulated in terms of disagreements between these two approaches. However, these two theories actually share many fundamental assumptions.

Neorealism is the more dominant theory. It argues that states act in accordance with the material structural incentives of the international system. State behaviour reflects the position of states within the international system. States' interests and strategies are based on calculations about their positions in the system. Thus, states seek to, at least, maintain their *relative* positions in the system. The greater a state's capabilities, the higher it is in the international hierarchy of power, and the greater its influence on the international stage. The structure of the international system is defined by this distribution of capabilities among states.

The neorealist understanding of state behaviour is underpinned by five core assumptions:

1   The first and most fundamental is the assumption of **anarchy**, a lack of overarching authority within the international system. This means that there is no power beyond states themselves that can enforce international agreements or protect the legitimate interests of states.
2   States possess military power and can be dangerous to each other. To some neorealists, power is reducible to military capabilities.
3   States can never be certain of the intentions of other states. An ally one day may be an enemy the next.
4   States are motivated by a concern with survival.
5   States are instrumentally rational actors.

Anarchy means that states must always be preoccupied with issues of **security** and their survival; they can rely only on themselves, and fear other states. If states do not act in accordance with the demands of anarchy, they will be weaker as a result. Using this logic, neorealists depict international cooperation as extremely difficult to achieve. States will avoid cooperation if other states benefit relatively more from a cooperative relationship.

Neoliberal institutionalism attempts to use the spare, self-interested rational actor assumptions of neorealism to show that cooperation under anarchy is possible within the international system. Neoliberals attribute this cooperation to the ability of international institutions and regimes to mitigate the effects of anarchy. Neoliberal institutionalists describe states as being *rational egoists* – they are narrowly self-interested and concerned only with increasing their own utility. When calculating their own utility, they have little interest in the utility functions of other states. Thus, if a cooperative endeavour is mutually beneficial, states may engage in that cooperative behaviour. Finally, it should be noted that neoliberals generally restrict their theory to economic interactions, believing the dynamics of cooperation to be much more difficult to achieve in security affairs.

Most neoliberals accept the neorealist characterisation of an anarchic international system. Again, anarchy indicates a lack of overarching authority which means a lack of enforcement mechanisms to ensure state compliance with international agreements. As a result, neoliberalism identifies a fear of cheating and defection as the major impediment to cooperation between states. This fear prevents cooperation even when it is rational for states to work together to their mutual benefit. Institutions or regimes address this fear in three distinct ways. First, they create a sense of legal liability (i.e. a sense of obligation between states to adhere to rules and agreements). Second, they reduce transaction costs between states (the cost of interactions both within and between issue areas, and the cost of rules being broken). Finally they provide transparency and information about issue areas and state actions. This is the most important function of regimes. The overall effect of regimes is to reduce uncertainty within the system, thereby allowing states to cooperate more fully. Thus, regimes mitigate the effects of anarchy. Neorealism and neoliberalism both study regimes as the instruments of states. The effectiveness of a regime is directly measured by the level of compliance with its rules by states.

*See also:* **anarchy; collective security; liberal internationalism; power; public goods; realism; regime**

*Further reading:* Baldwin, 1993; Grieco, 1990; Jervis, 1999

# ROGUE STATE

A state that regularly violates international standards of acceptable behaviour. Over the last decade Afghanistan, Cuba, Iran, Iraq, Libya, and North Korea have all been given this highly pejorative label. It evokes images of a state that is outwardly aggressive, a threat to international peace, highly repressive, xenophobic, and arrogant, and which has no regard for the norms of **international society**. It is no accident, then, that the term has found a home among some American policymakers. To refer to a state as a rogue is a way of justifying certain policy options, as well as mobilising public support for political action against such a state. What should not be lost sight of, however, is that in most cases it is the leadership that is rogue, and not the general populace. The term does not differentiate in this regard and, in most cases, it is the people who ultimately pay the price when the international community takes collective action against the rogue state. This is particularly evident in the case of Iraq.

The sort of behaviour that the international community regards as 'rogue behaviour' includes the development of chemical and biological weapons, attempting to buy the materials necessary for the construction of nuclear weapons, drug trafficking, failure to live up to international treaties, sponsorship of **terrorism**, invasion or the unwarranted provocation of neighbouring states, and the construction of long-distance missile delivery systems. A good example of rogue behaviour is North Korea's missile test flight over Japanese air-space in the mid-1990s. But the rogue state *par excellence* is undoubtedly Iraq. According to the United States, the Ba'athist regime has been involved in just about all the activities listed above. In April 2003, the US invaded Iraq in an attempt to uncover and destroy the weapons of mass destruction that Saddam Hussein was reported to be stockpiling. However, as of the summer 2007, inspectors have yet to uncover any weapons of mass destruction, which has raised concern about the strategic value of rogue state.

While not generally referred to as rogue states, a number of states are involved in some of the activities listed above. They are, in US foreign policy parlance, 'countries of concern'. Serbia is a good example. The distinction between rogue states and countries of concern highlights the fact that the United States, and by extension the international community, is willing to tolerate certain violations of **international law** by certain states without labelling them as rogues.

The international community has two main strategies for dealing with rogue states, namely containment or accommodation. Containment is, of course, a continuation of a **cold war** policy applied to particular states. A major component of this policy includes the imposition of **sanctions**. Many scholars believe that there is no guarantee that they can be successful. Iraq's government has demonstrated over the past few years that it has managed to survive the imposition of sanctions even if many Iraqi citizens have not.

Offering material rewards for complying with the wishes of the international community is another strategy that has been used against rogue states. This, of course, can be interpreted as a crude form of **appeasement**. Again, it is difficult to determine whether such a policy works. It remains to be seen, for example, whether the American attempt to convince North Korea to halt its nuclear weapons programme in return for aid and technical assistance will succeed.

One of the problems in treating particular states as rogues, pariahs, or 'backlash' states is that the international community must bear some of the responsibility for their recalcitrant behaviour. This is why there is something disingenuous about policymakers who use this language to describe certain states. For example, the United States has been only too willing to prop up and court unsavoury dictators, sell them advanced military hardware, and ignore their uncivilised and repressive behaviour if it served its interests to do so. It should be noted that rogue states are partly a product of an inequitable distribution of **power** and wealth in the international system. The best way to ensure that states like Iran, Libya, and Iraq do not become rogues in the first place is through strategies of inclusion, restraint in the sale of weaponry, debt cancellation, and a more ethical approach to the **Third World** by the international community.

*See also:* **appeasement; axis of evil; Bush doctrine; containment; failed state; sanctions; terrorism; weapons of mass destruction**

*Further reading:* Hoyt, 2000; Klare, 1995; Lake, 1994; Tanter, 1998

## SAFE HAVEN

The term 'safe haven' or, as it is sometimes called, 'safe *area*', refers to an area within a country of origin where would-be **refugees** are safe from **war** or persecution, thus creating an alternative to asylum outside the country. The idea was inaugurated with Operation Provide Comfort, the creation of a safe haven in northern Iraq in 1991. At the time, about 400,000 Iraqi Kurds were at or near the Turkish border, fleeing Saddam Hussein's armed forces. Until then, the traditional response under such circumstances had been for the country of first asylum, usually a contiguous country, to open its borders and provide at least temporary protection, and for the international community to lend support both with the costs of maintaining asylum and with seeking durable solutions. The international community not only offered support to promote first asylum, but also, if need be, exerted great pressure on first asylum countries not to push refugees back.

Operation Provide Comfort changed all that. Led by the United States, Britain, and France, and backed by **United Nations** (UN) Security Council Resolution 688, which spoke of Iraqi refugees themselves as posing a threat to international peace and **security**, the international community decided to introduce an international military force into northern Iraq to protect the Kurds where they were. This enabled Turkey, which had a major security concern with its own Kurds, to push the Iraqi Kurds away from its territory without risk of committing *refoulement*, the forcible return of refugees to persecution. It should be noted that Operation Provide Comfort never challenged Saddam Hussein's underlying sovereign claims to northern Iraq.

In 1991 Saddam Hussein had already been beaten by coalition forces at the time the safe haven was declared. He was in no position to resist, and the coalition ground troops did not have to fight their way into northern Iraq. Predictably, as time passed, the international community reduced its military forces in northern Iraq, and the security umbrella began to develop leaks. By 1996, when Iraqi forces penetrated the safe haven, entering the northern capital Irbil and arresting hundreds and summarily killing scores of people, it became clear that the international community would not guarantee the safety of the area. Under pressure from American **non-governmental organisations**, the US government relented and agreed to evacuate about 6,500 threatened Iraqis, mostly Kurds, who had been associated either with the humanitarian assistance programme or with the US government's political and security operations in the region. Turkey agreed to allow them to pass through its territory only in order to be flown to Guam, a US territory in the Pacific.

Operation Provide Comfort, despite its fundamental flaws, was not only the first, but for a time was the most effective of the safe havens created in the 1990s. Indeed, the United States continues to monitor Iraqi air forces to ensure that they do not enter so-called no-fly zones over northern and southern Iraq.

Although the safe haven idea remained attractive to host countries, and the international community persisted with attempts to implement it, the standard for safety in such areas steadily declined. As safe havens became less safe, governments' ulterior motive of blocking refugee flows to relieve them of the asylum burden became increasingly obvious.

This became particularly evident with the deterioration of the safe haven concept in former Yugoslavia. In 1992, as **ethnic cleansing** took its toll and displacement escalated, European governments began imposing visa restrictions and other obstacles to prevent the flow of more Bosnian refugees to their territories. Justifying the entrapment of would-be refugees inside Bosnia, the UN Security Council adopted two resolutions in 1993 guaranteeing the safety of Srebrenica and other safe areas. Unlike Operation Provide Comfort, however, safe havens in Bosnia were more rhetoric than reality. The international community was not willing to provide the requisite military force to protect the inhabitants of the safe areas from the imminent threat to their lives. Thus the Bosnian safe areas became some of the most dangerous places on earth. In Bosnia, the international community also demonstrated an unseemly willingness to substitute humanitarian assistance for genuine protection. In short, the international community was willing to keep the Bosnians from starving, but could not muster the will to prevent them from being killed by snipers and artillery. As the numbers of people in safe areas grew, Serb forces cut off these enclaves and besieged, shelled, and starved their inhabitants. When Serb forces closed in on Srebrenica and Zepa, UN **peacekeepers** failed to protect their charges. Serb soldiers separated men from their families, moved the women and children out of the towns, and massacred the men.

At first, the option of a safe haven looks attractive. Keep people within their own country, easing the burden on host countries; insist on citizens' right to remain, thus opposing ethnic cleansing; and guarantee their safety where they are. In practice, however, the safe havens have not lived up to their name. They have compromised the right of people fleeing persecution to seek asylum outside their countries and ultimately endangered the very lives of the people whose safety they were pledged to protect. For example, in 1994 France created Operation Turquoise in southwest Rwanda. While ostensibly a safe humanitarian zone, it clearly served political purposes: to protect members of the deposed government, the pro-French architects of the **genocide**. Armed Hutu militia members operated openly, killing Tutsis living there and intimidating Hutus who wanted to go home. In April 1995, after France had turned over the operation to the UN, the Rwandan Patriotic Army (RPA) moved to force the displaced out of Kibeho, the largest camp in the zone for displaced persons. Machete-wielding Hutu extremists in the camp provoked a violent confrontation with undisciplined RPA troops who, in full view of UN peacekeepers and humanitarian relief organisations, massacred hundreds if not thousands of people.

The ultimate contradiction and danger of safe havens is that they lure frightened people into places where the international community continues to recognise the sovereignty of their persecutors. Such places often become death traps.

*See also:* **ethnic cleansing; genocide; humanitarian intervention; peacekeeping; refugees; United Nations; wars of the third kind**

*Further reading:* Durch, 1997; Gourevitch, 1998; Klinghoffer, 1998; Rieff, 1995; Rohde, 1998

## SANCTIONS ✓

Many people consider sanctions a peaceful and effective means to enforce **international law**. Under Article 41 of the **United Nations** (UN) Charter, the Security Council may call on member states to apply measures not involving the use of armed force to give effect to its decisions. Typically, sanctions cut off trade and investments, preventing a target country from buying or selling goods in the global marketplace. Sanctions may aim at particular items like arms or oil. They may cut off air traffic, suspend or drastically curtail **diplomatic** relations, block movement of persons, bar investments, or freeze international bank deposits. Increasingly, critics charge that sanctions are cruel and unfair. International law has developed no standards on which sanctions can be based or their destructive impact limited. Ironically, then, sanctions are used to enforce law, but themselves are outside the law.

Sanctions can be imposed unilaterally or **multilaterally**. Unilateral sanctions always have some impact, both on the state that imposes them and on the target country. In recent years US sanctions have clearly weakened the economies of Cuba and Iraq, slowed investment in Libya and Iran, and hurt Pakistan, which used to receive substantial US economic and military assistance. But it is also important to contemplate the side effects of unilateral sanctions. These consequences transcend lost exports, profits, and jobs. In the case of Cuba, US sanctions may have made it easier for the Castro regime to maintain control over the Cuban economy and society. There and elsewhere (including Iraq), American sanctions have been used to justify repression and excuse incompetence. Indeed, sanctions may have had the perverse effect of weakening civilian rule in Pakistan and increasing its focus on nuclear weaponry.

As a rule, unilateral sanctions tend to be little more than statements or expressions of opposition, except in those instances in which the tie between the state that initiates them and the target is so extensive that the latter cannot adjust. Over time, economic sanctions tend to lose their bite. In a global economy, the target state can usually find substitute sources of supply and financing. Even advocates of unilateral sanctions would admit that their impact is second best. The problem is that it is often extremely difficult to garner international support for particular sanctions. Prospects for succeeding in bringing others on board tend to reflect a range of factors, including commercial stakes, policy preferences, and the availability of funds to compensate for lost revenues.

In recent years the United Nations has tried to coordinate multilateral sanctions against a number of states. The UN Security Council imposed only two sanctions **regimes** in its first 45 years. Surprisingly enough, both are generally considered effective. They targeted Southern Rhodesia (now Zimbabwe) and South Africa. In the decade after the end of the **cold war**, the Security Council followed with sanctions against 11 more states: Iraq (1990), the former Yugoslavia (1991), Libya, Somalia, and Liberia (1992), Haiti and Angola (1993), Rwanda (1994), Sudan and Burundi (1996), and Sierra Leone (1997).

Sanctions impose hardship by affecting ordinary people far more than leaders. As evidence has accumulated on the harsh effects of sanctions, particularly in Iraq, experts have increasingly recognised this negative side of sanctions and questioned whether human suffering can be justified by the original purpose. According to the UN Charter, the imposition of sanctions may only follow after the determination of an aggressive act as defined in Article 39. However, the phrase 'determination of an aggressive act' is not clearly defined. As a result, critics argue that sanctions are too often imposed unfairly, using standards that are unevenly applied or biased. All too often, the whims or interests of the mighty, not clear rules of international law, determine the targets of sanctions and the harshness of the sanctions regime.

Sanctions are meant to bring about a change of behaviour – they are not supposed to represent a form of punishment or retribution. When sanctions were imposed on Iraq to induce its withdrawal from occupied Kuwait, sceptics pointed out that many other invasions and occupations had not resulted in sanctions. Israel, Morocco, Turkey, and Indonesia, for example, all avoided sanctions when they invaded neighbours and occupied territory, even though they had been censured by the Security Council and called upon to withdraw.

Once UN sanctions are in place, a sanctions committee of the Security Council, which operates secretively, supervises them. This makes the ongoing sanctions process highly political and open to pressure from permanent members. Sanctions may begin with one justification and continue with others.

Sanctions often fail because they are not enforced. The UN has not been given the means to enforce sanctions in its own right. It must depend on voluntary compliance by member states and by traders and businesses. Not surprisingly, 'sanctions busting' has flourished. Sanctions also cause hardship outside the target country. They hurt countries that are neighbours or major trading partners who lose export markets, government revenues, and employment opportunities. Sanctions may also harm big business interests and they tend to cause suffering among the poorest and most vulnerable.

For all the pain they impose, sanctions rarely succeed. **League of Nations** sanctions, imposed in 1935, failed to force Italy to pull out of Ethiopia. More recently, UN sanctions have failed to induce Iraq to modify its policies substantially. Many experts believe that targeted sanctions can be more humanitarian and more effective. Targeting implies sanctions that deliver pressure where it is most effective. Arms embargoes are one type that is commonly used. Another type seeks to severely hit key groups like the business or political elite.

Sanctions tend to work best when an international political consensus exists and non-targeted countries that must bear an economic cost as a result of the sanctions are compensated. In most instances, other governments prefer no or minimal sanctions. In addition, it is often argued that economic interaction is desirable because it promotes more open political and economic systems. Such thinking makes achieving multilateral support for sanctions diffcult. It usually takes something truly egregious – Saddam's invasion and occupation of Kuwait, Libya's support of terrorism such as at Lockerbie, the brazen rejection of Haiti's election results and associated widespread **human rights** abuses – to overcome this anti-sanctions bias. Economic sanctions currently lie in a twilight zone between war and peace that is inadequately defined and regulated under international law. This lack of a permanent legal framework has contributed to their overall low level of success in the past.

*See also:* **League of Nations; rogue state; terrorism; United Nations**

*Further reading:* Cortright and Lopez, 1995; Doxy, 1996; Nossal, 1994; Pape, 1997; Weiss *et al.*, 1997

## SECESSION

Like revolution or emigration, secession is a way of challenging political authority. But secession presents that challenge in its own distinctive way. The aim of the political revolutionary is to overthrow the existing government or to force very basic changes in the constitutional, economic, and/or sociopolitical system. By contrast, the secessionist aims not at dissolving (or radically altering) the state's **power** but at restricting the jurisdiction of the state in question. Unlike the revolutionary, secessionists do not deny the state's political authority as such, but only its authority over them and the other members of their group and the territory they occupy. Emigration offers another way in which a group may challenge or free itself from the authority of a state. Members of a religious or **ethnic** group may claim a right to emigrate from a state and thus remove themselves from the state's jurisdiction without thereby challenging the state's claim to authority as such (that is, without challenging the state's authority over citizens who remain behind). Unlike a right of revolution, a right of emigration challenges not the state's authority *per se* but only the state's authority to control exit from the state's territory. Secession, by contrast, is an effort to remove oneself from the scope of the state's authority, not by moving beyond the existing boundaries of that authority, but by redrawing the boundaries so that one is not included within them. The contrast between emigration and secession reveals a crucial point about secession: unlike emigration, secession necessarily involves a claim to territory.

Different kinds of secession can be distinguished. Typically, minority groups undertake secession, but this need not be the case: the path of secession can be taken by a majority of people. Further, the secessionists may not only constitute the majority of the people of the existing state; they may also lay claim to the larger share of the existing state's territory. Finally, the right to secede is usually claimed to be held by groups rather than by individuals.

There is a wide range of arguments that might be advanced as justification(s) for a right to secede. Perhaps the most important and rhetorically powerful pro-secessionist argument is based on the idea that every people is entitled to its own state: thus, as a matter of right, cultural boundaries and political boundaries should coincide. The **United Nations** General Assembly Resolution 1514 explicitly endorses this **nationalist** principle of **self-determination**, declaring that 'all peoples have the right to self-determination; by virtue of that right they freely determine their political status and freely pursue their economic, social and cultural **development**'. But the principle of self-determination is either too indeterminate to be of much use (since the word 'people' is so ambiguous) or it is implausible because it leads to so much fragmentation (since ethnic pluralism is so much a part of modern **nation-states**). Often, the popular appeal of this principle depends precisely on its vagueness.

A much better justification for secession comes into play when a group secedes in order to rectify past injustices. This argument has application to many actual secession movements in the world, notably those of the Baltic Republics in the early 1990s. By this rationale, a region has a right to secede if that region was unjustly incorporated into the existing state. The argument for secession as a way to rectify past injustices is powerful because in such cases secession is simply the reappropriation, by the legitimate owner, of stolen property. The argument from rectificatory justice is perhaps the most potent grounding for a right to secede because this sort of justification directly delivers one crucial desideratum of a claim to secede: a valid claim to territory.

Indeed, so important is the territorial claim component to any putative right of secession, and so directly is that component delivered by the argument from rectificatory justice, that one might believe that secession could only be justified by a rectificatory claim to territory. However, there are non-rectificatory justifications for secession. For example, a group may have a right to secede if that group is seeking to secede from a state in order to protect its members from extermination by that state itself. Thus self-defence can in some cases provide a compelling justification for a group's right to secede. Note that in self-defence cases, the pro-secession justification does not itself rest on a valid territorial claim: the concern is not about territory but that the group avoids **genocide**. Therefore, there are powerful moral justifications for a right to secede that, while not founded on a valid territorial claim, can nonetheless generate one.

In the twenty-first century, we can expect much more attention to be paid to the theory and practice of secession than it has received thus far. The collapse of the Soviet Union, the violent dissolution of Yugoslavia, and the rise of claims to self-determination in multiethnic states such as Indonesia, have generated intense discussions about the morality and consequences of secession. As yet, there is little prospect of achieving any **diplomatic** consensus on these issues since the international community continues to be wary of a doctrine that threatens further fragmentation of its member states.

*See also:* **ethnic cleansing; ethnicity; international law; irredentism; nation-state; nationalism; self-determination; sovereignty**

*Further reading:* Bartkins, 1999; Buchanan, 1991; Lehning, 1998; Meadwell, 1999; Moore, 1998; Welhengama, 2000

## SECURITY

To be secure is to be safe from harm. Of course, no one is or can be perfectly secure. Accidents happen, resources become scarce, individuals lose their jobs, and **wars** start. What is indisputable is that the need to feel secure is a core human value and a prerequisite for being able to live a decent life. What is also generally true is that individuals living in the **OECD** world are far more secure than those living in the **Third World**, where conflict and resource scarcity are far more prevalent.

Security studies is a key area of inquiry within the field of international relations. During the **cold war**, the **realist** view dominated. For realists, the most important actors in the international system are not individuals *per se* but states, whose primary motive is to protect their **sovereignty**. Because, according to realists, states are worried about the prospect of going to war, security is a primary concern. Achieving it, however, is not an easy matter. The fact of **anarchy** means that states cannot totally rely on other states to protect them. Certainly, they will form **alliances**, sign treaties, and often undertake cooperative ventures in order to enhance their security. But this is not enough. If states are to survive they must provide for their self-defence.

States attack their neighbours for a number of reasons. They may seek to enhance their **power** position; they may want to improve access to important resources; they may be concerned that a neighbouring state is becoming too powerful; or they may simply **misperceive** the intentions of another state's actions. Regardless of the motivation, states are endemically insecure and this leads them to place a premium on military power. Certainly, realists acknowledge other forms of power, including wealth and **geopolitical** advantage. But in the final analysis, the more militarily powerful a state, the more secure it is likely to be.

This assessment of the character of international relations leads realists to offer a number of prescriptive insights. If states are to survive, they have to maintain large standing armies, they must be vigilant about their defence, never trust the word of other states, and always act in the **national interest**. In essence, realists believe that threats to the security of the state are usually posed by other states. During the cold war, realist security thinking focused primarily on the possibility of a nuclear exchange between the Soviet Union and the United States. Concepts such as **deterrence**, first strike, and **mutually assured destruction** (MAD) are all part of the realist security lexicon.

With the end of the cold war, there has been something of a revolution in the field of security studies, with scholars and policymakers beginning to move away from the traditional state-centric approach to a more expansive understanding of the concept of security. Some **regime** theorists, for example, are beginning to examine emerging **regional** security arrangements in Asia and Europe. A more radical perspective, however, suggests that security should be conceived in such a way as to embrace all of humanity, not just states, and should focus on sources of harm other than just military threats to states.

The rationale for this shift in perspective relies on two main arguments. First, while interstate war is still possible, the most violent conflicts in the world today are within states. It is not the national interest that is at stake in many of these conflicts but group identity and culture. This perspective suggests that the realist view of security is too narrowly formulated. Second, the capacity of the state to provide security for its citizens has been eroded by a range of non-military threats such as environmental problems, **population growth**, disease, **refugees,** and resource scarcity.

This more radical approach to the issue of human security reflects a holistic concern with human life and dignity. The idea of human security invites us to focus on the individual's need to be safe from hunger, disease, and repression, as well as protected against events likely to undermine the normal pattern of everyday existence. It also implies a need for a significant redistribution of wealth from the rich to the poor at a global level.

One of the interesting aspects of this new articulation of security is the extent to which it has been embraced by some middle powers. Canada, for example, has developed the idea of human security into a major foreign policy objective. Whether this is ultimately compatible with Canadian sovereignty is something that realists would undoubtedly question. But for those who believe that this way of thinking about security promises much, the fact that some states are beginning to take it seriously must be a satisfying development.

Within intellectual circles, however, the story is far less clear-cut. A fierce debate is underway between those who argue that security can only be meaningfully discussed in terms of interstate behaviour and those who seek to push our understanding of security in a more universal direction. Regardless of the outcome of this debate, there is no doubt that many of the threats that affect states today are global threats that require a global effort to overcome them.

*See also:* **cold war; collective security; global warming; globalisation; power; realism; security dilemma**

*Further reading:* Baldwin, 1995; Buzan, 1991; Klare and Chandrani, 1998

## SECURITY DILEMMA

This concept rests on the assumption that **security** is something for which states compete. In an **anarchical** international system lacking any authority capable of ensuring **order**, states have to look to their own efforts for protection. Striving to obtain this, they are driven to acquire more and more power in order to escape the impact of the power of other states. This, in turn, makes the others more insecure and encourages them to prepare for the worst. Since no state can ever feel entirely secure in such a world of competing states, competition follows, and the result is a rising spiral of insecurity among states. The security dilemma describes a condition in which efforts to improve national security have the effect of appearing to threaten other states, thereby provoking military counter-moves. This in turn can lead to a net decrease in security for all states.

The security dilemma encapsulates one of the many difficult choices facing some governments. On the one hand, they can relax defence efforts in order to facilitate peaceful relations; the problem here is that they may make their country more vulnerable to attack. On the other hand, they can strengthen defence preparations, but this can have the unintended consequence of undermining long-term security by exacerbating international suspicions and reinforcing pressures for arms racing. The result can be military conflict, and many commentators have argued that a paradigmatic example of the security dilemma led to the First World War (1914–18).

It is important to note that the security dilemma arises primarily from the alleged structure of the international system rather than the aggressive motives or intentions of states. This structural basis is exacerbated by the understandably conservative inclinations of defence planners to prepare for the worst and focus on the capabilities of their rivals rather than rely on their benign intentions. Ignorance and competition among different branches of the armed forces for government funds can fuel worst-case analysis. Thus while the structure of the international system must be seen as a fundamental precondition for the security dilemma, its intensity is a consequence both of the inherently violent nature of military capabilities and the degree to which states perceive others as threats rather than allies. Since these two factors are variable over space and time, the intensity of the security dilemma is very unevenly distributed among states. It is worth noting how each of them can vary.

First, the intensity of the security dilemma varies depending both on the degree to which one can distinguish between *defensive* and *offensive* weapons, as well as the relationship between them. Other things being equal, and acknowledging that weapons can be used offensively and defensively, some types of weapons are more suited to defence than offence. Defensive force configurations emphasise firepower with limited mobility and range (e.g. anti-tank missiles), and offensive configurations emphasise mobility and range (e.g. fighter-bombers). Advocates of what is called *non-offensive* defence believe that the security dilemma can be muted by the adoption of force configurations that are least likely to provoke counter-measures by other states. In part this depends on the degree to which defensive military technology is superior to offensive capabilities. If potential enemies each believe that the best form of defence (and **deterrence**) is preparing to attack, it is not difficult to see how they could be locked into a vicious circle of mutually reinforcing suspicions.

Second, the intensity of the security dilemma varies depending on the political relationship between states. Capabilities should not be examined in a political vacuum. The degree of trust and sense of common interest in the international system is neither fixed nor uniform. There is no security dilemma between Australia and New Zealand because neither state considers the other a threat to its national security.

At the beginning of the twenty-first century, there remains no consensus about the severity of the security dilemma, particularly between states that possess nuclear weapons. On the one hand, the phenomenon of **mutually assured destruction** on the basis of a secure second-strike capability would seem to ensure the supremacy of defence over offence. On the other hand, there remains doubt over the credibility of a defensive capability that offers little choice between suicide and surrender. Some scholars argue that the security dilemma is particularly weak amongst the **great powers**, simply because the strategic and economic gains from expanding one's territorial control are very few. In an age of economic **interdependence**, and in light of the degree of economic **integration** that exists today, it could be argued that what is called a security community exists, at least in North America, Western Europe, Australasia, and among some states in East Asia. A security community is one whose members are confident that the likelihood of force being used to resolve conflicts between them is extremely low. In other parts of the world, however, particularly in sub-Saharan Africa and the Middle East, the dynamics of the security dilemma remain a potent danger.

*See also:* **anarchy; collective security; disarmament; misperception; prisoners' dilemma; realism; regime; ; war**

*Further reading:* Jervis, 1978; Rotberg and Rabb, 1989; Webber, 1990; Wheeler and Booth, 1992

## SELF-DETERMINATION

At the start of the twenty-first century, the principle of self-determination is in dire need of creative analysis and far greater flexibility in the manner of its expression than it has received thus far. Prior to the end of the **cold war**, self-determination was limited to its close identification with the process of **decolonisation**. Since that process is now complete, at least in a formal sense, both the meaning of 'the self', and how that self determines how it should be governed, are ripe for imaginative reinterpretation. Unfortunately, although the principle has been the focus of renewed scholarly attention in recent years, this has yet to be translated into effective global policy. As a result, which groups get to enjoy self-determination and which do not remains in large part a function of violence and the visibility of particular political struggles.

Today, the principle of self-determination is proclaimed by, and on behalf of, non-state populations as diverse as the Kurds, the Québécois, the Basques, the Palestinians, the Tibetans, and the Tamils. Although the international community bestows a measure of **legitimacy** on some of these struggles, it does so in a haphazard manner. In part this is because self-determination struggles have appealed to opposing values of community and individuality that coexist uneasily. Self-determination involves conflict between two competing selves. As an expression of democracy, the principle is apparently a simple one: let the people rule! As has often been said, however, the people cannot rule until it is decided who *are* the people. And that decision, once taken, bestows upon the representatives of the people a great deal of leeway in limiting popular participation in the political process. It should also be noted that self-determination has adopted expansionist as well as disintegrative forms throughout history. It has been used as an imperial doctrine to justify the expansion of the United States through 'manifest destiny', the conquests of Napoleonic France and, most notoriously, Hitler's quest for a greater Germany. Since the end of the cold war it has taken on disintegrative forms in the former Soviet Union and, of course, Yugoslavia.

In the **United Nations**, the promotion of the principle of self-determination is sometimes celebrated as one of the organisation's main purposes. The Charter of the United Nations (1945) begins by affirming a 'respect for the principle of equal rights and self-determination of peoples'. At the same time, however, the liberal and democratic values that underpin the appeal of self-determination were muted as the principle was implemented solely as an instrument of decolonisation. It is a measure of how insignificant self-determination was thought to be by the drafters of the Charter that it appears only twice in the whole document. Certainly no right to self-determination flowed directly from the Charter. Prior to 1945, **international law** knew of no specific right to self-determination, and within the Charter the principle is clearly subordinate to the prohibition on the use of force, to the right to territorial integrity (Article 2), and to the general commitment to ensuring peace and **security** (Ch. VII).

The two decades following the drafting of the Charter and the 1948 Universal Declaration on Human Rights were marked by the end of **imperialism**. Most of the colonial powers became increasingly committed to divesting themselves of their colonial territories, and an Afro-Asian bloc began to find its voice in the United Nations. In 1960 and again in 1970, the General Assembly passed two Resolutions that provided the principle of self-determination with some international legal status even as they limited the scope of its application. Both the Declaration on the Granting of Independence to Colonial Countries and Peoples (1960) and the Declaration on Friendly Relations (1970) explicitly link self-determination to decolonisation. They do not recognise any right to what might be called *internal* self-determination (i.e. the right to representative government), nor do they recognise any need to alter territorial frontiers between ex-colonies that had been determined by Europeans with little or no consideration of the wishes of their subjects.

Since the end of decolonisation, it has become clear that the diplomatic compromises that facilitated the transfer of political authority during that era are now obsolete. Today, the principle of self-determination lacks both definition and applicability. Saving it from a complete descent into incoherence will require a renewal of the links between autonomy, democracy, **human rights**, and the right to self-determination. Central to cultivating this renewal should be the adoption of a more liberal and expansive interpretation of the meaning of self-determination. Self-determination does not have to mean **irredentism**, **secession**, and the violent renegotiation of territorial frontiers. The promotion of minority rights, devolution, federalism, and greater acknowledgement of the legitimacy of cultural self-expression are all expressions of self-determination. The recognition of group rights at the expense of individual ones, however, is not consistent with the ethical attraction of this much-abused concept.

*See also:* **ethnicity; nation-state; nationalism; recognition; secession; sovereignty; United Nations**

*Further reading:* Freeman, 1999; Hannum, 1990; Heraclides, 1992; Philpott, 1995; Shehadi, 1993; Tamir, 1991

# SOVEREIGNTY

The concept of sovereignty originated with the **Peace of Westphalia** in 1648, when governments ceased to support co-religionists in conflict with their own states. Recognising the territorial jurisdiction of kings and princes entailed following a policy of non-interference within their claimed and defined territorial boundaries. Thus the **extraterritorial** authority of the Roman Church in particular was severely weakened, giving rise to the development of the secular **nation-state**. The mutual **recognition** by the European princes of each other's sovereignty in the important matter of religious belief meant that they were willing to forgo certain political objectives in return for internal control and stability.

Thus the word 'sovereignty' harks back to an era when a single individual – the sovereign or king – governed states. The vestiges of this original meaning of the word remain in our modern usage with the tendency to treat sovereign states as individuals. However, the locus of sovereignty has gradually been seen to rest with the people or commonwealth (*popular* sovereignty), and not with an individual sovereign (as in *dynastic* sovereignty). The people's acknowledgement of a central governing authority within a specified geographical territory, combined with the recognition of its status by other states, confers on the state its sovereignty. However, and this is a key point, the recognition of a central authority, whether domestic or international, does not imply approval of that government. An unpopular and oppressive totalitarian government is no less sovereign than a popularly elected, democratic republic. Sovereignty flows from the recognition of the **legitimacy** of some central governing **power** and not the acceptance of the moral or legal validity of the acts carried out by the central authority.

Sovereign states are, in **international law**, equal, and sovereign equality is the basis upon which the **United Nations** (UN) operates. This principle of sovereign equality is what guarantees equal participation by all states in international relations. This sovereign equality has as its content the following elements:

1   States are legally equal.
2   Every state enjoys the rights inherent in full sovereignty.
3   Every state is obligated to respect the fact of the legal entity of other states.
4   The territorial integrity and political independence of a state are inviolable.
5   Each state has the right to freely choose and develop its own political, social, economic, and cultural systems.

6    Each state is obligated to carry out its international obligations fully and conscientiously and to live in peace with other states.

One point to notice here is that sovereignty is not entirely absolute. States can have international obligations. They accrue these obligations when they enter into international treaties and agreements. Of course, states are free not to enter into these agreements to begin with, but once they do, they relinquish a certain measure of sovereignty to the international community.

As a consequence of sovereignty, political lines upon maps assumed great importance. The concept of the powerful city-state, radiating and concentrating power, and of overlapping circles of influence, was replaced with the idea of homogeneity within linear territorial borders.

This novel political idea was to be transplanted to every corner of the earth as European colonialists imposed their worldview through military might upon the militarily backward civilisations of the Americas, Africa, and Asia. With great care and detail, the European colonialist drew lines upon maps, thus delineating nations where none had existed before, or dividing nations as if they had never existed.

The claim of sovereignty within a bordered territory brought with it powerful legitimising factors for an incumbent ruling class. Cultural, religious, and political conformities could be imposed using the state in a more systematic and efficient manner. **Nationalism** becomes the claim that political power should reflect cultural homogeneity in every corner of the sovereign territory; thus nationalism extends and deepens the scope of sovereignty to require certain kinds of cultural conformity for citizenship.

In recent years the concept of sovereignty has been the subject of intense debate after many years of relative neglect. Empirically, scholars have explored the degree to which sovereignty is changing in an era of alleged **globalisation** of economic activities. There is also a growing literature on *quasi*-states and **failed states**. If the issue for advanced industrialised states is the degree to which their effective sovereignty is being eroded, the question for many poorer states is the degree to which they ever enjoyed effective sovereignty. Robert Jackson distinguishes between *negative* and *positive* sovereignty. He suggests that many **Third World** states achieved the former through **decolonisation**, but not the latter. Negative sovereignty refers to the legal right to demand that other states refrain from interfering in a state's internal affairs. Positive sovereignty refers to the ability of the state to exercise effective control in the arena of its formal jurisdiction. Sovereignty is also being re-examined in a normative sense. If sovereign states systematically abuse the **human rights** of their citizens, should they continue to enjoy the privileges of sovereignty in international law? This issue is at the heart of debates over whether **humanitarian intervention** should play a greater role in international law than is currently the case.

It used to be said that sovereignty was like marriage. As a legal status, it stayed the same regardless of the relationship between married partners (in this case, law and autonomy). As such, sovereignty was not a very interesting concept. Today, that is no longer the case as scholars and states themselves explore variations in different dimensions of sovereignty over time and space.

*See also:* **extraterritoriality; failed state; functionalism; global governance; globalisation; humanitarian intervention; imperialism; nation–state; nationalism; Peace of Westphalia; self-determination; United Nations**

*Further reading:* Biersteker and Weber, 1992; Jackson, 1990; Krasner, 1999; Lyons and Mastanduno, 1995

## STRUCTURAL ADJUSTMENT PROGRAMME (SAP) ✔

A set of political and economic measures instituted by the **International Monetary Fund** (IMF) in cooperation with the **World Bank** to help states confronting chronic balance of payments deficits. The nature of the 'rescue' package varies from country to country, but it generally includes structural adjustment loans (SALs) and a range of strategies and conditions designed to improve the country's overall balance of payments position. These measures usually include a reduction in government spending, the removal of subsidies to local industries, the privatisation of state-owned assets, currency devaluation, a reduction in welfare spending, the removal of restrictions on foreign investment, and deregulation reforms designed to cut costs and to increase efficiency and competitiveness. At their core, IMF-supported programmes seek three main goals:

1   to assist a state in securing sustainable external financing;
2   adopting demand-restraining measures consistent with available financing;
3   proceeding with structural reforms to promote long-term economic growth.

The fundamental goal of SAPs is to enable indebted countries to increase their earnings so that they are able to meet their obligations to overseas banks and other international institutions. Before a country is eligible for any loan assistance it has to abide by the IMF's recommendations. This generally entails a reorientation of the economy away from domestic consumption towards production for export. The view of the IMF and the World Bank is that by increasing their exports, indebted countries will be able to 'earn' their way out of their economic problems.

There are a number of reasons why countries such as Mexico, Argentina, Brazil, Nigeria, and Indonesia have had to undertake structural adjustment in recent years. The most common reason is their excessively high levels of debt and dwindling export earnings. This was certainly the case during the 1980s, when international banks were happy to lend huge sums of money to **Third World** countries. But recession, falling commodity prices, and currency devaluations made it increasingly difficult for these countries to meet their repayments. The first sign that Third World debt was becoming a major international problem was in August 1982, when Mexico announced that it could no longer afford to repay its existing loans. Since the early 1980s SAPs have played an increasingly important role in the activities of the International Monetary Fund and the World Bank. Before 1980, the IMF's adjustment lending was limited to short-term financing to stabilise exchange rates. Today, almost all IMF funding in poor countries goes to adjustment. Similarly, before 1980 the World Bank devoted a negligible amount of lending to SAPs. Today, more than half of all new World Bank loans are linked to such programmes.

SAPs are highly controversial. Not surprisingly, the criticisms tend to increase when the international financial system faces a **crisis**, as was the case with the **debt trap** of the 1980s, the collapse of the centrally planned economies of Eastern Europe and the former Soviet Union, and most recently, the financial crises in East Asia in the late 1990s.

First, it is often argued that SAPs are too rigid and inflexible and that they fail to accommodate the differing and changing circumstances of countries that encounter balance of payments difficulties. Indeed, some writers have argued that they exacerbated the Asian financial collapse in the late 1990s.

Second, even if they work in a narrow economic sense, it is often claimed that SAPs promote unsustainable forms of **development**. Countries will export whatever they can in order to earn hard currency, regardless of the long-term consequences to the environment. As more countries become involved in export–oriented development, prices will fall for their products. Paradoxically, this will make it more difficult for indebted countries to meet their repayments. Indebted countries will need to raise exports even further to compensate, adding to the damage to the environment and to local communities.

Third, SAPs are often criticised for increasing inequality in Third World states, particularly between men and women. For example, as domestic spending falls, and development shifts towards exports, funds are diverted away from the provision of basic needs such as health, education, sanitation, and the like, leading to the further impoverishment of local communities.

Finally, one should note a growing contradiction between the IMF and the World Bank's commitment to **democratisation** and the instigation of SAPs. The essence of democracy is that people have a say in the issues that affect them. Yet, in most cases, the population at large is never consulted about the content of structural adjustment programmes.

Despite such criticisms, structural adjustment programmes are not likely to disappear in the near future, although there is evidence that the IMF and the World Bank are trying to respond to the criticisms without losing sight of the fundamental goals that SAPs are intended to achieve.

*See also:* **debt trap; foreign aid; International Monetary Fund; structural violence; Third World; World Bank**

*Further reading:* Feldstein, 1998; Harvey, 1995; Killick, 1995

## STRUCTURAL VIOLENCE

This is a key concept in the field of **peace studies** and was first coined by one of the pioneers in the field, Johan Galtung. Most of us think of peace intuitively in negative terms, as the absence of **war** or armed conflict. Peace is the opposite of what is observable, measurable, and very real in its direct effects – war. Thus throughout the years of the **cold war** between the former Soviet Union and the United States, many of those observers who supported nuclear **deterrence** and the condition of **mutually assured destruction** (MAD) claimed that whatever its costs, it helped to maintain a 'long peace' between the two main antagonists. However, the idea of structural violence (and its associated term 'positive peace') refers not merely to the observable use of force between states, but anything avoidable that prevents or impedes human fulfilment or self-realisation. In turn, the latter is usually conceived by peace researchers in terms of the satisfaction of fundamental human needs, which can be physiological, ecological, economic, and spiritual. The concept of structural violence, therefore, is much broader than the conventional focus of students in the Anglo–American study of international relations on war and the use of direct, physical armed force between states.

More specifically, the term alludes to the structures that maintain the dominance of one group at the centre of **power** over another group, usually the majority, at the periphery. For the latter, structural violence can manifest itself as low wages, illiteracy, poor health, few legal or political rights and very limited control over their lives. If they resist or try to change their condition of misery by direct action, they may encounter direct violence.

The concept of structural violence was first used in the context of colonial situations. Galtung himself drew upon his fieldwork in Rhodesia under British colonial rule. Today, the concept is used more widely to encompass the enduring and often insidious ways in which harm is inflicted upon individuals by repressive political, economic, and cultural structures.

In comparison with direct violence, structural violence works slowly but some would argue that it kills many more people in the long term. One way of measuring structural violence is to subtract average life expectancy for the world from the highest national life expectancy, year by year, and divide by the highest life expectancy to provide a rough indicator of preventable, premature deaths. This translates into at least 17 million people per year: usually children in the Third World, who die from hunger or preventable disease.

Of course, death is not the only effect of structural violence on its victims. There are four types of violence in global politics:

1   *Classical violence* of the conventional literature refers to the deliberate infliction of pain, such as in war, torture, or inhuman and degrading punishment.
2   *Deprivation* of our fundamental material needs for shelter, clothing, food, and water.
3   *Repression* refers to the loss of human freedoms to choose our beliefs and speak out on their behalf.
4   *Alienation* is a form of structural violence against our identity and our non-material needs for community and relations with others.

Structural violence refers to the second, third, and fourth types of violence. It does not need to be observed taking place between a perpetrator and a victim. Rather, it may be built into a social **order** or political and economic structure.

Just as the absence of war (or negative peace) is the preferred alternative to direct violence, positive peace is preferred to structural violence. In essence, positive peace involves the presence of structures that provide increasing degrees of political liberty and social justice.

The concept of structural violence has little explanatory use, however. It is simply a way of describing what, in the Third World in particular, is a familiar, if depressing, reality. There is no obvious link between structural and direct violence – poverty and oppression do not necessarily lead to revolt. The concept of structural violence was an interesting concept in helping to define the scope of peace studies and it remains a useful rhetorical device for activists who seek to justify struggles against economic oppression. One might argue, however, that the concept is far too broad. Not only are there perfectly good terms to describe what often is called structural violence (e.g. injustice, alienation, oppression, etc.), but there is also something distasteful in conflating such phenomena with Nazi genocide. Nevertheless, for revolutionaries, structural violence provides a good reason for armed struggle. By blurring the distinction between direct violence and other forms of 'violence', use of the former to end the latter is thereby 'justified'.

*See also:* **distributive justice; failed state; peace-building; peace studies; war; wars of the third kind**

*Further reading:* Eckhardt, 1992; Galtung, 1985; Lawler, 1995; Ryan, 1995

## SUPERPOWER ✓

How do we know a superpower when we see one? This question is not as easy to answer as it might seem. Indeed, some scholars doubt that the concept has any analytical utility in the twenty-first century.

The term was first coined by William Fox in 1944. Recall that at the time, Germany, Italy, and Japan (the Axis powers) were all but defeated, most of Europe was in tatters, and China was in the midst of a civil **war**. Fox defined a superpower as a state that possessed great **power** 'plus great mobility of power'. He argued that only the United States, the Soviet Union, and Britain deserved to be called superpowers because in his view these three states would be responsible for shaping the post-1945 world. In a sense he was right. Not only did the 'Big Three' set out the conditions for Germany's surrender in 1945, but they also presided over the subsequent division of Europe and were instrumental in setting up the **United Nations**.

Yet it would be a mistake to think that these were three states of equal power. While it is true that the Soviet army almost singlehandedly defeated the Germans on the Eastern Front, it should not be forgotten that the United States provided it with 15,000 aircraft, 7,000 tanks, 52,000 jeeps, and 376,000 trucks. In other words, the former Soviet Union's mobility of power was substantially underwritten by North American industrial and economic might. Of course, any doubt about the status of the Soviet Union as a superpower evaporated in 1949 when it detonated its first nuclear device.

Similarly, the American Lend-Lease Act was a critical factor in allowing Britain to prosecute the war in Europe and eventually prevail over Germany. Moreover, at the end of the Second World War Britain was almost bankrupt and many of its people were on the verge of starvation. Fox justified the reference to Britain as a superpower by suggesting that its vast human and material resources, advanced technology, and leadership in the Commonwealth set it apart from other, mere regionally dominant states. Despite this, it is hard to draw the conclusion that Britain ever really deserved to be called a superpower. In hindsight, the only real superpower in 1944 was the United States. As the 'arsenal of democracy', it had bankrolled the war effort, enjoyed a monopoly in the possession of nuclear weapons, and had the only functioning economy of any global significance. Despite protestations from Britain and the former Soviet Union, the United States also developed the regulatory framework for the postwar international economy.

The term 'superpower' implies that there is a hierarchy of power among states. It is a state that plays a crucial leadership role in the international system and is able to gain the allegiance of other states. Within its sphere of influence, a superpower can impose its political will on smaller states with relative impunity. Not only does a superpower have the capacity to project effective military power far from its territory, but it also has enormous military resources at its disposal. Finally, one might argue that a superpower has special duties with respect to the maintenance of international **order** and holds a privileged status in international forums such as the United Nations.

Some scholars argue that the term does not add anything significant to the much older concept of a **great power**. In anticipation of this criticism, Fox argued that there was a qualitative difference between the superpowers of the post-1945 era and the European great powers of the eighteenth and nineteenth centuries such as France, Spain, and Britain. For one thing, the latter were much smaller and carried on their activities in close proximity to one another. Even though they were significant international actors, they never had the global reach and influence of the United States and the Soviet Union. Today, after the collapse of the Soviet Union, there appears to be only one superpower for the foreseeable future – the United States.

*See also:* **cold war; great powers; hegemony; power**

*Further reading:* Fox, 1944, 1980; Sharp, 1992

## SUSTAINABLE DEVELOPMENT ✓

Despite the fact that this concept has become common currency, it is a confused and sometimes contradictory idea and there is no widespread agreement as to how it should work in practice. According to advocates of sustainable development, three priorities should be incorporated into all **development** programmes:

1   Maintenance of ecological processes
2   Sustainable use of resources
3   Maintenance of biodiversity.

Sustainable development gained credence thanks to the World Commission on Environment and Development (WCED; also known as the Brundtland Commission after its chair, Gro Harlem Brundtland of Norway), which was formed by the **United Nations** (UN) in 1983 and reported four years later. The Commission emphasised that the **integration** of economic and ecological systems is crucial if sustainable development is to be achieved, and the Commission defined sustainable development as that which meets the needs of the present without compromising the ability of future generations to meet their own needs. Although this definition is fairly concise, it is nonetheless open to varying interpretations. What exactly is a *need*, for example, and how can it be defined? Something that is considered a need by one person or cultural group may not necessarily be thought of as such by another person or cultural group. Needs may also vary through time, as does the ability of people to meet their needs. Likewise, the meaning of 'development' can be interpreted in many different ways.

Despite the difficulties in pinning down sustainable development and understanding how it should be applied, calls for its adoption have been made by various international lobby groups, notably at the UN Conference on Environment and Development (UNCED), otherwise known as the Earth Summit, in Rio de Janeiro in 1992. But although use of the term 'sustainable development' has gained common currency, the fact remains that it is still an ambiguous concept. Perhaps this should not be surprising, since the word 'sustainable' itself is used with different connotations. When we sustain something, we might be supporting a desired state of some kind, or, conversely, we might be enduring an undesired state. These different meanings have allowed the concept to be used in varying, often contradictory ways.

Further confusion over the meaning of the term 'sustainable' stems from its use in a number of different contexts, such as ecological/economic sustainability. A central tenet of ecological sustainability is that human interaction with the natural world should not impair the functioning of natural biological processes. Hence concepts such as 'maximum sustainable yield' have been developed to indicate the quantity of a renewable resource that can be extracted from nature without impairing nature's ability to produce a similar yield at a later date. Economic sustainability, however, tends to give a lower priority to ecosystem functions and resource depletion.

One strength of the sustainability idea is that it draws together environmental, economic, and social concerns. In practice, most would agree on a number of common guiding principles for sustainable development:

- continued support of human life;
- continued maintenance of environmental quality and the long-term stock of biological resources;
- the right of future generations to resources that are of equal worth to those used today.

Much research and thinking about sustainable development has focused on modifying economics to better integrate its operation with the workings and capacity of the environment, to use natural resources more efficiently, and to reduce flows of waste and pollution. The full cost of a product, from raw material extraction to eventual disposal as waste, should be reflected in its market price, although in practice such a 'cradle to grave' approach may prove troublesome for materials such as minerals.

A key issue in the sustainable development debate is the relative roles of economic growth (the quantitative expansion of economies) and development (the qualitative improvement of society). In its first report, the WCED suggested that sustainability could only be achieved with a fivefold to tenfold increase in world economic activity in 50 years. This growth would be necessary to meet the basic needs and aspirations of a larger future global population. Subsequently, however, the WCED has played down the importance of growth. This makes some sense, because many believe that it has been the pursuit of economic growth that has created most of the environmental problems in the first place.

The change of thinking on economic growth has been reflected in the two types of reaction to calls for sustainability that have been made to date: on the one hand, to concentrate on growth as usual, although at a slower rate; and on the other hand, to define sustainable development as development without growth in 'throughput beyond environmental capacity'. The idea of controlling 'throughput' refers to the flow of environmental matter and energy through the socioeconomic system. This does not necessarily mean that further economic growth is impossible, but it does mean that growth should be achieved by better use of resources and improved environmental management rather than by the traditional method of measuring economic 'throughput'.

One indication of the degree of change necessary to make this possible is in the ways we measure progress and living standards at the national level. For example, the gross national product (GNP) is essentially a measure of economic throughput and it has severe limitations with respect to considerations of environmental and natural resources. The calculation of GNP does not take into account any depletion of natural resources or adverse effects of economic activity on the environment, which feed back costs on such things as health and welfare. Indeed, conventional calculations of GNP frequently regard the degradation of resources as contributing to wealth, so that the destruction of an area of forest, for example, could be recorded as an increase in GNP. The need to introduce environmental parameters is now widely recognised, and some scholars believe that suitably adjusted measures of 'green GNP' could provide a good measure of national sustainability.

*See also:* **capitalism; development; global warming; tragedy of the commons**

*Further reading:* Kenny and Meadowcroft, 1999; Myers and Simon, 1994; World Commission on Environment and Development, 1987, 1992

## TERRORISM

Terrorism refers to the unpredictable and premeditated use of violence or the threat of violence to achieve identifiable goals. Because of the 9/11 terrorist attacks on the World Trade Center and Pentagon, terrorism has become arguably the most critical global issue in the post-9/11 era, posing one of the gravest threats to states. Today, virtually all states and the UN recognise the critical nature of this threat and have pledged to stop it.

Broadly speaking, terrorism includes attacks against tourists, embassy staff, military personnel, aid workers, and employees of **multinational corporations** (MNCs). It can be used by individuals and groups against governments, and it can be used and sponsored by governments against particular groups. There are four relatively distinct kinds of terrorism.

The first is *transnational organised crime*. Drug cartels may use terrorism to protect their private interests by attacking governments and individuals who attempt to reduce their activity and influence. The Italian Mafia, for example, has used terrorism to halt efforts on the part of the Italian government to curtail its criminal activities. The second type is *state-sponsored terrorism*. Afghanistan, Libya and Iraq are three of the major state sponsors of international terrorism to further their particular aims. State-sponsored terrorism is a method of warfare whereby a state uses agents or surrogates to create political and economic instability in another country. States also sponsor terrorism by giving logistical support, money, weapons and allied equipment, training, and safe passage to terrorists. The third major type of terrorism is *nationalistic*. Terrorism has often been used in the initial stages of anticolonial movements, or by groups wishing to **secede** from a particular state (examples include the Basque movement in Spain, Sikh nationalists in India, and a number of Palestinian movements). The fourth major type is *ideological*, in which terrorists use terror either to change a given domestic policy (for example, on abortion laws) or to overthrow a particular government. The latter would include groups such as the Red Army Faction in Germany and the Muslim Brotherhood in Egypt. Thus terrorism is far from being a mindless, irrational force. Acts of terrorism are typically well planned and carried out with military precision. The terrorist's greatest advantage is that he or she can easily blend into a crowd.

The methods used by terrorists vary considerably. Aircraft hijacking has been common since the late 1960s, but kidnapping, destruction of property, hostage-taking, bombings, and assassinations have also been used. There is an important correlation between the methods used by terrorists and their ultimate goal. The more spectacular the method, the more attention the act itself will receive. The kidnapping of a homeless person does not have the same impact as the kidnapping of a head of state or the hijacking of an aircraft. This is because the goal of terrorism is primarily psychological. It is meant to induce panic, fear, and alarm in the general population. In doing so, it puts pressure on its real targets (usually governments) to capitulate to the demands of the terrorists.

Terrorist attacks on civilians are primarily intended to be symbolic. A terrorist bombs a building not so much because he or she seeks to kill indiscriminately but because the act will be publicised across the globe and will draw attention to the cause. In this sense, the mass media can become an unwitting ally of the terrorist. The newsworthiness of terrorist attacks has led some writers to argue that there should be a complete news blackout on such acts.

Terrorism is not a new phenomenon. In 996, the Zealots sought to expel the Romans from Palestine through a campaign of terror. Since then, terrorism has been a constant feature of the political landscape. It is sometimes said that terrorism is a weapon of the powerless. Modern terrorism started to become a major international problem in the late 1960s, with numerous incidents occurring around the world, many of them associated with the Arab–Israeli conflict. In recent years, the number of terrorist attacks against the United States has increased dramatically. One of the major concerns about terrorism today is that a group might develop and use **weapons of mass destruction**. Chemical or biological weapons are relatively cheap to manufacture and could potentially kill hundreds of thousands of people depending on environmental conditions at the time of detonation. There is some debate whether this is a realistic possibility. But contested or not, the thought of such a weapon falling into the hands of a group of terrorists is a frightening one.

In response, a concerted international effort has been underway to try to reduce the number of attacks. This has involved the formation of counter-terrorist agencies, the funding of think-tanks and research, the training of personnel, the exchange of information between states, the use of military force, infiltration of terrorist cells, the use of **sanctions** and other punitive measures against countries that harbour terrorists, improved **security** at airports, embassies, and other vulnerable sites, and the strengthening of **international law**.

In recent years, the number of officially recorded terrorist incidents has increased markedly. Between 1968 and 1989, 35,150 acts of terrorism were recorded, an average of 1,673 per year. Between 1990 and 1996, the figure jumped to an average of 4,389 attacks per year. And by 2004, there were 651 attacks that killed 1,907 people. Much more important, global terrorism, in the aftermath of the 9/11 attacks, has called attention to the global jihadist struggle carried out by Al Qaeda, which has included attacks on London on 7 July 2005 and on Spain on 11 March 2004, and the ongoing suicide bombings in Iraq from 2005 to 2007. There are a number of specific reasons why terrorism can be expected to remain the single most important global issue. First, terrorism has proved very successful in attracting publicity, disrupting the activities of government and business, and causing significant death and destruction. Second, arms, explosives, supplies, financing, and secret communications technology are readily available. Some observers warn of new forms of terrorism in an age of **globalisation**. Sometimes referred to as **postmodern** terrorism, it would exploit information technology, use high-tech communications and computer equipment, and its targets would be data warehouses and computer network servers. Finally, an international support network of groups and states exists that greatly facilitates the undertaking of terrorist activities. In short, a world without some form of terrorism is highly unlikely and it is up to governments, individually and collectively, to seek ways to minimise the risk that it poses to their citizens.

*See also:* **rogue state; sanctions; security; weapons of mass destruction**

*Further reading:* Chalk, 1999; Harmon, 2000; Lacqueur and Alexander, 1987; Taylor and Horgan, 2000

## THEORY ✓

The word 'theory' is used in a bewildering variety of ways in the study of international relations. It is applied to propositions and arguments at varying levels of abstraction, and debates over its most appropriate meaning have proceeded apace with little consensus achieved. If there is no agreement on how best to understand this term, let alone how best to engage in developing and criticising the existing stock of international relations theory, there is much greater consensus over the ways in which the term is used. Three in particular stand out.

First, for most scholars a theory is simply an explanation of an event or pattern of behaviour in the 'real' world. This is otherwise known as *empirical* theory. A theory explains such patterns by elaborating on why they take place. In one (in)famous expression, a theory explains laws of behaviour. According to this conception, theories are useful instruments. If we know why and how events relate to each other, we may then be able to intervene and perhaps change reality to suit our purposes. This conception of empirical theory rests on two important assumptions. First, there is a categorical distinction between theory and practice. The world consists of an apparently random collection of facts that need to be described and studied to discern how they are related. Theory and practice are linked by empirical propositions that summarise the degree to which certain facts are connected to other facts. Only when we have a large body of such propositions can we engage in the hard work of attempting to explain them. Second, theories are never true or false in any absolute sense. Whilst theories must always be tested against the evidence, they can only be replaced by better theories that are either more coherent or more comprehensive in the scope of their explanatory power than their rivals.

It should be noted that the sheer variety of empirical theory in the study of international relations is very wide indeed. It is common to distinguish between *middle-range* theory and *grand* theory. For example, there is a big difference between a theory that tries to explain single events like the Iraqi invasion of Kuwait in August 1990, a theory that tries to account for the variation of patterns of **war** and peace among the **great powers** over the last 200 years, and a theory that attempts to explain why war itself takes place.

Second, it is common to come across the phrase *normative* theory. Unlike empirical theory, normative theory is concerned with how to elaborate the ethical standards used to judge international conduct. Today, there exists a large body of normative theory concerned with the use of force (**just war** theory) and **distributive justice** in international relations. When is it right or appropriate to use military force? Is the present distribution of global wealth and income fair? These are the kinds of questions that normative theory seeks to answer.

Third, the term is sometimes used in a constitutive sense. Unlike empirical or normative theory, this use of the term is perhaps best expressed through other concepts, such as *paradigm*, *worldview*, or *framework of analysis*. Some of the terms used in this book, such as **realism**, **critical theory**, and **liberal internationalism** are examples of *constitutive* theory in the study of international relations.

In addition to this familiar trilogy of meanings, it is important to understand an important distinction between theory and metatheory. The latter refers to the criteria that are used to adjudicate among the different meanings of theory and which privilege particular meanings over others. It is fair to say that over the last 20 years there has been rather more metatheoretical debate in the field than theoretical elaboration.

*See also:* **constructivism; critical theory; distributive justice; feminism; modernisation theory; postmodernism; world-system theory**

*Further reading:* Booth and Smith, 1995; Brown, 1992b; Hollis and Smith, 1990; Walt, 1998

## THIRD WORLD

This term is used (loosely) to refer to the economically underdeveloped countries of Asia, Africa, Oceania, and Latin America, considered as an entity with common characteristics, such as poverty, high birthrates, and economic **dependence** on the advanced countries. The First World is the developed world – US, Canada, Western Europe, Japan – and the **newly industrialising countries** (Hong Kong, Singapore, South Korea, and Taiwan), Australia and New Zealand. The Second World is the ex-**communist** world led by the former Soviet Union (USSR). With the demise of the USSR and the communist bloc, there is of course no longer a Second World. The Third World is the underdeveloped world – agrarian, rural, and poor. Many Third World countries have one or two developed cities, but the rest of the country is poor. Many parts of Central and Eastern Europe should probably be considered part of the Third World. Today, Russia could also be considered a Third World country with nuclear weapons. China has always been considered part of the Third World. In general, Latin America, Africa, and most of Asia are still considered parts of the Third World.

The term 'Fourth World' applies to some of the very poorest countries, especially in Africa, that have no industrialisation, are almost entirely agrarian (based on subsistence farming), and have little or no hope of industrialising and competing in the world market.

The term 'Third World' is not universally accepted. Some prefer other terms such as 'the South', 'non-industrialised countries', 'less-developed countries', or 'emerging nations'. Nonetheless, the term 'Third World' is probably the one most widely used in the media today. Of course, no term adequately describes all non-'First World', non-industrialised, non-'Western' countries accurately.

In so far as one can make useful generalisations, the underdevelopment of the Third World is marked by a number of common traits: distorted and highly dependent economies devoted to producing primary products for the developed world and to providing markets for their finished goods; traditional, rural social structures; high **population growth**; and widespread poverty. Nevertheless, the Third World is sharply differentiated, for it includes countries at various levels of economic **development**. And despite the poverty of the countryside and the urban shanty-towns, the ruling elites of most Third World countries are wealthy.

This combination of conditions in Asia, Africa, Oceania, and Latin America is linked to the absorption of the Third World into the international **capitalist** economy, by way of conquest or indirect domination. The main economic consequence of Western domination was the creation, for the first time in history, of a world market. By setting up throughout the Third World sub-economies linked to the West, and by introducing other modern institutions, industrial capitalism disrupted traditional economies and, indeed, societies.

Because the economies of underdeveloped countries have been geared to the needs of industrialised countries, they often comprise only a few modern economic activities, such as mining or the cultivation of plantation crops. Control over these activities has often remained in the hands of large foreign firms. The prices of Third World products are usually determined by large buyers in the economically dominant countries of the West, and trade with the West provides almost all the Third World's income. Throughout the colonial period, outright occupation severely limited the accumulation of capital within the foreign-dominated countries. Even after **decolonisation** (in the 1950s, 1960s, and 1970s), the economies of the Third World developed slowly, or not at all, owing largely to the deterioration of their terms of trade – the relation between the cost of the goods a state must import from abroad and its income from the exports it sends to foreign states. Terms of trade are said to deteriorate when the cost of imports rises faster than income from exports. Since buyers in the industrialised countries determined the prices of most products involved in international trade, the worsening position of the Third World was scarcely surprising. After 1973, only the oil-producing countries succeeded in escaping the effects of the Western domination of the world economy.

No study of the Third World could hope to assess its future prospects without taking into account population growth. In 2000, the earth's population was more than 6 billion, 80 per cent of whom lived in the Third World. This population growth will surely prevent any substantial improvements in living standards there as well as threaten people in stagnant economies with worsening poverty.

The Bandung conference, in 1955, was the beginning of the political emergence of the Third World. China and India, two states whose social and economic systems were sharply opposed, played a major role in promoting that conference and in changing the relationship between the Third World and the industrial countries, capitalist and communist. As a result of decolonisation, the **United Nations**, at first numerically dominated by European countries and countries of European origin, was gradually transformed into something of a Third World forum. With increasing urgency, the problem of underdevelopment then became the focus of a permanent, although essentially academic, debate. Despite that debate, the unity of the Third World remains hypothetical, expressed mainly from the platforms of international conferences.

**Foreign aid**, and indeed all the efforts of existing institutions and structures, have failed to solve the problem of underdevelopment. The United Nations Conference on Trade and Development (UNCTAD), held in New Delhi in 1971, suggested that 1 per cent of the national income of industrialised countries should be devoted to aiding the Third World. That figure has never been reached, or even approximated. In 1972 the Santiago (Chile) UNCTAD set a goal of a 6 per cent economic growth rate in the 1970s for the underdeveloped countries. But this, too, was not achieved. The living conditions endured by the overwhelming majority of the people who inhabit the poor countries have either not noticeably changed since 1972 or have actually deteriorated.

Whatever economic development has occurred in the Third World has not been distributed equally between countries or among population groups within them. Most of the countries that have managed to achieve substantial economic growth are those that produce oil: Algeria, Gabon, Iran, Iraq, Kuwait, Libya, Nigeria, Oman, Saudi Arabia, the United Arab Emirates, and Venezuela. They had the money to do so because after 1973 the Organisation of Petroleum Exporting Countries (OPEC), a cartel, succeeded in raising the price of oil drastically. Other important raw materials are also produced by underdeveloped countries who have tried to form cartels similar in form to OPEC. For example, Australia, Guinea, Guyana, Jamaica, Sierra Leone, Surinam, and Yugoslavia formed the Bauxite International Association (BIA) in 1974; and Chile, Peru, Zaire, and Zambia formed a cartel of copper-producing countries in 1967. But even strategic raw materials like copper and bauxite are not as essential to the industrialised countries as oil, and these cartels therefore lack OPEC's strength; while the countries that produce cocoa and coffee (and other foods) are even less able to impose their will.

All international agencies agree that drastic action is required to improve conditions in Third World countries, including investment in urban and rural public work projects to attack joblessness and underemployment, institutional reforms essential for the redistribution of economic power, agrarian reform, tax reform, and the reform of public funding. But in reality, political and social obstacles to reform are part of the very nature of the international order and of most Third World governments.

*See also:* **debt trap; decolonisation; dependency; development; distributive justice; failed state; foreign aid; humanitarian intervention; imperialism; modernisation theory; multinational corporation; newly industrialising countries; population growth; structural adjustment programme; sustainable development; women in development**

*Further reading:* Clapham, 1992; Dorraj, 1995; Goldgeier and McFaul, 1992; Harrison, 1993; Haynes, 1996; Neuman, 1998; Thomas, 1999

## TORTURE ✓

Of the many issues of the post-9/11 era, none is perhaps more volatile than torture. Torture as defined by the Torture Convention (1977), is as follows:

> any act by which severe pain or suffering, whether physical or mental, is intentionally inflicted on a person for such purposes as obtaining from him or a third person information or a confession, punishing him for an act he or a third person has committed or is suspected of having committed, or intimidating or coercing him or a third person, or for any reason based on discrimination of any kind, when such pain or suffering is inflicted by or at the instigation of or with the consent or acquiesence of a public official or other person acting in an official capacity.

As such, this legal definition remains broad and somewhat ambiguous, even though it is often linked to the more specific elements of a crime against humanity and **war crimes**. On a sociological and historical level, torture, it could be said, remains widespread – with its official use dating back to medieval times. During the Spanish inquisition, for instance, Savanarola, a Catholic inquisitor, used torture openly to extract confessions from suspected apostates. At this time, torture was widely accepted by the Church and other sects as a necessary extension of God's will. It was only during the Enlightenment era that the use of torture came to be questioned as an immoral form of legalised punishment, or rather, as a cruel and unusual form of punishment. For example, the first French National Assembly (1793) actively sought to outlaw any use of torture; whilst the framers of the Bill of Rights added the eighth amendment to the US Constitution, which outlaws cruel and unusual punishment. Despite these early examples of legal proscription, however, torture continued to exist in the form of institutionalised slavery, as well as colonialism, particularly during the colonial wars, including the French–Algerian War (1955–62).

Clearly, torture extends deep into history and the human psyche. A scientific experiment conducted by a Stanford University professor in the early 1970s, for instance, demonstrated that even college-educated people were capable of imposing torture in a very short period of time. The psychological test or issue here was not whether torture was morally reprehensible, but rather, how it constituted a seemingly repressed desire or fear of the human psyche; hence, a repressive mechanism for asserting control and power under conditions of severe duress or threat. Thus, while torture remains legally condemned in many countries, in practice, it remains fairly widespread. This is to say that while most developed civil societies or states with traditions of the rule of law have established safeguards against this practise, many countries continue to practice torture.

There are thus two underlying issues of torture that need to be addressed. The first is the ambiguous legal definition of torture whose effects cut across cultures and nation-states. Complicating matters in this regard is that torture can extend into many areas of life including the workplace, in the form of forced overtime labour (mental stress). More visibly, female mutilation, while considered a potentially cruel form of treatment, appears to be an acceptable practice for many parts of the Sudan. This is not to diminish the substantive value of the definition and elements encoded in the International Criminal Tribunal statutes, the Torture Convention and the Geneva Convention; but rather to demonstrate the difficulty of effectively outlawing torture, especially when there is conflict between international and national customs. This problem nonetheless underscores the importance of clarifying the elements of torture so that global enforcement can assume a more effective and credible role.

A second underlying issue is whether torture serves a necessary, overriding strategic purpose in severe **crises**. As the most extreme necessitating example, the ticking time-bomb model, in which a terrorist knows the whereabouts of a nuclear bomb that is set to go off in a densely-populated urban centre (that would kill millions of people), points to the extreme circumstances under which a civil society might elect to justify torture to save countless other lives. Yet it is precisely this general idea of a crisis situation or extenuating circumstances of war that characterises the overriding logic of the Bush administration's decision to impose harsh interrogation tactics on the prisoners being detained at Guantanamo Bay prison and other CIA prisons around the world.

But as the Abu Ghraib scandal has shown, such harsh interrogation tactics can regress into torture. This is one reason why the term **enemy combatants** remains so controversial, since it removes the legal guarantees against torture afforded under **international law**. Many who have criticised the harsh treatment of detainees have been quick to assert the breakdown in reciprocity concerning the rules of war encoded in the Geneva Convention. They argue that the US's engagement in torture will only encourage other states to torture US prisoners of war.

On a more encouraging level, there are various institutional mechanisms for redressing torture. The US Alien Torts Claim Act, for instance, allows aliens or non-citizens residing in the US to seek monetary and civil claims against their torturers. In addition to the Torture Convention, there is also the **International Criminal Court** which entered into force in July of 2002. Its statute, for instance, contains many elements of the crime of torture (crimes against humanity). It is hoped that the ICC's effectiveness will help to deter would-be torturers. However, one of the issues surrounding torture is whether there should be universal jurisdiction exercised over the crime. The ICC, for instance, does not exercise universal jurisdiction, which means that stopping torture will ultimately reside in a state's willingness to enforce the proscriptive norms against torture.

*See also:* **Bush doctrine; enemy combatants; human rights; international law; International Criminal Court; war crime; war on terror**

*Further reading:* Danner, 2004; Levinson, 2004; McCoy, 2006; Ratner and Abrams, 2001

## TRAGEDY OF THE COMMONS

The world has become a very unbalanced place in terms of human welfare and environmental quality. Much attention has focused on how economic and political forces have produced global imbalances in the way human society interacts with the environment, not just between city and countryside, but between groups within **international society** with different levels of access to **power** and influence (e.g. women and men, different states). On a global scale, there are clear imbalances between richer states and poorer states. In general terms, the wealthiest few are disproportionately responsible for environmental pollution, but at the other end of the spectrum the poorest are also accused of a responsibility that is greater than their numbers warrant.

The imbalance between human activities and the environment stems from differential ownership of certain resources and the values placed on them. Individuals own some environmental resources while others are under common ownership. One **theory** argues that resources under common ownership are prone to overuse and abuse for this very reason – the tragedy of the commons. The example often given to illustrate this principle is that of grazing lands that are commonly owned in pastoral societies. It is in the interest of an individual to graze as many livestock as possible, but if too many individuals all have the same attitude, the grazing lands may be overused and degraded; the rational use of a resource by an individual may not be rational from the viewpoint of a wider society. The principle can also be applied to explain the misuse of other commonly owned resources, such as the pollution of air and water or catching too many fish in the sea.

It is important to note, however, that common ownership does not necessarily lead to the exploitation of resources. In many areas where resources are commonly owned, strong social and cultural rules have evolved to control the use of resources. In situations like this, resource degradation usually occurs because the traditional rules for the control of the resource break down for some reason. Reasons include migration to a new area, changes in ownership rights, and global **population growth**. In examples like overfishing of the open oceans, by contrast, the tragedy of the commons applies because there is no tradition of rules developed to limit **exploitation**.

A related concept is the undervaluation of certain resources. Air is a good example. For all intents and purposes, air is a commonly owned continuous resource that, in practice, is not given an economic value. The owner of a windmill does not pay for the moving air that the windmill harnesses, nor does the owner of a factory who uses the air as a sink for the factory's wastes. Since air has no economic value it is prone to be overused. A simple economic argument suggests that if an appropriate economic value were put on the resource, the workings of the market would ensure that as the resource became scarce, so the price would increase. As the value of the resource increased, theory suggests that it would be managed more carefully. Putting a price on environmental assets and services is one of the central aims of the discipline of environmental economics. This can be done by finding out how much people are willing to pay for an aspect of the environment or how much people would accept in compensation for the loss of an environmental asset. One of the justifications of environmental pricing is the fact that money is the language of government treasuries and big business, and thus it is appropriate to address the tragedy of the commons in terms that such influential bodies understand.

There are problems with the approach, however. People's willingness to pay depends on their awareness and knowledge of the resource and of the consequences of losing it. Information, when available, is open to manipulation by the media and other interest groups. In instances where the common resource is unique in world terms – such as an endangered species, or a feature like the Grand Canyon – who should be asked about the willingness to pay? Should it be local people, national groups, or an international audience? Our ignorance of how the environment works and of the nature of the consequences of environmental change and degradation also presents difficulties. In the case of climatic change caused by human-induced atmospheric pollution, for example, all we know for certain is that the atmospheric concentrations of greenhouse gases have been rising and that human activity is most likely to be responsible. However, we do not know exactly how the climate will change nor what effects any changes may have upon human society. We can only guess at the consequences, so we can only guess at the costs.

*See also:* **capitalism; development; global warming; public goods; sustainable development**

*Further reading:* Anderson, R., 1991; Hardin, 1968

## UNILATERALISM

Unilateralism is a process in which one state acts independently of other states to implement and enforce its foreign policy objectives. Unilateralism, in this sense, is closely tied to promoting the national interests of one state, even if it means unduly disrupting the peace and security achieved on other issues. The process of acting unilaterally, as this applies to the **Bush**

**doctrine**, partakes of two overarching objectives: (1) to project the **hegemon**'s power interests in the most efficient manner; and (2) to create a new world **order** that is most favourable to securing the interests of the hegemon and the principles of freedom, security, and democracy.

During the twentieth century, the latter objective has come to be defined in terms of the major powers acting in concert to create a new democratic order. The most notable case during the post-**cold war** era occurred in 1990–1, when the first Bush administration led a UN multinational force to drive out Iraqi forces from Kuwait. Another example includes the US-led Kosovo invasion in the spring of 1999, in which the goal was to drive out Milosevic's forces from the region of Kosovo, where ethnic cleansing was reported to have taken place. Unlike unilateralism, then, **multilateralism** reflects how several powers act in concert, or coordinate policy, in order to achieve a stated goal. Typically, multilateralism operates within the framework of the **United Nations** or other international organisations.

As we have seen in recent years, the Bush administration has acted unilaterally to promote US national security interests. But it is important to stress that unilateralism is not unique to the foreign policy of the Bush administration. In fact, it has played an important role in previous US administrations, including the Clinton administration's decision to retaliate for the 1998 US embassy bombings in Kenya, and the Reagan administration's attack on Libya in 1986. It should also be noted that only under certain conditions of self-defence does **international law**, or the UN Charter in this case, sanction unilateral actions. Thus, countries acting unilaterally for the sake of preventing an act of aggression often operate outside, or in violation of international law, thereby making unilateralism a difficult process to justify on legal and moral grounds. By making unilateralism a pillar of its doctrine, then, the Bush administration has, in this sense, become defiant of customary international law.

Given these factors, we can identify three central conditions of unilateralism:

1   A country possesses the power and capabilities to act alone in accordance with its own perceived **national interests**.
2   The exigencies of the situation necessitate decisive and timely action by another country. Under this condition, a country must act unilaterally in order to forgo the time-lag associated with reaching consensus and implementing and enforcing measures.
3   Lastly, when a threat unduly threatens the values and interests of one hegemonic state, the hegemonic state may wish to exaggerate the extent and level of the threat in order to necessitate the need for quick, decisive, and **pre-emptive** action.

The consequences of unilateralism, though, can be severe. Indeed, the unilateralism of the Bush doctrine undermines many of the strategic benefits of multilateralism. Not only does multilateralism serve to isolate the enemy, it also confers and sustains the **legitimacy** of the country leading the action. The main consequence of unilateralism, therefore, is that it tends more often that not to undermine the legitimacy of the player acting unilaterally, which in this case is symptomatic of the hegemon's willingness to do what it wishes to do to promote its national **security** interests. In addition, unilateralism means that third party mediation and constructive dialogue is sidelined in favour of an active, aggressive approach. This can, as we have seen in the recent case of the Iraq War, keep one state from listening to the concerns or voices of other countries, which may have some direct political ties to that country's affairs. It may also create long-term grievances and ill will among the peoples in the region towards the hegemonic power.

*See also:* **Bush doctrine; hegemony; legitimacy; pre-emption; security; sovereignty; United Nations; war; war on terror**

*Further reading:* Malone and Khong, 2003; Prestowitz, 2003; Weiss and Crahan, 2004

## UNITED NATIONS (UN)

Two years after the outbreak of the Second World War the British Prime Minister Winston Churchill met with President Roosevelt of the United States. Between them they issued a document called the Atlantic Charter, setting out their **war** aims. Apart from the defeat of Nazi Germany, they sought peace, freedom, collaboration, and **security** between states, overseen by a wider and permanent system of general security. The Atlantic Charter contained the seeds of the United Nations, whose principles were adopted by 26 states in January 1942 when they signed a Declaration of the United Nations. In 1944, representatives of the **great powers** (the Soviet Union, the United States, China, and Britain) met at Dumbarton Oaks in the United States to draw up firm proposals for the new international organisation, the successor to the **League of Nations**. In 1945, 51 states met at the United Nations Conference in San Francisco to debate the terms of the UN Charter.

The UN has its headquarters in New York. Here it sets about achieving its three main purposes: to maintain international peace, to develop friendly relations among states, and to cooperate internationally in solving international economic, social, cultural, and humanitarian problems and in promoting respect for human rights and fundamental freedoms. The UN has six major organs. They are:

1    the General Assembly;
2    the Security Council;
3    the UN Secretariat;
4    the Economic and Social Council;
5    the International Court of Justice;
6    the Trusteeship Council.

The only time that all member states meet together is in the General Assembly. Here representatives from each of the 187 states that make up the UN gather every year to discuss the world's problems in a global parliamentary setting. Much of the Assembly's work goes on in its six committees:

- First Committee – disarmament issues, outer space, political, and security issues;
- Second Committee – economic and financial issues;
- Third Committee – social, humanitarian, and cultural matters;
- Fourth Committee – colonial matters;
- Fifth Committee – administrative and budgetary matters;
- Sixth Committee – legal issues.

The Assembly has little influence in world politics. It can debate any issue it chooses, adopt Resolutions with a two-thirds majority, help elect members of other UN bodies, and vote on the UN budget. Ultimately, whatever **power** it has depends on its moral authority as a reflection of global opinion.

The Security Council is the most important agency in the UN, particularly in fulfilling its primary purpose. It remains ready to meet at any time whenever there is a threat to international peace and security. There are 15 members of the Security Council. Five are permanent (the P5), and ten non-permanent members are elected for a period of two years from regional groups within the UN: Africa, Asia, Eastern Europe, Latin America, Western Europe, and Oceania. The P5 are the United States, Russia, China, France, and Britain. Decisions of the Council have to be accepted by a majority of members, and must include the P5, each of which is able to veto a decision.

Without doubt, the General Assembly and the Security Council are the most important bodies in the UN. Apart from the other four organs, the UN includes a variety of bodies known as Specialised Agencies, which regulate specific activities and set world standards. They include the **International Monetary Fund** (IMF), the **World Bank**, the World

Health Organisation (WHO), the Food and Agriculture Organisation (FAO), the United Nations Educational, Scientific, and Cultural Organisation (UNESCO), the UN International Children's Emergency Fund (UNICEF), the UN High Commission for Refugees (UNHCR), and the United Nations Environment Programme (UNEP).

Over the last half-century, the United Nations has had a chequered history. During the cold war, it was paralysed from playing a major role in maintaining international peace and security because of the constant use of the veto by the great powers. Without their cooperation, the Security Council was unable to fulfil the ambitions of those who had designed it to be more effective than its predecessor, the League of Nations. Nonetheless, the UN did oversee the complex process of **decolonisation**, which led to a rapid expansion in the number of member states in the 1950s and 1960s. It also developed the practice of **peacekeeping**, which was in part designed to prevent the **superpowers** from intervening in conflicts that might then escalate into a direct confrontation between them.

From 1988 to 1992, the United Nations enjoyed a brief period of success, although this was a direct consequence of the end of the cold war. No longer did the threat of a great power veto produce either gridlock or an ineffectual compromise. The United Nations reached its peak of popularity, especially in the United States, after the Gulf War in 1991 by providing the auspices for successfully challenging Iraq's conquest and annexation of Kuwait. This aura of achievement was reinforced by a series of seemingly successful mediation efforts from 1988 to 1990 related to long-festering regional conflicts: Iran–Iraq, Afghanistan, Cambodia, Namibia, and El Salvador. This string of successes lent some temporary credibility to expectations of what United States President George Bush called a new world **order**. The world would be guided by **international law** and peace would be upheld by a robust United Nations that would be strengthened gradually as public confidence in its effectiveness increased.

In a few short years, the number of UN peacekeeping operations doubled to nearly 20, the annual budget for peacekeeping quadrupled to almost US$4 billion, and the number of peacekeepers deployed around the globe skyrocketed to almost 80,000. By 1993, tens of thousands of blue-helmeted soldiers were viewed as instruments of salvation in areas ranging from Kuwait and Somalia to Bosnia and the Great Lakes region in Central Africa. These soldiers were the clear expression of the Clinton administration's devotion to a policy that Madeleine Albright, then its UN Ambassador, had christened assertive multilateralism.

Within months of coming to office, however, the Clinton administration had turned the United Nations from an instrument of global salvation into the new international 'bogeyman'. A badly mishandled military operation in the streets of Somalia's capital, Mogadishu, left 18 American soldiers dead. Although the operation had been conducted by American troops under sole US command and without the UN's knowledge or involvement, President Clinton and Congress placed the blame firmly on the UN Secretary General at the time, Boutros Boutros-Ghali. The failure of the UN Protection Force in Bosnia to provide the citizens of that unfortunate country with much in the way of protection only added to Washington's disillusionment with the United Nations.

As a result of this change of heart, US policy towards the UN underwent two profound changes. First, in May 1994 the Clinton administration adopted new guidelines restricting the likelihood of its support for future UN peacekeeping operations. As a first indication of this new stringency, Washington argued against bolstering the small UN force in Rwanda, even though its commander pleaded for 5,000 troops to halt a **genocide** that would eventually take the lives of some 800,000 Rwandans. Second, there was growing reluctance in the US Congress to pay for the exploding costs of large UN peacekeeping operations, particularly since Washington (as the UN's largest member) was responsible for 31 per cent of the total cost. Instead of paying its share (which in the mid-1990s ran to more than US$1 billion), Congress balked, appropriating only a small percentage of the total. As a result, US debts to the organisation mounted through the 1990s. In 1999 the US Congress finally agreed to begin paying its debts, although the decision was a close one which reflected the failure of the United Nations to build on its early post-cold war success.

There are three main reasons for the decline of the United Nations in the 1990s. First, patterns of war have changed. The Charter of the UN is based on the principles of **sovereignty** and non-intervention in the internal affairs of states. The UN is unable to respond effectively to armed conflict that blurs the line between civil and interstate war. Second, despite the end of the cold war, the UN is only as effective as its member states, particularly the P5, allow it to be. The UN lacks its own military forces, and therefore relies on member states to make forces available to the Secretary General on request. It is slow to respond to crises, and cannot act in those areas that are regarded as legitimate spheres of influence by any of the P5, especially the United States, Russia, and China. Third, the UN is wholly funded by its member states, particularly the P5. This enables them to use their financial power to promote their own **national interests** at the UN.

In recent years, there has been much discussion about how to reform the UN. Proposals have been put forward to make the organisation more representative of the changing balance of power in world politics. In April 2005, Kofi Annan put forth his proposal for UN reform, calling for an increase in the number of sitting members on the Security Council from 15 to 25 and the creation of a new humanitarian council. Annan's proposal also calls for an increase in the number of permanent members from five to seven, in order to reflect the shifting balance of power in international politics over the past several years. Here some commentators argue that Japan, Germany, and India deserve greater recognition and status in the Security Council. In addition, there has been much debate over whether and how to provide the UN with more financial and military power to respond to crises deemed to be within its remit. Unless the United Nations is reformed, the gap between expectation and performance is unlikely to be closed. This would be unfortunate, since the United Nations remains the only international organisation that approximates a form of **global governance**.

*See also:* **cold war; collective security; decolonisation; great powers; humanitarian intervention; League of Nations; peacekeeping; sovereignty**

*Further reading:* Annan, 2005; Baehr and Gordenker, 1999; Roberts and Kingsbury, 1992; Taylor, 1997

# WAR

The use of armed forces in a conflict, especially between countries. The conventional view is that for a conflict to be classified as a war, it should culminate in at least 1,000 battle deaths. This definition allows for the inclusion of other wars such as a civil war *within* a state. Although every war is unique, it is useful to distinguish between three categories of war as an organised set of hostilities conducted by states and initiated by the sending of large armed forces across an international boundary.

The first of these three categories comprises wars that may be called 'rational'. These are wars that are deliberately initiated by one or more governments in the expectation that this war will be instrumental in achieving some national purpose. In the nineteenth century, wars of this kind were frequent and the calculations leading to them were not unrealistic. Between 1816 and 1911, four-fifths of all wars were won by the states that initiated them. Thus, starting a war in the nineteenth century seemed to be a rational business.

The second type of war is that of drift or collision. In these instances governments become involved in wars because of gross misjudgements or a failure to perceive some particular course of events. Such wars have outcomes that are difficult to forecast. In the twentieth century, only two-fifths of wars were won by the country initiating them, while three-fifths were lost. In other words, after 1911 we find that if a government started a war, the likelihood was that it would lose. This raises the question of whether it is the case that governments have become more stupid; whether they have become over-burdened by the pressures of domestic politics; or whether the international system has become progressively more complicated and therefore harder to understand and control.

There is a third category of war that cuts across the first two categories. These are wars that are initiated because the government concerned is afraid of peace; it feels that if it does not go to war now, the result of several more years of peace would be more intolerable. For example, there is plenty of evidence to suggest that such fears lay behind Japan's decision to bomb Pearl Harbor in 1941.

There are a number of **theories** that seek to explain patterns of war and peace between states in the international system. Some scholars argue that the underlying causes of war can be found in the structure of **power** and **alliances** in the international system or in the way that the structure changes over time. Others trace the roots of war to political, economic, social, and psychological factors internal to the state. Some scholars argue that liberal democratic states are inherently peaceful, whereas authoritarian states are more warlike. Others believe that war results from the tendencies of **capitalist** states to expand in search of external markets, investment opportunities, and raw materials. Particular wars have also been traced to attempts by political leaders to solve their internal problems through the adoption of aggressive foreign policies on the assumption that external conflict will promote internal harmony. Wars have also been explained as a consequence of **misperception** and the effects of stress on **crisis** decision-making.

There is no single persuasive theory of war. In seeking its causes, it is important to distinguish between three separate issues: the *conditions* in the absence of which war would not be possible, *patterns* of war and peace over space and time, and finally, explanations of *particular* wars. In his famous survey of the literature on the causes of war, Kenneth Waltz (1959) noted that although the absence of world government made war possible, no particular war could be explained without examining factors at different **levels of analysis**.

Despite the difficulties of explaining war, it is important to note three key changes in patterns of war and peace in contemporary international relations. First, the prospect of war between the **great powers** of the twenty-first century is remote, particularly if the United States retains its military dominance and political **hegemony** in the international system. Prior to the modern era that began some time in the late seventeenth century, it was difficult to distinguish between periods of peace and war. With the rise of the modern state, industrialisation, and the application of advanced technology to weapons of war, the latter became increasingly destructive but also less frequent. Today, in part because of the existence of nuclear weapons, some scholars suggest that war has become obsolescent in relations among advanced industrialised states. Hopefully the Second World War will be the final 'total war' of the modern era. This is not to say that relations between Russia, China, Europe, and the United States will be harmonious, merely that it would be hard to imagine the conditions under which it would be rational for them to use force against each other to protect their perceived **national interests**.

If conventional or nuclear war seems increasingly unlikely between the most powerful states, this benign prospect does not necessarily apply to relations between strong and weak states in the system, or between states other than the great powers. Such wars never ceased during the period of the cold war, which is sometimes misleadingly called the 'long peace'! One of the most noted changes in conventional wars involving the United States is the so-called *Revolution in Military Affairs* (RMA). Many US strategic planners believe that by the end of the twenty-first century, war involving the United States will be fully automated and increasingly soldier–less. Much of the fighting will take place high above the battlefields using unmanned fighters, bombers, and missiles launched from semi-submerged submarine/ships. Distant commanders will watch the action on video in real time, pressing buttons to destroy the targets that appear on their screens. American soldiers in the field will also be 'online', able to destroy targets with a click of their field laptops. Present trends suggest that twenty-first-century war may be as much about information as bullets. The Pentagon is already planning advanced forms of information warfare, including computer-based sabotage of an enemy's computing, financial, and telephone systems before a shot is fired in anger. This would be backed up by 'cyber attacks' on command and control centres, possibly with the aid of killer satellites. The aim would be to effectively blindfold enemy commanders by robbing them of communication with their troops and knowledge of their positions before physical hostilities begin.

The political implications of the RMA are as yet unclear. Although many observers believe that advanced technology will bring about wars that are increasingly destructive, one must distinguish between destroying people and infrastructure. On the one hand, there is evidence to suggest that advanced military technology produces very precise and discriminating weapons. 'Smart' bombs are capable of selecting precise targets and avoiding others, thereby restoring the distinction between combatants and non-combatants that had been eroded over the course of the twentieth century. Thus **NATO** claimed with some justification during the Kosovo War in 1999 that it was not targeting civilians, but only troops and their military installations. On the other hand, the ability of the United States to wage war without large numbers of American deaths may tempt it to use force unnecessarily in order to 'resolve' its conflicts with weaker states in the international system. Furthermore, just because the RMA promises to reduce civilian casualties during a war does not mean that it will reduce damage to industrial infrastructures, which in turn will lead to large numbers of civilian deaths after the war has finished. Indeed, there is plenty of evidence in Iraq and Serbia to suggest the opposite.

Finally, a third major change in warfare concerns the relationship between war and the state. In the past, war between states in Europe was itself part of the 'state-making' project, helping to unify states internally and facilitating the expansion of European colonialism during the era of the 'classical' **balance of power** system. Today, it would be diffcult to argue that contemporary patterns of armed conflict in much of the **Third World** will produce a similar outcome. Some scholars distinguish between 'zones' of peace and war. The former exist in North and South America, Western Europe, and large parts of the Asia-Pacific. The latter dominates the regional politics of the Middle East and Sub-Saharan Africa. Today we are witnessing a return to private enterprise in the conduct of war in those parts of the world where states are disintegrating – as in Africa, where warring factions are trying to control the state simply to promote their personal interests in extracting wealth from their 'citizens'.

*See also:* **cold war; democratic peace; failed state; great powers; historical sociology; humanitarian intervention; just war; war on terror; wars of the third kind**

*Further reading:* Holsti, 1991, 1996; Orme, 1997/8; Van Creveld, 1991

## WAR CRIME √

Shorthand for a body of law that arose more than 500 years ago, although it has been substantially shaped by the experience of the Second World War and the Holocaust, war crimes are those violations of the laws of **war** that incur individual criminal responsibility. The first trial for war crimes is generally considered to be that of Peter von Hagenbach, who was tried in 1474 in Austria and sentenced to death for wartime atrocities. By the First World War, many states accepted that certain violations of the laws of war (which had been codified in the Hague Conventions of 1899 and 1907) were indeed crimes. The 1945 Charter of the International Military Tribunal at Nuremberg defined war crimes as 'violations of the laws or customs of war', including murder, ill-treatment, or deportation of civilians in occupied territory; murder or ill-treatment of prisoners of war; killing of hostages; plunder of public or private property; wanton destruction of municipalities; and any devastation that was not militarily necessary.

The 1949 Geneva Conventions marked the first attempt to codify war crimes in a humanitarian law treaty. War crimes were defined as 'grave breaches' of each of the four Conventions (on wounded and sick on land, wounded and sick at sea, prisoners of war, and civilians). They include:

- wilful killing;
- torture or inhuman treatment;
- wilfully causing great suffering;
- wanton destruction of property unjustified by military necessity;
- compelling civilians or prisoners of war to serve the hostile power;
- wilfully depriving civilians or prisoners of war of a fair trial;
- unlawful deportation or confinement of civilians;
- the taking of hostages.

In 1977 an additional protocol expanded the protections of the Geneva Conventions, and charged states with the duty to prosecute persons accused of war crimes or to hand them over to a state willing to do so.

It should be noted that all the above war crimes only apply in interstate armed conflicts. **International law** has fewer rules regulating the conduct of internal conflicts that many states consider part of their domestic jurisdiction. Nonetheless, one could argue that this situation is changing in light of the international response to the horrific violence attending the break-up of Yugoslavia in the 1990s, as well as the atrocities committed against the Tutsi population in Rwanda in 1994. When the **United Nations** Security Council established the Yugoslavia war crimes tribunal in 1993, and followed it up in 1994 with the International Criminal Tribunal for Rwanda, it ensured their jurisdiction over a range of crimes.

First, these **international criminal tribunals** have jurisdiction over the crime of **genocide**. The word genocide evokes the Holocaust, but it now has a specific legal description. The essence of the crime of genocide requires the specific intent to destroy, in whole or in substantial part, a national, **ethnic**, racial, or religious group through killing, torture, or other means. The element of *specific intent* is a key part of the crime of genocide, and remains one of the toughest to prove in a court. Second, these tribunals have jurisdiction over crimes against humanity. War crimes can be considered a subset of crimes against humanity, but the latter make no distinction between wars within states and wars between states. They include such atrocities as murder, enslavement, deportation, torture, and rape. International war crimes tribunals are meant to try the most heinous crimes known to humankind. These are crimes that deserve the universal condemnation of all states.

A moral issue arises when those accused are brought to trial for war crimes. Can they receive a fair trial? Are war criminal trials little more than a 'victor's peace'? The trials of captured German and Japanese military personnel and civilian officials at the end of the Second World War have never satisfied everyone that they produced justice and did not merely exact vengeance. Today, however, war crimes tribunals are comprised of judges who come from a variety of countries and receive their authority from the United Nations, not from a set of states victorious in war. It remains to be seen whether the experience of recent tribunals set up to investigate war crimes in specific countries will lead to the setting up of a permanent war crimes tribunal. This would take the form of a permanent international criminal court that would have jurisdiction over genocide, widespread or systematic crimes against humanity, and large-scale war crimes.

*See also:* **ethnic cleansing; genocide; human rights; International Criminal Court; international criminal tribunals; international law; just war; war; wars of the third kind**

*Further reading:* Beigbeder, 1999; Best, 1994; Robertson, 2000; Walzer, 1992

## WAR ON TERROR

The war on terror is a US-led global military campaign to eliminate the threat of terrorism. The word **'war'** was first used in the immediate aftermath of the September 11 attacks, when US authorities referred to these attacks as 'acts of war' on Western civilisation. Consequently, the war on terror has been labelled as a new kind of war: a campaign that operates across state borders and, in many respects, operates outside the scope of international criminal law. As such, it breaks with conventional approaches to criminalising **terrorism** against a state.

The war on terror is of course the centrepiece of the Bush administration's foreign policy. It is possible to identify four general strategic priorities of the war: first, is the seizure of all financial assets of the terrorists, particularly the assets tied to Osama Bin Laden's inherited fortune, which has helped to finance the operations of Al Qaeda; second, to pressure those states that harbour terrorists, thereby rendering the abetting or aiding of terrorists a guilt by association; third, to spread democracy to the areas of the Middle East where authoritarian governments have long clamped down on individual political and civil rights – even if this means imposing democracy or pressuring states to adopt democratic measures; and lastly, to fight against poverty and social deprivation in countries where these factors have become sources of recruitment for terrorists.

Given these four strategic priorities, the war on terrorism showcases a new brand of **realism**: a mix of neo-conservative and liberalist thinking. Many who have favoured the second priority also supported the US-led invasion of Afghanistan, the first official war of the war on terror. Here, the UN Security Council gave the Bush administration a blank cheque of military engagement, agreeing that the invasion constituted a necessary act of self-defence against the suspected perpetrators of the attacks. The second so-called war of the war on terror was of course the Iraq War. Widely perceived as an unsuccessful and unnecessary war, the Iraq War has quickly led to an erosion of UN and international support.

To be sure, the political fallout from the war has been significant. The US's **unilateralism** in this case has not only divided consensus over the operations of the war, but has reflected growing hostility towards the Bush administration. Critics of the war point out, among other things, that the war lacks a clear-cut focus or public enemy. This has raised the following questions: What actually constitutes a war on terror? And if terrorism is endemic to state **power** politics, what does it mean to win the war? Is it realistic to proclaim that terrorism has been uprooted when the means to attack the **imperial** power continue to increase in sophistication and in numbers?

Given these unanswered questions, it is important to emphasise the unclear or ill-defined parameters of the war, including the indefinite nature of the war and the seeming unsustainability of the political and **coercive** tactics used to conduct the war. The Bush administration, for instance, has long persisted in using the war on terror as a means of contesting the relevance of civil society norms, including the Geneva Conventions. But even if the Iraq War has proved unsustainable, or if the war is merely a campaign, not a war *per se*, the war on terror remains an enduring challenge for promoting peace, **security**, and the rights of citizens.

*See also:* **Bush doctrine; enemy combatants; pre-emption; security; sovereignty; unilateralism; war**

*Further reading:* Clark, 2004; Dolan, 2005; McInness, 2003; Mead, 2004

# WARS OF THE THIRD KIND

Most armed conflicts are neither nuclear nor mechanised conventional **wars** between states. Instead, they fall into a very broad category which Edward Rice (1990) first identified as 'wars of the third kind'. Such wars are usually fought in what used to be called the **Third World** and rely heavily, although not exclusively, on guerrilla warfare. The concept is more accurate than the term 'low-intensity conflicts', which sanitises what can be extremely intense armed conflicts. They are often neither exclusively interstate conflicts nor confined within existing territorial boundaries. In each year of the 1980s and 1990s, there have been between 30 and 40 wars of the third kind in progress. Until the break-up of the former Soviet Union and Yugoslavia in the 1990s, virtually all of them occurred in **developing** countries, typically between governments and opponents aspiring to take control over the state or to achieve some degree of territorial autonomy.

There are two broad types of such wars. First, there are ideological struggles, where usually two competing military forces are linked to civilian populations through a shared political commitment, such as in the liberation wars of Eritrea and Nicaragua. The second type are more fragmented conflicts, where violence becomes decentralised and its political economy extractive and **exploitative** (e.g. in Somalia, Liberia, and the Congo). The two types are not mutually exclusive, since during the course of a relatively structured ideological struggle, political factionalisation may cause fragmentation; equally, it cannot be assumed that the factions in such conflicts lack an ideological base.

Once started, wars of the third kind are very difficult to bring to a definitive end, whether by decisive military victory or by **diplomatic** and political negotiation. Weapons are easily available. The state is usually fragmented. Sections of the population, especially the young, are alienated from existing systems, and rival groups easily and quickly become polarised. There is no general theory of conflict applicable to wars of the third kind. Their roots cannot typically be found in one set of issues or attributed to one particular event. Every war has its own historical setting interacting with internal and external factors in a unique configuration. In the growing literature on these wars, some common causes or factors can be identified:

- *The colonial legacy*. Colonial states were typically imposed by force, with few roots among the indigenous people of colonised regions. In this process, colonial authorities commonly resorted to violence to compel compliance with their rule. Today's post-independence states are often external structures forcibly imposed from above. They have inherited colonial instruments of violence and used them to subjugate their populations.

- *Ethnicity and religion*. Conflict between **ethnic** groups has proliferated in recent years. While ethnic identity has been emphasised as a crucial tenet in wars of the third kind, many of these ethnic conflicts have their roots in the history of colonial state formation. By categorising social classes along ethnic lines and deeming some groups as deserving of preferential treatment, colonial authorities facilitated the structuring of relationships between dominant and subordinate ethnic groups. This laid the foundation for long-term hatred among the groups disadvantaged by such political arrangements. Rwanda is a classic example.

- *Uneven development*. Within many developing countries there may be an uneven and unequal geographical spread of economic activity, **modernisation**, and receptivity to change.

- *Poverty*. Poverty can be both a cause and effect of wars of the third kind. Governments with violent tendencies as well as their opponents can recruit supporters and operatives whose lowest common denominator is socio-economic opportunism and desire for economic gain.

- *Poor leadership*. Many poorer states lack competent leaders. Some have conducted themselves as tribal chieftains with a belief in violence as a legitimate instrument of policy. For their political survival they have depended on the support of military and paramilitary agencies.

- *Foreign intervention*. The speed of **decolonisation** has left many developing countries with **dependent** economies based on the production of primary products and the import of manufactured goods. Poor commodity prices and large debt burdens have exacerbated wars of the third kind. More directly, foreign states have often intervened directly by supplying arms. This was particularly the case during the **cold war**, when conflicts in Angola, Afghanistan, and El Salvador (to name but three) were prolonged by the intervention of the **superpowers** and their support for different factions.

- *Militarism*. This means much more than the presence of the military. It refers to the dominating influence of military values, ideology, and patterns of behaviour over the political, social, economic, and foreign affairs of the state.

- *The state and political development*. Many poorer states remain weak not only in an economic sense, but also in terms of their internal coherence, popular **legitimacy** of rulers, and the development of a sense of citizenship that is shared by the vast majority of the population.

Many observers argue that wars of the third kind will continue to be the dominant form of armed conflict in the next century. Unless they threaten to spill over into the perceived sphere of influence of a great power, or take place in an area of strategic importance to more powerful states, they are unlikely to attract the sustained diplomatic efforts of the international community. Tragically, there remains a large gap between the academic interest in understanding new forms of armed conflict and policymakers' interest in responding to them.

*See also:* **arms trade; ethnic cleansing; ethnicity; failed states; foreign aid; humanitarian intervention; mercenary; refugees; safe haven; United Nations; war crime**

*Further reading:* Berdal and Malone, 2000; Holsti, 1996; Mueller, 2000; Neuman, 1998; Rice, 1990

## WEAPONS OF MASS DESTRUCTION

One of the depressing side-products of modern technological innovation, these are weapons capable of causing unparalleled damage and loss of life. Fortunately, the end of the **cold war**, a significant reduction in the size of the nuclear arsenals of the United States and Russia, and treaties such as the Nuclear Non-Proliferation Treaty (NPT) have helped to diminish the threat of total annihilation from nuclear weapons of mass destruction.

But nuclear weapons are not the only weapons of mass destruction. Chemical and biological weapons (CBW) also fall under this rubric. Now that the cold war is over, many observers consider that these weapons pose the greatest danger to world **security**. They are portable, relatively easy to make, cheap to produce, and are therefore perfect weapons for **rogue states** and **terrorists**.

While chemical weapons were first used with devastating effect during the First World War, the use of biological agents in **war** goes back to at least the fourteenth century when the Tatars catapulted the bodies of plague victims into the besieged city of Kaffa (in the Ukraine). Other graphic instances highlight the insidious nature of these weapons:

- In the eighteenth century, the British army deliberately gave smallpox-infected blankets to American Indians, hoping that an epidemic would reduce their military effectiveness.
- During the First World War, German agents infected animal feed, live-stock, and cavalry horses with biological materials.
- Between 1932 and 1945 in Manchuria, the Japanese undertook extensive research into the military uses of anthrax and other biological agents. In 1941, due to a lack of proper equipment and training, 1,700

Japanese soldiers died of cholera. It is also estimated that 3,000 prisoners died as a consequence of the experiments associated with the Japanese weapons programme.

Since 1945, there has not been any recorded use of biological agents during wartime. Even though Saddam Hussein is known to have 'weaponised' a number of biological agents, including anthrax, there is no evidence to suggest that he has used these weapons against his enemies. The same cannot be said for the use of chemical weapons, however. Iraq is known to have used them against the Kurds and during the Iran–Iraq war (1980–9).

The agents capable of being used in biological weapons fall into three main categories: plant, animal, and microbial. Within these categories, the variety of toxic agents is extensive and defies easy summary. This is partly because there are a number of strains within a single disease. Brucellae, for example, include four strains that are toxic to humans, while botulinus has seven. Agents that have been developed for weapons include anthrax, botulinum toxin, tularemia, brucellae, the plague, and smallpox.

The toxicity of these agents varies. Some induce serious illness; others are lethal. Anthrax (*Bacillus anthracis*) is potentially the most toxic to humans. According to the United States Office of Technology Assessment, for example, 100 kilograms of anthrax spores spread over an area of 300 square kilometres on a calm evening could kill between 1 and 3 million people. Given that there has never been a biological weapons attack on a densely populated area, the figures are largely conjectural. Nevertheless they underscore the potential hazard that these weapons represent to human beings, especially given that most of us live in or near heavily populated cities.

As a consequence of the use of biological and chemical agents during the First World War, attempts were made to outlaw the use of these weapons. The 1925 Geneva Protocol for the Prohibition of the Use in War of Asphyxiating, Poisonous or Other Gases, or of Bacteriological Methods of Warfare was the first such attempt. Despite the significance of this treaty, it was conceptually flawed. There was no legal prohibition against the production of biological weapons; the treaty did not apply to states outside the **League of Nations** framework; and there were no institutional mechanisms for inspecting or regulating these weapons.

In the late 1960s significant advances occurred in the regulation and monitoring of weapons of mass destruction. Over 100 states, including the United States and the former Soviet Union, signed a 1972 Convention prohibiting the development, production, and stockpiling of chemical and biological weapons. Indeed, during this period the US destroyed its entire stockpile of biological agents. A number of states have still not signed the Convention and are suspected of having chemical and biological weapons. North Korea, Iran, and Syria are thought to possess a chemical weapons capability, while Iraq's CBW programme has, in the aftermath of the US invasion of Iraq in the spring of 2003, yielded no evidence of any stockpiles of chemical weapons. Equally worrying is the number of states that are developing long-range delivery systems that would give them the capacity to project fear and terror across national boundaries. This is precisely the reason why the United States has sponsored the Missile Technologies Control Regime (MTCR). On a positive note, however, efforts are underway to enhance the procedures and mechanisms for compliance with the various conventions. The comprehensive Chemical Weapons Convention (CWC) of 1997 is a step in this direction. In its first review conference held in May 2003 at the Hague, the 151 member states of the convention declared their intentions to strictly enforce all the provisions amidst growing concern of chemical stockpiles that might be used by terrorists.

It is important to recognise that in the hands of sub-state actors, chemical and biological weapons present a very different challenge to policymakers. Policies and strategies designed to keep the peace during the cold war are inappropriate to these new and changing circumstances. It may still be possible to deter a rogue state through the threat of massive retaliation, but these strategies are inappropriate in dealing with political extremists. Chemical and biological weapons are 'weapons of the weak' and as such require very different strategies to combat their spread. They can be discharged from a light aircraft, or exploded in a busy street or a rubbish bin by remote control. Most alarming is the fact that someone with a basic degree in biology or chemistry has the know-how to manufacture these agents in large quantities. The infrastructure of most states is inadequate to cope with an attack of this kind. There is not enough vaccine or gas masks/suits to protect a densely populated city from even a small-scale attack, let alone a large one.

It is easy to become alarmed about these weapons, especially when one considers that Russia has stockpiled enough smallpox virus to infect every man, woman, and child on the planet. Moreover, accidents do happen. Sixty-four people died as a consequence of an accidental release of anthrax in Sverdlovsk (Russia) in 1979. But it is also important to remember that the **United Nations**, the World Health Organisation, and other agencies around the world are working tirelessly to monitor sub-state actors and to devise ways to limit the spread of weapons of mass destruction. The real danger is complacency.

*See also:* **arms control; nuclear proliferation; rogue state; terrorism**

*Further reading:* Betts, 1998a; Cole, 1997; Guillemin, 1999; Lederberg, 1999; Price, 1997; Zilinskas, 1999

## WOMEN IN DEVELOPMENT (WID)

Since its creation in 1945, the **United Nations** (UN) has sought to alleviate poverty and to improve the standard of living of the world's poorest states. The overall strategy has been to fund a wide range of aid and **development** programmes. Until the 1970s, however, none of these programmes specifically took into account the role of women in the development process. In recognition of this problem, the UN embarked on a vigorous campaign to advance the position of women within the development community. This included measures to improve their access to funding, to make gender equity a priority, and to ensure that UN development programmes would lead to more gender-sensitive outcomes for women. To facilitate this, special units were set up within institutions such as the **World Bank**. Moreover, **foreign aid** began to target women's issues, and women began to have more input at the strategic planning level.

The most important initiative, however, was the *International Decade for the Advancement of Women*. Lasting from 1976 to 1985, the Decade helped to open up a space for dialogue and debate about issues of concern to women. It did this in at least three ways.

1   A number of conferences were held during the period which provided women with an opportunity to discuss their individual experiences, to take part in workshops, and develop information networks.
2   Two specialised agencies within the UN were established: the *United Nations Development Fund for Women* (UNIFEM) and the *United Nations International Research and Training Institute for the Advancement of Women* (INSTRAW).
3   The Decade provided an important impetus for an emerging feminist literature on Women in Development (WID).

Much of this literature remains highly critical of the United Nations for the gender-biased character of its aid and development programmes that allegedly fail to take account of issues central to women's lives, such as reproduction, health, and child-rearing. Moreover, the programmes have done little to overcome the large inequalities between men and women in the **Third World**. The WID literature argues that women are integral to development but that they rarely benefit from it, largely because of a lack of access to markets, funding, decision-making, and education. The goal of the WID literature, therefore, is to highlight the importance of women's roles and to help establish strategies to reduce gender inequality. The WID critique has helped to establish a presence for women within the development debate, as well as in the planning and decision-making process. In this sense, the WID literature has made a lasting contribution to Third World development and towards correcting the institutional bias against women in the United Nations and elsewhere. In addition, the WID literature was an important starting point for feminist incursions into development studies and **international political economy**. It was the first body of literature to draw attention to the need of women for better access to aid and development, gender equity, and gender-sensitive development planning.

*See also:* **development; modernisation theory; United Nations; World Ban**k

*Further reading:* Boserup, 1989; Kabeer, 1994; Sen and Grown, 1987; Tinker and Jaquette, 1987

# WORLD BANK

Like the **International Monetary Fund**, the World Bank is a product of the **Bretton Woods** system. Originally called the International Bank for Reconstruction and Development (IBRD), it commenced operations in 1946 with a membership of 38 states, including the United States, Britain, and France. The initial task for the Bank was to provide loans to the shattered economies of Europe. During the 1950s and 1960s, as Europe began to recover from the Second World War, the Bank turned its attention to Africa, Asia, and Latin America, offering loans, guarantees, technical assistance, investment advice, and **political risk** management to middle-income countries seeking to modernise and **develop**. Over the past decade this commitment has extended to East European countries as well. The Bank now has a membership of more than 180 states and is headquartered in Washington, DC. It is one of the key agencies of the **United Nations**.

Since the 1950s, four specialised organisations have been created to assist the Bank in its work. In 1956, the World Bank created the International Finance Corporation (IFC). This agency offers loans to private developers (mainly **multinational corporations**) as a way of attracting other private investment capital. The International Development Association (IDA) was the second of the specialised institutions created by the Bank. It came into being in 1960 to offer long-term, interest-free loans to the poorest countries in the world. In

1966, the International Centre for the Settlement of Investment Disputes (ICSID) was set up to mediate disputes between governments and investors. In 1988, the Multilateral Investment Guarantee Agency (MIGA) was formed to insure private investments against expropriation, coups, and other forms of political risk.

In principle, the main goal of the World Bank is laudable. It seeks to reduce the level of poverty in the **Third World**. The Bank tries to live up to this lofty ideal by targeting projects likely to stimulate economic growth and raise the standard of living of the recipient country. Generally, the Bank concentrates its efforts on large infrastructure projects such as dams, roads, telecommunications networks, ports, and bridges. But the IDA is involved in more modest projects such as water purification, sanitation, health, family planning, agricultural production, and the training of educators. It is important to note, however, that the Bank lends only a proportion of the funds required for particular projects. The remainder must be raised from private investors, taxation, and capital markets.

The Bank itself is funded from a number of sources. It borrows from commercial institutions and it receives interest on its loans and investments. The Bank also sells bonds to pension funds, insurance companies, and multinational corporations. The most steady source of income, however, has been the annual contributions of its member countries. The United States is the largest donor, contributing more than US$50 billion to the Bank since 1945.

The day-to-day running of the bank is handled by an Executive Board consisting of 22 directors. Five of these are appointed by the largest donor countries (the United States, Japan, Germany, Britain, and France) and the rest are elected by the member countries. Above the executive directors are the President and the Board of Governors. The Board includes a representative from each of the member countries. Voting power is proportional to contributions made. This gives the United States the largest number of votes. The President of the Bank is appointed by the executive directors, generally for a five-year period.

The World Bank has many critics. At one extreme are those who see it as a 'wolf in sheep's clothing'. From this vantage-point, the Bank is primarily an institution for opening up Third World markets for the First World rather than being devoted to reducing world poverty. Today, indebtedness in the Third World is approaching US$2 trillion. Some countries now have a lower per capita income than they did before becoming involved with the Bank. In the early 1980s an estimated 130 million people were living in poverty, but by 2005 the figure had risen to an estimated 210 million people. These are grim statistics, especially given the enormous sums of money that have already been loaned. One of the interesting things about these figures is that they are used by critics on both the left and the right of the political spectrum. The left highlight the growing poverty in order to mount a case for the cancellation of Third World debt and a redistribution of wealth from the rich to the poor countries. Those on the right use the same statistics to discredit the Bank and to push for its abolition, believing that economic prosperity can only come about when the market is left to itself.

Other writers have been critical of the Bank's 'large project' mentality, arguing that it has failed to consider local issues such as the environment and the role of **women in development**. The Bank has attempted to address some of these issues in recent years. For example, it has funded projects specifically designed to improve the position of women in Third World countries.

One of the most controversial projects in recent years has been the Bank's involvement in a US$160 million loan to resettle nearly 58,000 Han Chinese and Chinese Muslim farmers in traditional Tibetan territory. The Tibetan community-in-exile argues that if the Bank grants such a loan, it will be supporting a policy of **ethnic cleansing**. However one views this particular case, it highlights the main problem for the World Bank: it is an institution that exists to serve the interests of states. As such, its commercial decisions will often prejudice the needs of non-state groups. It is likely, therefore, that the Bank will always be mired in controversy. It will never be able to live up to its **cosmopolitan** ideals as long as it remains subordinate to the most powerful states in the international system, particularly the United States.

*See also:* **Bretton Woods; debt trap; dependency; development; foreign aid; International Monetary Fund; Third World; women in development**

*Further reading:* Danaher, 1994; Kapur, 1997; Sharufk, 1999

# WORLD-SYSTEM THEORY ✓

Students of international relations often come to their subject matter with a number of preconceptions and assumptions. Among the most entrenched of these is the idea that they are studying a world whose most important characteristic is division. We may harbour a desire to study international relations in order to bring states and peoples closer together, but the starting point is a potentially united world that is actually divided in political, economic, and cultural terms. Although world-system theorists would not deny that such divisions exist, they would argue that the best way of understanding them is by locating them in the context of unity. The concept of a world-system suggests that the most meaningful primary unit of social constraint and social decision-making is this world-system rather than the **nation-states** that have been traditionally used as units of analysis.

The term world-system is synonymous with the term 'capitalist world-economy'. Based on the German word *Weltwirtschaft*, it refers to an entity within whose boundaries there is a single overarching division of labour but which in fact includes a number of separate state structures. This entity, according to world-system theorists, is a historical system whose structures operate at a different level from any existing political unit.

Although inspired by radical **dependency** theories of under-development in the 1950s as well as the French *Annales* school of historiography, the foremost pioneer of contemporary world-system theory is Immanuel Wallerstein. It was he who located the origins of the modern world-system in what he called 'the long sixteenth century', from around 1450 to 1670. Before this period, Western Europe was feudal, and economic production was based almost entirely on agriculture. From 1300 onwards, however, agricultural production fell rapidly as changes in the European climate contributed to a rapid increase in the incidence of epidemics among the peasant population. It was not until the 1500s that Europe moved towards the establishment of a capitalist world economy, in which production was oriented towards exchange in the market rather than seasonal consumption, those who produced goods earned less than their value, and the driving force of capitalism became the endless accumulation of material goods.

Economic growth in the new era entailed the expansion of the geographical scope of the market, the development of different forms of labour control, and the rise of strong states in Europe. The new world economy that emerged differed from previous empires in that it co-existed with a multiplicity of political jurisdictions and was characterised by a new single international division of labour between core and periphery.

The core of the world-system refers to those regions that benefited most from change. In the period of initial expansion, this included most of northwestern Europe (France, England, and Holland). The region was characterised by strong central governments and large **mercenary** armies. The latter enabled the bourgeoisie to control international commerce and extract economic surplus from trade and commerce. The growth of urban manufacturing was fed by movements of landless peasants from the countryside to the cities, whilst improvements in agricultural technology ensured continuous increases in agricultural productivity. The core of the world-system is where capital is always concentrated in its most sophisticated forms. Banks, the professions, trade, and skilled manufacturing are all sufficiently widespread to sustain a wage-labour economy.

The periphery, in contrast, refers to regions lacking strong central governments, dependent on coercive rather than wage labour, and whose economies depend on the export of raw materials to the core. Latin America and Eastern Europe were key peripheral zones in the sixteenth century. In Latin America, the Spanish and the Portuguese conquests destroyed indigenous political leaders and replaced them with weak bureaucracies under European control. Indigenous populations were killed or enslaved. African slaves were imported to work the land and the mines, and the local aristocracy was complicit with a system that kept it in power while it presided over the production of goods primarily for consumption in Europe. In the periphery, extensive cultivation and coercive control of labour sustain low-cost agricultural production.

In addition to the important distinction between core and periphery, world-system theory identifies regions known as *semi-peripheries*. These can be geographically located in the core but are undergoing a process of relative decline, or they can include rising economies in the periphery. They are **exploited** by the core, but in turn take advantage of the periphery. The semi-periphery is a crucial buffer between core and periphery.

Historically, two stages in particular mark the evolution of the modern world-system from the sixteenth to the twenty-first century. Up to the eighteenth century, the system was characterised by a strengthening of European states, following the failure of the Habsburg Empire to convert the emerging world-economy to a world empire. Increasing trade with the Americas and Asia enriched small merchant elites at the expense of wage-labourers in Europe, whilst its monarchs expanded their power to collect taxes, borrow money, and expand their militias to support the absolute monarchies. Local populations in Europe became increasingly homogeneous as minorities were expelled, particularly Jews.

In the eighteenth century, industrialisation replaced the emphasis on agricultural production, and European states embarked on an aggressive search for new markets to exploit. Over the last 200 years new regions have been absorbed into the modern world-system, such as Asia and Africa, thereby increasing the available surplus. However, it was not until the early years of the twentieth century that the world-system became truly global.

For world-system theorists, the capitalist world-economy is characterised by four fundamental contradictions, which will ultimately bring about its demise even as it appears to consolidate its global control with the collapse of the Soviet Union and the end of the **cold war**. First, there is a continuing imbalance between supply and demand. So long as decisions about what and how much to produce are made at the level of the firm, the imbalance will be an unintended consequence of continuous mechanisation and commodification. Second, whereas in the short term it is rational for capitalists to make profits by withdrawing the surplus from immediate consumption, in the longer term the further production of surplus requires a mass demand that can only be met by redistributing the surplus. Third, there are limits to the degree to which the state can co-opt workers to maintain the **legitimacy** of the capitalist system. Finally, there is the contradiction between the one and the many, the co-existence of a plural states system within one world-system. Whilst this co-existence facilitated the expansion of the system, it also impedes any attempt to develop greater cooperation to counter systemic **crises**.

*See also:* **capitalism; dependency; development; globalisation; historical sociology; modernisation theory**

*Further reading:* Denemark, 1999; Frank and Gills, 1993; Hopkins, 1982; Wallerstein, 1974–89; Zolberg, 1981

## WORLD TRADE ORGANISATION (WTO) √

The WTO came into existence on 1 January 1995, as one result of the agreement reached in the seven-year-long Uruguay round of **multilateral** trade negotiations that was completed the previous year. Its history, however, extends much further back, at least to the proposed International Trade Organisation (ITO) that was designed in the mid-1940s alongside the other **Bretton Woods** institutions, the **International Monetary Fund** (IMF), and the **World Bank**. The ITO was never approved, and part of its intended purpose was served instead by the General Agreement on Tariffs and Trade (GATT), which had been agreed upon originally as only a temporary measure pending approval of the ITO.

The GATT sponsored a series of rounds of trade negotiations, with the Doha round, which was started in 2001 (and is still ongoing as of 2007) and whose agenda is to slash barriers and subsidies in farming, being the most recent. Early rounds were primarily intended to reduce tariffs, the most successful of these being the Kennedy Round that was completed in 1967. It was followed by the Tokyo Round, begun in 1974 and completed in 1979. Unlike GATT, the WTO is a formal organisation that is not restricted to promoting trade liberalisation solely in manufactured goods. The institutional structure of the WTO contains three components: a revised GATT, the General Agreement on Trade in Services (GATS), and the Agreement on Trade-Related Intellectual Property Issues (TRIPS).

These components collectively enable the WTO to fulfil four important functions in international trade.

First, it constitutes a forum for the exchange of information, consultation, and negotiation among its 135 member states. At the highest level, the trade ministers from the member countries meet every two years to discuss trade policies. Members also communicate through ongoing working groups on particular issue-areas such as the environment or competition policy. In addition, members of the WTO are obliged to notify it whenever they engage in policies in a variety of areas that might be trade restricting. Technical regulation, for example, must be notified to the WTO Secretariat with suffcient lead-time for exporters to adapt to the new rules.

Second, the WTO constrains the trade policy actions of member states. Underlying the entire WTO and its GATT predecessor is the single principle of non-discrimination: that economic welfare is greatest if policies do not discriminate among suppliers and among demanders of economic goods and services. The WTO spells out in some detail a long list of constraints on member state behaviour – things that they either must do or must not do in order to be viewed as cooperating. Many of these constraints appeared as provisions of the original GATT agreement of 1947, which took the form of a treaty and consisted of 35 Articles of Agreement. These Articles have been revised, extended, and supplemented with additional agreements in the rounds of negotiation that have occurred since then. For example, the WTO requires countries to commit not to raise tariffs above levels that they negotiate on entry or in multilateral trading rounds. These levels are called tariffs bindings. It also constrains states from imposing a variety of **non-tariff barriers** to trade.

Third, the WTO specifies and permits a list of exceptions from the constraints for prescribed reasons and with prescribed means. Complex agreements among national governments must permit a fair amount of flexibility. Any rules that are adopted will inevitably be subject to interpretation, and the effect of these rules on the economy can never be known with certainty. Therefore, international trade agreements typically include some sort of escape clause that allows the parties to back partially out of the agreement in the event that it proves to be more injurious than expected. The WTO specifies in great detail the criteria that states must follow in order to avoid the constraints without penalty.

Finally, the WTO offers a mechanism for the settlement of disputes among member states. Agreements are worthless without enforcement, because states may depart from them whenever they perceive it to be in their interest to do so. When one country believes that another country is violating any aspect of a trade agreement, the complaining country first requests consultation with the alleged offender, and the two seek to resolve the dispute on their own. If consultation fails, then the complaining country requests establishment of a panel, consisting of three persons with appropriate expertise from states not party to the dispute. This panel assesses the evidence in the context of its interpretation of the WTO rules and issues a report. The report is automatically accepted unless all WTO members decide against its adoption, or if one of the parties to the dispute appeals. The WTO has established an Appellate Body composed of seven members, of whom three will serve on any given case. It also issues a report that must be accepted except by a unanimous decision to reject it by member states.

Once this process is completed, states are expected to implement any recommendations of the panel report. If they do not, then complaining countries are entitled to compensation from them, or to use suspension of trade concessions against them. Concessions that the offended country had previously made to the offending party can be withdrawn. In practice, this means that selected trade barriers will be raised against (and only against) the offending country.

In short, the WTO represents a major attempt to provide a more institutionalised and regulatory system for the conduct of international trade. The scope and extent of regulation have increased with the inclusion of new issues and more detailed and obligatory substantive regulations. It remains to be seen how effective the new organisation will be. On the one hand, its membership has increased dramatically over the last decade, and many observers have welcomed the formal entry of China after years of negotiation. On the other hand, the organisation also faces some difficult challenges in the years ahead. This became clear in 1999 when member states met in Seattle to kickstart a new round of trade talks designed to increase free trade and reduce barriers to international trade. Preliminary talks in Geneva revealed such a sharp division among the participants that it proved impossible to create an agenda for the meetings. In other words, the members were so divided that they could not even agree on what ought to be discussed. For example, the United States wants Europe to cut its subsidies of farm products so that it can sell more products to Europe. The Europeans are refusing, since **free trade** between US and European agriculture would devastate Europe's farmers. Developing countries want to be excused from further liberalisation of their trade policies. Labour unions in advanced industrial countries want to set minimum labour standards in the **Third World**, which would make the Third World a less attractive investment. The Third World wants to do without the labour unions' solicitude. Further trade liberalisation depends upon whether member states can negotiate fruitfully on a global basis, or whether they will focus more on regional forms of cooperation.

*See also:* **Bretton Woods; embedded liberalism; free trade; liberal internationalism; managed trade; non-tariff barriers; regime; regional trade blocs**

*Further reading:* Bernard and Kosteck, 1995; Bhagwati, 1994; Jackson, 1989; Preeg, 1995

# APPENDIX
## International relations web sites

The world wide web (www) is an important research tool for students of international relations. This is because we are concerned with events and issues that change from day to day and that take place across the globe. Internet web sites often provide us with up-to-date information. But the web is important for other reasons as well. It allows us to keep up with the latest scholarly research, to converse with individuals who have similar academic interests to our own, and makes it possible to participate in a professional community of scholars. This is not to say that none of this was possible before the internet, but the speed at which it is now possible to retrieve information provides us with an incredibly powerful learning tool. It is not the only source we should use, however; there is no substitute for high-quality, written publications. Internet web sites should therefore be viewed as one information source, among many.

The following is a list of web sites that will be useful to all students of international relations. It has been divided into ten categories to facilitate easy use. They are:

- Area Studies;
- International Organisations;
- International Relations Resources;
- Issues and Subjects;
- Journals;
- News and Current Affairs Networks;
- Non-governmental Organisations;
- Professional Associations and Conferences;
- Research Centres, Institutes, and Think-tanks;
- Resources for Students.

Obviously, there are literally thousands of international relations web sites and it would be impossible to list them all. Our goal has been to develop a representative list of some of the best-known and useful sites in the field. They should be viewed as a launching pad for further exploration and as gateways to other sites on the internet. Most of the sites listed below have links that will take students to other interesting sites.

At the time of publication, all these sites were active. One of the most difficult problems with the internet is that web sites drop out or change their addresses. The ones listed here have been active for a number of years.

## AREA STUDIES

Area Studies and Ethnic Studies
*http://www.usg.edu/galileo/internet/area/areamenu.html*

Asian Studies
*http://www.coombs.anu.edu.au/WWWVL-AsianStudies.html*

Digital Librarian: Africana
*http://www.digital-librarian.com/africana.html*

Digital Librarian: Asian Resources
*http://www.digital-librarian.com/asian.html*

Digital Librarian: Latin America
*http://www.digital-librarian.com/latinamerican.html*

Digital Librarian: The Middle East
*http://www.digital-librarian.com/middle.html*

European Union Internet Resources
*http://www.lib.berkeley.edu/GSSI/eu.html*

World Area Studies
*http://www.wcsu.ctstateu.edu/socialsci/area.html*

## INTERNATIONAL ORGANISATIONS

Academic Council on the United Nations System
*http://www.yale.edu/acuns*

Arab League
*http://www.arab.de/arabinfo/league.htm*

Association of South East Asian Nations (ASEAN)
*http://www.asean.or.id/*

Asia Development Bank
*http://www.adb.org*

Asia Pacific Economic Cooperation (APEC)
*http://www.apec.org/*

Bank for International Settlements
*http://www.bis.org/*

Council of Europe
*http://www.coe.fr/index.asp*

European Union (EU)
*http://europa.eu.int/*

G8 Information Centre
*http://www.g7.utoronto.ca/*

INGO's and IGO's Web Sites
*http://www.uia.org/website.htm*

International Atomic Energy Agency (IAEA)
*http://www.iaea.org.at*

International Court of Justice (ICJ)
*http://www.icj-cij.org/*

International Inter-governmental Organisations Web Page Finder
*http://www.libsci.sc.edu/bob/IGOs.htm*

International Monetary Fund (IMF)
*http://www.imf.org*

North American Free Trade Association (NAFTA)
*http://www.mac.doc.gov/nafta/nafta2.htm*

North Atlantic Treaty Organisation (NATO)
*http://www.nato.int/*

Organisation of African Unity (OAU)
*http://www.oau-oua.org/*

Organisation for Economic Cooperation and Development (OECD)
*http://www.oecd.org/*

Organisation of Petroleum Exporting Countries (OPEC)
*http://www.opec.org*

Organisation for Security and Cooperation in Europe (OSCE)
*http://www.osce.org/*

Partnership for Peace
*http://www.nato.int/pfp/pfp.htm*

United Nations (UN)
*http://www.un.org/*

World Bank
*http://www.worldbank.org*

World Health Organisation (WHO)
*http://www.who.int/*

World Trade Organisation (WTO)
*http://www.wto.org*

## GENERAL INTERNATIONAL RELATIONS RESOURCES

Academic Information
*http://www.academicinfo.net/poliscied.html*

CaseNet International Affairs
*http://csf.colorado.edu/CaseNet/index.html*

Central Intelligence Agency
*http://www.cia.gov/*

Columbia International Affairs Online
*http://www.ciaonet.org*

Constitutions, Treaties, and Declarations
*http://www.psr.keele.ac.uk/const.htm*

Country Indicators for Foreign Policy
*http://www.carleton.ca/~dcarment/presents/cifp/sld003.htm*

Country Studies
*http://lcweb2.loc.gov/frd/cs/*

Global Interactive Academic Network
*http://www.indiana.edu/~global/giant.htm*

InfoManage International
*http://www.infomanage.com/*

Information on Governments and Political Leaders
*http://www.psr.keele.ac.uk/govinfo.htm*

International Affairs Network – Virtual Library
*http://www.etown.edu/vl/*

International Relations Data Page
*http://home.regent.edu/kevipow/data.html*

International Relations Resources of the Canadian Forces College
*http://www.cfcsc.dnd.ca/links/intrel/intrel.html*

International Relations Resources on the Web
*http://mitpress.mit.edu/journals/INOR/deibert-guide/TOC.html*

Jane's
*http://www.janes.com/*

Keele University Guide to International Affairs
*http://www.keele.ac.uk/depts/por/irbase.htm*

Offstats: Statistics on Countries around the World
*http://www.auckland.ac.nz/lbr/stats/offstats/OFFSTATSmain.htm*

Social Science Information Gateway to International Relations
*http://sosig.ac.uk/roads/subject-listing/World/intrel.html*

University of British Columbia International Relations Resources
*http://www.library.ubc.ca/poli/international.html*

Weatherhead Centre for International Affairs
*ttp://data.fas.harvard.edu/cfia/links*

World Governments
*http://www.polisci.com/almanac/world.htm*

Yale Library Selected Internet Resources
*http://www.library.yale.edu/ia-resources/resource.htm*

Your Nation
*http://www.your-nation.com/*

## ISSUES AND SUBJECT AREAS

### *Arms control and disarmament*

Arms Control Association
*http://www.armscontrol.org/home.htm*

Arms Conversion Project
*http://www.gn.apc.org/acp/*

Arms Sales Monitoring Project
*http://sun00781.dn.net/asmp/*

Conventional Arms Transfer Project
*http://www.clw.org/cat/*

Major International Instruments on Disarmament and Related Issues
*http://www.unog.ch/frames/disarm/distreat/warfare/.htm*

United Nations and Disarmament
*http://www.un.org/Depts/dda/index.html*

United States Arms Control and Disarmament Agency
*http://dosfan.lib.uic.edu/acda/*

### *Cold war*

CNN's Cold War Site
*www.cnn.com/SPECIALS/cold.war/*

Cold War International History Project (CWIHP)
*http://cwihp.si.edu/default.htm*

Harvard Project on Cold War Studies
*http://www.fas.harvard.edu/~hpcws/*

### Culture and ethnicity

Cultural Survival
*http://www.cs.org/*

Ethnic World Survey
*Http://www.partal.com/ciemen/ethnic.html*

Global and Cross-cultural Issues
*http://www.etown.edu/vl/global.html*

Islamic Gateway
*http://www.ummah.org.uk/*

### Development

Centre for Development and Population Activities
*http://www.cedpa.org/*

Earth Council
*http://www.ecouncil.ac.cr/*

Institute of Development Studies
*http://www.ids.ac.uk*

International Development Studies Network (IDSNet)
*http://www.idsnet.org*

International Institute for Sustainable Development
*http://iisd1.iisd.ca/*

United Nations Development Program
*http://www.undp.org/*

Women in Development
*http://www.iadb.org/sds/WID/index_wid_e.htm*

Women in Development Network
*http://www.focusintl.com/widnet.htm*

### Diplomacy and foreign policy

Diplomacy Resources of the Canadian Forces College
*http://www.cfcsc.dnd.ca/links/intrel/diplo.html*

### Environment

Digital Librarian: The Environment
*http://www.digital-librarian.com/environment.html*

European Network on Environment and Security
*http://www.keele.ac.uk/depts/spire/Research/cres/eunes/eunes_home.htm*

Greenpeace
*http://www.greenpeace.org/*

World Resources Institute
*http://www.wri.org/wri/*

Worldwatch Institute
*http://www.worldwatch.org/*

### Gender and international relations

Digital Librarian: Women's Resources
*http://www.digital-librarian.com/women.html*

United Nations Division for the Advancement of Women
*http://www.undp.org/fwcw/daw.htm*

Women, Gender and World Politics: Library and Internet Resources
*http://www.libraries.wright.edu/libnet/subj/gen/pls470.html*

Women in Development Network
*http://www.focusintl.com/widnet.htm*

Women in International Security
*http://www.puaf.umd.edu/WIIS/*

Women's Foreign Policy Group
*http://www.wfpg.org/*

### Genocide

Holocaust and Genocide Studies
*http://www.webster.edu/~woolflm/holocaust.html*

Internet Resources on Genocide and Mass Killings
*http://www.ess.uwe.ac.uk/genocide.htm*

The Simon Wiesenthal Centre
*http://www.wiesenthal.com/*

### Global governance

Commission on Global Governance
*http://www.cgg.ch/*

Global Policy Forum
*http://www.globalpolicy.org/*

### Globalisation

Globalisation
*http://www.uq.edu.au/jrn/global/*

Kiran C. Patel Center of Global Solutions
*http://www.cas.usf.edu./GlobalResearch*

### Health

Centre for Disease Control and Prevention
*http://www.cdc.gov/*

Global Health Network
*http://www.pitt.edu/HOME/GHNet/*

Health Netlinks
*http://www.jhuccp.org/netlinks/*

World Health Organisation Library Reference Desk
*http://www.who.int/hlt/virtuallibrary/English/virtuallib.htm*


## HUMAN RIGHTS/INTERNATIONAL LAW

Academic Info: Human Rights
*http://www.academicinfo.net/human.html*

Amnesty International
*http://www.amnesty.org*

Freedom House
*http://www.freedomhouse.org/*

Human Rights Interactive Network
*http://www.webcom.com/hrin/welcome.html*

Human Rights Library
*http://www.umn.edu/humanrts/*

Human Rights Resources at the Canadian Forces College
*http://www.cfcsc.dnd.ca/links/intrel/hum.html*

Human Rights Watch
*http://www.hrw.org*

International Court of Justice
*http://www.icj-cij.org/*

International Criminal Court
*http://www.icc-icp int/home.htmles=en*

International Law
*http://www.cfcsc.dnd.ca/links/intrel/intlaw.html*

J. W. Long Law Library: Foreign and International Law
*http://www.willamette.edu/law/longlib/forint.htm*

Public International Law
*http://www.law.ecel.uwa.edu.au/intlaw/*

United Nations High Commission for Human Rights (UNHCHR)
*http://www.unhchr.ch/*

### Indigenous people

Centre for World Indigenous Studies
*http://www.cwis.org/*

Indigenous Issues
*http://www.nativeweb.org/*

Minority Rights Group International
*http://www.minorityrights.org/*

Separatist and Independence Movements
*http://www.constitution.org/cs_separ.htm*

Unrepresented Nations and Peoples Organisation
*http://www.unpo.org/*

### Intelligence

Central Intelligence Agency
*http://www.cia.gov/index.html*

Centre for the Study of Intelligence
*http://www.odci.gov/csi/index.html*

Online Intelligence Project
*http://www.interaccess.com/intelweb/*

Strategic Forecast
*http://www.stratfor.com/*

Strategic Intelligence
*http://www.loyola.edu/dept/politics/intel.html*

### International political economy

Economic Policy Institute
*http://www.epinet.org/*

IANWEB: International Political Economy
*http://www.pitt.edu/~ian/resource/ipe.htm*

Institute for the Economy in Transition
*http://www.online.ru/sp/iet/index.html*

International Business Resources on the Web
*http://ciber.bus.msu.edu/busres.htm*

International Political Economy Network (IPNet)
*http://csf.colorado.edu/ipe/*

### Landmines

International Campaign to Ban Landmines
*http://www.icbl.org/*

### Mercenaries

Executive Outcomes
*http://www.fas.org/irp/world/para/executive_outcomes.htm*

MPRI
*http://www.mpri.com*

Sandline International
*http://www.sandline.com/site/index.html*

### Multinational corporations

Multinational Monitor
*http://www.essential.org/monitor/*

### North–South issues

Council on Hemispheric Affairs
*http://www.coha.org/*

North–South Institute
*http://www.nsi-ins.ca/*

One World Net
*http://www.oneworld.org/*

### Nuclear weapons

Academic Info: Nuclear Studies and Resources
*http://www.academicinfo.net/histnuke.html*

Coalition to Reduce Nuclear Dangers
*http://www.clw.org/coalition/*

Loose Nukes: Investigating the Threat of Nuclear Smuggling
*http://www.pbs.org/wgbh/pages/frontline/shows/nukes*

Race for the Superbomb
*http://www.pbs.org/wgbh/pages/amex/bomb*

### Peacekeeping

Canadian Peacekeeping Training Centre
*http://www.cdnpeacekeeping.ns.ca/*

Peacekeepers Homepage: A Canadian Site
*http://pk.kos.net/*

Peacekeeping and Related Operations
*http://www.unbsj.ca/library/subject/peace1.htm*

United Nations Peacekeeping
*http://www.un.org/Depts/dpko/dpko/home_bottom.htm*

United Nations Peacekeeping Operations: Past and Present
*http://www.clw.org/pub/clw/un/unoperat.html*

### Peace research and conflict resolution

Carnegie Commission for Preventing Deadly Conflict
*http://www.ccpdc.org/*

Conflict and Conflict Resolution Resources
*http://www.cfcsc.dnd.ca/links/intrel/confli.html*

Conflict Prevention Web
*http://www.caii-dc.com/ghai/welcome.htm*

European Platform for Conflict Prevention and Transformation
*http://www.oneworld.org/euconflict/*

Institute for Global Cooperation and Conflict
*http://www-igcc.ucsd.edu/*

International Crisis Group
*http://www.itnl-crisis-group.org/*

International Peace Research Institute, Oslo
*http://www.prio.no*

Peace Resource Centre
*http://www1.umn.edu/humanrts/peace/*

PeaceNet
*http://www.igc.org/igc/gateway/pnindex.html*

Program on International Peace and Security Online Database
*http://www.ssrc.org/search/ipsintro.htm*

Project Ploughshares
*http://www.ploughshares.ca/*

Search for Common Ground
*http://www.sfcg.org/*

Stockholm International Peace Research Institute
*http://www.sipri.se*

TRANET
*http://www.nonviolence.org/tranet/104-3.htm*

UNESCO's Transdisciplinary Project: Towards a Culture of Peace
*http://www.unesco.org/cpp/uk/*

World Views
*http://www.igc.org/worldviews/index.html*

### Population

Demography and Population Resources
*http://www.pstc.brown.edu/resources.html*

Popnet
*http://www.popnet.org/*

World Population Clock
*http://www.census.gov/cgi-bin/ipc/popclockw*

### Poverty

HungerWeb
*http://www.brown.edu/Departments/World_Hunger_Program/*

PovertyNet
*http://www.worldbank.org/poverty/*

United Nations Development Program: Towards the Elimination of Poverty
*http://www.undp.org/poverty/*

World Hunger Year
*http://www.worldhungeryear.org/*

World Neighbours
*http://www.wn.org/*

### Refugees and migration

Refugees and Migration Resources
*http://www.cfcsc.dnd.ca/links/intrel/refu.html*

### Religion

Academic Info: Religion
*http://www.academicinfo.net/religindex.html*

### Risk

Country Risk Analysis
*http://www.duke.edu/~charvey/Country_risk/couindex.htm*

### Security, strategy, and defence

Centre for Defence Information
*http://www.cdi.org/*

Centre for Defence and International Security Studies
*http://www.cdiss.org/hometemp.htm*

Centre for Military and Strategic Studies
*http://www.stratnet.ucalgary.ca/*

Centre for Strategic and International Studies
*http://www.csis.org/*

Digital National Security Archive
*Http://nsarchive.chadwyck.com/*

International Institute for Strategic Studies
*http://www.isn.ethz.ch/iiss/*

International Relations and Security Network
*http://www.isn.ethz.ch/*

National Security Archive
*http://www.gwu.edu/~nsarchiv/*

Security and Strategy Resources
*ttp://www.cfcsc.dnd.ca/links/intrel/sec.html*

Security Studies Program at MIT
*http://web.mit.edu/ssp/*

Women in International Security
*http://www.puaf.umd.edu/WIIS/*

### Terrorism

Terrorism
*http://www.cdiss.org/terror.htm*

Terrorism Research Centre
*http://www.terrorism.com/*

Terrorism Resources
*http://www.cfcsc.dnd.ca/links/intrel/terror.html*

### War and conflict

Armed Forces of the World
*http://www.cfcsc.dnd.ca/links/milorg/index.html*

Contemporary Conflicts
*http://www.cfcsc.dnd.ca/links/wars/index.html*

INCORE – Conflict Data Service
*http://www.incore.ulst.ac.uk/cds/countries/index.html*

Institute on Global Conflict and Cooperation
*http://www-igcc.ucsd.edu/*

Military Spending Clock
*http://www.cdi.org/msc/clock.html*

Peace and Conflict Studies
*http://www.library.utoronto.ca/pcs/*

SIPRI Military Expenditure
*http://www.sipri.se/projects/Milex/introductrion*

Spotlight on Military News and International Affairs
*http://www.cfc.dnd.ca/spotlight.en.html*

### Weapons of mass destruction

Bradford Project on Strengthening the BTW Convention
*http://www.brad.ac.uk/acad//sbtwc/home.htm*

Chemical and Biological Information Analysis Centre
*http://www.cbiac.apgea.army.mil/*

Organisation for the Prohibition of Chemical Weapons
*http://www.opcw.nl/*

SIPRI: Biological and Chemical Weapons Project
*http://www.sipri.se/projects/group-cw/*

## ACADEMIC JOURNALS IN INTERNATIONAL RELATIONS

*Alternatives: Global, Local and Political*
*http://www.rienner.com/viewbook.cfm?BookID=1585*

*American Diplomacy*
*http://www.unc.edu/depts/diplomat/*

*American Political Science Review*
*http://www.ssc.msu.edu/~apsr/*

*Antipodium*
*http://www.vuw.ac.nz/atp/*

*Arms Control Today*
*http://www.armscontrol.org/ACT/act.html*

*Bulletin of the Atomic Scientists*
*http://www.bullatomsci.org/*

*Consequences: The Nature and Implications of Environmental Change*
*http://www.gcrio.org/CONSEQUENCES/introCON.html*

*Current History*
*http://www.currenthistory.com/*

*Electronic Green Journal*
*http://egj.lib.uidaho.edu/*

*Electronic Journal of Africana Bibliography*
*http://sdrc.lib.uiowa.edu/ejab/*

*European Journal of International Relations*
*http://www.sagepub.co.uk/journalsProdDesc.nav?Prodid=Journal 20094*

*Far Eastern Economic Review*
*http://www.feer.com/*

*Foreign Affairs*
*http://www.foreignaffairs.org/*

*Foreign Policy*
*http://www.foreignpolicy.org/*

*Global Governance*
*http://www.rienner.com/viewbook.cfm?BookID=1310*

*Harpers Monthly*
*http://www.harpers.org/*

*Human Rights and Human Welfare*
*http://www.du.edu/gsis/hrhw/*

*Intermarium: Online Journal of East Central European Postwar History and Politics*
*http://www.columbia.edu/cu/sipa/REGIONAL/ECE/intermar.html*

*International Journal of Human Rights*
*http://www.periodicals.com/tandf.html*

*International Negotiation: A Journal of Theory and Practice*
*http://www.business.carleton.ca/interneg/reference/journals/in/*

*International Organization*
*http://www.journals.cambridge.org/IO*

*International Politics*
*http://www.palgrave-journals.com/ip*

*International Security*
*http://mitpress.mit.edu/journal-home.tcl?issn=01622889*

*International Studies Perspectives*
*http://www.blackwell-synergy.com/loi/insp/*

*International Studies Quarterly*
*http://www.public.iastate.edu/~isq/*

*International Studies Review*
*http://www.blackwell-synergy.com/loi/insr/*

*Journal of World Systems Research*
*http://csf.colorado.edu/jwsr/*

*Military History*
*http://www.thehistorynet.com/MilitaryHistory/*

*Millennium: Journal of International Studies*
*http://www.lse.ac.uk/Depts/intrel/millenn/*

*Mother Jones*
*http://motherjones.com/magazine/MA01/index.html*

*National Security Studies*
*http://www.georgetown.edu/sfs/programs/nssp/nssq/index.html*

*Negotiation Journal*
*http://www.pon.harvard.edu/publ/negojnl/index.html*

*New York Review of Books*
*http://www.nybooks.com/*

*OJPCR: Online Journal of Peace and Conflict Resolution*
*http://www.trinstitute.org/ojpcr/*

*Peacemagazine*
*http://www.peacemagazine.org/*

*Political Science Quarterly*
*http://www.psqonline.org/*

*Review of International Studies*
*http://www.journals.cambridge.org/RIS*

*The Atlantic Monthly Online*
*http://www.theatlantic.com/*

*The History Net*
*http://www.thehistorynet.com/*

*The Nation*
*http://www.thenation.com/*

*The National Review*
*http://www.nationalreview.com/*

*The New Republic*
*http://magazines.enews.com/magazines/tnr/*

*The Washington Monthly*
*http://www.washingtonmonthly.com/*

*World Politics*
*http://muse.jhu.edu/journals/world_politics/*

## NEWS AND CURRENT AFFAIRS NETWORKS

All Africa
*http://www.africanews.org/*

Arabic News
*http://www.arabicnews.com/*

Asia Times Online
*http://www.atimes.com/*

BBC World Service
*http://www.bbc.co.uk/worldservice/index.shtml*

China Daily
*http://www.chinadaily.net/*

CNN Network
*http://www.cnn.com*

Documents in the News
*http://www.lib.umich.edu/libhome/Documents.center/*

Earth Times
*http://www.earthtimes.org/*

Economist
*http://www.economist.com*

Financial Times
*http://news.ft.com/*

Guardian Unlimited
*http://www.guardianunlimited.co.uk/*

Internet Press
*http://www.wwideweb.com/link40.htm*

Jerusalem Report
*http://www.jrep.com/*

Media Links: Online Media Directory
*http://emedia1.mediainfo.com/emedia/*

Muslim News Online
*http://www.muslimnews.co.uk/*

New York Times
*http://www.nytimes.com/*

Newsweek
*http://www.newsweek.com/*

Omnivore Daily News and Information Service
*http://way.net/omnivore/*

Pacific Rim Review
*http://pacificrim.bx.com/*

Palestine Times
*http://www.ptimes.com/*

Time Magazine
*http://www.time.com/*

## NON-GOVERNMENTAL ORGANISATIONS

CARE
*http://www.care.org/*

International Chamber of Commerce
*http://www.iccwbo.org/*

International Committee of the Red Cross
*http://www.icrc.org/*

Médecins sans Frontières
*http://www.msf.org/*

Nobel Foundation
*http://www.nobel.se/*

Non-Profit Organisations
*http://www.digital-librarian.com/nonprofits.html*

OXFAM
*http://www.oxfam.org/*

## PROFESSIONAL ASSOCIATIONS AND CONFERENCES

African Studies Association
*http://www.africanstudies.org/*

American Political Science Association
*http://www.apsanet.org/*

Asiatica Association
*http://www.asiatica.org/*

Australasian Political Science Association
*http://www.une.edu.au/apsa/main.htm*

British International Studies Association
*http://www.bisa.ac.uk/*

Canadian Political Science Association
*http://www.sfu.ca/igs/cpsares.html*

Central and East European International Studies Association (CEEISA)
*http://ian.vse.cz/ceeisa/*

International Studies Association
*http://www.isanet.org*

Latin American Studies Association
*http://lasa.international.pitt.edu/*

Peace Studies Association
*http://sobek.colorado.edu/SOC/ORGS/peace.html*

Political Studies Association
*http://www.psa.ac.uk*

Royal Institute for International Affairs
*http://www.riia.org/*

## RESEARCH CENTRES, INSTITUTES, AND THINK-TANKS

Brookings Institution
*http: www.brook.edu*

Canadian Institute of Strategic Studies
*http://www.ciss.ca/*

Carnegie Council on Ethics and International Affairs
*http://www.cceia.org*

Carter Center
*http://www.cartercenter.org*

CATO Institute
*http://www.cato.org/*

Council on Foreign Relations
*http://www.foreignrelations.org*

Henry L. Stimson Centre
*http://www.stimson.org/*

Heritage Foundation
*http://www.heritage.org/*

Hoover Institute on War, Revolution and Peace
*http://www.hoover.org/*

Nixon Center
*http://www.nixoncenter.org/*

Rand Corporation
*http://www.rand.org/*

Soros Foundation
*http://www.soros.org/*

United States Institute for Peace
*http://www.usip.org*

W. Alton Jones Foundation
*http://www.wajones.org/*

Woodrow Wilson Center
*http://wwics.si.edu*

World Directory of Think Tanks
*http://www.nira.go.jp/ice/tt-info/nwdtt99/*


## RESOURCES FOR STUDENTS

Acronym Finder
*http://www.acronymfinder.com/*

Association of Commonwealth Universities
*http://www.acu.ac.uk/*

Association of Professional Schools of International Affairs
*http://www.apsia.org/*

Braintrack University Index
*http://www.braintrack.com/*

College and University Homepages by State
*http://www.mit.edu:8001/people/cdemello/geog.html*

Commonwealth Resource Centre: Grants and Scholarships
*http://www.commonwealth.org.uk/resource/reslists/grants.htm*

Digital Librarian: College and University
*http://www.digital-librarian.com/college.html*

Embassy Web
*http://www.embpage.org/*

Foreign Government Links
*http://www.lib.berkeley.edu/GSSI/foreign.html*

Fulbright Program
*http://www.iie.org/fulbright/*

Grants and Scholarships Index
*http://www.ala.org/work/awards/grtscidx.html*

GrantsNet
*http://www.grantsnet.org/*

John F. Kennedy School of Government, Harvard University
*http://www.ksg.harvard.edu*

Library of Congress: Collections and Services
*http://www.loc.gov/library/*

Perry-Castaneda Map Collection
*http://www.lib.utexas.edu/Libs/PCL/Map_collection/Map_collection.html*

Study and Work Abroad
*http://www.etown.edu/vl/study.html*

UK Universities and Colleges
*http://www.scit.wlv.ac.uk/ukinfo/alpha.html*

Universities and Colleges
*http://www.universities.com/*

Universities Worldwide
*http://geowww.uibk.ac.at/univ/*

World Wide Web Library Directory
*http://www.webpan.com/msauers/libdir/*

## ACADEMIC SEARCH ENGINE

Google
*http://www.google.com/*

# BIBLIOGRAPHY

Adelman, M. (1995) *The Genie out of the Bottle: World Oil since 1970*, Cambridge, MA, MIT Press.

Adler, E. (1992) *The International Practice of Arms Control*, Baltimore, MD, Johns Hopkins University Press.

—— (1997) 'Seizing the middle ground: constructivism in world politics', *European Journal of International Relations* 3: 319–63.

Aggarwal, V. (1998) *Institutional Designs for a Complex World*, Ithaca, NY, Cornell University Press.

Allen, C. (1999) 'Warfare, endemic violence and state collapse in Africa', *Review of African Political Economy* 81: 367–84.

Allison, G. (ed.) (1996) *Avoiding Nuclear Anarchy: Containing the Threat of Loose Russian Nuclear Weapons and Fissile Material*, Cambridge, MA, MIT Press.

Allison, G. and Zelikow, P. (1999) *Essence of Decision*, 2nd edn, Reading, MA, Addison-Wesley.

An-Na'im, A. (1987) 'Islamic law, international relations, and human rights: challenges and response', *Cornell International Law Journal* 32: 317–35.

Anderson, B. (1991) *Imagined Communities: Reflections on the Origin and Spread of Nationalism*, 2nd edn, London, Verso.

—— (1998) The Spectre of Comparison, London, Verso.

Anderson, P. (1992) *A Zone of Engagement*, London, Verso.

Anderson, R. (ed.) (1991) *Commons without Tragedy*, London, Shepheard-Walwyn.

Annan, K. (2005) '"In larger freedom": decision time at the UN', *Foreign Affairs* 84(3): 63–74.

Archibugi, D., Held, D. and Kohler, M. (eds) (1998) *Re-imagining Political Community*, Cambridge, Polity Press.

Arnett, E. (ed.) (1994) *Implementing the Comprehensive Test Ban*, Oxford, Oxford University Press.

Arnold, G. (1999) *Mercenaries*, Basingstoke, Palgrave.

Arthur, J. and Shaw, W. (eds) (1991) *Justice and Economic Distribution*, 2nd edn, Englewood Cliffs, NJ, Prentice-Hall.

Asch, R. (1997) *The Thirty Years' War: The Holy Empire and Europe 1618–48*, New York, St Martin's Press.

Ashcroft, B., Griffiths, G. and Tiffin, H. (1998) *Key Concepts in Post-Colonial Studies*, London, Routledge.

Ashley, R. and Walker, R. (eds) (1990) 'Speaking the language of exile: dissidence in international studies', Special issue, *International Studies Quarterly* 34: 259–417.

Ashworth, L. and Long, D. (eds) (1999) *New Perspectives on International Functionalism*, New York, St Martin's Press.

Axelrod, R. (1984) *The Evolution of Cooperation*, New York, Basic Books.

Axelrod, R. and Keohane, R. (1985) 'Achieving cooperation under anarchy: strategies and institutions', *World Politics* 38: 226–54.

Axtmann, R. (1997) *Liberal Democracy into the Twenty-First Century: Globalization, Integration and the Nation-State*, Manchester, Manchester University Press.

Ayoob, M. (2002) 'Humanitarian Intervention and State Sovereignty, *The International Journal of Human Rights* 6(1): 81–102.

Badsey, S. (ed.) (2000) *The Media and International Security*, London, Frank Cass.

Baehr, P. and Gordenker, L. (1999) *The United Nations at the End of the 1990s*, 3rd edn, Basingstoke, Macmillan.

Baldwin, D. (ed.) (1993) *Neorealism and Neoliberalism: The Contemporary Debate*, New York, Columbia University Press.

—— (1995) 'Security studies and the end of the cold war', *World Politics* 48: 117–41.

Banks, M. (1985) 'The inter-paradigm debate', in Light, M. and Groom, A. (eds), *International Relations: A Handbook of Current Theory*, London, Pinter.

—— (1987) 'Four conceptions of peace', in Sandole, S. and Sandole, I. (eds), *Conflict Management and Problem Solving: Interpersonal to International Applications*, New York, New York University Press.

Barkin, J. and Cronin, B. (1994) 'The state and the nation: changing norms and the rules of sovereignty in international relations', *International Organization* 48: 107–30.

Barnet, R. and Cavanagh, J. (1994) *Global Dreams: Imperial Corporations and the New World Order*, New York, Simon & Schuster.

Barnett, M. (1998) *Dialogues in Arab Politics: Negotiation in Regional Order*, New York, Columbia University Press.

Barry Jones, R. and Willetts, P. (1984) *Interdependence on Trial: Studies in the Theory and Reality of Contemporary Interdependence*, London, Pinter.

Barston, R. (1996) *Modern Diplomacy*, Harlow, Addison-Wesley Longman.

Bartkins, V. (1999) *The Dynamics of Secession*, Cambridge, Cambridge University Press.

Bassiouni, C. (2000) 'Negotiating the Treaty of Rome on the Establishment of the International Criminal Court', *Cornell International Law Journal* 41: 57–89.

Baubock, R. (1996) 'Introduction', in Baubock, R., Heller, A. and Zolberg, A. (eds), *The Challenge of Diversity*, Aldershot: Avebury.

Baylis, J. and Smith, S. (eds) (1997) *The Globalisation of World Politics*, Oxford, Oxford University Press.

Bayne, N. and Putnam, R. (2000) *Hanging in There: the G8 and Global Governance*, Aldershot, Ashgate.

Bebler, A. (1999) *The Challenge of NATO Enlargement*, Westport, CT, Praeger.

Beck, U. (1992) *Risk Society: Towards a New Modernity*, London, Sage.

Becker, S. (1986) *Reciprocity*, Chicago, IL, University of Chicago Press.

Beder, V. (1995) 'Transnational citizenship', *Political Theory* 23(2): 211–46.

Beigbeder, Y. (1999) *Judging War Criminals*, Basingstoke, Macmillan.

Beitz, C. (1979) *Political Theory and International Relations*, Princeton, NJ, Princeton University Press.

Bell-Fialkoff, A. (1996) *Ethnic Cleansing*, New York, St Martin's Press.

Berdal, M. (1993) *Whither UN Peacekeeping?* Adelphi Paper No. 281, London, International Institute for Strategic Studies.

—— (1996) *Disarmament and Demobilisation after Civil Wars*, Oxford, Oxford University Press.

Berdal, M. and Malone, D. (eds) (2000) *Greed and Grievance: Economic Agendas and Civil Wars*, Boulder, CO, Lynne Rienner.

Berger, P. and Luckmann, T. (1966) *The Social Construction of Reality: A Treatise in the Sociology of Knowledge*, New York, Anchor.

Bergsten, F. and Henning, C. (1996) *Global Economic Leadership and the Group of Seven*, Washington, DC, Institute for International Economics.

Berki, R. (1983) *Insight and Vision: The Problem of Communism in Marx's Thought*, London, J. M. Dent & Sons.

Bernard, H. and Kosteck, M. (1995) *The Political Economy of the World Trading System*, Oxford, Oxford University Press.

Bernstein, P. (1998) *Against the Gods: The Remarkable Story of Risk*, New York: John Wiley & Sons.

Bernstein, R. and Munro, R. (1997) *The Coming Conflict with China*, New York, Knopf.

Best, G. (1994) *War and Law since 1945*, Oxford, Clarendon Press.

Betts, R. (1998a) 'The new threat of mass destruction', *Foreign Affairs* 77: 26–39.

—— (1998b) *Decolonization*, London, Routledge.

Bhagwati, J. (1994) 'The world trading system', *Journal of International Affairs* 48: 279–85.

Bhalla, A. and Bhalla, P. (1997) *Regional Blocs*, Basingstoke, Macmillan.

Biersteker, T. and Weber, C. (eds) (1992) *State Sovereignty as Social Construct*, Cambridge, Cambridge University Press.

—— (eds) (1996) *State Sovereignty as Social Construct*, Cambridge, Cambridge University Press.

Binder, L. (1971) *Crises of Political Development*, Princeton, NJ, Princeton University Press.

Black, C. E. (1966) *The Dynamics of Modernization*, New York, Harper & Row.

Blackburn, R. (ed.) (1991) *After the Fall: The Failure of Communism and the Future of Socialism*, London, Verso.

Blair, D. (1993) *Trade Negotiations in the OECD*, London, Kegan Paul International.

Blomstrom, M. and Hettne, B. (1984) *Development Theory in Transition: The Dependency Debate and Beyond*, London, Zed Books.

Bohman, J. and Lutz-Bachman, M. (eds) (1997) *Perpetual Peace: Essays on Kant's Cosmopolitan Ideal*, Cambridge, MA, MIT Press.

Booth, K. (ed.) (1991) *New Thinking about Strategy and International Security*, London, Harper Collins Academic.

—— (ed.) (1998) *Statecraft and Security: The Cold War and Beyond*, Cambridge, Cambridge University Press.

Booth, K. and Smith, S. (eds) (1995) *International Relations Theory Today*, Cambridge, Polity Press.

Bornschier, V., Chase-Dunn, C. and Rubinson, R. (1984) 'Cross-national evidence of the effects of foreign investment and aid on economic growth and inequality', *American Journal of Sociology* 78: 651–83.

Boserup, E. (1989) *Women's Role in Economic Development*, London, Earthscan.

Bothe, M., Ronzitti, N. and Rosas, A. (eds) (1997) *The OSCE in the Maintenance of Peace and Security*, The Hague, Kluwer Law International.

Boulding, E. (1995) 'The dialectics of peace', in Boulding, E. and Boulding, K. (eds) *The Future: Images and Processes*, Thousand Oaks, CA, Sage.

Boutros-Ghali, B. (1992) *An Agenda for Peace*, New York, United Nations.

Braden, K. and Shelley, F. (1998) *Geopolitics*, London, Longman.

Bretherton, C. and Vogler, T. (1999) *The European Union as a Global Actor*, London, Routledge.

Brewer, A. (1980) *Marxist Theories of Imperialism*, London, Routledge.

Broomhall, B. (2004) *International Justice & the International Criminal Court: Between Sovereignty and the Rule of Law*, Oxford, Oxford University Press.

Brown, C. (1992a) *International Relations Theory: New Normative Approaches*, New York, Columbia University Press.

—— (1992b) 'Marxism and international ethics', in Nardin, T. and Mapel, D. (eds), *Traditions of International Ethics*, Cambridge: Cambridge University Press.

—— (1994) 'Turtles all the way down: anti-foundationalism, critical theory and international relations', *Millennium: Journal of International Studies* 23: 213–36.

—— (1999) 'History ends, worlds collide', *Review of International Studies* 25: 41–58.

Brown, M., Lynne-Jones, S. and Miller, S. (eds) (1996) *Debating the Democratic Peace*, Cambridge, MA, MIT Press.

Brzezinski, Z. and Sullivan, P. (1997) *Russia and the Commonwealth of Independent States: Documents, Data and Analysis*, London, M. E. Sharpe.

Buchanan, A. (1991) *Secession: The Morality of Political Divorce from Fort Sumter to Lithuania and Quebec*, Boulder, CO, Westview Press.

Bull, H. (1995) *The Anarchical Society*, 2nd edn, Basingstoke, Macmillan.

Burchill, S. (1996) 'Liberal internationalism', in Burchill, S. and Linklater, A. (eds), *Theories of International Relations*, Basingstoke, Macmillan.

Burtless, G., Lawrence, R., Litan, R. and Shapiro, R. (eds) (1998) *Confronting Fears about Open Trade*, Washington, DC, Brookings.

Butfoy, A. (1993) 'Collective security: theory, problems and reformulations', *Australian Journal of International Affairs* 47: 1–14.

Butler, F. (1997) 'Regionalism and integration', in Baylis, J. and Smith, S. (eds), *The Globalisation of World Politics*, Oxford, Oxford University Press.

Buzan, B. (1991) *People, States and Fear: The National Security Problem in International Relations*, 2nd edn, Boulder, CO, Lynne Rienner.

—— (2004) *From International to World Society?*, Cambridge: Cambridge University Press.

Byman, D. and Waxman, M. (2002) *The Dynamics of Coercion*, Cambridge, Cambridge University Press.

Cameron, G. (1999) *Nuclear Terrorism: A Threat Assessment for the 21st Century*, Basingstoke, Palgrave.

Caney, S. (2001) 'Review article: international distributive justice', *Political Studies* 49(5): 974–97.

Caporaso, J. (ed.) (2000) 'Continuity and change in the Westphalian order', special issue of the *International Studies Review* 2: 1–210.

Carlsnaes, W. (1992) 'The agency-structure problem in foreign policy analysis', *International Studies Quarterly* 36: 245–70.

Carment, D. and James, P. (1995) 'Internal constraints and interstate ethnic conflict: towards a crisis-based assessment of irredentism', *Journal of Conflict Resolution* 39: 82–109.

Carr, E. H. (1946) *The Twenty Years Crisis: 1919–1939*, 2nd edn, London, Macmillan.

Casebeer, W. (2004) 'Knowing evil when you see it: uses for the rhetoric of evil in IR', *International Relations* 18(4): 441–51.

Chabot, C. (1998) *Understanding the Euro: The Clear and Concise Guide to the New Trans-European Currency*, New York, McGraw-Hill.

Chafetz, G., Spritas, M. and Frankel, B. (eds) (1999) *Origins of National Interests*, London, Frank Cass.

Chalabi, F. (1989) *OPEC: At the Crossroads*, New York, Pergamon Press.

Chalk, P. (1999) 'The evolving dynamic of terrorism in the 1990s', *Australian Journal of International Affairs* 53: 151–68.

Chatterjee, P. (1994) *Nationalist Thought and the Colonial World: A Derivative Discourse*, London, Zed Books.

Chazan, N. (ed.) (1991) *Irredentism and International Politics*, Boulder, CO, Lynne Rienner.

Chimkin, C. (1992) 'The law and ethics of recognition', in Keal, P. (ed.), *Ethics and Foreign Policy*, St Leonards, NSW, Allen & Unwin.

Cigar, N. (1995) *Genocide in Bosnia: The Policy of Ethnic Cleansing*, Texas, Texas A&M University Press.

Cimbala, S. (1998) *The Past and Future of Nuclear Deterrence*, Westport, CO, Praeger.

Claes, D. (2000) *The Politics of Oil-Producer Cooperation*, Boulder, CO, Westview.

Clapham, C. (1992) *Third World Politics*, London, Routledge.

Clark, A. (1995) 'Non-governmental organisations and their influence on international society', *Journal of International Affairs* 48: 507–26.

Clark, R. (2004) *Against All Enemies: Inside America's War on Terror*, New York, Free Press.

Claude, I. (1967) *Power and International Relations*, New York, Random House.

Clemens, W. (1998) *Dynamics of International Relations: Conflict and Mutual Gain in an Era of Global Interdependence*, New York, Rowman & Littlefield.

Cochran, M. (1995a) 'Cosmopolitanism and communitarianism in a post-cold war world', in MacMillan, J. and Linklater, A. (eds), *Boundaries in Question: New Directions in International Relations*, London, Pinter.

—— (1995b) 'Postmodernism, ethics and international political theory', *Review of International Studies* 21: 237–50.

Cohen, B. (1996) 'Phoenix risen: the resurrection of global finance', *World Politics* 48: 268–96.

Cohen, J. (1995) *How Many People Can the Earth Support?*, New York, Norton.

Cohen, R. (ed.) (1995) *The Cambridge Survey of World Migration*, Cambridge, Cambridge University Press.

—— (1997) *Global Diasporas: An Introduction*, Seattle, WA, University of Washington Press.

Coicaud, J. (2002) *Legitimacy and Politics*, Cambridge: Cambridge University Press.

Cole, L. (1997) *The Eleventh Plague: The Politics of Biological and Chemical Warfare*, New York, W. H. Freeman.

Coleman, W. and Underhill, G. (eds) (1998) *Regionalism and Global Economic Integration*, London, Routledge.

Conybeare, J. (1984) 'Public goods, prisoners' dilemma, and the international political economy', *International Studies Quarterly* 28: 5–22.

Cooper, A., Higgot, R. and Nossal, K. (1993) *Relocating Middle Powers: Australia and Canada in a Changing World Order*, Vancouver, University of British Columbia Press.

Cortright, D. and Lopez, G. (1995) *Economic Sanctions: Panacea or Peacebuilding in a Post-Cold War World?*, Boulder, CO, Westview Press.

Coulon, J. (1998) *Soldiers of Diplomacy: The United Nations, Peacekeeping, and the New World Order*, Toronto, University of Toronto Press.

Cowles, M. and Smith, M. (eds) (2000) *The State of the European Union*, Oxford, Oxford University Press.

Cox, M., Ikenberry, G. and Inoguchi, T. (eds) (2000) *American Democracy Promotion*, Oxford, Oxford University Press.

Cox, R. (1981) 'Social forces, states and world orders: beyond international relations theory', *Millennium: Journal of International Studies* 10: 126–55.

Cox, R. and Sinclair, T. (1996) *Approaches to World Order*, Cambridge, Cambridge University Press.

Craft, C. (1999) *Weapons for War, Weapons for Peace*, London, Routledge.

Craig, G. and George, A. (1990) *Force and Statecraft*, 2nd edn, Oxford, Oxford University Press.

Crawford, R. (1996) *Regime Theory in the Post-Cold War World: Rethinking Neoliberal Approaches to International Relations*, Aldershot, Dartmouth.

—— (2000) *Idealism and Realism in International Relations*, London, Routledge.

Crockatt, R. (1995) *The Fifty Years War*, London, Routledge.

Croft, S. (1993) *Cooperative Security in Europe*, London, Brassey's.

Cummings, B. (2004) *Inventing the Axis of Evil: The Truth about North Korea, Iran and Syria*, New York: New Press.

Dahl, R. (1989) *Democracy and Its Critics*, New Haven, CT, Yale University Press.

Danaher, K. (1994) *50 Years Is Enough: The Case against the World Bank and the International Monetary Fund*, London, South End Press.

Danner, A. (2003) 'Enhancing the legitimacy and accountability of prosecutorial discretionary power at the International Criminal Court', *American Journal of International Law* 97: 510–52.

Danner, M. (2004) *Torture and Truth: America, Abu Ghraib, and the War on Terror*, New York, New York Review of Books.

Davidson, D. (1983) *Nuclear Weapons and the American Churches: Ethical Positions on Modern Warfare*, Boulder, CO, Westview Press.

De Grauwe, P. (1997) *The Economics of Monetary Union*, Oxford, Oxford University Press.

Denmark, R. (1999) 'World system history: from traditional international politics to the study of global relations', *International Studies Review* 1: 43–75.

Dent, M. and Peters, B. (1999) *The Crisis of Poverty and Debt in the Third World*, Aldershot, Ashgate.

Deudney, D. and Ikenberry, G. (1999) 'The nature and sources of liberal international order', *Review of International Studies* 25: 179–96.

Devetak, R. (1995) 'The project of modernity and international relations theory', *Millennium: Journal of International Studies* 24: 27–51.

Dewitt, D. (1994) 'Common, comprehensive and cooperative security', *Pacific Review* 7: 1–15.

Diamond, L. (1996) 'Is the third wave over?', *Journal of Democracy* 7: 20–38.

Dicken, P. (1998) *Global Shift: Transforming the World Economy*, 3rd edn, London, Sage.

Diehl, P. (1997) *The Politics of Global Governance: International Organisations in an Interdependent World*, Boulder, CO, Lynne Rienner.

Diez, T. and Steans, J. (2005) A useful dialogue? Habermas and international relations', *Review of International Studies* 31(1): 1–25.

Difilippo, A. (2005) 'US Policy and the nuclear weapons ambitions of the axis of evil countries', *New Political Science* 28(1): 101–23.

Dinan, D. (1999) *Ever Closer Union: An Introduction to European Integration*, Boulder, CO, Lynne Rienner.

Dobkowski, M. and Wallimann, I. (1998) *The Coming Age of Scarcity: Preventing Mass Death and Genocide in the Twenty-First Century*, Syracuse, NY, Syracuse University Press.

Dodds, K. and Atkinson, D. (2000) *Geopolitical Traditions*, London, Routledge.

Dolan, C. (2005) *In War We Trust: The Bush Doctrine and the Pursuit of Just War*, Aldershot: Ashgate.

Dombrowski, P. and Payne, R. (2003) 'Global debate and the limits of the Bush doctrine', *International Studies Perspectives* 4: 395–408.

Donnelly, J. (2000) *Realism and International Relations*, Cambridge, Cambridge University Press.

—— (2007) *International Human Rights*, 3rd edn, Boulder, CO, Westview Press.

Doremus, P., Keller, W., Pauly, L. and Reich, S. (1998) *The Myth of the Global Corporation*, Princeton, NJ, Princeton University Press.

Dorraj, M. (ed.) (1995) *The Changing Political Economy of the Third World*, Boulder, CO, Lynne Rienner.

Doxy, M. (1996) *International Sanctions in Contemporary Perspective*, 2nd edn, Basingstoke, Macmillan.

Doyle, M. (1983) 'Kant, liberal legacies, and foreign affairs', *Philosophy and Public Affairs* 12: 205–54.

—— (1986) *Empires*, Ithaca, NY, Cornell University Press.

—— (1997) *Ways of War and Peace: Realism, Liberalism, and Socialism*, New York, Norton.

Drainville, A. (1998) 'The fetishism of global civil society: global governance, transnational urbanism and sustainable capitalism in the world economy', in Smith, M. and Guarnizo, L. (eds), *Transnationalism from Below*, New Brunswick, NJ, Transaction.

Drake, F. (2000) *The Science of Climate Change*, London, Edward Arnold.

Drollas, L. and Greenman, J. (1989) *Oil: The Devil's Gold*, London, Duckworth.

Drury, S. (1992/3) 'The end of History and the new world order', *International Journal* 48: 80–99.

Dunn, L. (1991) *Containing Nuclear Proliferation*, Adelphi Paper no. 263, London, International Institute for Strategic Studies.

Dunne, T. (1998) *Inventing International Society: A History of the English School*, New York, St Martin's Press.

Dunne, T. and Wheeler, N. (eds) (1999) *Human Rights in Global Politics*, Cambridge, Cambridge University Press.

Dunning, J. (1993) *The Globalisation of Business*, London, Routledge.

Durch, W. (ed.) (1997, 2000) *United Nations Peacekeeping, American Politics, and the Uncivil Wars of the 1990s*, New York, St Martin's Press.

Dyker, D. (ed.) (1999) *Foreign Direct Investment and Technology Transfer in the Former Soviet Union*, Cheltenham, Edward Elgar.

Eban, A. (1998) *Diplomacy for the Next Century*, New Haven, CT, Yale University Press.

Eckhardt, W. (1992) 'Death by courtesy of governments', *Peace Research* 24: 51–5.

Edwards, S. (ed.) (1997) *Capital Controls, Exchange Rates, and Monetary Policy in the World Economy*, Cambridge, Cambridge University Press.

Eldon, S. (1994) *From Quill Pen to Satellite*, London, Royal Institute of International Affairs.

Elias, R. and Turpin, T. (eds) (1994) *Rethinking Peace*, Boulder, CO, Lynne Rienner.

Enloe, C. (1990) *Bananas, Beaches and Bases: Making Feminist Sense of International Politics*, Berkeley, CA, University of California Press.

Esposito, J. (2002) *Unholy War: Terror in the Name of Islam*, Oxford, Oxford University Press.

Etzioni, A. (2004) *From Empire to Community*, New York, Palgrave Macmillan.

Evans, G. (1993) *Cooperating for Peace: The Global Agenda for the 1990s and Beyond*, Sydney, Allen & Unwin.

Evans, L. (1998) *Feeding the Ten Billion*, Cambridge, Cambridge University Press.

Evans, P., Jacobson, H. and Putnam, R. (eds) (1993) *Double-Edged Diplomacy: International Bargaining and Domestic Politics*, Berkeley, CA, University of California Press.

Falk, R. (1995) *On Human Governance: Towards a New Global Politics*, Cambridge, Polity Press.

—— (1999) *Predatory Globalization: A Critique*, Cambridge, Polity Press.

—— (2004) 'Legality to legitimacy: the revival of the Just War framework', *Harvard International Review* 31: 40–5.

Fawcett, L. and Hurrell, A. (eds) (1995) *Regionalism in World Politics: Regional Organization and International Order*, Oxford, Oxford University Press.

Feldstein, M. (1998) 'Refocusing the IMF', *Foreign Affairs* 77: 20–33.

Ferguson, Y. and Mansbach, R. (2004) *Remapping Global Politics: History's Revenge and Future Shock*, Cambridge, Cambridge University Press.

Finger, J. (ed.) (1993) *Antidumping: How It Works and Who Gets Hurt*, Ann Arbor, MI, University of Michigan Press.

Finnemore, M. (1996) *National Interests in International Society*, Ithaca, NY, Cornell University Press.

Forsythe, J. (2004) *Human Rights in International Politics*, Cambridge, Cambridge University Press.

Fowler, K. (2000) *Medieval Mercenaries*, Oxford, Blackwell.

Fox, W. (1944) *The Superpowers: The United States, Britain, and the Soviet Union – Their Responsibility for Peace*, New York, Harcourt Brace.

—— (1980) 'The superpowers then and now', *International Journal* 35: 417–36.

Franceschet, A. (1999) 'The ethical foundations of liberal internationalism', *International Journal* 54: 463–81.

Franck, T. (1990) *The Power of Legitimacy among Nations*, Oxford, Oxford University Press.

Frank, A. and Gills, B. (eds) (1993) *The World System: Five Hundred Years or Five Thousand Years?*, London, Routledge.

Frankel, J. (1997) *Regional Trading Blocs in the World Economic System*, New York, Institute for International Economics.

Freedman, L. (1981) *The Evolution of Nuclear Strategy*, Basingstoke, Macmillan.

—— (ed.) (1998) *Strategic Coercion: Concepts and Cases*, Oxford, Oxford University Press.

Freeman, M. (1999) 'The right to self-determination in international politics', *Review of International Studies* 25: 355–70.

Fukuyama, F. (1992) *The End of History and the Last Man*, London, Hamish Hamilton.

Gaddis, J. (1982) *Strategies of Containment*, Oxford, Oxford University Press.

—— (1997) *We Now Know: Rethinking Cold War History*, Oxford, Oxford University Press.

Gallagher, N. (1998) *Arms Control: New Approaches to Theory and Policy*, London, Frank Cass.

Gallie, W. (1979) *Philosophers of Peace and War*, Cambridge, Cambridge University Press.

Galtung, J. (1985) 'Twenty-five years of peace research: ten challenges and some responses', *Journal of Peace Research* 22: 141–58.

Gamble, A. and Payne, A. (eds) (1996) *Regionalism and World Order*, New York: St Martin's Press.

Garran, R. (1998) *Tigers Tamed: The End of the Asian Miracle*, Honolulu, HI, University of Hawaii Press.

Garten, J. (1992) *A Cold Peace: America, Japan, Germany and the Struggle for Supremacy*, New York, Times Books.

Geiger, T. and Kennedy, D. (1996) *Regional Trade Blocs: Multilateralism and the GATT*, New York, Pinter.

Gellner, E. (1983) *Nations and Nationalism*, Oxford, Blackwell.

George, A. and Holl, J. (1997) *The Warning-Response Problem and Missed Opportunities in Preventive Diplomacy*, Washington, DC, Carnegie Commission.

George, A. and Simons, L. (1994) *The Limits of Coercive Dipolomacy*, 2nd edn, Boulder, CO, Westview Press.

George, J. (1994) *Discourses of Global Politics: A Critical (Re)Introduction to International Relations*, Boulder, CO, Lynne Rienner.

George, S. (1988) *A Fate Worse than Debt*, Harmondsworth, Penguin.

—— (1991) *The Debt Boomerang*, London, Pluto Press.

Giboa, Eytan (2005) 'Global television news and foreign policy: debating the CNN effect', *International Studies Perspectives* 6(3): 325–41.

Gill, G. (1996) *The League of Nations from 1929–46*, New York, Avery.

Gill, S. (1995) 'Globalisation, market civilization, and disciplinary neoliberalism', *Millennium: Journal of International Studies* 24: 399–423.

Gill, S. (ed.) (1997) *Globalization, Democratization and Multilateralism*, New York, St Martin's Press.

Gill, S. and Mittelman, J. (eds) (1997) *Innovation and Transformation in International Studies*, Cambridge, Cambridge University Press.

Gilligan, M. (1997) *Empowering Exporters: Reciprocity, Delegation, and Collective Action in American Trade Policy*, Ann Arbor, MI, University of Michigan Press.

Gilpin, R. (1981) *War and Change in World Politics*, Cambridge, Cambridge University Press.

—— (1987) *The Political Economy of International Relations*, Princeton, NJ, Princeton University Press.

—— (1994) 'The cycle of great powers: has it finally been broken?', in Lundestad, G. (ed.), *The Fall of Great Powers: Peace, Stability, and Legitimacy*, Oslo, Scandinavian University Press.

Goldgeier, J. and McFaul, M. (1992) 'A tale of two worlds: core and periphery in the post-cold war era', *International Organization* 46: 467–91.

Gong, G. (1984) *The Standard of 'Civilization' in International Society*, Oxford, Clarendon Press.

Gorry, J. (2000) 'Just War or just war? The future of a tradition', *Politics* 20: 177–83.

Goulding, M. (1993) 'The evolution of UN peacekeeping', *International Affairs* 69: 451–64.

Gourevitch, P. (1998) *We Wish to Inform You that Tomorrow We Will Be Killed with Our Families: Stories from Rwanda*, New York, Farrar, Straus & Giroux.

Gowa, J. (1989) 'Rational hegemons, excludable goods, and small groups', *World Politics* 41: 307–24.

—— (1995) 'Democratic states and international disputes', *International Organization* 49: 519–22.

Gray, C. (2000) *Geopolitics, Geography and Strategy*, London, Frank Cass.

Greene, O. (1999) 'Environmental issues', in Baylis, J. and Smith, S. (eds), *The Globalization of World Politics*, Oxford, Oxford University Press.

Greenfeld, L. (1992) *Nationalism: Five Roads to Modernity*, Cambridge, MA, Harvard University Press.

Greider, W. (1998) *One World, Ready or Not: The Manic Logic of Global Capitalism*, New York, Touchstone.

Grieco, J. (1990) *Cooperation among Nations*, Ithaca, NY, Cornell University Press.

Griffiths, M. (1992) 'Order and international society: the real realism?', *Review of International Studies* 18: 217–40.

—— (1995) *Realism, Idealism and International Politics*, London, Routledge.

—— (1999) *Fifty Key Thinkers in International Relations*, London, Routledge.

Griffiths, M. and O'Callaghan, T. (2001) 'The end of international relations?', in Crawford, M. and Jarvis, D. (eds), *International Relations: Still an American Social Science?*, Albany, NY, State University of New York Press.

Grunberg, I. (1990) 'Exploring the myth of hegemonic stability', *International Organization* 44: 431–77.

Guibernau, M. and Jones, R. (eds) (1997) *The Ethnicity Reader: Nationalism, Multiculturalism and Migration*, Cambridge, Polity Press.

Guillemin, J. (1999) *Anthrax: The Investigation of a Deadly Outbreak*, Berkeley, CA, University of California Press.

Gutmann, M. (1988) 'The origins of the Thirty Years War', *Journal of Interdisciplinary History* 18: 749–70.

Guzzini, S. (1998) *Realism in International Relations and International Political Economy: The Continuing Story of a Death Foretold*, London, Routledge.

Haacke, J. (1996) 'Theory and praxis in international relations: Habermas, self-reflection, rational argumentation', *Millennium: Journal of International Studies* 24: 255–89.

Haas, E. (1953) 'The balance of power: prescription, concept or propaganda?', *World Politics* 5: 442–77.

—— (1964) *Beyond the Nation-State: Functionalism and International Organization*, Stanford, CA, Stanford University Press.

Habermas, J. (1994) *On the Logic of the Social Sciences*, Cambridge, MA, MIT Press.

—— (1999) 'Does Europe need a new constitution?', *New Left Review* 11: 5–22.

Haggard, S. (1990) *Pathways from the Periphery: The Politics of Growth in the Newly Industrializing Countries*, Ithaca, NY, Cornell University Press.

Hajnal, P. and Meikle, S. (1999) *The G7/G8 System: Evolution, Role and Documentation*, Aldershot, Ashgate.

Hall, T. and Ferguson, J. (1998) *The Great Depression: An International Disaster of Perverse Economic Policies*, Ann Arbor, MI, University of Michigan Press.

Halliday, F. (1992) 'International society as homogeneity: Burke, Marx, and Fukuyama', *Millennium: Journal of International Studies* 21: 435–61.

Handelman, H. (1999) *The Challenge of Third World Development*, Englewood Cliffs, NJ, Prentice-Hall.

Hannum, H. (1990) *Autonomy, Sovereignty and Self-Determination: The Accommodation of Conflicting Rights*, Philadelphia, PA, University of Pennsylvania Press.

Hardin, G. (1968) 'The tragedy of the commons', *Science* 162: 1243–8.

Hardin, R. (1982) *Collective Action*, Baltimore, MD, Johns Hopkins University Press.

Harmon, C. (2000) *Terrorism Today*, London, Frank Cass.

Harrison, P. (1993) *Inside the Third World*, Harmondsworth, Penguin.

Harvey, C. (1995) *Constraints on the Success of Structural Adjustment Programmes in Africa*, New York, St Martin's Press.

Hasenclever, A., Mayer, P. and Rittberger, V. (1997) *Theories of International Regimes*, Cambridge, Cambridge University Press.

Hasou, T. (1985) *The Struggle for the Arab World: Egypt's Nasser and the Arab League*, London, KPI.

Hawes, M. (1990) 'Assessing the world economy: the rise and fall of Bretton Woods', in Haglund, D. and Hawes, M. (eds), *World Politics: Power, Interdependence and Dependence*, Toronto, Harcourt Brace Jovanovich.

Hayden, P. and Lansford, T. (2003) *America's War on Terror*, Aldershot, Ashgate.

Haynes, J. (1996) *Third World Politics: An Introduction*, Oxford, Blackwell.

Heater, D. (1996) *World Citizenship: Cosmopolitan Ideas in the History of Western Political Thought*, New York, St Martin's Press.

Heilbroner, R. (1994) *Twenty-First Century Capitalism*, New York, W. W. Norton.

Held, D. (1995) *Democracy and the Global Order: From the Modern State to Cosmopolitan Governance*, Cambridge, Polity Press.

—— (2002) 'Law of states, law of peoples: three models of sovereignty', *Legal Theory* 8: 1–44.

Helleiner, E. (1996) *States and the Reemergence of Global Finance: From Bretton Woods to the 1990s*, Ithaca, NY, Cornell University Press.

Heller, F. (1992) *NATO: The Founding of the Atlantic Alliance and the Integration of Europe*, New York, St Martin's Press.

Helman, G. and Ratner, S. (1992–93) 'Saving failed states', *Foreign Policy* 89: 3–20.

Heraclides, A. (1990) 'Secessionist minorities and external involvement', *International Organization* 44: 341–78.

—— (1992) 'Secession, self-determination and nonintervention', *Journal of International Affairs* 45: 399–420.

Herzog, R. (1999) *Preventing the Clash of Civilizations: A Peace Strategy for the New Century*, New York, St Martin's Press.

Higgins, R. (1995) *Problems and Process: International Law and How We Use It*, Oxford, Clarendon Press.

Hobbes, T. (1988) *The Leviathan*, New York, Prometheus Books.

Hobsbawm, E. (1991) *Nations and Nationalism since 1780: Programme, Myth, Reality*, Cambridge, Cambridge University Press.

Hobson, J. A. (1965) *Imperialism: A Study*, Ann Arbor, MI, University of Michigan Press.

Hobson, J. (1998) 'The historical sociology of the state and the state of historical sociology in international relations', *Review of International Political Economy* 5: 284–320.

Hodder, D., Lloyd, S. and McLachlan, K. (1997) *Land-Locked States of Africa and Asia*, London, Frank Cass.

Hoffman, M. (1987) 'Critical theory and the inter-paradigm debate', *Millennium: Journal of International Studies* 16: 231–49.

Hoffmann, S. (1998) 'The crisis of liberal internationalism', *Foreign Policy* 98: 159–77.

Holbraad, C. (1984) *Middle Powers in International Politics*, New York, St Martin's Press.

Hollis, M. and Smith, S. (1990) *Explaining and Understanding International Relations*, Oxford, Clarendon Press.

Holsti, K. (1991) *Peace and War: Armed Conflict and International Order, 1648–1989*, Cambridge, Cambridge University Press.

—— (1992) 'Governance without government: polyarchy in nineteenth-century European international politics', in Rosenau, J. and Czempiel, E. (eds), *Governance without Government: Order and Change in World Politics*, Cambridge, Cambridge University Press.

—— (1996) *The State, War, and the State of War*, Cambridge, Cambridge University Press.

Holton, R. (1998) *Globalization and the Nation-State*, Basingstoke, Macmillan.

Holzgrefe, J.L. and R. Keohane (2003) *Humanitarian Intervention: Ethical, Legal and Political Dilemmas*, Cambridge: Cambridge University Press.

Homer-Dixon, T. and Blitt, J. (1998) *Ecoviolence: Links Among Environment, Populations, and Security*, Lanham, MD, Rowman & Littlefield.

Hopf, T. (1998) 'The promise of constructivism in international relations theory', *International Security* 23: 171–200.

Hopkins, T. (1982) *World-Systems Analysis: Theory and Methodology*, Beverly Hills, CA, Sage.

Horowitz, D. (1992) 'Irredentas and secessions: adjacent phenomena, neglected connections', *International Journal of Comparative Sociology* 23: 118–30.

Houghton, J. (1997) *Global Warming: The Complete Briefing*, 2nd edn, Cambridge, Cambridge University Press.

Hourani, A. (1991) *A History of the Arab Peoples*, Cambridge, MA, Harvard University Press.

Howlett, D. (1999) 'Nuclear proliferation', in Baylis, J. and Smith, S. (eds), *The Globalization of World Politics*, Oxford, Oxford University Press.

Hoyt, P. (2000) 'The "rogue state" image in American foreign policy', *Global Society* 14: 297–310.

Human Security Report (2006) *Human Security Report 2005*, Oxford, Oxford University Press.

Huntington, S. (1968) *Political Order in Changing Societies*, New Haven, CT, Yale University Press.

—— (1993) 'The clash of civilizations?', *Foreign Affairs* 72: 22–49.

—— (1996) *The Clash of Civilizations and the Remaking of World Order*, New York, Simon & Schuster.

Hurrell, A. (1990) 'Kant and the Kantian paradigm in international relations', *Review of International Studies* 16: 183–205.

Hurrell, A. and Woods, N. (eds) (1999) *Inequality, Globalization, and World Politics*, Oxford, Oxford University Press.

Hutchings, K. and Dannreuther, R. (eds) (1999) *Cosmopolitan Citizenship*, New York, St Martin's Press.

Hutchinson, J. and Smith, A. (eds) (1996) *Ethnicity*, Oxford, Oxford University Press.

Hyde-Price, A. (1991) *European Security beyond the Cold War: Four Scenarios for the Year 2010*, London, Royal Institute of International Affairs.

Ikenberry, J. (2002) 'America's imperial ambition', *Foreign Affairs* 8(5): 44–60.

Intergovernmental Panel on Climate Change (2007) Intergovernmental Panel on Climate Change Report. Geneva.

Isaacs, J. and Downing, T. (1998) *The Cold War*, London, Bantam Press.

Ishay, M. (2004) *The History of Human Rights: From Ancient Times to the Globalization Era,*. Berkeley, CA, University of Californian Press.

Ito, T. and Krueger, A. (eds) (1997) *Regionalism versus Multilateral Trade Arrangements*, Chicago, IL, University of Chicago Press.

Jackson, J. (1989) *The World Trading System*, Cambridge, MA, MIT Press.

Jackson, R. (1990) *Quasi-States: Sovereignty, International Relations and the Third World*, Cambridge, Cambridge University Press.

—— (2000) *The Global Covenant*, Oxford, Oxford University Press.

Jackson, R. and James, A. (eds) (1993) *States in a Changing World*, Oxford, Clarendon Press.

Jackson, R. and Sorensen, G. (1999) *Introduction to International Relations*, Oxford, Oxford University Press.

Jahn, B. (1998) 'One step forward, two steps back: critical theory as the latest edition of liberal idealism', *Millennium: Journal of International Studies* 27: 613–41.

Janis, I. (1972) *Victims of Groupthink*, Boston, MA, Houghton Mifflin.

Jarvis, A. (1995) 'Societies, states, and geopolitics: challenges from historical sociology', *Review of International Studies* 15: 281–93.

Jarvis, D. (2000) *International Relations and the Challenge of Postmodernism: Defending the Discipline*, Columbia, SC, University of South Carolina Press.

Jervis, R. (1976) *Perception and Misperception in International Politics*, Princeton, NJ, Princeton University Press.

—— (1978) 'Cooperation under the security dilemma', *World Politics* 30: 167–214.

—— (1988) 'Realism, game theory and cooperation', *World Politics* 40: 317–49.

—— (1999) 'Realism, neoliberalism, and cooperation: understanding the debate', *International Security* 24: 42–63.

—— (2003) 'Understanding the Bush doctrine', *Political Science Quarterly* 118: 365–88.

Jervis, R., Lebow, R. and Stein, J. (1985) *Psychology and Deterrence*, Baltimore, MD, Johns Hopkins University Press.

Jett, D. (2000) *Why Peacekeeping Fails*, New York, St Martin's Press.

Joffe, J. (1998) *The Future of the Great Powers*, London, Phoenix.

Johnson, J. (1984) *Can Modern War Be Just?*, New Haven, CT, Yale University Press.

Jones, A. (1996) 'Does gender make the world go round?', *Review of International Studies* 22: 405–29.

Jones, C. (1999) *Global Justice: Defending Cosmopolitanism*, Oxford, Oxford University Press.

Jones, S. (1997) *The Archaeology of Ethnicity: Constructing Identity in the Past and Present*, London, Routledge.

Kabeer, N. (1994) *Reversed Realities: Gender Hierarchies in Development Thought*, London, Verso.

Kahler, M. (ed.) (1998) *Capital Controls and Financial Crises*, Ithaca, NY, Cornell University Press.

Kaldor, M. (1999) *New and Old Wars: Organized Violence in a Global Era*, Cambridge, Polity Press.

—— (2000) 'Europe at the millennium', *Politics* 20: 55–62.

Kamali, M. (2002) *Freedom, Equality and Justice in Islam*, Cambridge, Islamic Texts Society.

Kaplan, E. (1996) *American Trade Policy 1923–95*, London, Greenwood.

Kaplan, R. (2000) *The Coming Anarchy*, New York, Random House.

Kapur, D. (1997) *The World Bank: Its First Half Century*, Washington, DC, Brookings.

Karl, T. (1990) 'Dilemmas of democratization in Latin America', *Comparative Politics* 23: 1–21.

Karp, R. (ed.) (1992) *Security without Nuclear Weapons*, Oxford, Oxford University Press.

Katzenstein, P. (ed.) (1996a) *The Culture of National Security: Norms and Identity in World Politics*, New York, Columbia University Press.

—— (1996b) 'Regionalism in comparative perspective', *Cooperation and Conflict* 31: 123–59.

Keane, J. (2003) *A Global Civil Society?*, Cambridge, Cambridge University Press.

Kegley, C. and Raymond, G. (1992) 'Must we fear a post-cold war multipolar system?', *Journal of Conflict Resolution* 36: 573–85.

—— (1999) *How Nations Make Peace*, New York, Worth.

Kenen, P. (1988) *Managing Exchange Rates*, New York, Council on Foreign Relations.

—— (1995a) *Economic and Monetary Union in Europe: Moving beyond Maastricht*, Cambridge, Cambridge University Press.

—— (1995b) *Understanding Interdependence*, Princeton, NJ, Princeton University Press.

Kennedy, P. (1987) *The Rise and Decline of Great Powers: Economic Change and Military Conflict from 1500–2000*, New York, Random House.

Kenny, M. and Meadowcroft, J. (eds) (1999) *Planning Sustainability*, London, Routledge.

Keohane, R. (1984) *After Hegemony: Cooperation and Discord in the World Political Economy*, Princeton, NJ, Princeton University Press.

—— (1986a) 'Reciprocity and international relations', *International Organization* 40: 1–27.

—— (ed.) (1986b) *Neorealism and its Critics*, New York, Columbia University Press.

Keohane, R. and Nye, J. (2000) *Power and Interdependence*, 3rd edn, Reading, MA, Addison Wesley.

Kerr. R. (2004) *The International Criminal Tribunal for the Former Yugoslavia*, Oxford, Oxford University Press.

Keylor, W. (1992) *The Twentieth Century World: An International History*, New York, Oxford University Press.

Khazanov, A. (1996) *After the USSR Collapsed*, Madison, WI, University of Wisconsin Press.

Kiely, R. and Marfleet, P. (1998) *Globalisation and the Third World*, New York, Routledge.

Killick, T. (1995) *IMF Programmes in Developing Countries: Design and Impact*, London, Routledge.

Kindleberger, C. (1973) *The World in Depression, 1929–39*, Berkeley, CA, University of California Press.

—— (1981) 'Dominance and leadership in the international economy: exploitation, public goods, and free-rides', *International Studies Quarterly* 25: 242–54.

Kissinger, H. (1994) *Diplomacy*, New York, Simon & Schuster.

Klare, M. (1995) *Rogue States and Nuclear Outlaws*, New York, Hill & Wang.

Klare, M. and Chandrani, Y. (eds) (1998) *World Security: Challenges for a New Century*, 3rd edn, New York, St Martin's Press.

Klare, M. and Lumpe, L. (1998) 'Fanning the flames of war: conventional arms transfers in the 1990s', in Klare, M. and Chandrani, Y. (eds), *World Security: Challenges for a New Century*, 3rd edn, New York, St Martin's Press.

Klinghoffer, A. (1998) *The International Dimension of Genocide in Rwanda*, New York, New York University Press.

Kliot, N. and Newman, D. (2000) *Geopolitics at the End of the Twentieth Century: The Changing World Map*, London, Frank Cass.

Knock, T. (1995) *To End All Wars: Woodrow Wilson and the Quest for a New World Order*, Princeton, NJ, Princeton University Press.

Kober, S. (1990) 'Idealpolitik', *Foreign Policy* 79: 3–24.

Kokotsis, E. (1999) *Keeping International Commitments: Compliance, Credibility and the G7, 1988–95*, London, Garland.

Kolakowski, L. (1978) *Main Currents of Marxism*, Volumes 1 and 2, Oxford, Oxford University Press.

Korten, D. (1995) *When Corporations Rule the World*, West Hartford, CT, Barett-Kohler/Kumarian.

Koslowski, R. and Kratochwil, F. (1994) 'Understanding change in international relations: the Soviet Union's demise and the international system', *International Organization* 48: 215–48.

Krasner, S. (1976) 'State power and the structure of international trade', *World Politics* 28: 317–45.

—— (1978) *Defending the National Interest*, Princeton, NJ, Princeton University Press.

—— (ed.) (1982) *International Regimes*, Ithaca, NY, Cornell University Press.

—— (1993) 'Westphalia and all that', in Goldstein, J. and Keohane, R. (eds), *Ideas and Foreign Policy*, Ithaca, NY, Cornell University Press.

—— (1999) *Sovereignty: Organized Hypocrisy*, Princeton, NJ, Princeton University Press.

Krause, K. (1992) *Arms and the State: Patterns of Military Production and Trade*, Cambridge, Cambridge University Press.

Kressel, N. (1996) *Mass Hate: The Global Rise of Genocide and Terror*, New York, Plenum Press.

Krugman, P. (ed.) (1986) *Strategic Trade Policy and the New International Economics*, Cambridge, MA, MIT Press.

Kuhn, T. (1970) *The Structure of Scientific Revolutions*, 2nd edn, Chicago, IL, University of Chicago Press.

Kupchan, C. (1998) 'After Pax Americana: benign power, regional integration, and the sources of a stable multipolarity', *International Security* 23: 40–79.

Kurti, L. and Langman, J. (eds) (1997) *Beyond Borders: Remaking Cultural Identities in the New East and Central Europe*, Boulder, CO, Westview Press.

Kymlicka, W. (1990) *Contemporary Political Philosophy*, Oxford, Clarendon Press.

—— (1995) *Multicultural Citizenship*, Oxford, Clarendon Press.

Lacqueur, W. and Alexander, Y. (eds) (1987) *The Terrorism Reader*, New York, New American Library.

Lafferty, W. and Meadowcroft, J. (eds) (2000) *Implementing Sustainable Development*, Oxford, Oxford University Press.

Lake, A. (1994) 'Confronting backlash states', *Foreign Affairs* 73: 45–55.

Lake, D. and Rothchild, D. (eds) (1998) *The International Spread of Ethnic Conflict: Fear, Diffusion, and Escalation*, Princeton, NJ, Princeton University Press.

Landes, D. (1999) *The Wealth and Poverty of Nations*, New York, Norton.

Lang, D. and Born, G. (eds) (1987) *The Extraterritorial Application of National Laws*, Deventer, Kluwer Law and Taxation Publishers.

Lapid, Y. (1989) 'The third debate: on the prospects of international theory in a post–positivist era', *International Studies Quarterly* 33: 235–54.

Lapid, Y. and Kratochwil, F. (eds) (1996) *The Return of Culture and Identity in IR Theory*, Boulder, CO, Lynne Rienner.

Laudan, L. (1996) *Beyond Positivism and Relativism: Theory, Method and Evidence*, Boulder, CO, Westview Press.

Laurance, E. (1992) *The International Arms Trade*, New York, Lexington.

Lawler, P. (1995) *A Question of Values: Johan Galtung's Peace Research*, Boulder, CO, Lynne Rienner.

Lawrence, R. (1996) *Single World, Divided Nations? International Trade and the OECD Labor Markets*, Washington, DC, Brookings.

Layne, C. (1993) 'The unipolar illusion: why new great powers will arise', *International Security* 17: 5–51.

Leaver, R. and Cox, D. (eds) (1997) *Middling, Meddling, Muddling: Issues in Australian Foreign Policy*, St Leonards, NSW, Allen & Unwin.

Lebow, R. (1990) *Between Peace and War: The Nature of International Crisis*, Baltimore, MD, Johns Hopkins University Press.

Lebow, R. and Stein, J. (1998) 'Nuclear lessons of the cold war', in Booth, K. (ed.), *Statecraft and Security: The Cold War and Beyond*, Cambridge, Cambridge University Press.

Lederberg, J. (1999) *Biological Weapons: Limiting the Threat*, Cambridge, MA, MIT Press.

Lee, R. (1998) *Smuggling Armageddon: The Nuclear Black Market in the Former Soviet Union and Europe*, New York, St Martin's Press.

—— (ed.) (1999) *The International Criminal Court: The Making of the Rome Statute*, The Hague, Kluwer Law International.

Lehne, S. (1991) *The Vienna Meeting of the Conference on Security and Cooperation in Europe, 1986–89: A Turning Point in East–West Relations*, Boulder, CO, Westview Press.

Lehning, P. (ed.) (1998) *Theories of Secession*, London, Routledge.

Lelyveld, J. (2007) 'No exit', *The New York Review of Books* LIV(2): 12–17.

Lenin, V. (1968) *Imperialism as the Highest Stage of Capitalism*, Moscow, Foreign Language Press.

Lepgold, J. and Weiss, T. (1998) *Collective Conflict Management and Changing World Politics*, New York, State University of New York Press.

Levinson, S. (2004) *Torture: A Collection*, Oxford, Oxford University Press.

Lewis, B. (2003) *The Crisis of Islam: Holy War and Untold War*, New York, Modern Library.

Leys, C. (1996) *The Rise and Fall of Development Theory*, Bloomington, IN, Indiana University Press.

Lijphart, A. (1974) 'The structure of the theoretical revolution in international relations', *International Studies Quarterly* 18: 41–74.

Linklater, A. (1992) 'The question of the next stage in international relations theory: a critical-theoretical point of view', *Millennium: Journal of International Studies* 21: 77–98.

—— (1998) *The Transformation of Political Community*, Cambridge, Polity Press.

Lipschutz, R. (1992) 'Reconstructing world politics: the emergence of global civil society', *Millennium: Journal of International Studies* 21: 389–420.

Litfin, K. (1999) 'Environmental security in the coming century', in Paul, T. and Hall, J. (eds), *International Order and the Future of World Politics*, Cambridge, Cambridge University Press.

Little, D. (2001) *Development Ethics: Justice, Well-Being, and Poverty in the Developing World*, Boulder, CO, Westview Press.

Little, R. (2000) 'The English School's contribution to the study of international relations', *European Journal of International Relations* 6(3): 395–422.

Litwak, R. (2000) *Rogue States and US Foreign Policy: Containment after the Cold War*, Baltimore, MD, Johns Hopkins University Press.

Livi-Bacci, M. and Ipsen, C. (1997) *A Concise History of World Population*, Oxford, Blackwell.

Loescher, G. (1992) *Refugee Movements and International Security*, Adelphi Paper No. 268, London, International Institute for Strategic Studies.

—— (1993) *Beyond Charity: International Cooperation and the Global Refugee Crisis*, New York, Oxford University Press.

Long, D. and Wilson, P. (1995) *Thinkers of the Twenty Years' Crisis*, Oxford, Clarendon Press.

Lukes, S. (1974) *Power: A Radical View*, Basingstoke, Macmillan.

—— (1996) *The Curious Enlightenment of Professor Caritat*, London, Verso.

Lund, M. (1995) *Preventing Violent Conflicts: A Strategy for Preventive Diplomacy*, Washington, DC, United States Institute of Peace.

Lundestad, G. (1997) *East, West, North, South*, 3rd edn, Oslo, Scandinavian University Press.

Lyons, G. and Mastanduno, M. (eds) (1995) *Beyond Westphalia? State Sovereignty and International Intervention*, Baltimore, MD, Johns Hopkins University Press.

Lyotard, J. (1984) *The Postmodern Condition: A Report On Knowledge*, Minneapolis, University of Minnesota Press.

McCoy, A. (2006) *A Question of Torture: CIA Interrogation from the Cold War to the War on Terror*, Oxford, Oxford University Press.

McDonough, F. (1998) *Neville Chamberlain, Appeasement and the British Road to War*, Manchester, Manchester University Press.

McInness, I. (2003) 'A different kind of war', *Review of International Studies* 29(2): 165–84.

McKinney, J. (1994) 'The world trade regime: past successes and future challenges', *International Journal* 49: 445–71.

McNamara, K. (1999) *The Currency of Ideas: Monetary Politics in the European Union*, Ithaca, NY, Cornell University Press.

McQuillan, L. (1999) *The International Monetary Fund*, Washington, DC, Hoover Institute Press.

Magnusson, L. (1995) *Mercantilism*, London, Routledge.

Makinda, S. (2000) 'Recasting global governance', in Thakur, R. and Newman, E. (eds), *New Millennium, New Perspectives: The United Nations, Security, and Governance*, Tokyo, United Nations University Press.

Malanczuk, P. (1997) *Akehurst's Modern Introduction to International Law*, 7th edn, London, Routledge.

Malekian, F. (1994) *The Concept of of Islamic International Criminal Law: Comparative Study*, The Hague, Graham & Trotman/Martinus Nijhof.

Malone, D. and Khong, Y. (2003) *Unilateralism and U.S. Foreign Policy: International Perspectives*, Boulder, CO, Lynne Rienner Publishers.

Mamdani, M. (2004) *Good Muslim, Bad Muslim: America, the Cold war, and the Roots of Terror*, New York, Pantheon Books.

Manzetti, L. (1994) 'The political economy of Mercosur', *Journal of Interamerican Studies and World Afffairs* 35: 1–23.

Maren, M. (1997) *The Road to Hell: The Ravaging Effects of Foreign Aid*, New York, Free Press.

Maresca, J. (1985) *To Helsinki: The Conference on Security and Cooperation in Europe, 1973–75*, Durham, NC, Duke University Press.

Martinez, J. (2004) 'Hamdi v. Rumsfeld', *American Journal of International Law* 98(4): 782–7.

Marx, K. (1976) *Capital*, Volume 1, New York, Penguin Books.

Marx, K. and Engels, F. (1999) *The Communist Manifesto*, Harmondsworth, Penguin.

Mason, T. and Turay, A. (1994) *Trilateral Cooperation or Confrontation*, New York, St Martin's Press.

Mastanduno, M. (1999) 'A realist view: three images of the coming international order', in Paul, T. and Hall, J. (eds) *International Order and the Future of World Politics*, Cambridge, Cambridge University Press.

Mathews, K. (2001) 'Birth of the African Union (AU)', *African Quarterly* 41(1–2): 113–20.

Matthew, R. and Zacher, M. (1995) 'Liberal international theory: common threads, divergent strands', in Kegley, C. (ed.), *Controversies in International Politics: Realism and the Neoliberal Challenge*, New York, St Martin's Press.

May, E. (1973) *Lessons of the Past: the Use and Misuse of History in American Foreign Policy*, Oxford, Oxford University Press.

Mayall, J. (1989) *Nationalism and International Society*, Cambridge, Cambridge University Press.

Mazrui, A. (1997) 'Islamic and Western values', *Foreign Affairs* 76: 118–32.

Mead, W. R. (2004) *Power, Terror, Peace and War: America's Grand Strategy in a World at Risk*, New York, Knopf.

Meadwell, H. (1999) 'Secession, states and international society', *Review of International Studies* 25: 371–87.

Mearsheimer, J. (1990) 'Back to the future: instability in Europe after the cold war', *International Security* 15: 5–56.

—— (1994/5) 'The false promise of international institutions', *International Security* 19: 5–59.

Mehmet, O. (1999) *Westernizing the Third World*, New York, Routledge.

Midlarsky, M. (ed.) (1992) *The Internationalization of Communal Strife*, London, Routledge.

Miller, D. (1989) *Market, State, and Community*, Oxford, Clarendon Press.

—— (1999) 'Justice and inequality', in Hurrell, A. and Woods, N. (eds), *Inequality, Globalization and World Politics*, Oxford, Oxford University Press.

Milner, C. (ed.) (1998) *Developing and Newly Industrializing Countries*, Cheltenham, Edward Elgar.

Milner, H. (1988) *Resisting Protectionism and the Politics of International Trade*, Princeton, NJ, Princeton University Press.

—— (1991) 'The assumption of anarchy in international relations theory', *Review of International Studies* 17: 67–85.

Milwertz, C. (1996) *Accepting Population Control*, London, Curzon Press.

Mitrany, D. (1975) *The Functional Theory of Politics*, New York, St Martin's Press.

Mittelman, J. (1996) 'Rethinking the "New Regionalism" in the context of globalization', *Global Governance* 2: 189–214.

Moeller, S. (1999) *Compassion Fatigue: How the Media Sell Disease, Famine, War and Death*, London, Routledge.

Mofidi, M. and Eckert, A. (2003) '"Unlawful combatants" or "prisoners of war": the law and politics of labels', *Cornell International Journal of International Law*, 36.

Monten, J. (2005) 'The roots of the Bush doctrine: power, nationalism, and democracy promotion in U.S. strategy', *International Security*, 29(4): 112–56.

Moore, M. (ed.) (1998) *National Self-Determination and Secession*, Oxford, Oxford University Press.

Moran, T. (1998) *Managing International Political Risk: New Tools, Strategies and Techniques for Investors and Financial Institutions*, Oxford, Blackwell.

Morgan, P. (2003) *Complex Deterrence*, Cambridge, Cambridge University Press.

Morgenthau, H. (1948) *Politics Among Nations: The Struggle for Power and Peace*, 1st edn, New York, McGraw-Hill.

Mueller, J. (1996) *Retreat from Doomsday: The Obsolescence of Major War*, New York, University of Rochester Press.

—— (2000) 'The banality of "ethnic" war', *International Security* 25: 42–70.

Mulhall, S. and Swift, A. (1992) *Liberals and Communitarians*, Oxford, Blackwell.

Murphy, C. (1996) 'Seeing women, recognising gender, recasting international relations', *International Organization* 50: 513–38.

Musah, A.-F. and Fayemi, J. (1999) *Mercenaries: An African Security Dilemma*, London, Pluto Press.

Myers, N. and Simon, J. (1994) *Scarcity or Abundance: A Debate on the Environment*, New York, Norton.

Nadia, G. (1996) 'How different are postcommunist transitions?', *Journal of Democracy* 7: 15–29.

Naimark, N. (2001) *Fires of Hatred: Ethnic Cleansing in Twentieth Century Europe*, Boston, MA, Harvard University Press.

Nash, M. (1989) *The Cauldron of Ethnicity in the Modern World*, Chicago, IL, University of Chicago Press.

Neale, A. and Stephens, M. (1988) *International Business and National Jurisdiction*, Oxford, Clarendon Press.

Nef, J. (1999) *Human Security and Mutual Vulnerability: The Global Political Economy of Development and Underdevelopment*, 2nd edn, Ottawa, International Development Research Centre.

Neufeld, M. (1993) 'Reflexivity and international relations theory', *Millennium: Journal of International Studies* 22: 77–88.

Neuman, S. (ed.) (1998) *International Relations Theory and the Third World*, Basingstoke, Macmillan.

Nordlinger, E. (1996) *Isolationism Reconfigured*, Princeton, NJ, Princeton University Press.

Norris, P. (2001) *Digital Divide: Civic Engagement, Information Poverty and the Internet Worldwide*, Cambridge, Cambridge University Press.

Nossal, K. (1994) *Rain Dancing: Sanctions in Canadian and Australian Foreign Policy*, Toronto, University of Toronto Press.

Nugent, N. (1994) *The Government and Politics of the European Union*, Basingstoke, Macmillan.

Nussbaum, M. (1997) *Cultivating Humanity*, London, Harvard University Press.

Nye, J. (1990) *Bound to Lead: The Changing Nature of American Power*, New York, Basic Books.

Ohmae, K. (1995) *The End of the Nation State: The Rise of Regional Economics*, New York, The Free Press.

Okpewho, I., Davis, C. and Mazrui, A. (eds) (1999) *The African Diaspora*, Bloomington, IN, Indiana University Press.

Olson, M. (1971) *The Logic of Collective Action*, Cambridge, MA, Harvard University Press.

O'Meara, P., Mehlinger, H. and Krain, M. (eds) (2000) *Globalization and the Challenges of a New Century*, Bloomington, IN, Indiana University Press.

Oommen, T. (1997) *Citizenship, Nationality and Ethnicity: Reconciling Competing Identities*, Cambridge, Polity Press.

Orme, J. (1997/98) 'The utility of force in a world of scarcity', *International Security* 22: 138–67.

Oudraat, C. (2000) 'Humanitarian intervention: the lessons learned', *Current History* 99: 419–29.

Oxley, A. (1990) *The Challenge of Free Trade*, New York, St Martin's Press.

Pape, R. (1996) *Military Coercion*, Ithaca, NY, Cornell University Press.

—— (1997) 'Why economic sanctions do not work', *International Security* 22: 90–136.

Paris, R. (2001) 'Human security: paradigm shift or hot air?', *International Security* 26(2): 87–102.

—— (2006) 'Bringing the leviathan back in: classical vs. contemporary studies of the liberal peace', *International Studies Review*, 8(3): 425–40.

Parker, C. and Rukare, D. (2002) 'The New African Union and its constitutive act', *American Journal of International Law* 96(2): 365–78.

Parker, G. (ed.) (1997) *The Thirty Years' War*, 2nd edn, New York, Routledge.

Parnwell, M. (1993) *Population Movements and the Third World*, London, Routledge.

Paterson, M. (1996) *Global Warming and Global Politics*, London, Routledge.

Patomaki, H. and Wight, C. (2000) 'The promises of critical realism', *International Studies Quarterly* 44: 213–37.

Paul, T. and Hall, J. (eds) (1999) *International Order and the Future of World Politics*, Cambridge, Cambridge University Press.

Paul, T., Harknett, R. and Wirtz, J. (eds) (1998) *The Absolute Weapon Revisited: Nuclear Arms and the Emerging International Order*, Ann Arbor, MI, University of Michigan Press.

Payer, C. (1991) *Lent and Lost: Foreign Credit and the Third World*, London, Zed Books.

Perlman, D., Adelson, G. and Wilson, E. (1997) *Exploring Values and Priorities in Conservation*, Oxford, Blackwell Science.

Peterson, M. (1997) *Recognition of Governments: Legal Doctrine and State Practice*, New York, St Martin's Press.

Peterson, V. (ed.) (1992) *Gendered States: Feminist (Re)Visions of International Relations Theory*, Boulder, CO, Westview.

Phillips, R. and Cady, D. (1995) *Humanitarian Intervention*, Oxford, Rowman & Littlefield.

Philpott, D. (1995) 'In defense of self-determination', *Ethics* 105: 352–85.

Pierre, A. (1997) *Cascade of Arms: Controlling Conventional Weapons Proliferation in the 1990s*, Washington, DC, Brookings Institute.

Pinkney, R. (1993) *Democracy in the Third World*, Buckingham, Open University Press.

Plaut, W. (1995) *Asylum: A Moral Dilemma*, Westport, CT, Praeger.

Pohl, J. (1999) *Ethnic Cleansing in the USSR, 1937–49*, London, Greenwood Press.

Polanyi, K. (1944) *The Great Transformation*, Boston, MA, Beacon Press.

Porter, G. and Brown, J. (1991) *Global Environmental Politics*, Boulder, CO, Westview Press.

Powell, R. (1994) 'Anarchy in international relations theory: the neorealist–neoliberal debate', *International Organization* 48: 313–44.

Powers, S. (2003) *A Problem from Hell: America and the Age of Genocide*, New York, Harper Perennial.

Preeg, E. (1995) *Traders in a Brave New World: The Uruguay Round and the Future of the International Trading System*, Chicago, IL, University of Chicago Press.

Prestowitz, C. (1988) *Trading Places*, New York, Basic Books.

—— (2003) *Rogue Nation: American Unilateralism and the Failure of Good Intentions*. New York: Basic Books.

Preusse, H. (2001) 'Mercosur: another failed move towards regional integration?', *World Economy* 24: 911–32.

Price, R. (1997) *The Chemical Weapons Taboo*, Ithaca, NY, Cornell University Press.

Puchala, D. (1988) 'The integration theorists and the study of international relations', in Kegley, C. and Wittkopf, E. (eds), *The Global Agenda*, New York, Random House.

Putnam, R. (2001) *Bowling Alone*, New York, Simon & Schuster.

Ralph, J. (2005) 'International society, the International Criminal Court and American foreign policy', *Review of International Studies* 31(1): 27–44.

Rapkin, D. (ed.) (1990) *World Leadership and Hegemony*, Boulder, CO, Lynne Rienner.

Rashid, S. (ed.) (1998) *The Clash of Civilizations? Asian Responses*, New York, Oxford University Press.

Ratner, S. and Abrams, J. (2001) *Accountability for Human Rights Atrocities in International Law: Beyond the Nuremburh Legacy*, 2nd edn, Oxford, Oxford University Press.

Rawls, J. (1971) *A Theory of Justice*, Harvard, MA, Belknap Press of Harvard University Press.

—— (1999) *The Law of Peoples*, Harvard, MA, Belknap Press of Harvard University Press.

Ray, J. (1995) *Democracy and International Conflict*, Columbia, SC, University of South Carolina Press.

Reiss, H. (ed.) (1991) *Kant's Political Writings*, 2nd edn, Cambridge, Cambridge University Press.

Reiss, M. (1995) *Bridled Ambition: Why Countries Constrain Their Nuclear Capabilities*, Washington, DC, Woodrow Wilson Center.

Reiter, D. (1996) *Crucible of Beliefs: Learning, Alliances and World Wars*, Ithaca, NY, Cornell University Press.

Rengger, N. (2000) *International Relations, Political Theory and the Problem of Order*, London, Routledge.

Reno, W. (1995) *Corruption and State Politics in Sierra Leone*, Cambridge, Cambridge University Press.

—— (2000) 'Clandestine economies, violence and the state in Africa', *Journal of International Affairs* 53: 433–59.

Reus-Smit, C. (2004) *The Politics of International Law*, Cambridge, Cambridge University Press.

Rhodes, C. (1993) *Reciprocity, US Trade Policy, and the GATT Regime*, Ithaca, NY, Cornell University Press.

Ricardo, D. (1996) *Principles of Political Economy and Taxation*, New York, Prometheus Books.

Rice, E. (1990) *Wars of the Third Kind: Conflict in Underdeveloped Countries*, Berkeley, CA, University of California Press.

Richmond, A. (1994) *Global Apartheid: Refugees, Racism, and the New World Order*, Toronto, Oxford University Press.

Rieff, D. (1995) *Slaughterhouse: Bosnia and the Failure of the West*, London, Vintage.

Ries, C. and Sweeney, R. (eds) (1997) *Capital Controls in Emerging Economies*, Boulder, CO, Westview.

Rise, T., Ropp, S. and Sikkink, K. (eds) (1999) *The Power of Human Rights*, Cambridge, Cambridge University Press.

Risse-Kappen, T. (1995) *Bringing Transnational Actors Back In: Non-State Actors, Domestic Structure, and International Institutions*, Cambridge, Cambridge University Press.

Roach, S. C. (2005a) *Cultural Autonomy, Minority Rights, and Globalization*, Aldershot, Ashgate.

—— (2005b) 'Humanitarian coercion: assessing the strategic role of non-state actors in the Kosovo war', *International Journal of Human Rights* 9: 435–48.

—— (2006) *Politicizing the International Criminal Court: The Convergence of Politics, Ethics, and Law*, Lanham, MD, Rowman & Littlefield.

—— (2007) *Critical Theory and International Relations: A Reader*, New York, Routledge.

Robbins, K. (1997) *Appeasement*, Oxford, Blackwell.

Roberts, A. and Kingsbury, B. (eds) (1992) *United Nations, Divided World*, 2nd edn, Oxford, Clarendon Press.

Roberts, R. (2000) *The Choice: A Fable of Free Trade and Protectionism*, 2nd edn, Englewood Cliffs, NJ, Prentice-Hall.

Robertson, G. (2000) *Crimes against Humanity*, Harmondsworth, Penguin.

Robinson, P. (2002) *The CNN Effect, the Myth of News and Foreign Policy*, London, Routledge.

Robinson, S. (1996) *The Politics of International Crisis Escalation: Decision-Making Under Pressure*, London, I. B. Taurus.

Roemer, J. (1982) *A General Theory of Exploitation and Class*, Cambridge, MA, Harvard University Press.

—— (1996) *Theories of Distributive Justice*, Cambridge, MA, Harvard University Press.

Roett, R. (ed.) (1999) *Mercosur: Regional Integration, World Markets*, Boulder, CO Westview.

Rogers, P. and Ramsbotham, O. (1999) 'Then and now: peace research – past and future', *Political Studies* 47: 740–54.

Rohde, D. (1998) *Endgame: The Betrayal and Fall of Srebrenica*, Boulder, CO, Westview Press.

Ronit, K. and Schneider, V. (2000) *Private Organisations in Global Politics*, London, Routledge.

Roper, S. and Barria L. (2006) *Designing Criminal Tribunals: Sovereignty and International Concerns in the Protection of Human Rights*, Burlington, VT, Ashgate.

Rosecrance, R. (1986) *The Rise of the Trading State: Commerce and Conquest in the Modern World*, New York, Basic Books.

—— (1992) 'A new concert of powers', *Foreign Affairs* 71: 64–82.

Rosenau, J. (1998) 'Governance and democracy in a globalizing world', in Archibugi, D., Held, D. and Kohler, M. (eds), *Re-imagining Political Community: Studies in Cosmopolitan Democracy*, Cambridge, Polity Press.

Rosenberg, J. (1994) *The Empire of Civil Society: A Critique of the Realist Theory of International Relations*, London, Verso.

Rostow, W. (1960) *The Stages of Economic Growth*, Cambridge, Cambridge University Press.

Rotberg, R. and Rabb, T. (eds) (1989) *The Origin and Prevention of Major Wars*, Cambridge, Cambridge University Press.

Ruggie, J. (1982) 'International regimes, transactions, and change: embedded liberalism in the postwar economic order', *International Organization* 36: 379–415.

—— (ed.) (1989) *Multilateralism Matters*, New York, Columbia University Press.

—— (1994) 'Trade protectionism and the future of welfare capitalism', *Journal of International Affairs* 48: 1–12.

—— (1997) *Winning the Peace: America and World Order in the New Era*, New York, Columbia University Press.

—— (1998) *Constructing the World Polity*, London, Routledge.

Rupert, M. and Solomon, S. (2005) *Globalization and the International Political Economy: The Politics of Alternative Futures*, Lanham, MD, Rowman & Littlefield.

Russett, B. (1993) *Grasping the Democratic Peace*, Princeton, NJ, Princeton University Press.

Ryan, S. (1995) 'Transforming violent intercommunal conflict', in Rupesinghe, K. (ed.), *Conflict Transformation*, New York, St Martin's Press.

Sagan, S. and Waltz, K. (1995) *The Spread of Nuclear Weapons: A Debate*, New York, Norton.

Said, E. (1994) *Culture and Imperialism*, New York, Vintage Press.

Sandler, T. and Harley, K. (1999) *The Political Economy of NATO: Past, Present, and into the 21st Century*, Cambridge, Cambridge University Press.

Saroosh, D. (1999) *The United Nations and the Development of Collective Security*, Oxford, Clarendon Press.

Schabas, W. (2006) *Introduction to the International Criminal Court*, 2nd edn, Cambridge, Cambridge University Press.

Schechter, M. (ed.) (1998) *Future Multilateralism*, Basingstoke, Palgrave.

Schelling, T. (1984) *Choice and Consequence*, Cambridge, MA, Harvard University Press.

Schild, G. (1995) *Bretton Woods and Dumbarton Oaks: American Postwar Planning in the Summer of 1944*, New York, St Martin's Press.

Schmidt, B. (1998) *The Political Discourse of Anarchy*, Albany, NY, State University of New York Press.

Scholte, J. (2000) *Globalization: A Critical Introduction*, Basingstoke, Macmillan.

Schulze, G. (2000) *The Political Economy of Capital Controls*, Cambridge, Cambridge University Press.

Schwartz, P. and Gibb, B. (1999) *When Good Companies Do Bad Things: Responsibility and Risk in an Age of Globalisation*, New York, John Wiley & Sons.

Searle, J. (1995) *The Construction of Social Reality*, New York, The Free Press.

Sen, A. (1999) *Development as Freedom*, New York, Knopf.

Sen, G. and Grown, C. (1987) *Development, Crises, and Alternative Visions: Third World Women's Perspectives*, New York, Monthly Review Press.

Servon, L. (2002) *Bridging the Digital Divide: Technology, Communication, and Public Policy*, London, Blackwell Publishing.

Sewall, S. and Kaysen, C. (eds) (2000) *The United States and the International Criminal Court*, Lanham, MD, Rowman & Littlefield Publishers.

Sewell, J. (ed.) (2000) *Multilateralism in Multinational Perspective*, Basingstoke, Palgrave.

Shai, S. (2005) *The Axis of Evil: Iran, Hizballah, and Palestinian Terror*, New Brunswick, NJ, Transaction Publishers.

Sharp, P. (1992) 'Adieu to the superpowers?', *International Journal* 47: 818–47.

—— (1999) 'For diplomacy: representation and the study of international relations', *International Studies Review* 1: 33–57.

Sharufk, R. (1999) *Do World Bank and IMF Policies Work?*, New York, St Martin's Press.

Shaw, M. (1994) *Global Society and International Relations*, Cambridge, Polity Press.

—— (1997) *International Law*, 4th edn, Cambridge, Cambridge University Press.

Shawcross, W. (2000) *Deliver Us from Evil*, London, Bloomsbury.

Shearer, D. (1998) *Private Armies and Military Intervention*, Oxford, Oxford University Press.

Shehadi, K. (1993) *Ethnic Self-Determination and the Break-up of States*, London, International Institute of Strategic Studies.

Simonovic, I. (1999) 'The role of the ICTY in the development of international criminal law', *Fordham International Law Journal* 23: 440–59.

Singer, J. (1969) 'The levels of analysis problem in international relations', in Rosenau, J. (ed.), *International Politics and Foreign Policy*, New York, Free Press.

Sjolander, C. and Cox, W. (eds) (1994) *Beyond Positivism: Critical Reflections on International Relations*, Boulder, CO, Lynne Rienner.

Slaughter, A. (2004) *A New World Order*, Princeton, NJ, Princeton University Press.

Sloan, E. (1998) *Bosnia and the New Collective Security*, New York, Praeger.

Sloss, D. (2004) 'Rasal v. Bush', *American Journal of International Law* 98(4): 788–97.

Smith, A. (1991) 'The nation: invented, imagined, reconstructed', *Millennium: Journal of International Studies* 20: 353–68.

—— (1995) *Nations and Nationalism in a Global Era*, Cambridge, Polity Press.

Smith, D. (1991) *The Rise of Historical Sociology*, Cambridge, Polity Press.

Smith, E. (2000) *Opposition beyond the Water's Edge: Liberal Internationalists, Pacifists and Containment, 1945–53*, London, Greenwood Press.

Smith, S. (1995) 'The self-images of a discipline: a genealogy of international relations theory', in Booth, K. and Smith, S. (eds), *International Relations Theory Today*, Cambridge, Polity Press.

—— (ed.) (1996) *Positivism and After*, Cambridge, Cambridge University Press.

—— (1999) 'Is the truth out there? Eight questions about international order', in Hall, J. and Paul, T. (eds), *International Order and the Future of World Politics*, Cambridge, Cambridge University Press.

Smith, T. (1979) 'The underdevelopment of development literature: the case of dependency theory', *World Politics* 31: 247–88.

Snidal, D. (1985) 'The game *theory* of international politics', *World Politics* 38: 25–57.

Snyder, G. H. (1997) *Alliance Politics*, Ithaca, NY, Cornell University Press.

Snyder, J. (1991) *Myths of Empire: Domestic Politics and International Ambition*, Ithaca, NY, Cornell University Press.

Spegele, R. (2001) 'Out with theory – in with practical reflection: towards a new understanding of realist moral skepticism', in Crawford, R. and Jarvis, D. (eds) *International Relations: Still an American Social Science?*, New York, State University of New York Press.

Spence, K. (2005) 'World risk society and war against terror', *Political Studies* 53(2): 284–302.

Spinner, J. (1995) *The Boundaries of Citizenship: Race, Ethnicity and Nationality in the Liberal State*, Baltimore, MD, Johns Hopkins University Press.

Stairs, D. (1998) 'Of medium powers and middling roles', in Booth, K. (ed.), *Statecraft and Security: The Cold War and Beyond*, Cambridge, Cambridge University Press.

Steans, J. (1997) *Gender and International Relations*, Cambridge, Cambridge University Press.

Steger, M. (2006) *Globalization: The New Market Ideology*, 2nd edn, Lanham, MD, Rowman & Littlefield Publishers.

Stein, A. (1982) 'When misperception matters', *World Politics* 34: 505–26.

Stopford, J. (2000) 'Multinational corporations', *Foreign Policy* 117: 12–20.

Strange, S. (1982) '*Cave! hic dragones*: a critique of regime analysis', *International Organization* 36: 479–96.

—— (1987) 'The persistent myth of lost hegemony', *International Organization* 41: 551–74.

—— (1996) *The Retreat of the State: The Diffusion of Power in the World Economy*, Cambridge, Cambridge University Press.

Strobel, W. (1996) 'The CNN effect', *American Journalism Review* 18: 33–37.

—— (1997) *Late-Breaking Foreign Policy*, Washington, DC, United States Institute of Peace Studies.

Strozier, C. and Flynn, M. (1998) *Genocide, War, and Human Survival*, Lanham, MD, Rowman & Littlefield.

Suhrke, A. (1999) 'Human security and the interests of states', *Security Dialogue* 30(3): 265–76.

Sullivan, M. (1990) *Power in Contemporary International Politics*, Columbia, SC, University of South Carolina Press.

Suny, R. (1997) *The Soviet Experiment: Russia, the USSR and the Successor States*, Oxford, Oxford University Press.

Sylvester, C. (1994) *Feminist Theory and International Relations in a Postmodern Era*, Cambridge, Cambridge University Press.

Tamir, Y. (1991) 'The right of self-determination', *Social Research* 58: 565–90.

Tanter, R. (1998) *Rogue Regimes: Terrorism and Proliferation*, Basingstoke, Macmillan.

Tarp, E. (2000) *Foreign Aid and Development*, London, Routledge.

Taylor, M. and Horgan, J. (eds) (2000) *The Future of Terrorism*, London, Frank Cass.

Taylor, P. (1997) 'The United Nations and international organisation', in Baylis, J. and Smith, T. (eds), *The Globalisation of World Politics*, Oxford, Oxford University Press.

Teschke, B. (2003) *The Myth of 1648: Class, Geopolitics and the Making of Modern International Relations*, London, Verso.

Thomas, C. (1999) 'Where is the third world now?', *Review of International Studies* 25: 225–44.

—— (2000) *Global Governance, Development and Human Security*, London, Pluto Press.

Thompson, J. (1992) *Justice and World Order: A Philosophical Inquiry*, London, Routledge.

Thucydides (1954) *History of the Peloponnesian War*, New York, Penguin Classics.

Tickner, J. (1992) *Gender in International Relations: Feminist Perspectives on Achieving Global Security*, New York, Columbia University Press.

—— (1997) 'You just don't understand: troubled engagements between feminists and IR theorists', *International Studies Quarterly* 41: 611–32.

Tieku, T. (2004) 'Explaining the clash and accommodation of interests of major actors in the creation of the African Union', *African Affairs*, 103: 249–67.

Tilly, C. (1990) *Coercion, Capital, and European States, A.D. 990–1990*, Cambridge, Blackwell.

Tinker, I. and Jaquette, J. (1987) 'UN Decade for Women: its impact and legacy', *World Development* 15: 419–27.

Tisch, S. and Wallace, M. (1994) *Dilemmas of Developmental Assistance: The What, Why and Who of Foreign Aid*, Boulder, CO, Westview Press.

Tornquist, O. (1998) *Politics and Development: A Critical Introduction*, London, Sage.

Totten, S., Parsons, W. and Charny, I. (1997) *Century of Genocide: Eyewitness Accounts and Critical Views*, New York, Garland.

Toulmin, S. (1990) *Cosmopolis: The Hidden Agenda of Modernity*, New York, Free Press.

Trubowitz, P. (1998) *Defining the National Interest*, Chicago, IL, University of Chicago Press.

Tsagourias, N. (2000) *The Jurisprudence of Humanitarian Intervention*, Manchester, Manchester University Press.

Tucker, R. (1978) *The Marx Engels Reader*, New York, W. W. Norton Company.

Tucker, R. and Hendrickson, D. (2004) 'Iraq and U.S. legitimacy', *Foreign Affairs* 83(6): 18–32.

Tyson, L. (1992) *Who's Bashing Whom? Trade Conflicts in the High Technology Industry*, Washington, DC, Institute for International Economics.

Ulam, A. (1992) *The Communists: The Story of Power and Lost Illusions 1948–1991*, New York, Scribner.

Ullock, C. (1996) 'Imagined community: a metaphysics of being or becoming?', *Millennium: Journal of International Studies* 25: 425–41.

UNHCR (2000) *The State of the World's Refugees: Fifty Years of Humanitarian Action*, Oxford, Oxford University Press.

Van Creveld, M. (1991) *The Transformation of War*, New York, Simon & Schuster.

—— (1999) *The Rise and Decline of the State*, Cambridge, Cambridge University Press.

Vayrynen, R. (1999) *Globalisation and Global Governance*, New York, Rowman & Littlefield.

Vertzberger, Y. (1998) *Risk Taking and Decisionmaking*, Stanford, CA, Stanford University Press.

Vogel, E. (1991) *The Four Little Dragons: The Spread of Industrialisation in East Asia*, Cambridge, MA, Harvard University Press.

Wade, H. (2002) 'Bridging the digital divide: new route to development or new form of depedency?', *Global Governance* 8: 443–67.

Waever, O. (1996) 'The rise and fall of the inter-paradigm debate', in Smith, S., Booth, K. and Zalewski, M. (eds), *International Theory: Positivism and Beyond*, Cambridge, Cambridge University Press.

Wagner, R. (1993) 'What was bipolarity?', *International Organisation* 47: 77–106.

Waites, B. (2000) *Europe and the Third World: From Colonisation to Decolonisation, c. 1500–1998*, New York, St Martin's Press.

Walker, M. (1993) *The Cold War and the Making of the Modern World*, London, Fourth Estate.

Wallerstein, I. (1974–89) *The Modern World-System*, 3 vols, New York, Academic Press.

—— (1979) *The Capitalist World-Economy*, Cambridge, Cambridge University Press.

Walt, S. (1987) *The Origins of Alliances*, Ithaca, NY, Cornell University Press.

—— (1997) 'Building up new bogeymen', *Foreign Policy* 109: 176–99.

—— (1998) 'One world, many theories', *Foreign Policy* 110: 29–45.

Walters, F. (1986) *A History of the League of Nations*, London, Greenwood.

Waltz, K. (1959) *Man, The State, and War*, New York, Columbia University Press.

—— (1979) *Theory of International Politics*, Reading, MA, Addison-Wesley.

Walzer, M. (1992) *Just and Unjust Wars*, 2nd edn, New York, Basic Books.

Warschauer, M. (2004) *Technology and Social Exclusion: Rethinking the Digital Divide*, Cambridge, MA, MIT Press.

Weart, S. (1998) *Never at War: Why Democracies Will not Fight Each Other*, New Haven, CT, Yale University Press.

Webb, M. (2000) 'The Group of Seven and political management of the global economy', in Stubbs, R. and Underhill, G. (eds), *Political Economy and the Changing Global Order*, 2nd edn, Oxford, Oxford University Press.

Webber, M. (1996) *The International Politics of Russia and the Successor States*, Manchester, Manchester University Press.

Webber, P. (1990) *New Defence Strategies for the 1990s: From Confrontation to Coexistence*, Basingstoke, Macmillan.

Weber, M. (1971) *Economy and Society*, Volume 1, Berkeley, CA, University of California Press.

Weiler, J. H. H. (2003) 'A constitution for Europe? Some hard choices', in Weiler, J. H. H., Begg, I. and Peterson, J. (eds), *Integration in an Expanding European Union: Reassessing the Fundamentals*, London, Blackwell Publishing.

Weine, S. (1999) *When History is a Nightmare*, New York, Rutgers University Press.

Weiss, T. and Crahan, M. (2004) *Wars on Terror and Iraq: Human Rights, Unilateralism, and the US Iraq Policy*, New York, Routledge.

Weiss, T., Cortright, D. and Lopez, G. (1997) *Political Gain and Civilian Pain*, Lanham, MD, Rowman & Littlefield.

Welch, D. (1989) 'Crisis decision making reconsidered', *Journal of Conflict Resolution* 33: 430–45.

Welhengama, G. (2000) *Minorities' Claims: From Autonomy to Secession*, Dartmouth, Ashgate.

Weller, M. (2002) 'Global constitutionalism: UN Security Council action', *International Affairs* 79: 693–711.

Wendt, A. (1987) 'The agent-structure problem in international relations theory', *International Organization* 41: 335–70.

—— (1992) 'Anarchy is what states make of it: the social construction of power politics', *International Organization* 46: 391–426.

—— (1999) *Social Theory of International Relations*, Cambridge, Cambridge University Press.

Westad, O. A. (ed.) (2000) *Reviewing the Cold War*, London, Frank Cass.

Westlake, M. (1994) *A Modern Guide to the European Parliament*, London, Pinter.

Wheeler, N. (2000) *Saving Strangers*, Oxford, Oxford University Press.

Wheeler, N. and Booth, K. (1992) 'The security dilemma', in Baylis, J. and Rengger, N. (eds), *Dilemmas of World Politics: International Issues in a Changing World*, Oxford, Clarendon Press.

Whittaker, D. (1999) *Conflict and Reconciliation in the Contemporary World*, London, Routledge.

Wight, M. (1991) *International Theory: The Three Traditions*, Leicester, Leicester University Press.

Wilkinson, D. (1999) 'Unipolarity without hegemony', *International Studies Review* 1: 141–72.

Wilkinson, R. (2000) *Multilateralism and the World Trade Organisation*, London, Routledge.

Williams, H., Mathews, G. and Sullivan, D. (eds) (1997) *Francis Fukuyama and the End of History*, Cardiff, University of Wales Press.

Williams, M. (2000) *International Relations Theory and European Integration: Power, Security and Community*, London, Routledge.

Wittner, L. (1995) *The Struggle Against the Bomb*, Stanford, CA, Stanford University Press.

Woodhouse, O. and Ramsbotham, T. (1996) *Humanitarian Intervention in Contemporary Conflicts*, Cambridge, Polity Press.

World Commission on Environment and Development (WCED) (1987) *Our Common Future*, Oxford, Oxford University Press.

—— (1992) *Our Common Future Reconvened*, London, WCED.

Wyn Jones, R. (ed.) (2001) *Critical Theory and World Politics*, Boulder, CO, Lynne Rienner Publishers.

Yergin, D. (1993) *The Prize*, New York, Simon & Schuster.

Yost, D. (1999) *NATO Transformed: The Alliance's New Roles in International Security*, New York, Institute of Peace.

Young, O. (1995) *International Governance: Protecting the Environment in a Stateless Society*, Ithaca, NY, Cornell University Press.

Zartman, W. (1995) *Collapsed States*, Boulder, CO, Lynne Rienner.

Zerubavel, E. (1993) 'Horizons: on the sociomental foundations of relevance', *Social Research* 60: 397–413.

Zilinskas, R. (1999) *Biological Warfare*, Boulder, CO, Lynne Rienner.

Zolberg, A. (1981) 'Origins of the modern world-system', *World Politics* 33: 253–81.

# INDEX